WASSERSTROM
JANUARY 2000
PORTLAND OR

Franz Xaver von Baader (1765–1841) is an enigmatic figure. Although his written output is largely undisciplined and his prolix rhetoric difficult to assimilate, he was widely admired by the early German Romantics and profoundly influenced their thinking. His reputation and influence, however, waned rapidly after his death. Today, he is only marginally known in the German-speaking world and virtually unknown outside of it.

In this monograph, the late Professor Ramón J. Betanzos organizes and articulates Baader's philosophy of love by systematically tracing it through a vast and complex maze of essays, articles, commentaries, lectures, reviews, manifestos, aphorisms, propositions, and fragments. In so doing, he also demonstrates how Baader reintroduced discarded and neglected philosophical traditions – particularly mysticism and theosophy – and made them intellectually respectable in a world where scepticism and rationalism prevailed.

Ramón J. Betanzos – born in 1933, died in 1995 – was a Professor of Humanities at Wayne State University in Detroit, Michigan.

FRANZ VON BAADER'S PHILOSOPHY OF LOVE

PHILOSOPHISCHE THEOLOGIE 6

Philosophische Theologie
Studien zu spekulativer Philosophie und Religion
Philosophical Theology. Studies in Speculative Philosophy and Religion

Ramón J. Betanzos

Franz von Baader's Philosophy of Love

Edited by Martin M. Herman

Passagen Verlag

Deutsche Erstausgabe

Die Deutsche Bibliothek – CIP-Einheitsaufnahme

Betanzos, Ramón J.:
Franz von Baader's philosophy of love / Ramón J.
Betanzos. Ed. by Martin M. Herman. – Dt. Erstausg. –
Wien : Passagen-Verl., 1998
   (Passagen Philosophische Theologie ; 6)
   ISBN 3-85165-213-4

ISBN 3-85165-213-4
© 1998 by Passagen Verlag Ges. m. b. H., Wien
Graphisches Konzept: Ecke Bonk
Druck: Manz, Wien

Table of Contents

IN MEMORIAM
RAMÓN J. BETANZOS
1933–1995

Editor's Introduction

Franz von Baader, Philosopher of Love

Knowledgeable students of German intellectual history regard Franz von Baader (1765–1841) as the Romantic thinker most responsible for formulating a comprehensive and compelling philosophy of love. For decades, the mystical Baader devoted vast amounts of time to the "science" or philosophy of love – even to an "erotic philosophy of love", as he sometimes described it – while drolly referring to himself as the "professor of love". And it was Baader who articulated and nurtured the Romantic conception of love – as both eros and agape – in its most persuasive and fully-developed form. Today, unhappily, Baader is only dimly remembered, even in the German-speaking world; outside of it, he remains virtually unknown. During his long and productive lifetime, however, both the man and his thought were highly regarded and widely respected. And his life time, it should be remembered, coincided with the golden age of German arts and letters.

Benedict Franz Xaver von Baader (1765–1841)

Born in Munich, Franz von Baader became an accomplished physician, mining engineer, and university professor during a long and peripatetic life. But he became many other things as well: philosopher, theologian, mystical theosophist, ecumenical Christian, social theorist, inventor, and founder of "Munich Romanticism". For more than five decades, this Bavarian Catholic polymath remained intensely engaged with a broad spectrum of current issues: above all, with philosophy and theology; but also with psychology, anthropology, and sociology – even economics and political science. As a theologian, his principal objective was to reconcile religion with science and politics, and to do so in a philosophically sound way: by avoiding an overdependence on rationalism or an excessive reliance on subjectivism. Although his written output (covering a vast range of topics) is undisciplined, and his often prolix rhetoric difficult to assimilate, his oral discourse was widely admired for its orderliness and lucidity. Like his two famous contemporaries, Goethe (1749–1832) and Beethoven (1770–1827), Baader's formative years were spent in the eighteenth century, but he came of age during the nineteenth. His mature works, like those of Goethe and Beethoven, were widely disseminated and debated by his contemporaries, and he too attempted – with some degree of success –to reconcile Enlightenment rationalism with Romantic sensibility. And like Beethoven and Goethe, he profoundly influenced the thinking of the Early German Romantics. Unlike Goethe and Beethoven, however, Baader's fame and influence waned rapidly after his death: the philosophical-theological equilibrium which he sought and tentatively achieved proved fleeting; his intellectual legacy, largely ignored by succeeding generations of unknowing and unsympathetic thinkers, has been accorded only passing notice in histories of philosophy published since the late nineteenth century; and modern dictionaries of national biography barely mention his name.

To his contemporaries, though, Baader ranked high among the intellectual elite of the early nineteenth century, and numerous reports attest to the profound impact which this gifted thinker made on his peers. He possessed an engaging personality, an extraordinary talent for extemporaneous speaking, and an acutely penetrating mind. Bettina von Arnim, for one, considered him "full to overflowing with intelligence". Hegel praised him for reviving the religious heritage of the past, especially the mystical tradition of the West, and stressed his own agreement with Baader on basic philosophical principles. After years of embracing a pantheistic philosophy rooted in Spinoza, Schelling – influenced principally by Baader – moved toward a theism based on the thought of Jacob Böhme. (Schelling also credited Baader with rediscovering the true nature of evil and providing the key to understanding its mystery.) For Novalis, "Baader was a true psychologist who spoke the genuine language of psychology". Joseph Görres considered him a "genius of electric power." Ringseis thought him a more profound and richer thinker than Schelling.

And Baader was widely admired, not only for the depth of his thought but also for the orderliness of his mind. He is frequently described as a speaker whose ideas were sharply defined and whose intellect was rigorously focused, an adroit debater who rarely missed a step in advancing an argument or developing a train of thought, a clear-headed thinker who never repeated himself. In verbal discourse, he was incisive and articulate, brilliant and well-organized, eloquent and convincing. But even Friederich Schlegel, who considered Baader "the most intelligent, the most profound man whom I have seen in a long time", was dismayed by his ineptitude as a writer. If Baader could only write as effectively as he spoke, Schlegel observed, people would soon forget Schelling and Fichte. Unhappily, Schlegel's assessment of Baader the writer has proven painfully accurate: despite his brilliance as a speaker, Baader's written work is verbose and redundant, undisciplined and abstruse. And this unhappy dichotomy – the sharp contrast between Baader the facile, persuasive speaker and Baader the awkward, tedious writer – has contributed significantly to his lack of posthumous recognition. Fame and influence are largely determined by the surviving (written) record, not by glowing accounts of verbal eloquence offered by contemporary supporters and apologists.

Nevertheless, Baader was a prolific author who published a prodigious number of essays, articles, commentaries, lectures, reviews, manifestos, aphorisms, propositions, and fragments – almost all of which are occasional in nature – during a long and productive life. But he never wrote a book. Even his larger and ostensibly more comprehensive works, those meant to transcend the aphoristic and fragmentary, are generally united by little more than a shared title. Indeed, many (perhaps most) of the items gathered in the collected edition of Baader's works – a sixteen-volume miscellany of the most diverse sort – carry titles which bear little resemblance to their content. The published diaries (*Tagebücher*), in which his thoughts were faithfully recorded for more than six decades, and the extensive correspondence which he carried on with the intellectual elite of the Western World and beyond complement the more formal body of published writings.

Baader produced this large corpus of written material during more than a half century of diligent labor, a period of time stretching from his early maturity until the year of his death, but he was neither intellectually disposed nor psychologically inclined to gather and organize it into a coherent body of thought. In fact, he stubbornly refused to do so. Though profoundly committed to the view that a valid philosophical system demanded a consistent and rigorous methodology, he never felt the need to demonstrate that his collected works, considered as a whole, constituted such a unified body of thought. To the contrary, substantial evidence suggests that he thought of himself principally as a sower or purveyor of ideas, not as the architect of a comprehensive philosophical system. When this perceived "shortcoming" was brought to his attention, he responded by noting that "nothing would be more foolish or more lacking in understanding than to reprove a seed-peddler for selling only seeds and not mature plants".

In view of Baader's inability to write fluently or effectively, his penchant for the aphoristic and fragmentary, and his dogged unwillingness to systematize a vast body of miscellaneous material, it is surprising – and gratifying – to discover that his thought did indeed possess a high degree of internal unity and consistency; it is, in fact, extraordinarily free of self-contradiction. (His fundamental ideas, to be sure, became more richly nuanced as he matured, but they did not change substantively in any appreciable way.) Since Baader never attempted to make this unity manifest, it can only be documented by rigorously tracing a specific topic through all of the material gathered in the collected edition, a truly formidable task.

Baader lived in an age of systematic philosophers and was rated (by his contemporaries) among the best of them, an evaluation clearly based on his ability as a speaker – not on his effectiveness as a writer. As a writer, the revealing insight – not the carefully-constructed argument – suited his temperament. He relied heavily on symbol and analogy, and he tended to express himself paradoxically, in an esoteric language drawn largely from the Bible, the Cabbala, alchemy, and the mystics. He found the "radical" rationalism of Enlightenment thought – particularly that of Kant, Spinoza, and Descartes – wanting because it accorded so little place to faith and mystery. Likewise, he found the "radical" subjectivism of Romantic thought – particularly that of such early Romantics as Rousseau, Jacobi, and the Pietists – equally wanting because it accorded so little place to logic and reason.

Despite all of these contradictions – the oral Baader versus the written Baader, the "systematic" Baader versus the "fragmentary and aphoristic" Baader – the German Romantics and Idealists took him very seriously and were considerably influenced by his thought. But it was Baader the living exemplar of Romanticism, rather than Baader the philosopher of Romanticism, who most captivated his like-minded friends and contemporaries. To them, he seemed the personification of their values and the embodiment of their worldview. He reintroduced mysticism and theosophy to a world of ideas in which skepticism and rationalism prevailed. And he returned these traditional but neglected modes of thought to philosophical respectability. Above all, he attempted to synthesize the old and the new, to expose the inadequacies of both Enlightenment rationalism and Romantic subjectivism, to foster an intellectual-spiritual climate in which reason and faith could coexist harmoniously. And he did so in a language of paradox, one which deemphasized methodology and systematic thought. Intellectually and spiritually he was a remarkable figure – even in a Germany at the height of its cultural development, even in a Germany where Goethe and Beethoven, Hegel and Schelling, the Schlegels and the Grimms were all simultaneously at work.

Ramón James Betanzos (1933–1995)

Ramón James Betanzos was an extraordinary human being. Endowed with a keen intellect and a penetrating mind, his vast erudition was complemented by a serene temperament and a giving nature. Personally, he was a devoted husband, a doting father, a loving grandfather, and a steadfast friend. Professionally, he was a consummate academic: an effective and caring teacher, a gifted and versatile scholar, a cherished and generous mentor, a highly-valued and widely-admired colleague. Spiritually, he was a devout Roman Catholic who remained vitally engaged with religion – in particular and in general – throughout his entire life, an exemplary member of the human community who steadfastly practiced love, generosity, and morality. And he did so selflessly, gracefully, and with unfailing kindness.

But fate was unkind to this sweet and gentle man. In February of 1995, he was prematurely taken from our midst at the age of sixty-one, at a moment of great personal happiness, at a time when his teaching and scholarly achievements had attained new levels of sophistication and respect.

Ray Betanzos was of Basque heritage, but the Betanzos family history in America reads like the quintessential immigrant success story. His father left Northern Spain in 1927 to look for work in Detroit. In 1929, after securing a job with the Ford Motor Company and purchasing a home, he sent for his wife and three young children – Peter, Mary, and Teresa. Three other children – Patricia, Ramón, and Luis – were born during the next seven years. Sadly, Ray's mother died unexpectedly when he was just three years old. A well-meaning friend offered to adopt the two younger boys (Ray and Luis, then only six months old), but the devout, hard-working father, who spoke virtually no English, elected to keep his large family together, the older teen-age children helping to care for and raise the younger ones. Some years later, Ray's father remarried and two additional children – Martha and Berta – were added to the family.

Though Ray was a native Michiganian, born (1933) in Dearborn and raised in Detroit, he was also a first-generation American raised in a Spanish-speaking household that proudly and fiercely celebrated its Basque roots. As one of the younger children in a large and devout Catholic family, he was given a traditional Catholic upbringing: his elementary-school years were spent at St. Gabriel in Detroit, and he attended high school at Sacred Heart Seminary, also in Detroit. In 1955, he received his Bachelor of Arts degree, with a major in philosophy, from Sacred Heart Seminary College. He was awarded a second baccalaureate degree in 1959, this one with a major in theology, from the Catholic University of America, and on June 6th of that year was ordained a Roman Catholic priest. (He served as a diocesan priest, in and around metropolitan Detroit, from 1959 until 1974.) Both of his graduate degrees, an M.A. (1963) and a Ph. D. (1968), were in history, and both were earned at the University of Michigan.

From 1968 until 1974, Ray served on the faculty of Sacred Heart Seminary College, his undergraduate alma mater, where he taught a wide range of courses in both history and philosophy. Concurrently, he held several administrative positions: Dean of Students (1969–1974) and Acting Dean of Admissions (1973–1974).

During his years as a faculty member at Sacred Heart Seminary, Ray spent most summers in Germany or Austria refining his knowledge of history, deepening his understanding of philosophy, and perfecting his command of German. He generally lived at a local parish or monastery, receiving room and board in exchange for such clerical assistance as preaching, saying Mass, and hearing confessions. His "spare time", eight to ten hours a day, was pleasantly and productively spent reading and studying. The summer of 1970, for example, found him in Vienna where he read the complete works of both Wilhelm Dilthey and José Ortega y Gasset. In 1971, he studied all of Kant, much of Nietzsche, and read Winston Churchill's *History of the English Speaking Peoples* while living with the Pallotine Fathers in a monastery overlooking Salzburg. He spent the summer of 1972 in Munich, completing his study of Nietzsche and immersing himself in the writings of Ernst Cassirer and Ernst Troelsch. (He had hoped, someday, to write a book about Troeltsch's notion of compromise.) The summer of 1973, spent in Salzburg, was devoted largely to the thought of Mircea Eliade, but a considerable amount of time was allotted to reading military history and reconsidering various approaches to the history of ideas.

These were happy and important interludes in Ray's life, idyllic "moments" when his mind was stimulated and his spirit nurtured. He read and studied, with few distractions, and eagerly grasped the opportunity to enlarge and refine his already extensive knowledge of philosophy, theology, and history. His responsibilities were minimal, and he was relatively free to travel – as he wished and where he wished. Ideally situated (geographically) to indulge his love of music, he regularly attended concerts offered by some of Europe's finest musical organizations and frequently witnessed productions mounted by several of the Continent's most highly regarded opera companies. How he relished those performances! And at the end of each summer, he set aside several weeks to accompany friends or family members on extensive tours of the Europe he had come to know so well and love so much.

Ray's life was altered dramatically in the summer of 1974 when he left the priesthood to marry his beloved Kathleen (Kay) and to become stepfather to her two daughters: thirteen-year old Colleen and eight-year-old Elizabeth. They were married on July 13, 1974, and a daughter, Mary, was born to them in 1977. Although Ray's position within the Church had clearly changed, his devotion to Catholicism had not. He remained a committed Catholic all of his life.

In the spring of 1974, Ray was appointed to the faculty of Monteith College's Division of Humanistic Studies. (The appointment was effective for the fall term.) Monteith College, an academic unit of Wayne State University dedicated to experimentation in general education, had been founded in 1958. (It was to be phased out by the University in 1981.) In 1977, two years after the Monteith phase-out had been decreed (1975) but four years before it had been fully implemented, Ray, together with a group of his Monteith colleagues, was transferred to the University's College of Liberal Arts. He was awarded tenure in 1978 and subsequently promoted to the rank of associate professor and then to that of full professor as a faculty member in that College's Department of Humanities. In 1993, he became chair of Humanities.

During an academic career which spanned more than a quarter of a century, Ray, motivated principally by personal interest and intellectual curiosity, acquired a sophisticated command of art, music, and literature to complement his rigorous and systematic training in history, philosophy, and theology. Because his interests ranged so broadly and his disciplinary competence was so extensive, he was ideally equipped – temperamentally and intellectually – to teach and to write in the areas of interdisciplinary humanistic studies and comparative arts, the curricular focus of the academic units in which he held professorial appointments at both Monteith College and the College of Liberal Arts. But beyond his mastery of broadly-based subject matter, Ray possessed a genuine talent for combining disparate materials – drawn largely from the humanistic disciplines and the arts – in strikingly original ways, and he excelled in communicating the results engagingly and effectively. His ready wit – featuring a special fondness for outrageous punning – and affable disposition neatly complemented his wide-ranging knowledge and permitted him to establish an easy and genuine rapport in the classroom and on the written page. And he did so without ever compromising academic integrity.

Ray's penchant for languages, and the ease with which he mastered them, proved a tremendous asset in his personal life and an invaluable tool during his academic career. Competence in Latin and Greek was achieved at the seminary, where he also learned some Hebrew. Fluency in Spanish, his first language, and the familiy's Basque heritage served him well when he studied and quickly became proficient in Italian and French. He became fluent in German while a student at the University of Michigan. Indeed, his command of German was honed and refined during the summers spent in Germany and Austria.

As a teacher, Ray excelled in every mode of instruction. Enthusiastic and exuberant, he taught with pleasure and conviction, but he demanded much of his students. (Those in need of assistance, however, invariably received patient and generous support.) He was blessed with a striking pedagogical gift: the ability to make even arcane subject matter relevant and accessible. And like all master teachers, he was admired for the skill with which he simplifed and summarized complex texts (whether historical, philosophical, literary, musical, or artistic) without violating their integrity or trivializing their subtleties. Colleagues marveled at the ease with which he distilled even the most complex ideas without misrepresenting them and eagerly sought his advice about matters pertaining to their own classes. He graciously served as mentor to the junior members of the departmental faculty, encouraging them as they struggled to master difficult subject matters and assisting them as they worked to refine their teaching skills. And he provided a splendid model for the entire faculty, generously collaborating with all of his colleagues in countless ways – notable attributes for one engaged in interdisciplinary and comparative teaching and scholarship, activities which place a heavy premium on cooperation and collaboration.

As a scholar, Ray's principal interests and major publications group themselves into three broad categories: (1) specialized studies – book-length translations, monographs, textual analyses, and critical essays – devoted to various aspects of modern (late eighteenth-, nineteenth-, and twentieth–century) German philosophy, theology, and intellectual history; (2) reflections about the philosophy and pedagogy of interdisciplinary humanistic studies and comparative arts; and (3) meditations aimed at "popularizing" complex moral and ethical issues.

In the area of specialized scholarship, Ray was particularly interested in modes of thought pursued by a number of German Catholic scholars who concerned themselves with such wide-ranging issues as the essence of being, the nature of world views, the organization of knowledge, and the periodization of history. Until recently, the work of these philosophers and historians was only marginally known in the English-speaking world for several reasons: on the one hand, their broad-based and holistic perspectives were not compatible with the pragmatic and "objective" orientation of contemporary scholarship; on the other, the academic prose in which they wrote was often dense and convoluted, the bane of even the most literate reader of German texts. By publishing accurate and intelligible translations of seminal studies written by a number of these scholars, and by complementing these translations with lucid, monograph-length introductions and critical essays, Ray contributed substantially to the renewed interest manifested by the intellectual community in their work. Among his most important contributions are book-length translations, each preceded by a substantial introductory essay, of major works by Wilhelm Dilthey (*Einleitung in die Geisteswissenschaften* as *Introduction to the Human Sciences*, copublished by Wayne State University Press in 1988 and Harvester-Wheatshaft the following year) and Heinz Heimsoeth (*Die sechs grossen Themen der abendländischen Metaphysik und der Ausgang des Mittelalters* as *The Six Great Themes of Western Metaphysics and the End of the Middle Ages*, published by Wayne State University Press in 1993). In addition, he was one of several translator-critics invited to participate in a major scholarly effort aimed at making Dilthey's most important work available in English: *Wilhelm Dilthey: Selected Works*, a six-volume set currently being issued by the Princeton University Press. Ray's contributions will appear in volumes scheduled for publication in the late 1990s.

Tangible contributions made by Ray to the philosophy and pedagogy of interdisciplinary humanistic studies and comparative arts include a number of thoughtful and pioneering articles published in the journal *Humanities Education* (now *Interdisciplinary Humanities*) and a striking body of innovative teaching materials – principally translations and commentaries – conceived and developed for several of the courses which he designed and taught.

"Popularizing", that much-maligned and undervalued branch of scholarship, is not held in high regard by the academy. Nevertheless, it is central to the academic enterprise and remains the stock in trade of the professoriate: education would be impossible without it, and academics spend much of their time practicing it. Skillfully done, popularizing is an important and legitimate form of scholarship; and Ray Betanzos was an accomplished practitioner. Indeed, he succeeded as a popularizer in precisely the same way that he succeeded as a master teacher and traditional scholar: by being precise and thorough; by being organized and systematic; and by simplifying without distorting. The substantial body of pastoral-homiletic meditations, which he wrote for a regional religious community and published locally, provide some notable examples. Straightforward and clear, but rigorous and skillfully nuanced, these thoughtful essays address such central issues of the human condition as: "The Problem of Evil", "What Human Beings Do to Each Other", "Recognizing the Good", etc. And they do so directly and simply – but never simplistically.

Ray Betanzos' entire scholarly output, a broadly-based body of work, is widely admired – not only for its "analytical rigor and dispassionate judgment", but also for the "intrinsic value of the [many different types of] subjects to which he devoted attention". Such is the judgment offered by referees who read the manuscripts submitted by Ray to various journals and presses, reviewers of his published books and articles, and external evaluators who assessed his candidacy for tenure and/or promotion. They unanimously praised all of his scholarly efforts – be they specialized translations and monographs, articles dealing with the philosophy and pedagogy of interdisciplinary humanistic studies and comparative arts, or pastoral-homiletic essays. Virtually all invited attention to Ray's acute "sense of what questions should be asked", noted how "edified" they were "by his answers", and commented about "the way in which he made extremely complex and difficult materials accessible to the reasonably sophisticated reader". As a translator (of Dilthey), he "felicitously rendered his source into English prose that is not only accurate, but intelligible and pleasing as well". The substantial introductions which precede the Dilthey and Heimsoeth translations display a "lucid quality of thought" and are characterized as "rigorous and accessible". His "thorough grounding in modern European philosophy" was widely admired; and his efforts on behalf of Baader, Dilthey, and Heimsoeth were hailed as truly significant because they brought "to the English-speaking world seminal and influential works of nineteenth- and twentieth–century German thought". A distinguished academic, currently teaching at one of America's most prestigious universities, summarized Ray's scholarly contributions in the following words: "This man thinks seriously, very seriously, about a wholistic [*sic*] philosophy of the humanities, and he is publicly engaged in its contemporary construction . . . He is a Philosopher of the humanities".

In truth, Ray Betanzos personified and exemplified the professor of decades past: his personal and professional lives were completely intertwined. Together, they embodied an unflagging commitment to study and learning. To Ray, teaching and scholarship, service and living were all related parts of an undivided whole, a seamless entity synonymous with strength of mind, intellectual vitality, dedication to the highest professional standards, and an abiding commitment to morality and ethical values.

Ramón J. Betanzos and Franz von Baader

Ray Betanzos first became acquainted with Franz von Baader while a graduate student at the University of Michigan. There, he was introduced to this overlooked and underestimated philosopher/theologian by Professor Stephen Tonsor, a distinguished member of the University's History Department who became Ray's faculty mentor. Ray was so struck by the richness of Baader's ideas and the depth of his imagination that he set himself the task of trying to unravel and understand Baader's concept of love, an undertaking which required tracing Baader's evolving thoughts about love through a vast and complex maze of written material. Expanded further, Ray's quest to identify a genuine philosophy of love in Baader's thinking, and to articulate it in a systematic and coherent way, developed into a doctoral dissertation written under the direction of Professor Tonsor.

After receiving his Ph.D. in 1968, Ray – as previously noted – accepted a position at Sacred Heart Seminary College where he hoped to continue exploring Baader's thought. Unfortunately, the large number of courses which he prepared and taught as a faculty member and the ever-increasing responsibility which he was asked to assume as priest and administrator proved so demanding that further work on Baader was, of necessity, abandoned – at least for the time being. After being appointed to the faculty of Wayne State University in the fall of 1974, Ray's principal efforts were focused in several different directions: mastering the interdisciplinary and comparative curriculum of Monteith College's Division of Humanistic Studies; and participating, with his faculty colleagues, in shaping the Division's future direction. The concentrated and sustained attention required by these activities left little time for anything else, and once again, the Baader project languished.

Following the phase-out of Monteith College in 1981, it took several years (early 1980s) for Ray – and those of his former Monteith colleagues who had been transferred with him – to become comfortable with their new assignments as faculty members in the Department of Humanities, an academic unit housed in the University's College of Liberal Arts. New curricula had to be developed, new courses had to be designed, and a new set of professional expectations – associated with a more traditional academic environment – had to be assimilated. A great deal of time and energy was spent adapting previous assumptions to changed circumstances and reorienting the intellectual compasses of both department and faculty members.

During the middle-late 1980s, after having finished the Dilthey book and while contemplating the Heimsoeth translation, Ray began, once again, to think seriously about Baader. In 1989, Professor Peter Koslowski, a distinguished Baader scholar who directs the Forschungsinstitut für Philosophie Hannover and who had read Ray's doctoral dissertation on microfilm, invited Ray to spend some time at the Institute. In late May and early June of 1989, at the beginning of a year-long sabbatical leave (academic 1989–90) to be spent in Salzburg working on a book in which differing worldviews would be compared and contrasted, Ray accepted Professor Koslowski's invitation and visited the Institute for several weeks. While in Hannover, Ray was invited to deliver a lecture on Baader. The lecture, entitled "Der Mensch als Bild Gottes bei Franz von Baader" ("Man as God's Image, According to Franz von Baader"), was well received, and Professor Koslowski – having heard the lecture and having now become personally acquainted with the man – urged Ray to turn his doctoral dissertation into a book. When Professor Koslowski organized a three-day conference in Munich in 1991 to commemorate the 150th anniversary of Baader's death, Ray was one of eighteen scholars (worldwide) invited to address the international audience assembled in honor of Baader. The lecture which he prepared and presented, "Franz von Baaders Philosophie der Liebe" ("Franz von Baader's Philosophy of Love"), was subsequently published – in somewhat revised form – as chapter 2 of P. Koslowski (Ed.): *Die Philosophie, Theologie und Gnosis Franz von Baaders: Spekulatives Denken zwischen Aufklärung, Restauration und Romantik*, Vienna (Passagen Verlag) 1993. Once again Ray's work was warmly received, and he was further encouraged to revisit the dissertation with an eye to turning it into a book. The entire experience convinced Ray that a book-length monograph devoted to Baader's philosophy of love was indeed a viable – and worthwhile – scholarly undertaking.

Between 1992 and 1994, Ray managed to devote some time to the project. Time, however, was in short supply during that two-year period. In the fall of 1993, Ray was appointed chair of Humanities; as a department chair, he was expected to assume a substantial amount of administrative responsibility in addition to maintaining many of his former teaching commitments. Nevertheless, he slowly began to revise the twenty-four-year-old dissertation, simultaneously incorporating new information about Baader which had appeared in print since 1968. A review of the scholarly literature revealed that only a dozen or so books and approximately three dozen articles about Baader had been published since 1968; none dealt specifically with Baader's philosophy of love in any substantial way.

Late in 1993, Ray requested an administrative leave of absence for the fall semester of 1994; the proposal which supported his request indicated that the time provided by the leave would be used to finish the book. Ray's proposal, enthusiastically supported by his departmental colleagues and endorsed by the Dean of Liberal Arts, described the Baader project, assessed its prospects for publication, and justified the need for a substantial block of uncommitted time in which to complete the task. The administrative leave was granted, and the Betanzos family prepared to leave Michigan (in late August of 1994) for a four-month stay in Vienna, the venue in which the project was to be completed. Several factors pointed to Vienna as the preferred site for the leave: library resources were excellent and readily available; and Passagen Verlag, a prospective publisher of the manuscript, was located there. (Professor Koslowski, editor of a series entitled "Philosophische Theologie" for Passagen Verlag, had expressed interest in publishing the Betanzos manuscript – in English – as a volume in that series.)

Unfortunately, these plans were never realized. Ray became seriously ill and was diagnosed with stomach cancer in late July of 1994. Following a heroic but debilitating battle with that dreadful disease, he died on Saturday, February 4, 1995. It was at that point that we – I and several of Ray's closest colleagues and friends – committed ourselves to editing the largely-completed manuscript and preparing it for publication. We vowed to produce a book which would simultaneously make an important contribution to scholarship and serve as a suitable memorial to a cherished colleague and dear friend. And it is to that end that we have directed our efforts.

Franz von Baader's Philosophy of Love: The Manuscript

At the time of Ray's death, the text of the manuscript – but not the appendices, index, or bibliography – was complete. It consisted of an Introduction, five

Chapters, and a Conclusion. In the Introduction, the book's thesis was proposed and an overview of the intellectual milieu in which Baader lived and worked was sketched. Chapter 1 surveyed Baader's life, outlined his philosophical positions, discussed his vast and disparate output, and described the laborious process by means of which information germane to the principal topic of the study – "God as Love" – had been extracted from a veritable mountain of source material. Chapters 2–6 were organizationally and methodologically similar: in each, pertinent information was gathered and arranged according to the topic specified in the chapter title. All began with introductory statements, continued by marshaling supporting evidence drawn from the relevant primary sources (passages quoted in English translation and connected by explanatory narrative), and concluded with summary statements offering further explanation and clarification. The monograph ended with a Conclusion in which the author's argument was summarized, Baader's influence on later thought was surveyed, and Baader's work, as a whole, was evaluated.

While the text of the manuscript was essentially complete at the time of his death, Ray had not yet fashioned a book from the dissertation; the major portion of that task was to have been undertaken in Vienna during the fall of 1994, during the leave of absence which unhappily never took place. As a result, the monograph – as presented here in its finished form – may seem excessively documented and may still read too much like an academic exercise. Extensive documentation, however, can be a virtue – particularly when, as with Baader, it offers a systematic survey of the literature (primary and secondary) related to an important figure under-represented in print; stylistic appropriateness, on the other hand, is most suitably evaluated in terms of how well it deals with the subject being addressed, not by a generic characterization. Be that as it may, the editor – for professional and technical reasons – felt it neither wise nor desirable to undertake a major recasting of the text.

Precisely what, then, did the editor contribute? With regard to the text proper, changes were basically limited to copy editing – particularly of the text's expository sections: the Introduction; Chapter 1; the introductory statements, summary statements, and explanatory narrative linking the quoted passages in Chapters 2–6; and the Conclusion. Other than minor changes in punctuation (to clarify meaning) and alterations of word order (to minimize ambiguity) the Betanzos translations of Baader stand as originally made. Ray's skill as a translator was widely recognized, and his philosophy of translation – being careful and precise but essentially literal – has been respected. The Index (of names and subjects) and the two Appendices are the work of the editor. Appendix 1 is an alphabetically–ordered list of Works Written By Baader Which Are Cited by Title in the Text; and Appendix 2 is an alphabetically-ordered list of Non-Critical Works (e.g. literature, philosophy, theology) Written by Predecessors,

Contemporaries, or Successors of Baader (e.g. Plato, Aquinas, Kant, Goethe, Camus, Faulkner) Which Are Cited by Title in the Text and which, for the most part, do not appear in the Bibliography. The Bibliography, begun by Betanzos, was completed by the editor. It has been updated to include books and articles published since 1968. Unfortunately, much of the recent material – items which post-date 1968 – is not as well integrated into the text as it would have been had Ray lived to complete the project.

Why Baader?

In view of Baader's "ambiguous" and "marginal" position as a philosopher and theologian, what justifies the publication of an entire monograph devoted to his philosophy of love? With information about Baader in English currently limited to generalizations found in a handful of encyclopedia articles, why should a major effort now be made to change the situation? Why, in short, is Baader sufficiently important to warrant reconsideration?

In general, it is worth remembering that Baader was a committed ecumenist and an out-spoken social critic who made at least three important contributions to nineteenth-century history: (1) he was, in all probability, the intellectual father and principal architect of the Holy Alliance Treaty of 1815; (2) he was the most prominent participant in the ecumenical effort undertaken in the 1820s to reunite the Catholic Church with the Protestant churches and the Russian Orthodox Church; and (3) he was an acute social analyst who identified many of the "human" problems associated with emerging capitalism – anticipating Marx, in this respect, by more than a decade – and championed the exploited proletariat of the new industrial age in its search for justice.

More specifically, he was a highly original and vital religious thinker. At a time when pantheistic philosophies were much in vogue (particularly among the early nineteenth-century German Idealists, Romantics, and Transcendentalists), he staunchly defended theism, and he did so by invoking tradition as well as by developing new and innovative arguments. He described the "malaise" of his age (subsequently labeled spiritual nihilism) in graphic detail, specifically relating it to nihilism, the death of God, and the rise of "absolute man" (superman). It is worth noting that these same issues also preoccupied Nietzsche, born three years after Baader died. Their respective analyses and proposed solutions, of course, differed radically.

In *Franz von Baader und die philosophische Romantik* (1927), David Baumgardt, by no means an uncritical Baader enthusiast, argues that Baader possessed one of the most powerful and original religious minds ever to emerge in Germany; and with respect to theology, he should rightfully be considered the consummate German Romantic. "Even Novalis's religiosity", Baumgardt maintains, "seems more artificial and Schleiermacher's more a matter of educational acquisition when compared to the deep and mighty natural power of Baader's religious struggle". Hugo Ball, a pioneer in twentieth-century Baader scholarship, claims – in *Zur Kritik der deutschen Intelligenz* (1919) – that Baader "is the only great Christian philosopher that Germany has [ever] had". And Friedrich Heer, the renowned historian, notes – in *Europa Mutter der Revolutionen* (1964) – that Baader "is still one of the great unknowns of the nineteenth century, although Hegel, his opposite pole, thought highly of him and important Russian and French thinkers held him in high esteem during his lifetime. Subsequently, Kierkegaard and Scheler found him appealing, and Berdaev bases himself completely on Baader". With regard to Baader's philosophy of love – and the role played by love in Baader's thought – Paul Kluckhohn, a distinguished scholar of German Romanticism, holds – in *Die Auffassung der Liebe in der Literatur des 18. Jahrhunderts und der deutschen Romantik* (³1966) – that Franz von Baader "brought the Romantic conception of love to its highest peak", and in *Das Ideengut der deutschen Romantik* (⁴1961) states that "Baader's aphorisms on love belong to the best that have ever been written about love and marriage".

For all of these reasons, it seems clear that a thinker of Baader's stature merits being introduced to the English-speaking world in a full-length study. And while the Betanzos book deals principally with Baader's philosophy of love, embedded in it one can find the most comprehensive overview of Baader and his philosophy available in English. Viewed collectively, the Introduction, Chapter 1, and the Conclusion provide a fine summary of Baader in general: he is carefully placed in his intellectual milieu – German Romanticism and German Idealism; a generous sketch of his life and works is offered; his "system of thought" is outlined; his influence on later thinkers is evaluated; the Baader literature is surveyed; and a critique of his work as a whole is presented.

The Betanzos Memorial Fund

Shortly after Ray died, friends and colleagues established a memorial fund to help underwrite costs associated with preparing and publishing this monograph. It is the sincere hope of those named below, all generous contributors to the Betanzos Memorial Fund, that this book will serve as a lasting memorial and loving tribute to his memory.

Contributors

Peter and Colleen Baird
Brian and Martha (Betanzos) Bennett
Kathleen Betanzos
Luis and Nancy Betanzos
Mary Kathleen Betanzos
Sandra Betanzos
Paul and Leah Blizman
Henry V. Bohm
Thomas Bonner
Al and Joanne Butts
Rosemary and Virginia Catanese
Andy and Mary (Betanzos) Chekerylla
Marc and Sarah Cogan
Community Mental Health Board,
   Ingam Counseling Center
Tom and Loretta Deku
William and Louise Dezur
Andrea Di Tommaso and Janet Langlois
Harold and Teresa (Betanzos) Dobson
Jack DuBois
Gerald and Nancy DuFresne
Donald and Winifred Esper
Frances Field and staff
Bernard and Carol Garbacik
Katz Gato and Lynne McNamara
Kim Gresham
Owen and Elizabeth McNamara Guthrie
Donald and Connie Haase
Yates and Gail Hafner
Leslie Hancz
Martin and Judith Herman
History Department,
   Wayne State University
Lou and Leslee Holtzman
Rudy and Pat (Betanzos) Horvat
Humanities Department,
   Wayne State University
Christopher and Lois Johnson
James and Betty Judge

Edward and Helen Kasparek
William and Javan Kienzle
Robert Kirtland
Fred and Sara Leopold
Thomas G. and Christine J. Litka
Lawrence Lombard
Jose Lopez and Berta Betanzos
Larry and Sandy Mackle
Jim and Irma Macy
Frank and Janice Mafrice
Rick and Donna Manley
Michael Martin
Sandra McCoy
Tom and Mary McLaughlin
Richard and Marlene McLaughlin
Christine McLaughlin
Jack and Sally McNamara
Kathleen McNamee
Charles and Peggy Peck
Philip and Janice Pokorski
Fred and Susan Schanne
John Schober
Linda Speck
John and Kathleen Stuart
Richard and Rose Studing
Robert and Richelle Szanter
Clare Tabor
Larry and Pat Teal
Mark and Pamela Thomas
Dennis Tini
Stephen Tonsor
Nola H. Tutag
Jay and Alexandra Vogelbaum
Richard and Sharon Wagner
Wayne State University Press
Melvin and Mary Wendrick
Charles and Marion Wetherill
Mark and Linda Weiss
Gene and Beverly Williams

Acknowledgements

So many people have helped bring this project to fruition that I am reluctant to acknowledge some for fear of inadvertently omitting others. I would be remiss, however, if I failed to recognize those whose assistance has been indispensable. Kay and Mary Betanzos have been unfailingly kind and supportive. Even during a protracted period of deep personal grief, their unstinting help and encouragement have been an inspiration. Javan Kienzle, experienced editor and one of Ray's close personal friends, read the original manuscript several times and offered a countless number of wise and helpful suggestions. I am particularly grateful for her enthusiasm and deeply indebted to her for the high level of professionalism with which she edited the manuscript. She assisted me in the same way she had assisted Ray with many of his previous scholarly projects: graciously and constructively. Marc and Sarah Cogan generously – indeed, heroically – provided the expert technical assistance needed to ready the manuscript for editing and to prepare the final, camera-ready copy of the completed monograph for publication. Professors Marc Cogan, Yates Hafner, Sara Leopold, Linda Speck, Richard Studing, and Jay Vogelbaum, all dear friends and colleagues of Ray Betanzos, graciously read numerous drafts of the "Editor's Introduction" and offered many helpful suggestions. Louise Dezur carefully and faithfully oversaw and administered the Betanzos Memorial Fund. Professor Peter Koslowski, director of the Forschungsinstitut für Philosophie in Hannover and editor of the series in which this monograph appears, initiated the project; following Ray's death, he encouraged us to complete it. At Passagen Verlag in Vienna, Kathrin Murr (from the beginning of the editorial process) and Thomas Hartl (during its latter and final stages) have been unfailingly kind and helpful. For more than two and a half years, their professionalism has been exemplary and their commitment total: a file drawer full of FAXes attests to that fact. Without their expert and sympathetic guidance, this book would never have been published. For all of us, the experience has been a genuine labor of love.

Introduction

In the introduction to his edition of Franz von Baader's collected writings, *Franz von Baader. Über Liebe, Ehe und Kunst*, Hans Grassl singles out "three significant contributions" that Baader made to the evolution of nineteenth-century thought and history. The first was the "very probable" influence that he exercised on the drafting of the text of the Holy Alliance document of 1815. The second was his failed journey to Russia in 1822–23, a journey undertaken to establish an academy in St. Petersburg with the ecumenical goal of reunifying the Greek Orthodox, Protestant, and Roman Catholic Churches. The third was his plea for justice on behalf of the exploited "proletariat"; tellingly, his analysis of the "social problem" anticipated Karl Marx's in far-reaching detail.[1]

Grassl's choices are good ones, but many other contributions made by Baader could plausibly have been added to the list. His theory of political economy, for example, anticipated in striking fashion the classic formulation of that theory set forth by Friedrich List in the *National-System der politischen Ökonomie* (1841).[2] More subtle than the others, yet in some ways exceeding them all in importance, was Baader's analysis of the profound spiritual malaise of his age, a malaise perhaps similar to that of our own. Baader identified *spiritual nihilism* as the root cause of this crisis. He viewed the separation of man from God and the divorce of human reason from faith as the seed of all destruction and dissolution. Though Baader's and Nietzsche's worldviews were poles apart, it is interesting to note the ways in which nihilism, the death of God, and the rise of absolute man – a veritable superman – preoccupied them both.[3]

---

1 H. GRASSL (Ed.): *Franz von Baader. Über Liebe, Ehe und Kunst*, Munich (Kösel) 1953, pp. 11–12.
2 See H. HARRAS: "Franz von Baader (1765–1841), ein Vorläufer und Geistesverwandter Friedrich Lists", *Ständisches Leben*, 4 (1931); J. SAUTER: "Die Grundlegung der deutschen Volkswirtschaftslehre durch Franz von Baader", *Jahrbuch für Nationalökonomie und Statistik*, 123 (1925). See also BAADER: *Sämtliche Werke* 6,191–192.
3 See E. BENZ: "Franz von Baader und der abendländische Nihilismus", *Archiv für Philosophie*, 3 (1949).

As disparate and variegated as these seemingly unrelated areas appear to be, there is, nevertheless, a single controlling idea behind Baader's approach to every one of them: his mystical notion of love. Christian nations should be united to one another in Christian love; that was the rationale behind the Holy Alliance concept. Christian love made the long-existing separation of the Churches intolerable; only love and understanding could make ecumenism work. Christian love forbade economic exploitation of the weak by the strong and the proletariat by the capitalists; a bloodless, soulless, heartless economic machine was the antithesis of love. But, can love and political economy be legitimately linked? In Baader's view they could, for society, as he understood it, was an organic union of men, a community whose organizational principle was a common love of all for God and one another. Finally, spiritual nihilism was the most blatant rejection of love possible, according to Baader's *Weltanschauung*, for nihilism results from, and consists in, man's repudiation of God – and God is love itself.

No one has more adequately summarized the contributions made by Franz von Baader to the thought of his time than Hegel. In the preface to the second edition of his *Enzyklopädie der philosophischen Wissenschaften im Grundrisse* (1827), he writes:

Scholarship has at its disposal the rich content which centuries and millennia of learning activity have delivered up to it. This content is not simply left over as a historical remain which only others have possessed, and which is past for us, something with which to stuff our memories or on which to test the acuteness of our critical literary faculties; it is not as though this content did not serve the interests of knowledge for our minds and the cause of truth. The most elevated, profound, and inward things have been brought to light in religions, philosophies, and works of art, in forms more or less pure, more or less clear or clouded, at times in a very shocking guise. We must consider it a matter of special merit that Herr Franz v. Bader [*sic*] continues not simply to recall such forms to memory, but with his profoundly speculative mind expressly to restore their content to scholarly respectability by exposing and establishing the philosophical idea they contain.[4]

---

4   G. F. HEGEL: *Hegels Sämtliche Werke*, ed. by G. LASSON and J. HOFFMEISTER, 21 volumes, Leipzig (Meiner) 1905ff., volume 5, pp. 18ff. The German text reads as follows:

Aber vor der Wissenschaft liegt der reiche Inhalt, den Jahrhunderte und Jahrtausende der erkennenden Thätigkeit vor sich gebracht haben, und vor ihr liegt er nicht als etwas Historisches, das nur andere besessen, und für uns ein Vergangenes, nur eine Beschäftigung zur Kenntniss des Gedächtnisses und für den Scharfsinn des Kritisirens der Erzählungen, nicht für die Erkenntniss des Geistes und das Interesse der Wahrheit wäre. Das Erhabenste, Tiefste und Innerste ist zu Tage gefördert worden, in den Religionen, Philosophien und Werken der Kunst, in reinerer und unreinerer, klarer und trüberer, oft sehr abschreckender Gestalt. Es ist für ein besonderes Verdienst zu

In his comprehensive study, *Baader und Kant*, Johannes Sauter asserts that Hegel's statement aptly describes Baader's place in the history of philosophy because "his [Baader's] chief effort was aimed at producing a great intellectual synthesis between the idealism of past times and German Idealism".[5] Hans Grassl emphasizes that it is particularly the mystical and occult heritage of the past which Baader tried to translate into the language of philosophical idealism. He states further that "it was through his kinship with the ancient traditions that Baader derived the decisive impulses and ideas that separate him from Romanticism and German Idealism in a fundamental way, despite all affinity with them on other counts".[6] Baader was a many-sided man, active in medicine and the physical sciences, in philosophy and theology, in public office and in private business enterprise. But "the essential Baader" is the Baader who tried to recapture and renew the religious heritage of the past, especially its mystical legacy.

If one delves more deeply into the core of this mystical heritage, it is the notion of love which emerges as central. In Baader's mystical view of reality, God, the ultimate mystery, is love; therefore, man, made in God's image, must also be teleologically defined in terms of love. The lot of nature, in turn, depends on the use or misuse its lord – i.e. man – makes of love. Thus, Baader's theology, his anthropology, and his cosmology are more profoundly affected by his concept of love than by any other single concept. Consequently, the present study has two principal aims: (1) to show that Baader's thought about God, man, and the world is fundamentally a "philosophy of love" – that is, to show how his notion of love is the key to all of Baader's thought; and (2) to present an exhaustive study of all that Baader has to say about love, either by direct citation or by reference to relevant passages. This second aim serves the purpose of concentrating materials scattered throughout fifteen volumes of Baader's *Sämtliche Werke* and four volumes of *Lettres inédites de Franz von Baader*.

No one who has studied Baader's work fails to mention the complexity of his thought, the diversity of intellectual currents that influenced him, the highly symbolic language and convoluted style in which he wrote, and the unsystematic character of his philosophy. These characteristics, juxtaposed with the fact

achten, dass Herr Franz v. Bader [*sic*] fortfährt, solche Formen nicht nur in Erinnerung, sondern mit tief spekulativem Geiste ihren Gehalt ausdrücklich zu wissenschaftlichen Ehren zu bringen, indem er die philosophische Idee aus ihnen exponirt und erhärtet.

5   J. SAUTER: *Baader und Kant*, Jena (Gustav Fischer) 1928, is the most complete study which has appeared to date dealing with Baader's relations to Kant and to German Idealism. See also F. LIEB: *Baader und Kant*, Basel (doctoral dissertation) 1923.
6   H. GRASSL (Ed.): *Franz von Baader. Über Liebe, Ehe und Kunst*, p. 14.

that Baader remains relatively unknown to most scholars, especially outside the German-speaking world, make it advisable to sketch briefly the major intellectual influences with which he contended. The chief idea-complexes to be considered in this connection are: Romanticism, German Idealism, Christianity, and Mysticism-Occultism.

Baader and German Romanticism

Nicolai Hartmann notes that "Romanticism is a tone of living of a peculiar kind. It is for that reason impossible to capture it in concepts".[7] Certainly, it is impossible to reduce Romanticism to a single univocal formula: it is much too complex and, in part, too self-contradictory to be defined simply.[8] The term "Romanticism" is used loosely to designate the numerous changes which took place in the arts and literature of Europe between the mid-eighteenth and mid-nineteenth centuries. But Romanticism is much more than an esthetic and literary phenomenon. It is a genuine cosmology, one which embodies a whole philosophy of man; no major area of intellectual and cultural life is irrelevant to it.

The German Romantic Movement crystallized toward the end of the 1790s. It took shape in Friedrich and August Wilhelm Schlegel's literary journal *Athenaeum* (1798–1802), in Novalis's fragments, and in the glorification of Germany's landscape and medieval heritage found in the literary works of Tieck and Wackenroder. Schelling's *Über die Weltseele* (1798), Novalis's *Christenheit oder Europa* (1799), and Schleiermacher's *Reden über die Religion* (1799), for example, were important products of incipient Romantic thought. Early German Romanticism blossomed largely in Jena and Berlin. With A. W. Schlegel's lectures *Über die schöne Kunst und Literatur* (Berlin, 1802–05), Romanticism flowered and achieved maturity, principally in Berlin and Heidelberg. A later phase was centered in Munich, Vienna, Dresden, and in the district of Schwaben.

The key to the entire Romantic worldview is the *organic idea*, the belief that reality is a living whole, all members of which – despite their diverse characteristics and functions – are immediately related to a common center and

---

7   N. HARTMANN: *Die Philosophie des deutschen Idealismus*, Berlin (Walter de Gruyter) ²1960, p. 160.
8   See, for example, A. O. LOVEJOY: "On the Discrimination of Romanticisms", in: *Essays in the History of Ideas*, chapter 12, New York (G. P. Putnam & Sons) 1948; and "Romanticism and the Principle of Plentitude", in: *The Great Chain of Being*, chapter 10, New York (Harper Torchbook) 1960.

through that center to each other. With regard to its organicism, there is no question about the utterly Romantic quality of Baader's thought. For him, as for all the Romantics, the concrete living whole provided a means for resolving all abstract antitheses. As Paul Kluckhohn notes:

The effort to resolve all antitheses in a higher third element, the impulse to synthesize, manifests itself as the fundamental drive of the Romantic feeling for life . . . The realm of understanding and the world of feeling, consciousness and unconsciousness, experience and idea, nature and spirit, sensual life and the yearning of the soul, personality and community, national uniqueness and universal range of vision, the special and the general, the finite and the infinite, this world and another world – all these pairs of opposites which the Enlightenment and kindred perspectives regarded as antinomies – the Romantics experienced and conceived as polarities, as correlatives that belong to each other and condition each other, entities whose interaction produces the stream of life's power, dualities that manifest primitive unity and that must be reunited in a higher unity.[9]

Baader was one with the Romantics in a great many ways. He believed, for example, in the ineffable uniqueness of the individual. He stressed the importance of history in speculation and believed that a process of dynamic development undergirds all reality. He appropriated Burke's view of the "social contract", considering it applicable to all persons living, dead, and still to be born (6,70; 8,219); it was, indeed, a view well-received among the Romantics generally. His theory of knowledge recognized the significant influence of feeling and will in the cognitive process, but he refused to reduce all knowledge worthy of the name to feeling, as Rousseau and Jacobi did. With many other Romantics, Baader considered speech a direct gift of God and poetry the original language of the human race. His dialectical understanding of all things led him to accept and elucidate the myth of androgyny, another favorite Romantic preoccupation. For Baader, and for many of the other Romantics, the world was a poem for man to interpret and enlarge in light of his own experience. Schlegel's or Schleiermacher's "yearning for the infinite" found its echo in Baader's "all things reach out toward the heart of God as toward their center" (14,485; 15,650). The interest manifested by many Romanics in alchemy, universal medicine, magnetism, and parapsychological phenomena was also shared by Baader. In their opposition to the mechanistic worldview and geometrizing spirit of the Enlightenment, the Romantics found in Baader one of their most effective champions. Baader supported Herder's Romantic stress on the unique character of each nation's *Volksgeist* (especially Germany's). He manifested a tragic sense of life in his own work, a deep feeling that man and nature were not comfortable

9   P. KLUCKHOHN: *Das Ideengut der deutschen Romantik*, Tübingen (Max Niemeyer) ⁴1961, p. 22.

with one another and that the spirit of evil is forever at work. And like many Romantics, who "began everything and finished nothing", Baader too was active in many fields; characteristically, he produced impressive fragments, never a finished whole. His language, like that of many Romantics, was a language of paradox and aphorism.[10]

But Baader differed with his Romantic colleagues on many points. For example: despite his high regard for feeling and will, he refused to surrender the claims of "calculating intelligence" as some Romantics did. He could never be styled an enthusiast or *Schwärmer*. He never subscribed to the apotheosis of the Ego, a notion which some Romantics appropriated from Fichte's metaphysics and built into a cult of the Promethean hero. Eventually, Romanticism as a whole began to place less emphasis on deifying the Ego and moved in the direction of stressing the organic interconnectedness of individuals in history, nature, the state, and religion. Many Romantics tended to overemphasize the purely *subjective,* as, for example, Schleiermacher and Novalis did in their religious views. Baader, on the other hand, emphasized the *objective* ground of being even more than the individual's response to it. One of his chief objections to the whole tradition of philosophy since Descartes was precisely its overwhelmingly subjective character.

Baader also differed from the many Romantics who felt that a return to the Roman Catholic Church was the only road to salvation; his approach was much more ecumenical and interdenominational. Whereas many Romantics idealized the past, especially the "golden age" of medieval Christianity, and indulged in the cult of ruins, Baader would have none of that. To him, this kind of cult was nothing less than *Mumiendienst* (mummy worship), fit for the churchyard but not for life. In his personal life, Baader did not share the bizarre eccentricities and unconventional attitudes that marked the lives of many Romantics. For example: he always clung to an institutional view of marriage; he never permitted the claims of feeling and inclination alone to become absolute; and he refused to become an "isolated, sad and noble soul", a rebel against social rules. In esthetics, he did not repudiate classical rules, but he did find a place for the genius "in whom the spirit of the rule resides" apart from any formalistic adherence to it.

Baader's principal contribution to Romanticism was to introduce and champion the organic idea, the very centerpiece of the Romantic *Weltanschauung.* He was the first of the Romantics to break with the eighteenth-century's mecha-

---

10   See J. NOHL: "Franz von Baader, der Philosoph der Romantik", *Euphorion,* 19 (1912), pp. 625ff., for a discussion of the ideas which Baader shared with Romanticism in general.

nistic view of the world and to replace it with an organic model.[11] His earliest essays – beginning with *Vom Wärmestoff, seiner Vertheilung, Bindung und Entbindung, vorzüglich beim Brennen der Körper* (1786) and followed by *Ideen über Festigkeit und Flüssigkeit zur Prüfung der physikalischen Grundsätze des Herrn Lavoisier* (1792), *Beiträge zur Elementar-Physiologie* (1797), and *Über das pythagoräische Quadrat in der Natur oder die vier Weltgegenden* (1798) – were pioneering works of Romantic philosophy. The latter two in particular made a considerable impact on such readers as Novalis, Goethe, and Schelling.[12]

Baader's role as a Romantic thinker and his contributions to Romantic philosophy are much more seminal than is generally acknowledged. In an article dated 1912, Johannes Nohl called Franz von Baader "the philosopher of Romanticism", a designation subsequently adopted by Paul Kluckhohn and Johannes Sauter.[13] Nohl explains:

When we call Baader the philosopher of Romanticism, we are justified in doing so not only because of the actual influence Baader exercised on the Romantics, but most of all because of the personality of the philosopher, its specifically Romantic pathos, its style, its relationship to nature, to life, and to work.[14]

Characterized in this way, Baader's life clearly reflects Hartmann's statement that "Romanticism is a tone of living of a peculiar kind". It was Baader as living examplar of Romanticism, even more than Baader as philosopher of Romanticism, who captivated his fellow Romantics. He seemed to them a truly Promethean hero, a magic personality, an inexhaustible font of creativity and life, and they left eloquent testimony to support this impression.

---

11 See, for example, H. GRASSL: "Franz von Baader als Nachfahre der Alchemisten und Rosenkreuzer", *Antaios: Zeitschrift für eine freie Welt*, 3 (1962). Grassl argues that "the decisive transformation of the mechanistic worldview of the Enlightenment into the organological one of Romanticism was accomplished in fully conscious adherence to Herder, to the alchemists, and to the Rosicrucians" (p. 334). Evidence of Baader's use of these sources is clear in his earliest work, *Vom Wärmestoff, seiner Vertheilung, Bindung und Entbindung, vorzüglich beim Brennen der Körper* (1786) and especially in *Beiträge zur Elementar-Physiologie* (1797). "The idea that Romanticism first came to Bavaria from Jena by way of Schelling is false". (H. GRASSL: "Franz von Baader als Nachfahre der Alchemisten und Rosenkreuzer", p. 339).

12 See J. SAUTER (Ed.): *Franz von Baaders Schriften zur Gesellschaftsphilosophie*, Jena (Gustav Fischer) 1925, p. 573.

13 J. NOHL: "Franz von Baader, der Philosoph der Romantik"; P. KLUCKHOHN: *Die deutsche Romantik*, Bielefeld and Leipzig (Velhagen and Klasing) 1924, p. 96; J. SAUTER: "Franz von Baaders Aesthetik", *Archiv für Geschichte der Philosophie*, new series, 38 (1927), p. 35.

14 J. NOHL: "Franz von Baader, der Philosoph der Romantik", p. 618.

The young Romantic genius Novalis found Baader a true psychologist who "speaks the genuine language of psychology" (15,35). He considered Baader, Fichte, Schelling, Ritter, and Schlegel "the philosophical directorate in Germany".[15] In a letter to Friedrich Schlegel, Novalis wrote:

> There is still one whom I would wish to have in our company, one whom I compare to you alone – Baader
>> It is his magic spell that reunites
>> What the sword of madness has rent asunder.
> . . . Could he not be invited to the Athenaeum? Join forces with Baader, my friend – the two of you could accomplish fantastic things![16]

So many Romantics testify to the overpowering personality of Baader that personal contact with him must have been a truly remarkable phenomenon. Thus, Friedrich Schlegel wrote to Sulpiz Boisserée in 1811:

> For some time now Baader has been here and, as you may easily imagine, I see him often. I do not just see him, however. I also hear him and perceive him . . . If only he could write as well as he can speak, people would not be talking about Schelling and Fichte for very long. It's strange that the ability to write is such an isolated gift . . . But the most remarkable, the most intelligent, the profoundest man whom I have ever seen in a long time is indeed Baader. He has made many things clear to me.[17]

Varnhage von Ense, friend of nearly all the best-known German Romantics, reports that for a long time after their meeting Schlegel lived exclusively in Baader's world of ideas and viewpoints (15,53). Such reactions were not exceptional. Von Ense himself, for example, was deeply affected by Baader's personality (15,101ff). Ludwig Tieck remarked that it was extremely rare for one to encounter a talent for extemporaneous speaking greater than that possessed by Baader (15,36). And Nicolas Lenau, the Austrian poet and dramatist, described his first meeting with Baader in the following words:

> Today [September 13, 1837 in Munich] stands as an important day for me: I have spoken with Franz Baader. Just as I expected – a great and mighty thinker. One grows by many years through

---

15 See D. BAUMGARDT: *Franz von Baader und die philosophische Romantik,* Halle/Saale (Max Niemeyer) 1927, p. 6, fn. 2.
16 See P. KLUCKHOHN: *Charakteristiken. Die Romantiker in Selbstzeugnissen und Äusserungen ihrer Zeitgenossen,* Stuttgart (Reclam) 1950, p. 167; D. BAUMGARDT: *Franz von Baader und die philosophische Romantik,* p. 6, fn. 2; J. SIEGL: *Franz von Baader, ein Bild seines Lebens und Wirkens,* Munich (Bayerisches Schulbuch) 1957, p. 67.
17 P. KLUCKHOHN: *Charakteristiken. Die Romantiker in Selbstzeugnissen und Äusserungen ihrer Zeitgenossen,* p. 169.

steady conversation with him. Thoughts really rise to the fore then! One's mind is expanded, really perceptibly greater, in order to be able to face up to this great interlocuter.[18]

Steffens thought that Baader was "as facile in speech as he was awkward in writing", and Bettina von Arnim found him "full to overflowing with intelligence (*voll Geist bis an die Spitzen seiner Lippen*) – he never utters an insignificant word . . . ".[19] Joseph Görres's reaction to Baader was enthusiastic: "No one will deny . . . that Baader is a great and acutely penetrating mind . . . in fact, he is really a genius of electric power (*ein eigentliches elektrisches Blitzgenie*)".[20] Ringseis, the Romantic physician who knew most of the great German Romantics personally, says of Baader: "In the richness and depth of his thoughts I consider him more significant than Schelling; in fact, he is perhaps matched by no one else in this regard . . . ".[21]

The French scholar, François Alexis Rio, who was in personal contact with a large segment of Germany's intellectual elite, compared him to Schelling in much the same way: he called Baader "his [Schelling's] rival, if not in popularity, at least in genius", and preferred Baader to Schelling as an intellectual guide.[22] Jean Paul expressed his admiration for Baader's power, as did Caroline Schlegel, Clemens Brentano, Wilhelm von Humboldt, and many others.[23] At times, enthusiasm for the man reached the level of sheer extravagance. Consider the description offered by the Swedish poet and philosopher, P. D. A. Atterbom, who wrote in his memoirs for January 21, 1818:

---

18 P. KLUCKHOHN: *Charakteristiken. Die Romantiker in Selbstzeugnissen und Äusserungen ihrer Zeitgenossen*, p. 173.
19 P. KLUCKHOHN: *Charakteristiken. Die Romantiker in Selbstzeugnissen und Äusserungen ihrer Zeitgenossen*, p. 169.
20 BAADER: *Sämtliche Werke*, introduction to volume 17, p. v.
21 See E. RINGSEIS (Ed.): *Erinnerungen des Dr. J. N. Ringseis*, 4 volumes, Regensberg 1886, volume 1, p. 305.
22 See E. SUSINI (Ed.): *Lettres inédites de Franz von Baader*, 4 volumes: volume 1, Paris (J. Vrin) 1942; volumes 2 and 3, Vienna (Herder) 1951; volume 4, Paris (Presses universitaires de France) 1967, volume 3, pp. 253ff. Susini cites Rio at considerable length about Baader and Schelling.
23 It is easily possible to multiply such references. See, for example, D. BAUMGARDT: *Franz von Baader, der Philosoph der Romantik*, introduction; P. KLUCKHOHN: *Charakteristiken. Die Romantiker in Selbstzeugnissen und Äusserungen ihrer Zeitgenossen* is made up entirely of such citations; J. NOHL: "Franz von Baader, der Philosoph der Romantik"; E. SUSINI (Ed.): *Lettres inédites*, notes and commentaries to volumes 2 and 3. It may be noted that Goethe read Baader's essay *Über das pythagoräische Quadrat in der Natur oder die vier Weltgegenden* when it appeared in 1798. He wrote to Schiller about it, saying that it pleased him very much, but also that he found it quite hard to understand. (See also BAADER: *Sämtliche Werke* 15,35.)

Today I met the most miraculous (*miraculösesten*) man whom I have ever seen and perhaps who exists anywhere in the whole world, since Swedenborg and St. Martin passed away. You can easily guess that this man is Franz von Baader . . . He discusses nothing but the most profound principles, antitheses, analogies, etymologies, physical experiments, and religious considerations, and all this just tumbles out of him, lightning bolt after lightning bolt, crack after crack, with indescribable enthusiasm; he is a man, however, who makes no mistakes in method or dialectic. He expresses his ideas with the sharpest definition; he does not miss a step in his argumentation; he leaves no gaps and makes no repetitions . . . In whatever language you like, he will speak with equal facility and, in fact, preferably in several at a time; for example: today they switched back and forth between German, French, English, Latin, Greek, and Chaldaic.[24]

On balance, then, one may indeed concur with Nohl's designation of Baader as: "the philosopher of Romanticism". He earned the title in several ways: in particular, by dint of his important contributions to the Romantic philosophy of nature; but also because of the powerful personal impact he made on such leaders of the Romantic movement as Friedrich Schlegel, Novalis, Schelling, and others. To the Romantics, Baader seemed the personification and living synthesis of their values. Still, he neither aligned himself with any single Romantic coterie nor subscribed completely to the complex of ideas associated with the Romantic movement as a whole. The mystical-occult flavor of his religious philosophy was something entirely unique.

Baader and German Idealism

1. Baader and Kant

Baader grew up in an atmosphere of Wolffian rationalism, but he never found it personally satisfying. Indeed, he strongly rejected Enlightenment rationalism throughout his life. In view of this antipathy, it is interesting to note that the first major philosopher with whose thought Baader seriously grappled for an extended period of time was Immanuel Kant; in fact, Johannes Sauter claims that "Baader . . . unfolded his whole world of ideas in constant altercation with Kant, inasmuch as he expanded and built further what was incomplete [in Kant's work]; he set aside the errors and contradictions, but he also assimilated the accomplishments".[25]

Baader's thought was most strongly influenced by Kant between 1786 and 1796. A close reading of Kant's work – during this ten-year period – caused

24 P. D. A. ATTERBOM: *Aufzeichnungen des schwedischen Dichters Pehr D. A. Atterbom über berühmte deutsche Männer und Frauen nebst Reiseerinnerungen aus Deutschland und Italien aus den Jahren 1817–1819*, German translation by F. MAURER, Berlin 1867, pp. 134ff.
25 J. SAUTER: *Baader und Kant*, p. viii.

Baader to fall more and more out of sympathy with his point of view. The appearance of *Über Kants Deduction der praktischen Vernunft und die absolute Blindheit der letztern* (1,1–23), an essay written in 1796 but not published until 1809, marked the culmination of Baader's dissatisfaction. It is a remarkably early critique of Kantian thought. His essay of 1813, *Über die Begründung der Ethik durch die Physik* (5,1–34), is yet another critique of Kant. Baader found great merit in Kant's fight against the claims of both rationalism and empiricism as exclusive avenues to truth and in his strong opposition to utilitarian ethics, but he also found serious flaws in the Kantian scheme. Sauter sums up the major areas of Baader's discontent:

> Baader, therefore, felt that he was forced to expose the weaknesses in Kant and his associates, most of all formalism and rigorism in ethics, absolute autonomy, absence of mystical thought, and ignoring emotional intentionalities.[26]

Beyond that, Baader was also unwilling to accept the core argument of the *Kritik der reinen Vernunft* because he was convinced that it levied a sentence of *de jure* blindness on all men forever. In Baader's eyes, Kant's whole enterprise in this *Kritik* was self-contradictory: how could Kant use reason itself as the tool to demonstrate that reason cannot reach actual knowledge of things as they really are? How could Kant state that one cannot, on principle, attain knowledge of the "thing-in-itself", yet, at the same time, proceed to describe the "thing-in-itself-of-the-mind" – i.e., its ultimate structure? Clearly, Kant's entire argument in the *Critique of Pure Reason* has no foundation unless it can describe the mind *as it truly is*, not only in Kant's case but in everyone else's as well. If we know only the appearances of things, how do we know the mind-in-itself? Indeed, if we know only *appearances*, does it make any sense, in the final analysis, to say that we know anything at all?

Kant's hylomorphic picture of the structure and workings of the mind was not congenial to Baader's thinking either – it was much too abstract. Concrete reality knows no form without content, nor content without form. "The principle: *quidquid implet per modum recipientis implet* (whatever fills something up fills it up after the manner of the recipient) is, in fact, one-sided and untrue if one does not complement it with: *quidquid impletur, per modum implentis impletur* . . . (whatever is filled up is filled up after the manner of the one doing the filling up)" (4,390).

---

26 See J. SAUTER: "Franz von Baaders romantische Sozialphilosophie", *Zeitschrift für die gesamte Staatswissenschaft*, (1926), pp. 469ff. Sauter develops the three points at some length: i.e., Kant's assault on rationalism, empiricism, and utilitarianism. The passage cited in the text appears in the footnote on pp. 468–69.

There is evidence, dating back even to 1786, that Baader's cast of mind and approach to truth were not well-suited to accept the Kantian notion of the "thing-in-itself" or Kantian formalism in general. (See also 11,15.) Sauter argues[27] that in going beyond Kant Baader did not really reject him totally, but simply took Kant at his own word: i.e., that the *Critiques* were only a *Propädeutik* to a positive philosophy; consequently, the true follower of Kant must take the step that leads beyond transcendental philosophy to transcendent philosophy, a philosophy of idealism. (If so, Baader would not be the only philosopher – especially if one considers Kant's immediate successors among the German Idealists – who attempted to complete the "preliminary" work done by Kant in his *Critiques*.) Sauter, in any case, regards Baader's philosophy as a continuation of Kant's thought, an elucidation of the metaphysics implicit in it. But, there is no doubt that Baader's thought required an extensive overhauling of Kant's critical philosophy: as Kant had found it necessary to "do away with knowledge in order to make room for faith", Baader found it necessary to "do away with Criticism in order to make room for knowledge".

2. Baader and Jacobi

Baader became acquainted with Friedrich Jacobi in 1796. They met in Hamburg, while Baader was en route to Munich from England. (It was during the years spent in England that Baader had composed his initial critique of Kant.) In Jacobi, Baader found a kindred spirit, one whose objections to Kant's philosophy were mainly concerned with the notion of the "thing-in-itself" and with the formal *a priori* in Kant's epistemology. They shared important grounds of agreement, particularly in their common emphasis on the "priority of the optative" (15,169): i.e., prayer and a preoccupation with mysticism. They agreed that faith is the *a priori* of knowledge (15,168) and that Kant's attack on rationalism did him great honor. Yet, they also differed sharply. Baader's essays, *Über den Affect der Bewunderung und der Ehrfurcht* (1804) and *Über die Behauptung: dass kein übler Gebrauch der Vernunft sein könne* (1807), were both aimed at Jacobi. Baader's attack on Jacobi's *Gefühlsdeismus* provided a companion piece to his blast against Kant's *Verstandesdeismus* (1,32 fn.). Baader regarded Jacobi's excessive stress on the role of feeling as an avenue to truth as obscurantism. He opposed Jacobi's subjectivism and his disparagement of intelligence. After Schelling's shift to a theistic worldview (a development strongly influenced by

27   J. SAUTER: *Baader und Kant.* For Sauter's thesis, see the foreword. For an example of Baader's claiming to go beyond Kant, precisely in the name of Kant's own principles, see BAADER: *Sämtliche Werke* 3,242 fn.

Baader), Baader supported Schelling's stand in favor of cooperation between faith and reason against Jacobi's "religion of the heart" position. Over time, these actions produced a complete rift between Baader and Jacobi.

3. Baader and Fichte

Baader never met Johann Gottlieb Fichte; nor, as far as is known, did they ever correspond. Baader's first contact with Fichte's thought came during his visit to Hamburg in 1796. He hailed Fichte's contributions toward understanding consciousness and acknowledged its importance to philosophy. In number fourteen of the *Vorlesungen über religiöse Philosophie im Gegensatz der irreligiösen älterer und neuerer Zeit,* he states:

Because German philosophy (since, and because of, Fichte) has directed its attention principally to the nature and essence of self-consciousness (of the mind), it has made it possible to grasp the concept of knowing more sharply and accurately than previously. (1,178ff.)

Everywhere he credits Fichte for his fine work in describing "the mechanics or instinctive operation of the human mind in its struggle for awareness (preservation of consciousness) within the temporal flow of what is transient" (3,244),[28] but they did not agree on everything. Baader's chief quarrel with Fichte's metaphysics of the Ego centered on the notion of the non-Ego. As Sauter notes: "The principal weakness of Fichte, in Baader's view, was that he made no distinction between the healthy and the sickly in the non-Ego (3,242ff.; 15,174) and likewise, no clear distinction between the individual Ego and the absolute [Ego]".[29] Indeed, Baader himself asks:

But what is this mysterious and protean thing or monstrosity, this non-Ego, which (as H. Fichte so beautifully and truly expresses himself) exists only when one does not grasp it (does not actively seize it) and which disappears as soon as one wishes to grasp it – by which it shows itself to be in practice (and what is all speculation if not conceptualized practice?) something everywhere and nowhere present, a resistance that is effective only in and through our ineffectiveness? (3,242ff.)

Baader charges Kant and Fichte with apotheosizing the Ego, because for each of them, but especially for Fichte, man becomes the supreme lawgiver and

---

28 Baader's words read: "Niemand hat übrigens den Mechanismus oder jene instinctartige Operation des menschlichen Geistes, in seinem Kampf um Besinnung (Bewusstseinserhaltung) inner dem Zeitstrom des Vergehenden, klarer und genauer bezeichnet, als Hr. Fichte".

29 J. SAUTER: *Baader und Kant,* p. 538.

ultimate source of morality. In effect, this makes man God (2,445). Nothing could be more opposed to Baader's Christian and mystical conception of man than to transpose the characteristics of finite consciousness and power into the absolute or vice-versa.

4. Baader and Schelling

Hans Grassl divides Baader's relationship to Friedrich Wilhelm Joseph von Schelling into three periods.[30] The first began in 1806, although both were acquainted with each other's work ten years earlier. Why, then, 1806? Sauter identifies that year as "a most significant turning-point in German Idealism" because it was in 1806 that Schelling broke with Fichte's philosophy and exchanged Spinoza for Böhme. But, Sauter adds, the fact that this turn to theism was taken under the influence of Baader is almost completely unknown.[31] It was at this time, notes Grassl,[32] that Schelling wrote "probably the most beautiful lines ever written about Baader":

I know someone who is by nature an underground-man, [one] in whom knowing has become part of his very nature and existence, a compact unity like the timbre and light in metals. This person is not so much a person who knows; rather is he a living, constantly active, yet complete personality of knowing.[33]

In a letter dated October 26, 1815, Schelling asked Baader for an appraisal of his (Schelling's) newest writing because, "There is perhaps no one who can grasp the hidden, the scientific, and other relationships in it in so immediate a way as you can".[34] And in his *Untersuchungen über das Wesen der menschlichen*

30 H. GRASSL (Ed.): *Franz von Baader. Über Liebe, Ehe und Kunst*, introduction, pp. 44ff.
31 J. SAUTER: *Baader und Kant*, pp. 539ff. J. E. ERDMANN: *Die Entwicklung der deutschen Spekulation seit Kant*, Stuttgart, 1931, volume 3, p. 289, makes it clear that Baader, who was ten years Schelling's senior, was far from being purely receptive vis-à-vis Schelling. "On the contrary, it was Baader especially who sought very early to steer Schelling away from Spinoza and toward Jacob Böhme, and it was his [Baader's] writings particularly through which Schelling passed en route to his study of Böhme. In his altered position, Schelling showed himself a disciple of Baader to a greater extent than Baader ever showed himself an adherent of the system of identity". See also D. BAUMGARDT: *Franz von Baader, der Philosoph der Romantik*, p. 31.
32 H. GRASSL (Ed.): *Franz von Baader. Über Liebe, Ehe und Kunst*, p. 28.
33 Schelling's words read: "Einen kenne ich, der ist von Natur ein unterirdischer Mensch, in dem das Wissen substantiell und zum Sein geworden ist, wie in den Metallen Klang und Licht zu gediegener Masse. Dieser erkennt nicht, sondern ist eine lebendige, stets bewegliche und vollständige Persönlichkeit des Erkennens". (F. W. SCHELLING: *Sämtliche Werke*, 6 volumes, Munich (Jubilaeum) 1927ff., volume 8, p. 247).
34 E. SUSINI (Ed.): *Lettres inédites* 4,108.

Freiheit (1809),[35] Schelling credits Baader with rediscovering the only correct notion of evil. To him, during this period, Baader was "a marvelous seer and excellent man".[36] Indeed, Schelling is purported to have said, during those years, that after speaking with Baader on philosophical matters it would always take him a few hours to rediscover his own position.[37]

Though the Schelling and Baader families were still on friendly — even close — terms during the second decade of the nineteenth century, Baader, as early as 1798, wrote to Jacobi: "I know Schelling, but I am not very satisfied with him" (15,181), explaining that Schelling's hypothesis about the polarity of nature's basic forces must be replaced by a triadic structure.[38] And despite Schelling's debts to Baader in the early years of their relationship, their views always differed substantially. For example: Schelling maintained that God's "center" (*Mitte*) was not in himself, but in the world; he argued that creation was necessary, not free, on God's part; he held no doctrine of Sophia. Baader disagreed with him on all these points. Whereas Schelling remained close to pantheism, even after his shift to theism, Baader always rejected pantheism completely, though one might argue that in essence he was a panentheist.

The second period of their relationship began about 1818. It was marked by an increasing personal coolness and a sharpening of their philosophical differences. It was becoming more and more evident that Schelling's commitment to Fichtean idealism did not mesh well with Baader's theosophical-mystical heritage and leanings. Baader's thought, after 1820, inclined progressively toward Hegel as it gradually grew more distant from Schelling. Indeed, Baader's *Bemerkungen über einige antireligiöse Philosopheme unserer Zeit* (1824; 2,443ff.) proved an especial affront to Schelling. The work seriously aggravated the ill feeling Schelling already entertained towards Baader because of Baader's journey to Russia in 1822-23. In a letter of December 4, 1824, Schelling — in effect — announced to Baader that their relationship had ended (15,421).

Thus began a third period, this one marked by open hostility. Schelling's antagonism remained intense, even into the last year of his life (1854), when he

---

35   F. W. SCHELLING: *Sämtliche Werke*, volume 4, p. 258.
36   See D. BAUMGARDT: *Franz von Baader, der Philosoph der Romantik*, p. 5, fn. 3.
37   J. SAUTER: *Baader und Kant*, p. 541. Pages 540–42 of this work bring together the various allusions to Baader made by Schelling and corroborate the fact of Schelling's dependence on Baader with testimony from Atterbom, Steffens, and Ringseis. See also note 27 above.
38   On this point, see also J. SAUTER: *Baader und Kant*, p. 541. It will be shown in many connections throughout this study that Baader adopts a triadic or trinitarian schema as the paradigm for totality. The supreme analogate for this schema is to be found in the divine trinity of persons who, in the fullness of their interrelationships, make up a substantial unity.

tried to prevent the publication of Baader's *Sämtliche Werke.*[39] At that time, both were professors at the University of Munich: Schelling arrived from Erlangen in 1827; Baader had been on staff from the University's inception in 1826. Baader charged many times that Schelling's thought had lost its vitality and creativity. (See, for example, 15,431ff., 445, 462, 464, 485, 688, 689.) One of Baader's major objections to the thought of both Schelling and Hegel was that it failed to be, as philosophy should, a science of existing reality: "beyond" the relativity of *Dasein*, one must search for *Sein* itself. Baader also held that both unjustifiably used the notion of existing, as it applies to God and to creatures, in a univocal way; the notion of analogy was evidently foreign to them.[40] More than anything else, however, it was Schelling's pantheism that Baader repudiated. It was, Baader felt, one of the major shortcomings of the nature-philosophers and the rationalists that they were unable to conceive of a "central-being" – i.e., an absolute – as having any individuality or singular character about it; they erroneously believed that "individuality and universality contradicted one another, although such a central being (*Centralwesen*) must be conceived, on the contrary, as the individual par excellence with respect to all subordinate, partial individuals" (2,510).

5. Baader and Hegel

While Baader was returning from his proposed trip to Russia, he stopped in Berlin, and remained there, from November of 1823 until April of 1824. A major highlight of his stay was meeting Georg Wilhelm Friedrich Hegel and engaging in an extended exchange of ideas with him. Both men respected each other highly. As a young man, Hegel had taken a great interest in theology and mysticism. He had been much impressed by Baader's quasi-mystical essay *Über das pythagoräische Quadrat in der Natur oder die vier Weltgegenden* (1798), a work which served as the chief inspiration for Hegel's *Vom göttlichen Dreieck* (1800).[41] What Hegel found so interesting in Baader's thought was its mysticism; what Baader admired so much in Hegel was his logic and the power of his speculative mind. Baader hailed Hegel's *Phänomenologie des Geistes* and *Wissenschaft der Logik* as works of which the German nation could be proud (2,1ff.), but he paid his greatest tribute to Hegel in the introduction to the first book of *Fermenta Cognitionis* (2,141ff.) where he credits Hegel with being responsible for a rebirth in philosophy.

39   J. SAUTER: *Baader und Kant,* p. 547, fn. 4.
40   J. SAUTER: *Baader und Kant,* pp. 548ff.
41   J. SAUTER: *Baader und Kant,* p. 551, fn.

And in fact, since Hegel has lit the dialectical fire (the *Auto da Fé* of previous philosophy) once and for all, there is no way to success except through it: i.e., a person has to conduct himself and his works through this fire – he cannot prescind from it or even go so far as to ignore it.

Their months of close and amicable contact in Berlin during late 1823 and early 1824 led to an extended period (1824–30) of genuine rapport between the two philosophers. Baader was very anxious to win Hegel's approval and to reach philosophical understanding with him (15,405). Hegel, for his part, was very interested in *Fermenta Cognitionis* (15,401), the bulk of which Baader had composed at Memel while waiting for permission to enter Russia – a permission that never came. Late in his life, Baader even recalled Hegel's enthusiasm at being introduced (by Baader) to the thought of Meister Eckehart (15,159).

Nevertheless, Baader had never been reluctant to criticize Hegel's thought, even in the first book of *Fermenta Cognitionis*; but, as time went on, the criticism intensified, especially after 1830. Still, Hegel and Baader managed to avoid the type of personal animosity which had developed between Schelling and Baader. Their disputes remained academic. Indeed, Hegel seems to have been much more inclined to stress the closeness of his thought to Baader's than to point out the differences. In the preface to the second edition of the *Enzklopädie der philosophischen Wissenschaften im Grundrisse* (1827), the same preface in which he had praised Baader's restoration of ancient philosophical love to scholarly respectability,[42] Hegel also noted:

I must consider it desirable to see both in the content of several recent writings of Herr von Bader [*sic*] , as well as in their explicit mention of many of my principles, his agreement with the latter. As for the majority of, or indeed easily all of what he disputes, it would not be difficult to come to an understanding with him: i.e., to show that in fact there is no real departure from his views.[43]

42 See above.
43 G. W. F. HEGEL: *Hegels Sämtliche Werke*, volume 5, p. 19, fn. Hegel's opening words in this footnote read: "Es muss mir erwünscht sein, sowohl durch den Inhalt der mehreren neuerlichen Schriften des Herrn v. Bader [sic], als in den namentlichen Erwähnungen vieler meiner Sätze die Zustimmung desselben zu ersehen; über das Meiste dessen oder leicht Alles, was er bestreitet, würde es nicht schwer sein, mich ihm zu verständigen, nämlich zu zeigen, dass es in der That nicht von seinen Ansichten abweicht". As Baumgardt points out, this remark of Hegel's (together with the one cited above in note 4) indicates a great deal, coming as it does from Hegel in his later years: D. BAUMGARDT: *Franz von Baader, der Philosoph der Romantik*, p. 5, fn. 2. See also BAADER: *Sämtliche Werke* 2,liv; H. A. FISCHER-BARNICOL (Ed.): *Franz von Baader: Vom Sinn der Gesellschaft. Schriften zur Sozialphilosophie*, Cologne (Hegener) 1966, pp. 38ff.

Baader, however, did not completely agree and in a brief essay entitled "Hegel über meine Lehre", *Religionsphilosophische Aphorismen*, number 15 (10,306ff.), responded expressly to this assertion:

Hegel would have it that we agree on essentials (*in der Hauptsache*). To be sure, I agree with Hegel on many things: i.e., in everything in which he shows the lack of understanding in Kant's, Fichte's and Schelling's philosophy; but in essentials we are not for that reason of one mind. I will single out just three points . . . (10,307)

He then proceeded to attack Hegel's dualism of concept and intuition, of subject and object, and his totally materialistic concept of nature. In fact, Baader and Hegel differed fundamentally in their views of God. (Baader even held that Hegel's God was no God at all.) For Baader, God is a free and personal ground of being for the world. Schelling and Hegel, as Baader saw it, simply added superstructure to a basically Spinozistic foundation. Baader (and Plato) believed that the creation of the world, far from being a sign of God's inadequacy unto himself, was a sign that the overflowing richness of God's love had found a need for itself to fulfill (2,348). Baader insisted on a God who was both immanent and transcendent; he maintained that the existence of all things in and through and because of God was not the same as the identity of God with all things (14,31). Although Baader always credited Hegel with great achievements in philosophy, and Hegel felt that his differences with Baader could be reconciled, they were, in fact, deeply divided on some basic issues. The insuperable disagreements between Baader and other German Idealists can be attributed, in considerable measure, to the fact that Baader was the only German Idealist philosopher of stature who never came under the influence of Spinoza's thought.[44]

Baader and Christianity

The simple fact that Baader was born and raised in Catholic Bavaria during the late eighteenth century is probably the single most important factor that influenced his thought, for his religious beliefs decisively shaped his basic worldview. They determined the kinds of philosophical problems with which he would grapple and the types of philosophical approaches that he would adopt. For him, there was never a question of hermetically separating reason and faith. He was convinced that neither would fare well without the other, and he considered it the chief aim of his philosophy to restore faith and reason

44   See J. SAUTER: *Baader und Kant*, p. 562.

to a proper working relationship. His great intellectual enemies were *rationalists*, who had no use for faith and feeling, and *sentimentalists* or Pietists, who refused reason its due. Martin Deutinger, perhaps the most brilliant and original of Baader's followers, judged that the heart of Baader's contribution to modern thought was the restoration of religion and revelation to their rightful places:

> ... one will not recognize Baader's significance correctly unless he has totally overcome and left behind the whole movement of modern philosophy, which from Bacon and Descartes through Schelling and Herbart has pursued just one and the same principle, that of denying all and every authority, the principle of unlimited emancipation of reason. One must look at philosophy not from the standpoint of sense experience or absolute reason but from that of religion and moral freedom. Only from this standpoint can one rightly understand Baader's significance ... Baader has undertaken a real transformation of knowledge (*Wissenschaft*) and has once again in all seriousness placed religion and revelation at the head of it, where they belong, and beneath them nature and reason, where they belong.[45]

In fact, Baader claims (*Lettres inédites* 4,367) to be "the first one since the introduction of Cartesian philosophy who opened up again the insight into a more profound alliance between the knowledge of natural and divine things". Though he assigns this contribution to himself, his claim is not substantially different than Hegel's claim on his behalf.[46] What Baader termed "the quintessence of my philosophy" reads: "How a man is related to God determines how he is related to himself, to other men, to his own nature and [to] the rest of nature" (15,469; *Lettres inédites* 4,219). To Baader, religion is the commanding dimension, the framework of life, value, and thought. In stark contrast to the abstract rationalist thought of his own time and the rest of the nineteenth century, Baader spoke the language of the Bible and of symbol. In place of absolute human autonomy, there was, for Baader, the God "in whom we live and move and exist" (Acts 17,28). In place of the generalized and vague longing for salvation that characterized most Romantic thought, Baader believed specifically in original sin, or man's fallen state, and yearned for a Redeemer sent from God. In place of hopes for the perfectibility of man, Baader believed in an historical perfect man, Jesus Christ, who serves as model and ideal for all men. In place of the eighteenth-century view of marriage, one in which the role of woman was so low in dignity, or the Romantic view, one in which – despite some

45   H. FELS: *Martin Deutinger. Auswahl seiner Schriften,* Munich (Kösel and Pustet) 1938, pp. 193–94. The second part of this work (pp. 115ff.) consists of selected writings of Deutinger himself.
46   See above.

religious overtones – the center of gravity remained the purely human and the purely earthly, Baader saw marriage as a sacramental union whose goal was to reestablish the integral humanity that God made in his own image.

Baader was a religious philosopher. What philosophy meant to him cannot be separated from what his religion meant to him, because his philosophy was about his religion. In this connection, Hans Grassl observes:

> To philosophize about the incarnate Word also means to stand in the midst of the mystery of light, the mystery of a world created by God, circumscribed by God, and redeemed by God, and to recognize that the measure of all knowledge of being (just as in the Middle Ages) is dependent on its relationship to God as bearer and sustainer of this mystery. Without God, there is no knowledge at all. *With* God, a man knows differently than *against* God.[47]

Grassl goes on to state that it was neither the lonely nostalgia of the Romantics nor the tragic feeling that spiritual integrity was no longer possible to man on earth that led Baader to philosophize.

> On the contrary, what made Baader a philosopher was the imperative that sprang up out of full possession of the mystery – to describe in the most speculative way the state of being penetrated by the ecstatic-luminous created world of God . . .[48]

In other words, the object of Baader's philosophy was speculation about the mysteries of his religion as he himself experienced them. As previously noted, Baader grew up in the religious atmosphere of late eighteenth-century Bavaria, and that atmosphere strongly influenced the type of religious experience to which he was exposed.[49] Above all, there was the strong Latin stamp of Bavarian baroque Catholicism. In addition, this hierarchically-structured Church, which filled such a central place in the lives of the faithful, accorded only a relatively small place to individualism. Yet, it was a Church whose ceremonies

---

47 H. GRASSL (Ed.): *Franz von Baader. Über Liebe, Ehe und Kunst,* p. 17. Grassl's words read: "Über den fleischgewordenen Logos zu philosophieren bedeutet denn auch, drinnenzustehen im Lichtmysterium einer göttlich geschlossenen, göttlich erlösten Welt und das Mass aller Seinserkenntnis wie im Mittelalter abhängig zu wissen vom Verhältnis zu Gott als dem Träger und Nährer dieses Mysteriums. Ohne Gott könnte es überhaupt keine Erkenntnis geben. *Mit* Gott erkennt der Mensch anders als *gegen* Gott".

48 H. GRASSL (Ed.): *Franz von Baader. Über Liebe, Ehe und Kunst,* p. 18. Grassl's words read: "Im Gegenteil, was Baader zum Philosophen machte, war das aus dem Vollbesitz des Mysteriums herkommende Gebot, die Durchgriffenheit von der ekstatisch-lichthaft erschaffenen Gotteswelt höchst spekulativ darzustellen . . ."

49 Hans Grassl is unique among Baader scholars in his throughgoing mastery of the Bavarian environment in which Baader lived, especially Munich Romanticism. See: H. GRASSL: *Aufbruch zur Romantik. Bayerns Beitrag zur deutschen Geistesgeschichte 1765–1785,* Munich (C.H. Beck) 1968. What follows in the text is also based largely on H. GRASSL (Ed.): *Franz von Baader. Über Liebe, Ehe und Kunst,* introduction, pp. 28ff.

48

served as the high points of people's lives, and it was a Church that stood as the organic center of communal unity. And it was a Church whose baroque art and devotional piety impressed the young Baader deeply. He was considerably influenced by the Benedictines, notably by Pater Kaindl,[50] and it may have been the Benedictines who sparked Baader's interest in medieval mysticism, a mode of thought that inspired his thinking for the rest of his life.[51]

Baroque Catholicism, however, did not hold undisputed sway in Bavarian religious life. The German Enlightenment, the *Aufklärung*, especially as it was embodied in the thought and activity of the Freemasons and the *Illuminati*,[52] served as a major opposing force. Klaus Epstein explains: "The purpose of Masonry was to spread *Aufklärung* in defiance of the existing patterns of social hierarchy, political authority, and traditionalist religion".[53] The Illuminati were a kind of secret society "pledged to engage in unremitting warfare against every form of tyranny, oppression, and superstition – or, to put matters concretely, against royal absolutism, feudal exploitation, and supernatural religion".[54] Baader was influenced by these movements, especially by such men as Eusebius Amort and Benedict Stattler, both of whom strongly advocated reconciliation of the divided Christian churches and emancipation from Rome. Neither point was lost on Baader, nor, for that matter, was the predilection of Masonry and Illuminationism for mystical and occult lore. In all probability, Baader himself was a Mason.[55] And while he remained a staunch foe of anything which attributed total autonomy to reason, he never failed to assign reason a very important place in his scheme of reality. He opposed obscurantism of every kind.

The Pietist movement exerted yet another important influence on religious life in Bavaria: it was "evangelical Christianity, the direct antithesis of the hierarchical, dogmatic, and ritualistic established Bavarian Church"; it emphasized

---

50 Johann Evangelist Kaindl published *Die Teutsche Sprache aus ihren Wurzeln,* 4 volumes, Sulzbach (Seidel) 1815–24, on which Baader based many etymologies. (See, for example, BAADER: *Sämtliche Werke* 13,219ff.) Kaindl's work is not scientific; indeed its data are often quite fanciful.

51 H. GRASSL (Ed.): *Franz von Baader. Über Liebe, Ehe und Kunst,* p. 32.

52 On Masonry, Illuminism, and *Aufklärung,* see: K. EPSTEIN: *The Genesis of German Conservatism,* Princeton, New Jersey (Princeton University Press) 1966, chapter 2, pp. 84ff; A. VIATTE: *Les Sources Occultes du Romantisme; Illuminisme-Theosophie 1770–1820,* 2 volumes, Paris (Honoré Champion) 1928, 1965; Hans Grassl also offers bibliographical leads: see both references cited in note 49; F. SCHNABEL: *Deutsche Geschichte im 19en Jahrhundert,* 4 volumes, Freiburg (Herder) ³1955, especially volume 4.

53 K. EPSTEIN: *The Genesis of German Conservatism,* p. 84.

54 K. EPSTEIN: *The Genesis of German Conservatism,* p. 90.

55 E. SUSINI (Ed.): *Lettres inédites* 3,60ff.; J. SAUTER: *Franz von Baaders Schriften zur Gesellschaftsphilosophie,* pp. 900ff.

49

the Bible, unstructured Christianity, practical Christian love in action, and the priesthood of all believers; and it opposed pilgrimages and indulgences. The best-known leaders of the Pietistic movement in Bavaria included Feneberg, Lindl, Gossner, and Boos.[56] They were powerful preachers, winning over such a large following in Bavaria that the movement almost took on the proportions of a schism.[57] Baader was acquainted with all these leaders and was a personal friend of Lindl and Gossner in particular; he acted as a mediator in arranging for the emigration of these men and others to Russia where they could pursue their religious work.[58] But Baader himself could never be considered a Pietist. He was committed to the concept of a visible Church with a collegial structure of authority; he opposed the onesideness of "religion of the heart".

Nevertheless, Bavarian Pietism left its mark on Baader, not least of all through the pronounced mystical preoccupations of many of its leaders. The spirituality of *The Imitation of Christ* and the mystical thought embodied in the works of many great medieval German philosophers, as well as the writings of John of the Cross and Teresa of Avila, were studied and expounded upon by the Pietists. In such matters, they found a willing listener in Baader.

Baader, Mysticism, and Occultism

Franz von Baader was, as Ernst Benz calls him, "the great rediscoverer of mysticism" in his time.[59] Baader was persuaded that the principles of true mysticism were precisely what was needed to reestablish religion in his day:

. . . it is only the hitherto prevailing aversion from true mysticism that has kept speculation as superficial as it is for the most part even now; for all such fear, whether it shows itself among Catholics or non-Catholics, whether it be rationalistic or pietistic in nature, can work only in a mystifying and obscuring way, since it bars or keeps us from access to the place in which those mysteries are still veiled. But it is now time to unveil them, without which a deeper grounding of religion is not possible. (Die zeugende, hervorbringende Liebe ist väterlich und mütterlich zugleich, *Religionsphilosophische Aphorismen*, number 32, 10,331–32)

56 See E. SUSINI (Ed.): *Lettres inédites* 3. The index has numerous references to these men. See also, H. GRASSL, both references cited in note 49; H. SCHIEL: *Johann Michael Sailer*, 2 volumes, Regensburg (Friedrich Pustet): volume 1, 1948, volume 2, 1952.

57 F. SCHNABEL: *Deutsche Geschichte im 19en Jahrhundert*, volume 4, p. 479.

58 See E. SUSINI (Ed.): *Lettres inédites* 3; for details on this subject, see index, pp. 599–600.

59 E. BENZ: *Schelling. Werden und Wirken seines Denkens*, Zürich (Rhein) 1955, p. 7. On Baader and mysticism, see further: J. SAUTER: *Baader und Kant*, pp. 564ff.; E. SUSINI: *Franz von Baader et le romantisme mystique. La philosophie de Franz von Baader*, 2 volumes, Paris (J. Vrin) 1942; D. BAUMGARDT: *Franz von Baader, der Philosoph der Romantik.*

Mystical preoccupations and ways of thinking, however, were not latter-day discoveries in Baader's life. As Johannes Sauter puts it:

. . . for it was not because he zealously studied the mystics that we find mystical themes in his thought; rather, he had such predilection for the mystics because he possessed the same thought-structure and the same thought-motivations as they did.[60]

Two things in particular attracted Baader powerfully toward mysticism: (1) "the special piety toward nature (*Naturandacht*) that breathes forth in the ancient writings" (3,236), their "faith in nature" (5,6); and (2) the *dynamism* of mystical religious thought.[61] The force of mysticism, in short, allowed Baader to feel a living unity between mind and nature, between himself and the world around him, as well as between himself and God. It ushered him into the mystery of life itself. His complaint against Enlightenment philosophizing was that it took no account of the wisdom of older philosophical and theosophical traditions. He would make it his business to expose its superficiality, a superficiality which had hitherto been concealed only by "the fig-leaf of critical philosophy"; and he would do so precisely by reviving the ancient philosophies of nature and religion (9,37ff.). Baader's notion of mysticism was not that of a mysticism based on feeling but one based on speculation. (See 4,314; 8,207.) He believed that profoundest speculation ends in mysticism:

All investigation into the ultimate grounds of our knowledge ends finally in mysticism (i.e., speculative mysticism), says Weishaupt . . . To that, one can only answer with Yes! and Amen! and with the psalmist's word: "My spirit must search". (13,392)

Between 1796 and 1809 Baader published little. In 1796, he had written to Jacobi (15,163) indicating that he intended to be still for a time in order to gather needed resources of power and knowledge. During these thirteen years, he busied himself intensely, not only with German Idealist philosophy but also with mysticism. Johann Friedrich Kleuker's *Magikon oder das geheime System einer Gesellschaft unbekannter Philosophen* (Frankfurt and Leipzig, 1784), in particular, had a considerable affect on Baader's orientation toward mysticism; it was a work which Baader treasured highly and studied with care.[62] *Magikon*, which

---

60 J. SAUTER: *Baader und Kant*, p. 583. The statement reads: ". . . denn nicht weil er (Baader) die Mystiker eifrig studiert, finden sich bei ihm mystische Denkmotive, sondern er hatte zu den Mystikern solche Vorliebe, weil er dieselbe Denkstruktur, dieselben Denkaffekte besass".

61 J. SAUTER: *Baader und Kant*, pp. 564–65.

62 See Baader's notes on *Magikon* (12,529ff.) and his letter to Kleuker (15,188ff.). See also 3,218; 7,192; 9,352; 12,65, 73; 15,291. See also E. SUSINI (Ed.): *Lettres inédites* 1 and 2 (index references in volume 3).

had so much to say about the theosophy and mysticism of Louis Claude de St. Martin (1743–1803), a prominent French illuminist,[63] proved of vital significance to Baader's intellectual development, and it did so for two principal reasons: (1) St. Martin directly influenced Baader's thought more than any other thinker except Jacob Böhme; and (2) St. Martin was probably responsible for leading Baader to his serious lifelong study of Böhme.[64] (Further, St. Martin played a key role in the revival of medieval mysticism in France, just as Baader did in Germany.) St. Martin, before becoming immersed in Böhme and – in later life – Emanuel Swedenborg, had initially been a disciple of the Jewish mystic Martinez Pasqualis.[65] And while St. Martin had been a theosophist –

63 It is difficult to say, precisely, why Baader was initially attracted to St. Martin's work. Sauter states that Baader was first made aware of St. Martin through *Magikon*. (See J. SAUTER: *Baader und Kant*, p. 568.) On the other hand, Grassl (H. GRASSL [Ed.]: *Franz von Baader. Über Liebe, Ehe, und Kunst*, p. 35) holds that "it also seems to have been Sailer who recommended that Baader read Saint-Martin, even before reading the Munich Pietist Karl von Eckartshausen". Grassl says: "Sailer scheint es auch gewesen zu sein, der Baader noch vor dem Müncher Pietisten Karl von Eckartshausen die Lektüre Saint-Martins empfahl". Grassl emphasizes the great influence which Sailer, who later became bishop of Regensburg, exercised on Baader for many decades (H. GRASSL [Ed.]: *Franz von Baader. Über Liebe, Ehe, und Kunst*, pp. 35-38). It was Sailer who recommended the reading of Klopstock, Claudius, Lavater, Herder, and Jacobi to Baader. Baader was certainly heavily influenced by Sailer, as his diary and correspondence show. On Sailer, see H. SCHIEL: *Johann Michael Sailer*, volumes 1 and 2; E. SUSINI (Ed.): *Lettres inédites* 3, (index, p. 615), cites a host of references and bibliography, as does H. GRASSL: *Aufbruch zur Romantik*. Baader's letter of 1804 to Kleuker says that he had read Kleuker's *Magikon* for the first time twelve years before. On the other hand, his diary for January 31, 1787 indicates that he had already read St. Martin's *Des Erreurs et de la Verité* (Lyon, 1775) and that he agreed with Claudius and the author of *Magikon* that it was not a reprehensible book. Regarding Baader's letter to Kleuker and the entry in his diary, referred to above, see: BAADER: *Sämtliche Werke* 11,126; 15,188ff.

64 Little is known regarding how and when Baader first became acquainted with the works of Böhme. (J. SAUTER: Baader und Kant, p. 573). Anton Lutterbeck, editor of the 16th volume of BAADER: *Sämtliche Werke*, says (p. 8): "On January 31, 1787 [Baader] mentions for the first time the writings of St. Martin (possibly made known to him through Kleuker's *Magikon* of 1784); they remained his faithful companions throughout his life. He was probably already acquainted with the writings of Jacob Böhme, as one can still see from a passage in his work *Über den Wärmestoff* (3,41)". That passage, however, makes no mention of Böhme or his work. The content is indeed similar to what one might find in Böhme, and so is the language, but their provenance remains uncertain. K. P. Fischer thinks Oetinger led Baader to Böhme. (See: K. P. FISCHER: *Zur hundertjährigen Geburtsfeier Franz von Baaders. Versuch einer Charakteristik seiner Theosophie*, Erlangen [Eduard Besold], 1865, p. 9.)

65 Baader wrote an essay, *Über des Spaniers Don Martinez Pasqualis Lehre*, in 1823 (4,115–32). He was especially interested in Pasqualis's number-theory (2,335; 15,314, 340,

even before becoming acquainted with Böhme's works – he managed, even after falling under the influence of Böhme, to maintain his own individuality. Still, he considered Böhme his greatest teacher, and his gnosiology was based on a Böhme principle often cited by Baader: "One must explain things through man, and not man through things" (11,233; 12,88, 264, 371–72; *Lettres inédites* 1,188).[66]

Baader especially admired St. Martin's skill in harmonizing the claims of nature and grace (1,67; 2,233). He also felt a profound kinship with St. Martin's feeling for the tragic and fallen character of man's present earthly condition, an elemental feeling that all is not well with man and the world, that nature and man are both "sick" and out of sorts. (See Baader's *Vorrede zu [D. G. H.] Schuberts Übersetzung von St. Martin de l'Esprit des choses*, 1,57-70, especially 63ff.) The contrast with Enlightenment optimism and apotheosis of reason is evident, but Baader did not adopt this attitude from St. Martin. As early as Christmas day, 1786, Baader wrote in his diary about man's need for a redeemer: this need presupposed that man is in captivity, which, in turn, indicated that man is presently "not a completely pure creature of God (*kein ganz reines Geschöpf Gottes*)" (11,110). St. Martin's philosophy of nature went even further than Herder's in the direction of "spiritualizing nature". Baader concurred, for "there is no spirit which is not an *esprit de corps*" (12,46). Johannes Sauter sums up:

St. Martin and Baader agree with one another, then, in epistemology and cosmology, in ethics and religion! The whole of nature is a giant palimpsest on which the original metaphysical text has been covered over by another text.[67]

It is uncertain when Baader began to study the thought of Jacob Böhme (1575–1624). His first mention of the "teutonic philosopher" (by name) in print did not occur until 1812 (1,69), but it is clear that his introduction to Böhme's work had taken place many years earlier. (He was acquainted with St. Martin's writings at least as early as January of 1787 [11,126], and it is unlikely that he would have neglected studying – for himself – a figure so highly extolled by St. Martin.) By 1800, it is probable that Baader's preoccupation with St. Martin had

---

365). See the index volume of BAADER: *Sämtliche Werke* and SUSINI (Ed.): *Lettres inédites* 3 (index), for further references.

66   This dictum appears in German in Baader's diary (11,233): "Man muss die Dinge durch den Menschen und nicht den Menschen durch die Dinge erklären". Hoffmann gives the French in a footnote: "Il faut expliquer les choses par l'homme et non l'homme par les choses". Baader uses the text in varying ways, sometimes in French and sometimes in German.

67   J. SAUTER: *Baader und Kant*, p. 573.

also led him to do some serious work on Böhme as well,[68] and by 1804, Ludwig Tieck could write: "Baader lives entirely in J. Böhme too".[69]

To understand the intellectual milieu of early nineteenth-century German Romanticism and Idealism, it is of great importance to realize what a huge impact Jacob Böhme's thought exercised on the elite of these two movements: for example, on Novalis and Tieck, and on Schelling and Hegel.[70] And Baader played a key role in this Böhme revival, especially as it influenced Schelling and Hegel.[71] August Wilhelm Schlegel dubbed Baader *Böhmius redivivus*, a nickname Baader prized highly.[72] Indeed, one of Baader's lasting ambitions was to publish a critical edition of Böhme's works, either in their entirety or singly. He never succeeded in doing so (see 15,244, 250, 254, 257, 446ff., 464, 476, 491, 541, 570–84, 655, 688), but a considerable portion of Baader's *Sämtliche Werke* is devoted to commentaries and study-books about Böhme.[73]

Böhme's deep intuition into the interrelationships that linked the world of nature with the world of spirit, and his thoroughgoing blend of naturalism and idealism, served as the focal point that "magnetically" attracted Baader to Böhme's thought. Baader considered Böhme and Paracelsus "the two greatest German philosophers of nature" (15,482, 632, 703), and Böhme, for him, was "the founder of true German physiology and theosophy" (9,304). Baader believed that Böhme had discovered a valid way to reconcile the unity of the first principle with the multiplicity of phenomena; he regarded Böhme's scheme of reality as coherent and dynamic, not merely a fanciful abstraction but a living unity. The way in which Böhme explained created nature, as the external figure of an internal world of the spirit, as well as Böhme's idea of an eternal nature in God Himself, appealed strongly to Baader. Although Böhme's thought, it has been claimed, embodied elements of pantheism, Baader was always convinced that Böhme was no pantheist (2,373; 3,390; 13,173). At a time when God and the world – spirit and nature – seemed on their way to becoming

---

68 J. SAUTER: *Baader und Kant*, p. 573. Hoffmann relates that Baader first found Böhme's works in a second-hand book store after much searching. Baader told him that his reaction to reading Böhme's work for the first time was very negative; he found it so abstruse and unintelligible that he threw the volume against the wall in disgust (l,lxiii; 16,8; J. SAUTER: *Baader und Kant*, p. 573; and elsewhere in the literature). Baader reported in a letter to Stransky (October 27, 1809) that he had received three complete editions of Böhme's works (15,235).

69 J. SAUTER: *Baader und Kant*, p. 573.

70 Sauter (J. SAUTER: *Baader und Kant*, pp. 574ff.) provides an extensive sketch outlining the great interest Romantics and Idealist philosophers had in Böhme's thought.

71 J. SAUTER: *Baader und Kant*, p. 575.

72 J. SAUTER: *Baader und Kant*, p. 575.

73 See especially volumes 3 and 13. Appeals to Böhme are very numerous throughout BAADER: *Sämtliche Werke*.

antithetical rather than complementary aspects of reality,[74] Baader felt that Böhme's synthesis of nature and spirit had much to offer. Böhme's ideas, he argued, were sufficiently powerful to serve as principles for a deeper foundation of Christian doctrine than ever before (2,367; 7,7, 78, 116; 13,161). Böhme's significance, Baader held, should not merely be relegated to the past, but should be permitted to reemerge and provide guidelines for the present and the future (15,572). Now, Baader believed, was the time for Böhme's ideas to flourish (15,280).

Baader apparently took great pleasure in citing the thought of Jacob Böhme, the humble and generally forgotten shoemaker from Görlitz in Saxony, and by so doing confounding the scholars in their own province: "I really enjoy vexing our worldly-wise fools often with this shoemaker" (15,381). But Baader also drew on other mystical-occult sources, particularly those that concentrated, as Böhme did, on speculating about nature. Paracelsus (1493–1541), for example, seriously occupied his interest, especially between the years 1812 and 1815 (15,243ff., 259). Baader cites him often, just as he does Friedrich Christoph Oetinger. During this period of his life, he also turned frequently to the Cabbala, "a torso of ancient philosophy of nature" (15,168ff.), and to alchemy.[75]

In addition to the stream of mysticism which centered about nature, there was another devoted purely to religion, and this stream also attracted much of Baader's attention. As a religious thinker, Meister Eckehart (ca. 1260–1327) held a position of eminence in Baader's thought analogous to that held by Böhme as a philosopher of nature. Baader regarded Eckehart as "the most enlightened of all medieval theologians" (14,93), notable not only for the boldness and depth of his speculation but also for his sheer religiosity (5,263); he is, for Baader, the commanding figure in medieval mysticism (15,457). Had Eckehart lived in Böhme's day, Baader held, he would have surpassed even Böhme's accomplishments (15,159). Baader cited Eckehart often, finding his work especially worthwhile in defining the status of creature vis-à-vis Creator in general (e.g., 1,208; 4,359); explaining man's need for grace (7,152); relating time and eternity (1,273; 10,116, 224); and addressing the "marriage" of the human soul with God in virtue of the image of God in man (7,153). But Baader also frequently mentioned other important figures and influences from this

---

74   The great preoccupation with the natural and supernatural (especially the strong tendency to transpose everything traditionally supernatural into natural terms and realities) during the period of Romanticism is the focus of an excellent analysis in M. H. ABRAMS: *Natural Supernaturalism: Tradition and Revolution in Romantic Literature*, New York (W. W. Norton) 1971.

75   See J. SAUTER: *Baader und Kant*, pp. 579ff. The index volume to BAADER: *Sämtliche Werke* lists copious references to Paracelsus, Oetinger, and other natural philosophers involved with Cabbalism, Alchemy, and the like.

tradition: e.g. Eckehart's disciple Tauler, as well as Angelus Silesius, Suso, Thomas à Kempis, Ruysbroek, and the "German Theology", etc.[76] Because he combined an innate personal proclivity toward mystical thought with an intensive, lifelong cultivation of the whole western mystical tradition – much of which had been generally forgotten – Baader became one of the most influential thinkers in early nineteenth-century Germany.

Hans Grassl remarks that "the ground of tradition on which Baader stands is one of incredible complexity, yes even contradictoriness".[77] And while the foregoing sketch of Baader's intellectual development suggests some of this complexity, many important aspects of his life and thought have been barely touched upon or not even mentioned at all. Nothing has been said, for example, about his early medical studies – training which led to a doctor's degree in medicine – nor has any reference been made to the years following, years devoted to becoming a mining engineer. No account has been given of the many years which he spent in the Bavarian civil service as inspector of mints and mines, nor of the glass-making factory which he ran, nor of the important new glass-manufacturing process which he invented. No mention has been made of the intellectual ties which linked him to such important foreign luminaries as Prince Gallitzin or Prince Mestchersky in Russia and to Montalembert and the *l'Avenir* circle in France, nor of the years spent in England studying technology and observing the factory system and the social problems it engendered. And no note has been taken of his extensive research into parapsychology, magnetism, somnambulism, and related phenomena, nor of the intensive study which he devoted to the Church Fathers and to Thomas Aquinas. In a word, Baader is not a man easily "labeled"; his interests were as wide-ranging as they were profound.

In the preceding pages, especially in the section dealing with Baader and Romanticism,[78] judgments made about Baader by many of his contemporaries have been noted. Without even citing the laudatory testimony offered by the editors of the *Sämtliche Werke* (who mince no words in praising Baader), it has been possible to suggest the force of Baader's personality and the impact which his intellectual accomplishments made on those who knew him and his work. By adding a second stage to this "publicity campaign" on behalf of Franz von Baader, a more up-to-date, objective, and balanced assessment can be made of a figure who has truly remained the "underground man" that Schelling called him.[79]

---

76 J. SAUTER: *Baader und Kant*, pp. 581ff.
77 H. GRASSL (Ed.): *Franz von Baader. Über Liebe, Ehe und Kunst*, p. 15.
78 See above.
79 See above.

Twentieth-century appraisals of Baader and his work, unlike those offered by his contemporaries, will not be affected by Baader's overwhelming personality. They can be based exclusively on the value of Baader's ideas, ideas which until recently have been inadequately understood, principally because of rhetorical problems associated with freeing them from a corpus of problematically-written essays. (Many of Baader's contemporaries, even those who attest to the richness of his skills in oral discourse, note the relative poverty of his writing ability.) Further, this century's assessments have the advantage of perspective. They are not as immediately conditioned by the chronological/environmental matrix out of which Baader's thought grew and, consequently, can help determine whether Baader's thought, so vitally important to his own age, has something of significance to offer ours as well.

What do more modern students of Baader have to say? In "Neues über Baader",[80] an article which appeared in 1929 and in which three then recent major works about Baader are reviewed, Eduard Winter credits Fritz Lieb (one of the three authors) with making important contributions to Baader's early history, but he devotes greater attention to the more comprehensive studies of Johannes Sauter and David Baumgardt. Sauter is lauded for having clarified the architectonic of Baader's whole thought-edifice. And in *Baader und Kant* (Jena, 1928), a book which "shows for the first time the richness of thought possessed by Baader, a richness that burst all barriers of language", Sauter holds:

[that] it was Baader who tried to unite Idealism, Romanticism, and Realism in a highest principle, and what he said about the relationship of religion, metaphysics, and love belongs to the most profound that can be taught about them.[81]

While Winter argues that Sauter tended to overestimate Baader's importance for German philosophy, David Baumgardt, he maintains, "must be labelled reserved (*nüchtern*)". Still, even Baumgardt does not shrink from saying:

Greater intensity of religious struggle [than Baader evidenced], more disciplined self-control over feelings of faith, is hardly to be encountered in the whole of Protestant literature of that time – even the Pietistic. Judged by the pithiness, the depth, and the enthusiasm of his being, Baader definitely belongs to the most powerful religious minds of the German people (*Deutschtums*). In fact, he surpasses the entire Romantic movement in this respect. Even Novalis's religiosity seems more artificial and Schleiermacher's more a matter of educational acquisition when compared to the deep and mighty natural power of Baader's religious struggle.[82]

---

80   E. WINTER: "Neues über Baader", *Hochland*, 26 (1929), pp. 433ff.
81   J. SAUTER: *Baader und Kant*, p. 466.
82   D. BAUMGARDT: *Franz von Baader und die philosophische Romantik*, p. 131.

Paul Kluckhohn, a distinguished scholar of German Romanticism, writes in *Die deutsche Romantik* that "Baader, more than any other man, deserves the designation 'the philosopher of the Romantic movement' ".[83] And in a large study entitled *Die Auffassung der Liebe in der Literatur des 18. Jahrhunderts und der deutschen Romantik,* he (Kluckhohn) concludes that Franz von Baader "brought the Romantic conception of love to its highest peak".[84] Kluckhohn's conclusion is based on a detailed demonstration of why Romantic notions of love and marriage are superior to those held in the eighteenth century.

Hugo Ball, a major twentieth-century contributor to Baader scholarship, not only provided impetus to Baader research by devoting an entire chapter of his *Zur Kritik der deutschen Intelligenz* to Baader, but also made this amazing claim on his behalf:

> He is the only great Christian philosopher that Germany has had, but he replaces whole schools and generations. He can, if only the young will understand him, become a magnet that will wrest the iron out of the hands of a whole people.[85]

Friedrich Heer, the highly-regarded Viennese historian of ideas, calls Baader "the richest and most comprehensive German Catholic thinker of the nineteenth century",[86] and he allots more space to Baader than to either Johann Adam Möhler or Joseph Görres. Nevertheless, Heer notes:

> Baader is still one of the great unknowns of the nineteenth century, although his opposite pole, Hegel, thought highly of him and important Russian and French scholars held him in high regard during his lifetime; later on, Kierkegaard and Scheler appealed to him. Berdyaev bases himself completely on him.[87]

Leopold Ziegler found it appropriate to dedicate his two-volume study, *Die Menschwerdung,* "to the shades of Jacob Böhme, Sören Kierkegaard, and Franz Baader",[88] and to include dozens of allusions to Baader's thought in the work. In *Die neue Wissenschaft,* Ziegler appeals to Baader in yet another way – by suggesting that he should serve as the guiding spirit in reconciling faith and

---

83 P. 96. Kluckhohn's use of the term is adopted from Johannes Nohl (see note 7 above).
84 P. 542.
85 H. BALL: *Zur Kritik der deutschen Intelligenz,* Bern (1919), p. 140. Ball's words are: "Er ist der einzige christliche Philosoph grossen Stiles, den Deutschland gehabt hat, doch ersetzt er . . . ganze Schulen und Generationen. Er kann, wenn nur die Jugend ihn verstehen will, zum Magnetberg werden, der einem ganzen Volke das Eisen aus den Händen windet".
86 F. HEER: *Europa Mutter der Revolutionen,* Stuttgart (Kohlhammer) 1964, p. 578.
87 F. HEER: *Europa Mutter der Revolutionen,* p. 578.
88 See Dedication. The work appeared in Olten in 1948.

reason and could provide the synthesis necessary for the unity of mind that Europe needed so desperately after World War II.[89]

Gerd-Klaus Kaltenbrunner considers Baader "the only great Catholic philosopher in the modern intellectual history of Germany, a history stamped above all by Protestantism and the secularization wrought by it".[90] According to Kaltenbrunner, Baader, along with Hamann in the Protestant sphere, was

the only great philosopher of Germany who self-consciously willed to do nothing else but to defend the entirety of Christian tradition – with love, but also with such ardor as to lead him to blustering rudeness.[91]

Eugène Susini, as sober and dispassionate a scholar as one can imagine, assesses Baader in a way highly reminiscent of Schelling: in Baader, "knowing has become a part of his very nature and existence, a compact unity".[92] Susini calls Baader "a philosopher for whom thought was a reality that penetrated his whole being, one who would brook no separation between abstract idea and concrete life, but rather one who lived his thought and thought his life".[93] Once again, it seems clear that Baader's strength and attractiveness are to be found, not in any abstract and systematic exposition of ideas, but in a concrete and dynamic synthesis of love and calculation, a genuine reconciliation of the irrational and the rational. And it was precisely such a view that led Max Pulver to publish selected *Schriften Franz von Baaders*; for Pulver, Baader's speculation spoke to life and experience in a way that truly enriched them both.[94]

To add additional witnesses to the roster testifying on Baader's behalf would be superfluous. Enough evidence has already been marshalled to support the claim that those who have paid the price – those who have wrestled with Baader's tortured, heavily symbolic, and overburdened prose and have waded through his unsystematized agglomeration of the most diffusely recondite and esoteric materials – have found much in Baader to ignite their enthusiasm and excite their imaginations. What further need then is there for additional testi-

---

89 P. 151. The work was published in Munich in 1951.
90 G-K. KALTENBRUNNER: "Socialrevolutionär, Politiker, und Laientheologe. Zum 200. Geburtstag Franz von Baaders", *Zeitwende*, new series, vol. 9,3 (1965), p. 151.
91 G-K. KALTENBRUNNER: "Socialrevolutionär, Politiker, und Laientheologe. Zum 200. Geburtstag Franz von Baaders", p. 152.
92 See above.
93 E. SUSINI (Ed.): *Lettres inédites* 2,472. Susini says: "Ce philosophe, pour qui la pensée etait une réalité pénétrant sa vie tout entiére, qui n'établissait pas de séparation entre l'idée abstraite et la vie concrète mais qui vivait sa pensée et pensait sa vie . . ."
94 M. PULVER (Ed.): *Schriften Franz von Baaders*, Leipzig (Insel) 1921, pp. v–xv.

mony? The "publicity campaign", it is hoped, has served to arouse interest in Baader's life and thought. The real justification for that interest, however, can manifest itself – with full intensity – only to those who respond to Baader's own invitation – by investigating his thought and attempting to understand it "in much the same fashion as one learns to swim: i.e., all at once, after one has tried long enough and felt his way around long enough" (10,296).

Chapter 1
Franz von Baader:
His Life and His Thought

Biographical Sketch[1]

Benedict Franz Xaver von Baader was born in Munich on the 27th day of March, 1765. His father, Josef Franz Paula Baader, was the Bavarian court physician; his mother was the former Rosalie von Schöpff. Franz was the third of thirteen children born to these parents of moderate means between the years 1762 and 1781.[2] Of the ten children younger than Franz, six died before completing their tenth year. Although none of his other surviving siblings became famous, Franz's two older brothers, Clemens Alois and Joseph Anton,[3] did become well-known in Bavaria. Clemens, the eldest of the Baader children, was a priest who made a name for himself by working on behalf of secularization and church reform in the spirit of Josephism: he favored, among other things, the abolition of mandatory sacerdotal celibacy. An accomplished writer, he authored a number of highly-regarded biographies and bibliographies dealing with Bavarian history. Joseph, the second son, became still better-known. As chief mining inspector and director of the royal fountains, he was widely

---

1 The principal sources for Baader's biography include: Franz Hoffmann's biography, found in BAADER: *Sämtliche Werke* 11,1–160; the diary kept by Baader himself, also found in the *Sämtliche Werke* 11; Baader's correspondence, found in the *Sämtliche Werke* 15,161–706, and E. SUSINI (Ed.): *Lettres inédites de Franz von Baader*, 4 volumes. Studies include: F. LIEB: *Baaders Jugendgeschichte*, Munich (M. C. Kaiser) 1926; D. BAUMGARDT: *Franz von Baader und die philosophische Romantik*, Halle/Saale (Max Niemeyer) 1927; J. SAUTER (Ed.): *Franz von Baaders Schriften zur Gesellschaftsphilosophie*, Jena (Gustav Fischer) 1925, pp. 565ff.; and J. SAUTER *Baader und Kant*, Jena (Gustav Fischer) 1928, pp. 1ff.; H. GRASSL (Ed.): *Franz von Baader. Über Liebe, Ehe und Kunst*, Munich (Kösel) 1953, pp. 11–59.

2 On Joseph Franz Baader's limited financial resources, see E. SUSINI (Ed.): *Lettres inédites* 4, appendix 4, pp. 415ff.

3 On Baader's brothers, see Hans Grassl's articles in the *Allgemeine deutsche Biographie*, I,476; BAADER: *Sämtliche Werke* 15,6ff., 275, 285; E. SUSINI (Ed.): *Lettres inédites* 3,592 (index); 4,597ff. (index); J. SAUTER (Ed.): *Franz von Baaders Schriften zur Gesellschaftsphilosophie*, pp. 566, 859ff.

recognized for his expertise in technological matters, especially for his pioneering work in railroads. His earliest plans and sketches for railroads date from 1807, nearly two decades before the first railroad was introduced into England.

As a child, Baader was physically weak and seemed to be somewhat mentally retarded. In his eleventh year, however, a dramatic change took place, occasioned, as Baader himself reports (15,25), by his looking at some theorems from Euclid's geometry. The developmental problems which had plagued him were resolved, and his schooling, marginal until that time, progressed so rapidly that by his sixteenth year he was able to attend the University at Ingolstadt with his older brother, Joseph. Between 1781 and 1785, Baader and his brother studied medicine at Ingolstadt and in Vienna, where they were taught by the then-renowned physician, Dr. Stoll. Both received their doctor's degrees, with highest honors, from Ingolstadt in 1785. Franz practiced medicine briefly with his father before discovering that medical work did not suit him. So, with his father's permission, he decided to study mining. He enrolled in a highly-regarded mining academy at Freiberg in Saxony where, like Novalis, he profited from the instruction of a famous man in the field, Abraham Werner. He remained in Freiberg from 1788 until 1792, but his studies in mining were not narrowly focused; during this four-year period, he also found time to study chemistry and mineralogy intensively. His student years at Freiberg were subsidized by the Bavarian government.

Baader's first publication, *Vom Wärmestoff, seiner Vertheilung, Bindung und Entbindung, vorzüglich beim Brennen der Körper* (3,1–180) appeared in 1786. It is a work "that can rightly be considered the first fruit of Romantic speculation about nature".[4] In this essay, he praises Herder as "one of the more exalted geniuses of our century, one whose deep, pure, and discreet understanding of nature I admire and honor in all his writings" (3,40). Baader's diary for this period reveals more of his high regard for Herder, especially in the area of philosophy of nature. (See, for example, 11,29ff.) While references to Kant appear in Baader's very first diary entry (11,4), and continue to reappear for decades to come, his serious preoccupation with Kant did not begin until the mid 1790s. Late in his Freiberg years (1791–92), Baader befriended Alexander von Humboldt, and before leaving Freiberg, published a highly-regarded essay on the use of explosives: *Versuch einer Theorie der Sprengarbeit* (1792; 6,153–66).[5]

4   H. GRASSL (Ed.): *Franz von Baader. Über Liebe, Ehe und Kunst*, p. 40.
5   For Henrik Steffen's report concerning the impression Baader made on a lady in Freiberg at this time, see BAADER: *Sämtliche Werke* 15,27 fn. 4. Though she seems to have been well beyond her youth, she "had never met a more interesting man" than Baader, who was then in his mid-twenties.

In the spring of 1792, Baader left Saxony for England and Scotland where he spent the next four years studying British mines, British factories, and matters of general technological interest. A look at the *Tagebücher*, however, reveals that Baader also had many things other than technology on his mind. For Baader, keeping a diary was no mere whim or fad; it was serious study, the object and *Leitmotiv* of which were the "Know Thyself" that he cites so often in its pages. During these early years, Baader worked hard at hammering out a personal and distinctive philosophy, one that profited from the most modern ideas and theories, but one which did not betray the deeply ingrained values he had derived from his Catholic faith and Bavarian heritage. By 1787, Baader was acquainted with St. Martin and Kleuker (11,126), and with Kant even earlier (11,4). He also read Hamann, though not as intensively as he read Herder. Once in England, he devoted a great deal of energy to an intensive study of the Kantian *Critiques*; passages excerpted from them and commentary based upon them occupy large sections of his diary (11,199, 207, 289ff., 312, 338–44, 347, 351, 354–61, 372–400). Grappling seriously with Kant constituted the first great intellectual struggle of Baader's life. Facing up to the Kantian synthesis, assimilating it critically, transcending it, and ultimately replacing it with his own philosophy occupied Baader for decades. Before leaving England in 1796, he had already written *Über Kants Deduction der praktischen Vernunft und die absolute Blindheit der letztern* (1,1–23), an essay that contains – in broad outline – key elements subsequently incorporated in Baader's mature worldview.[6] Franz Hoffmann, principal editor of the *Sämtliche Werke*, takes pains to point out the many instances in the diary and other early writings which show that Baader's thought did not undergo any substantial alterations or major changes during the more than fifty years of his adult life.

In England, Baader also read such English philosophers as Reid, Berkeley, Locke, Hobbes, and Hume. Although he became a strong critic of Adam Smith's principles of political economy, he cites Godwin's writings favorably – and at considerable length (11,210ff.) – as he does those of Jean Jacques Rousseau (11,250–434 *passim*). Entries made in the very first year of his diary indicate

6 J. SAUTER: *Baader und Kant*, p. 36; J. SAUTER (Ed.): *Franz von Baaders Schriften zur Gesellschaftsphilosophie*, p. 571; Sauter states that Baader's essay was:

perhaps the best that could be brought against Kant at that time; at the same time, it was the most fundamental of all Baader's writings (*zugleich auch die prinzipiellste aller Baader-Schriften*). This writing is basic for understanding Baader, because it already clearly expresses the epistemological, metaphysical, and ethical principles of his later philosophy.

By 1795, Baader had already written an essay in English to introduce Kant's thought to the English-speaking world (*Sämtliche Werke* 11,405–434).

Baader's heavy emphasis on reading the Bible and on prayer.[7] Indeed, the impact of the Bible on Baader's life and thought is evident on nearly every page he wrote. The late 1780s and the early 1790s saw Baader caught up in a maelstrom of intellectual and spiritual influences. These were times of crisis and tension for Baader as he strained to establish a satisfactory intellectual-spiritual platform for his life. (See, for example, 11,199ff., 280, 281, 290 fn.; 16,8.)

In England, Baader suffered from homesickness (11,199); and he left it, in June of 1796, after refusing an attractive offer to take over the management of a silver and lead mine in Devonshire. His route back to Munich took him first to Hamburg, where he stayed for several months. There he met the mercantilist economist Büsch (see 6,174ff., especially 181ff.) as well as Matthias Claudius and Friedrich Jacobi, and it was there that he first began to study the Cabbala (15,31, 168). It was also at Hamburg that he first became acquainted with the work of Fichte and Schelling (15,32), the beginnings of German Idealism in philosophy. Baader finally arrived in Munich in December of 1796.

Baader's early essays, *Beiträge zur Elementar-Physiologie* of 1797 (3,203–46) and *Über das pythagoräische Quadrat in der Natur oder die vier Weltgegenden* of 1798 (3,247–68), are the first published works that won him recognition among the intelligentsia of Germany.[8] It was St. Martin, in particular, who heavily influenced his thought towards the end of the century. From 1788 until 1809, Baader published little, but he studied Böhme and St. Martin carefully and in great detail. Throughout this period, he was in active personal contact with many of German Romanticism's leading figures.

In 1797, Baader became a member of the board for the royal mint and mines. By 1807, he had advanced to its highest position (*Oberstbergrat*), an office which he held until 1820. In 1800, he married Francisca von Reisky, a young woman from Prague. Guido and Julie, the future wife of Ernst von Lasaulx, were their only children. In 1802, Baader was invited to serve as a corresponding member of the *Conseil des mines* of Paris. (He had become a corresponding member of the Munich Academy of Sciences in 1801, and in 1808 was elected to full membership in the Academy.) The same year he was made a Knight of the newly established Civil Service Order of Nobility (15,41); a permanent patent of knighthood was conferred upon him in 1813. His mandated duties included lecturing on mining techniques (15,40), but he also found time to compose technical essays on such topics as iron foundries, mining, and timber cultivation. (See, for example, 6,193ff.)

---

7   Baader styled his entire philosophy a "philosophy of prayer" (15,536). He wrote often about the vital role played by prayer in his life and thought. See, for example, BAADER: *Sämtliche Werke* 2,500–16; 5,343ff.; 11,8; 12,210, etc.

8   J. SAUTER (Ed.): *Franz von Baaders Schriften zur Gesellschaftsphilosophie*, p. 573.

Glass manufacturing was an area of particular interest to Baader. He had a glass factory of his own at Lambach, near Regensburg, and through experimentation made an important contribution to the field: by partially substituting Glauber's salt (sodium sulphate) for the more expensive potash, he devised a way to make glass manufacturing considerably less expensive. This partial substitution also doubled the speed at which glass could be manufactured. As a result, much timber was saved in the melting process, and the glass produced was of higher quality. In 1811, the Austrian government bought his idea for 12,000 Gulden.[9] By 1812, his success as a businessman and inventor enabled him to purchase some property in Schwabing near Munich (15,243) where he and his family lived until 1832.

Franz Hoffmann describes the extraordinarily powerful impression Baader made on Ludwig Tieck when the latter come to Munich from Jena in 1804 (15,36). Baader tried hard to interest Tieck in Jacob Böhme's mysticism but, if one may judge from a remark made by Baader about Tieck in 1840, his regard for Tieck's speculative capacity was not very high (15,661).

In 1806, Schelling and Baader met for the first time; the overwhelming impact of Baader's personality and ideas on Schelling is clear from Schelling's own testimony.[10] The most important result of that early meeting was Schelling's philosophical reorientation from pantheism to theism.[11] The repercussions of Schelling's reorientation on the entire German Romantic movement were substantial. While one cannot say that Schelling, as the "herald of early Romanticism", caused the shift from pantheism to theism in the Romantic movement as a whole, his action must have had a significant impact on the elite of Romanticism, among whom his philosophical reputation was so great.[12]

Friedrich Schlegel was yet another important personage dazzled by Baader's power and insights during this period. They met in Vienna, where Baader resided (from December of 1810 until November of 1811) while engaged in experiments that led to the Austrian government's acceptance of his glass invention.[13] Baader and Schlegel corresponded and maintained contact after Baader left Vienna. (See, for example, 15,311, 352, 431; *Lettres inédites* 3, index, p. 618; 4, index, pp. 597ff.)

---

9 On Baader's glass-making invention, see BAADER: *Sämtliche Werke* 6,227–72; 15,44ff.; E. SUSINI (Ed.): *Lettres inédites*, especially volume 2, most of which is devoted to the subject. Also see the index volume of the *Sämtliche Werke*.

10 See above, Introduction. See also J. SAUTER (Ed.): *Franz von Baaders Schriften zur Gesellschaftsphilosophie*, pp. 579ff.

11 J. SAUTER (Ed.): *Franz von Baaders Schriften zur Gesellschaftsphilosophie*, p. 581.

12 J. SAUTER (Ed.): *Franz von Baaders Schriften zur Gesellschaftsphilosophie*, p. 582.

13 J. SAUTER (Ed.): *Franz von Baaders Schriften zur Gesellschaftsphilosophie*, pp. 584ff. Viennese Romanticism and Baader's contacts with it are discussed on pages 586ff.

From 1803 to 1808, Baader corresponded extensively with Josef Wilhelm Ritter, the Romantic physicist and researcher. (See 15,187–235; *Lettres inédites* 3, index, p. 614.) Gotthilf Heinrich Schubert, philosopher and scientist, was another kindred spirit whom Baader had met while on a business trip to Nürnberg in 1809; they corresponded frequently throughout the next decade. (See 15,238–350; *Lettres inédites* 3,73-75, 138–40, 149–51, 159–61, 170–71.) Schubert's first impression of Baader is recorded by Hoffman (15,42). Baader persuaded Schubert to study St. Martin and eventually to translate the French thinker's *De l'Esprit des choses* into German, a translation for which Baader himself supplied a Foreword (1,57ff.).

Ritter, Schubert, and Baader shared a feverish interest in the esoteric forces of nature and mind with many of Romanticism's intellectual elite. Their correspondence is filled with passages dealing with such parapsychological themes as "animal magnetism" (*Tiermagnetismus*), *actio in distans*, somnambulism, and the like, and several of Baader's essays deal with related subjects.[14] In fact, Baader's earliest works had suggested the close unity and interpenetration of mind and nature and the all-pervasiveness of the organic model for reality. (The two essays which he published in 1813, *Gedanken aus dem grossen Zusammenhang des Lebens* (2,9–26) and *Über die Begründung der Ethik durch die Physik* (5,1–34), amount to manifestos proclaiming that some mysterious unity links mind, nature, and God.) Such an approach to reality made the whole field of parapsychology seem worthy of serious and careful consideration.

By 1813, clear signs of the incipient dissolution of Napoleon's hegemony over Europe were appearing on the horizon; the disastrous Russian campaign and the "Battle of the Nations" at Leipzig were both significant harbingers. The changing political situation moved Baader to consider seriously how he

---

14 See *Über die Ekstase oder das Verzücktsein der magnetischen Schlafredner, (drei Stücke)* (1817; 4,1–40); *Fragment aus der Geschichte einer magnetischen Hellseherin* (1818; 4,41–60); *Über Divinations- und Glaubenskraft* (1822; 4,61–92); *Randglossen zu Schriften: Die Symbolik des Traumes, von J. H. Schubert* (1821; 14,351–58); *Über den inneren Sinn im Gegensatze zu den äussern Sinnen* (1822; 4,93–106); *Über die Abbreviatur der indirecten, nicht intuitiven, reflectirenden Vernunfterkenntniss durch das directe, intuitive und evidente Erkennen* (1822; 4,107–14); *Randglossen zu Schriften: Die Seherin von Prevorst, von Justinus Kerner* (1829; 14,358–66); *Über den Begriff der Ekstasis als Metastasis* (1830; 4,147–162); *Über Swedenborg* (1832; 4,201–08); *Über eine bleibende und universelle Geisterscheinung hienieden* (1833; 4,209–20); *Über die Incompetenz unserer dermaligen Philosophie zur Erklärung der Erscheinungen aus dem Nachtgebiete der Natur* (1837; 4,303–24); *Randglossen zu Schriften: Die Schutzgeister, oder merkwürdige Blicke zweier Seherinnen in die Geisterwelt, von Heinrich Werner* (1839; 14,367–81). The works cited above do not constitute an exhaustive listing of all that Baader has to say on the subject. See also J. SAUTER (Ed.): *Franz von Baaders Schriften zur Gesellschaftsphilosophie*, pp. 715ff.

might contribute to establishing a truly Christian polity in Europe after Napoleon's power had been shattered. In an action reminiscent of Leibniz's memorandum (*Über die Sicherheit des Reiches*, 1670) to the German Princes, Baader sent three identical memoranda to the rulers of Russia, Prussia, and Austria in the summer of 1814. He did so again in the spring of 1815. The views expressed are substantially the same as those found in an essay which he had published in 1815: *Über das durch die französische Revolution herbeigeführte Bedürfnis einer neuen und innigeren Verbindung der Religion mit der Politik* (6,11–28). The Russian Czar, Alexander I, was deeply interested in religious matters, particularly in mysticism, and his favorable view of Baader's proposals significantly contributed to their being adopted in the text of the Holy Alliance document.[15] It should be noted, however, that Baader's intention was not to provide concrete and practical guidelines for regulating state policies; it was, rather, to describe the spirit in which politics should be conducted.[16]

In the years that followed the signing of the Holy Alliance document, Baader studied mysticism with special diligence, concentrating not only on the thought of Böhme and St. Martin, but also on that of such great medieval mystics as Eckehart, Tauler, Suso, Angelus Silesius, and Ruysbroeck. (He devoted less time and effort during this period to the thought of Kant, Fichte, Schelling, and Hegel.) His main goal, throughout, was to revivify and transform German phi-

---

15   The most important work dealing with Baader's participation in drafting the Holy Alliance document is E. BENZ: *Die abendländische Sendung der östlich-orthodoxen Kirche*, Mainz (Akademie der Wissenschaften und der Literatur) 1950. Despite its title, this book is almost entirely about Baader. Benz treats Baader's connections with Russia in all the Russia-related works listed under his name in the bibliography. Earlier studies, such as those by Hildegard Schäder and Franz Büchler (see bibliography), have been rendered obsolete by E. SUSINI (Ed.): *Lettres inédites* 1, Paris 1942, which made Benz's work possible. Volumes 2 and 3 of the *Lettres inédites*, Vienna 1951, comprise only notes and commentaries on the first volume. Volume 4, Strasbourg 1967, has more recent material about Baader's relations to Russia in appendix 1 (pp. 361ff.), mostly his views about the political and religious mission of Russia, but it is quite brief and adds nothing substantial to what had already been known. See also H. GRASSL (Ed.): *Franz von Baader. Gesellschaftslehre*, Munich (Kösel) 1957, pp. 26ff. and pp. 330ff. On Alexander I as a messianic figure, see E. BENZ, *Die abendländische Sendung der östlich-orthodoxen Kirche*, pp. 584ff. Baader's dream of a Europe united in faith was the same in substance as that of Novalis in his *Christenheit oder Europa* of 1799.

16   See J. SAUTER (Ed.): *Franz von Baaders Schriften zur Gesellschaftsphilosophie*, p. 592:

People have said that Baader's "Romantic" sense shows up precisely in the fact that he wanted to make kings into philosophers and hoped by so doing to secure a better world. On the contrary, Baader started from the completely realistic psychological consideration that the state is built on the souls of its citizens and that politics must be in harmony with the order of objective values.

losophy by reintroducing the spirit of mysticism and other philosophical traditions of the past. Baader wanted to create a synthesis that would do justice to both the new and the old, one that would harmoniously juxtapose reason and faith. His new positive philosophy, he hoped, would decisively expose the inherent inadequacies of both Enlightenment rationalism and obscurantist Pietism at their extremes. A correlative purpose was to counteract the effects of excessive rationalization in both society and politics, a practice whose harmful effects produced a mechanical, loveless, and soulless perception of man and society; the deification of money as an absolute value; and the corresponding uprooting of natural ties to soil and home.[17] In short, the subordination of all values to economics or to *raison d'état* had to be reversed. To Baader, these evils all stemmed from erroneously making the demands of abstract reason supersede the claims of life as a totality. His goal was to renew philosophy and Christian society.

Baader was already 56 years old when he began to study Thomas Aquinas. His published study-notes (14,197-348) indicate great respect for Aquinas's thought, but not an uncritical acceptance of it. Baader's writings also show considerable acquaintance with the Church Fathers, especially Augustine, and he marshaled vast amounts of material from patristic sources in attempting to prove that the papacy was not an original institution of Christianity but a later accretion.[18]

Contacts with Russia did not cease with the signing of the Holy Alliance document.[19] In 1815, Alexander I commissioned Baader to write a textbook on

17 J. SAUTER: "Franz von Baader", *Süddeutsche Monatshefte*, 32 (1935) perverts the intent and spirit of all that Baader says about love of the soil and one's home. Sauter apparently wrote this article to please the National Socialists, not to supplement his fine earlier work on Franz von Baader. No one should have known better than Sauter that it was folly to seek forerunners of National Socialist themes in the work of Baader. To my knowledge, no one else attempted to do likewise. Sauter himself mentions only what he regards as kindred ideas, but he indicates no specific historical influence of Baader on Nazism.

18 See, for example, *Der morgenländische und abendländische Katholicismus . . .* (1841; 10,89–254, especially pp. 148ff). Martin Deutinger notes, however, that the citations used in this essay were thoroughly falsified ("not even a tenth part of them is correct"), as anyone can verify by simply checking the sources. Deutinger blames Baader's unbounded gullibility for uncritically accepting these citations. He adds, however, that such carelessness should not be taken as characteristic. Baader's scholarship, in general, was as thorough as it was profound. See H. FELS: *Martin Deutinger. Auswahl seiner Schriften,* Munich (Kösel and Pustet) 1938, p. 219.

19 See the sources mentioned in note 15, especially those of E. BENZ and E. SUSINI (Ed.): *Lettres inédites.* Susini deals with all of Baader's important Russian contacts, especially in volume 3. Many are also dealt with in E. BENZ: *Die abendländische Sendung der östlich-orthodoxen Kirche*; see, for example, entries for Gallitzin, Uvarov, the Stourdzas,

science and religion for the Russian clergy.[20] In 1816, Baader was busy making arrangements on behalf of Prince Gallitzin, president of the Holy Synod and head of the Russian Bible Society, to have young Catholic priests from Germany work in Russia (*Lettres inédites* 1,292ff.). Starting in 1818, Baader was paid a monthly stipend of 140 rubles to serve as literary correspondent of Prince Gallitzin, who became Russian Minister of Cults that year. Baader was to report all significant developments associated with the intellectual, religious, and political life of Germany. (August von Kotzebue, assassinated in 1819 by Karl Sand,[21] was one of Baader's "colleagues" in this effort.) During these years, Baader's interest in Russian affairs was very strong; it remained so for the rest of his life.

In 1820, the various mining enterprises operated by the Bavarian state were reorganized. As a result, both Franz and Joseph Baader were retired from active service; they were, however, awarded pensions and permitted to retain their titles. Though Baader very much resented losing his post (15,436), he thereby acquired time to devote all of his energies to creating a new philosophy and building a genuinely Christian society. He still had twenty years to live, two decades in which his most important ideas would be committed to writing.

Baader was simultaneously experiencing difficulties in other areas of his life. Despite his important contributions to the technology of glass manufacturing, he never became financially successful. During the Continental Blockade, several of his debtors declared bankruptcy; the general level of business activity had indeed declined substantially as a result of the Napoleonic wars. By 1821, Baader was ready to sell his factory at Lambach; his business had failed to improve satisfactorily, even after the Restoration of 1815. (See 15,237, 246, 250, 384ff., 390ff.) As Baader grew older, his interests in technology, the natural sciences, and business gave way to a preoccupation with philosophy, religion, and the problems of society. For the rest of his life, he often found himself short of money.[22]

Mestchersky, Paulucci, and Sevyrev. For one of Mestchersky's love-poems based on Baader's ideas, see E. SUSINI (Ed.): *Lettres inédites* 3,310ff.

20   As was the case with many of Baader's projects, this one also remained incomplete. His essays *Sur la notion du tems* [*sic*], 1818 (2,47–68) and *Sur l'Eucharistie*, 1815 (7,1–14) may be considered fragments which would have been incorporated in the complete book, had it ever been written.

21   See E. BENZ: *Franz von Baader und Kotzebue. Das Russlandsbild der Restaurationszeit*, Mainz/Wiesbaden (Akademie der Wissenschaften und der Literatur) 1957. Benz shows that Kotzebue's murder was related to his position as literary correspondent of Gallitzin, the same role played by Baader.

22   Baader's correspondence confirms this fact. The evidence, however, is not as clear as it should be. (See, for example, the correspondence found in volume 15 of BAADER:

The memoranda which Baader had written to the emperors in 1814-15 stressed his conviction that one of the chief needs of the age was to establish a closer relationship among religion, learning, and the arts, but he was also committed to the reconciliation of the Catholic, Orthodox, and Protestant churches. In 1834, he would write to the Bavarian Academy of Sciences urging it to strive for the goal of reconciling tradition, the Bible, and science "so that the destruction that came out of Wittenberg could be made good again at Munich" (15,516). But Baader's real hopes were centered on Russia. On April 28, 1822, he wrote that he was thinking about founding a philosophical-religious missionary society, one which would do in a good cause what the Masons and Jesuits had done in a bad one (15,378). He hoped to establish an academy at St. Petersburg which would strive to unite religion, science, and art – just as the Encyclopedists had divided them (15,96ff., 379). It would, furthermore, be the nucleus of a new effort to reunite the churches. Russia was the best place to start the process of reunification because it had been least corrupted – by history – since the Reformation.

An opportunity came in 1822 to do something about all of these convictions – or so it appeared.[23] Baron Boris von Üxküll, a disciple of Hegel from the Baltic area, invited Baader to accompany him back to his estates, whence he could then continue on to St. Petersburg. Baader had been disturbed by the amount of surveillance to which he was being subjected by Count Pahlen, head of the Russian embassy in Munich, and he was bothered by the fact that his reports to Gallitzin had been tampered with. He set out with Üxküll, first toward Berlin and then toward the Baltic states, but was held up at Memel for seven long months awaiting permission to enter Russia. Paulucci, the governor of Riga, thoroughly distrusted Baader. He considered him a "liberal and a demagogue". Politically, Paulucci was a thoroughgoing reactionary determined to secure the downfall of Gallitzin and the whole bevy of Pietistically-oriented people who were upsetting the religious life of Russia. (Joseph de Maistre was one of Gallitzen's mentors.) Paulucci was able to persuade the Czar – a more conservative man in his later years, especially after the assassination of Kotzebue – to refuse Baader permission to enter Russia.

During his seven-month stay in Memel, Baader knew little about what was transpiring elsewhere; he was under constant police surveillance. Gallitzin was

---

Sämtliche Werke.) Hoffmann, as Susini repeatedly shows (Lettres inédites 3,602–03, index), often suppressed references to Baader's debts. The Lettres inédites themselves provide much more evidence of Baader's perpetual financial difficulties.
23 See E. BENZ: Die abendländische Sendung der östlich-orthodoxen Kirche, pp. 620ff., as well as the documents cited in E. SUSINI (Ed.): Lettres inédites.

out of favor and could not help. Baader, as usual, was short of money; he was to have been aided by Gallitzin in covering his travel expenses, but the expected assistance and promised support never materialized. Any correspondence he attempted with Gallitzin was confiscated. Meanwhile, his family in Munich needed him. In retrospect, these were among the worst months of his life. "The whole north is for me nothing but a barren snow and ice field", he wrote to Üxküll on July 19, 1823 (15,400). After all prospects of gaining entry into Russia had vanished, Baader departed Memel for Berlin. He arrived in November, 1823.

The hard days at Memel had by no means been a total loss. It was, for Baader, a time of great productivity and intellectual illumination; he wrote a large part of *Fermenta Cognitionis*, one of his most ambitious and important works, at Memel. A passage from a letter which Baader addressed to Baron von Üxküll on July 28, 1823 illustrates the ambivalent state of misery and joy which he experienced in intellectual accomplishment:

If it is the condition of a prophet to be outwardly in hell and inwardly in heaven, then really there is something of the prophet in me. For the clarity of knowledge that has come over me this summer and winter, the precious truths I have wrested from the future, which glisten before me like the germs of stars in my mind, only to ascend to the permanent firmament of human wisdom and knowledge in their own time and from there also to illumine my mind like a crown of glory – this deeper and higher knowledge, I say, at which I would not have arrived without the deepest loneliness, can really be compared to heaven, one that only few among the few, however, would envy me. (15,402)[24]

Hegel had read *Fermenta Cognitionis* and was eager to talk to Baader about it (15,401, 405).[25] Baader was no less anxious:

24   The text reads as follows:

Wenn es übrigens der Zustand eines Propheten ist, von aussen in der Hölle, innerlich im Himmel zu sein, so bin ich wahrlich ein Stück eines solchen Propheten, denn die Klarheit des Wissens, die mir aufging diesen Sommer und Winter über, die *vérités précieuses, que j'ai arrachées a l'avenir*, und die wie Gestirnsamen in meinem Geiste mir entgegenfunkeln, um in das bleibende Firmament des menschlichen Wissens und Erkennens sich zu ihrer Zeit emporzuheben, und von dort auch meinem Geiste als eine Ehrenkrone zu leuchten, diese tiefere und höhere Erkenntniss, die ich ohne die tiefste Einsamkeit erlangt hätte, ist wohl gleich einem Himmel zu achten, um den mich freilich unter den Wenigen nur Wenige beneiden würden.

25   The first five parts of *Fermenta Cognitionis* were completed by the time Baader left Memel. They were published in Berlin, 1822–24. Part six was published in Leipzig in 1825.

In Berlin, I will be linked to Hegel in mind and (God willing) in heart. For I respect him highly, and for that reason I love him. If he had had the training in religion that I received, we would have come to reasoned agreement with each other long ago (15,405).[26]

Baader remained in Berlin from November of 1823 until April of 1824; he and Hegel conversed long and often during this six-month period. Baader notes that he pleased Hegel especially by introducing him to the thought of Meister Eckehart (15,159). While in Berlin, Baader renewed his friendship with Varnhagen von Ense and his wife, Rachel. He also met the eminent Protestant theologian Marheinecke and visited Friedrich Schleiermacher several times (15,105).[27] On his journey from Berlin to Munich, Baader visited Adam Müller, the Romantic political theorist, at Leipzig. Müller was then in the Austrian civil service, and he proposed using his influence to obtain a post for Baader similar to the one he held in the consulate. Baader declined the offer and proceeded to Munich. He arrived at the end of May, 1824, quite demoralized about the failure of his proposed enterprise in Russia (15,412, 414).

In March of 1824, Baader had sent a memorandum to King Friedrich Wilhelm III in which he stressed the need for a positive theology if the good of state and society were to be served. He pointed out that a great deal of revolutionary and anti-religious instruction was taking place in the Prussian states, and he urged the king to do something about it (15,67ff.). In a letter to Eschenmayer (15,422), he called the situation an "anti-Christian scandal". Baader's memorandum was filed away innocuously by Altenstein, the Prussian Minister of Worship and Education (15,68).

There is no doubt about what was occupying Baader's mind in 1824 and the years following. He was doing all in his power to make society Christian again, to reconcile faith and philosophy, and to reinstate positive Christian values in

26 Baader's words read: "Ich werde allerdings in Berlin mit Hegel Geist- und (wills Gott) auch Herz-verwandt werden. Denn ich hochachte ihn, und eben darum liebe ich ihn; wenn er den Unterricht über Religion erhalten hätte, den ich erhielt, so würden wir uns schon längst einverstanden oder einvernünftigt haben".

27 Three years later, Marheinecke wrote of Baader:

Herr von Baader belongs indisputably among the most brilliant writers in the nation, not indeed as far as external form or writing style is concerned, but rather in consideration of the intensity of his wit and his thought. He understands the art of saying a great deal in few words.

See E. WINTER: "Neues über Baader", *Hochland* 26 (1929), p. 433. Marheinecke and Baader became friends, but Schleiermacher and Baader did not. As J. Sauter observes, it is noteworthy that Schleiermacher is the only one of the important Romantics who did not study Jacob Böhme. (J. SAUTER: *Baader und Kant*, p. 574; and J. SAUTER [Ed.]: *Franz von Baaders Schriften zur Gesellschaftsphilosophie*, p. 604.)

public life. He felt that the anti-religious tide of the Enlightenment could end only in an abyss of nihilism. The titles of several essays written between 1824 and 1835 show clear evidence of his concern: *Bemerkungen über einige antireligiöse Philosopheme unserer Zeit* (1824; 2,443–96.); *Über das durch unsere Zeit herbeigeführte Bedürfnis einer innigeren Verbindung der Wissenschaft mit der Religion* (1824; 1,81–96.); *Alles, was dem Eindringern der Religion in die Region des Wissens sich widersetzt oder selbes nicht fördert, ist vom Bösen* (1825; 7,47–52.); *Über Religions-und religiöse Philosophie im Gegensatze sowohl der Religionsunphilosophie als der irreligiösen Philosophie* (1831; 1,321–38); *Über den Zwiespalt des religiösen Glaubens und Wissens als die geistige Wurzel des Verfalls der religiösen und politischen Societät in unserer wie in jeder Zeit* (1833; 1,357–82); *Über das Verhalten des Wissens zum Glauben. Auf Veranlassung eines Programms des Herrn Abbé Bautain: Enseignement de la Philosophie en France, Strasbourg, 1833* (1833; 1,339–56). In a letter to Windischmann, written on April 6, 1824, he calls nihilism itself the greatest problem facing religion and society (*Lettres inédites* 1,374). He wrote to Alexander I of Russia (May 1, 1825) that Protestantism had become "nihilist and even anti-evangelical" (*Lettres inédites* 1,386). A letter to Count Armansperg, written on November 28, 1826, contrasts Prussian Nihilism with Austrian Obscurantism (*Lettres inédites* 1,394). Essays and letters dating from the mid 1820s are filled with phrases like "Christophobia", "theophobia", and "nihilism".[28]

Schelling took umbrage at the *Bemerkungen über einige antireligiöse Philosopheme unserer Zeit;* he thought that it had been directed at him. Consequently, a serious rift developed between Schelling and Baader. Although the essay's content applied as much to Hegel as it did to Schelling, Hegel and Baader, nevertheless, managed to remain on good terms. Baader was so thoroughly aroused by the need to combat the spirit of irreligion and nihilism that he often called it his proper "vocation" or "occupation" (*Beruf*) to do so. (See, for example, 8,301; 15,335, 379, 417, 435-36, 444, 643; *Lettres inédites* 1,380; 4,202, 207.) It was a preoccupation that defined a central part of his mature life.

Although Baader's efforts to pursue this aim were frustrated in both Russia and in Prussia, he tried to do what he could in Bavaria. The educational system

---

28 See E. BENZ: "Franz von Baader und der abendländische Nihilismus", *Archiv für Philosophie*, 1949, p. 33. It should be noted that Baader used the term "nihilism" as early as April 6, 1824 (*Lettres inédites* 1,374); he is the first one to introduce the term into philosophical usage in Germany (BENZ: "Franz von Baader und der abendländische Nihilismus", p. 32). This contradicts the not uncommon view that Turgeniev invented the term in his novel, *Fathers and Sons* (1862). See, for example, A. CAMUS: *The Rebel*, New York (Vintage Books) 1956, where Camus says (p. 154): "We know that the very term nihilism was invented by Turgeniev in his novel *Fathers and Sons . . .* "

there was being restructured at the time of Baader's return. He and Bishop Sailer spearheaded the effort to combat the anti-religious books then being used as the basis for instruction.[29] One of Baader's favorite ideas was that society as a whole demanded the close cooperation of priests, rulers, and scholars: i.e., church, state, and university. (See, for example, 1,150ff.)

In 1826, the Bavarian university was moved from Landshut to Munich, where it was renamed the Ludwig Maximilian University. Supported by a recommendation from Bishop Sailer, Baader was invited to teach philosophy and theology at the University; unfortunately, he was not appointed a regular professor, merely an honorary one. His colleagues included Joseph Görres, G. H. Schubert, Oken, Schelling, Döllinger, and Ringseis. In his campaign against irreligion, Baader counted especially on Görres's support (15,431). As Ringseis reports, it was taken for granted that Baader would supply philosophical leadership to the cause: "We did not need to look for a Catholic philosopher. We sat, after all, in the midst of the shower of intellectual sparks that came from Franz von Baader".[30]

Baader's inaugural address at the university was published in 1826 under the title: *Über die Freiheit der Intelligenz* (1,133–50). His first lecture, *Vorlesungen über religiöse Philosophie im Gegensatz der irreligiösen älterer und neuerer Zeit* (1,151ff.), appeared in print the following year. Numerous lectures on theory of knowledge and philosophy of religion followed. (Many of Baader's university lectures can be found in *Vorlesungen über speculative Dogmatik* [8,1–368; 9,1–288].) He lectured extensively on theology until, in 1838, the government prohibited all laymen from teaching theology. After 1838, his lectures were principally devoted to psychology and anthropology.[31] Franz Hoffmann, himself a student of Baader before becoming editor of Baader's *Sämtliche Werke*, has left a vivid description of the electrifying effect Baader had on his students (15,109ff.).[32]

29 J. SAUTER (Ed.): *Franz von Baaders Schriften zur Gesellschaftsphilosophie*, pp. 608ff.
30 E. RINGSEIS (Ed.): *Erinnerungen des Dr. J. N. Ringseis*, volume 2, p. 226. The text reads: "Um einen katholischen Philosophen hatten wir nicht zu suchen. Sassen wir doch mitten im Sprühregen von Franz von Baaders Geistesfunken".
31 To a large extent, the new course descriptions were in fact camouflage: Baader continued to teach a great deal of theology, for without it, nothing else made sense to him. It is frequently the case that the titles of Baader's essays do not really reveal their contents. Schelling also continued to teach theology after the prohibition; he even retained the earlier title of his course: *Offenbarungslehre*.
32 Baader was always plagued with what Sauter calls his "hereditary error" of disorganization. He seemed incapable of presenting a complete whole. His material seemed to dominate him, rather than vice-versa. Descriptions of his delivery, for example, abound with expressions like "lightning bolts", "rushing torrents" of ideas, "volcanic outpourings", etc. It was partly this characteristic that suggested to the Romantics – as an ideal to be sought – that Baader had identified his person with his ideas, his philosophy with his life: his thought was one with what he was and vice-versa.

Baader's contacts in this period included some important French intellectuals In 1831, he wrote to Prince von Löwenstein-Wertheim that the editors of *l'Avenir* – as a token of their regard – had begun sending him their publication daily because they believed Baader to be the only German philosopher "taking the offensive for Christianity instead of the miserable and cowardly defense mounted heretofore" (15,467). Baader's French correspondents included Montalembert, Victor Cousin, and the mystic Divonne. He was, of course, also familiar with the works of de Maistre, Bonald, Bautain, Lamennais, and others.[33] In his sixty-sixth year, Baader was seriously considering a trip to Paris to confer with the editors of *l'Avenir* (15,467). He had travelled so much in his lifetime that the Hegelians called him "the traveling philosopher".[34]

Visitors to the Baader home in Schwabing included not only members of the local intelligentsia – e.g. Ringseis, Görres, Schubert, Ritter, Haneberg, and Döllinger – but also many important people from outside Munich or Bavaria – e.g. Varnhagen von Ense, Ludwig Tieck, Friedrich Schlegel, Montalembert, Lamennais, Alexander Stourdza, and Professor Sevyrev.[35] A regular Baader Circle or *Kongregation* began to develop. Its members, all interested in mysticism and religious philosophy, regarded Baader, the *philosophus per Fulgur*, as their cynosure. The *Kongregation* appropriated the periodical *Eos: Münchener Blätter für Poesie, Literatur und Kunst*, adopting it as its "official" organ. While *Eos* had been published since 1818, in 1828 it became the mouthpiece of Munich Romanticism, then under the leadership of Görres and Baader. (See 15,444, 454.) The goal of *Eos* was similar to that of Schlegel's *Concordia* (1820–23): the reconciliation of church and state; the reunification of religion, society, science, and art.[36] By 1830, however, Baader found it necessary to disassociate

---

33 Consult the index volume of BAADER: *Sämtliche Werke* as well as the indexes in volumes 3 and 4 of the *Lettres inédites*; see also J. SAUTER: *Baader und Kant*, pp. 548ff.; and S. LÖSCH: *Döllinger und Frankreich. Eine geistige Allianz 1823-1871*, Munich (C. H. Beck) 1955. The *Sämtliche Werke* include Baader's *Randglossen zu Schriften: Les Soirées de Saint-Petersbourg, par J. de Maistre, (Abendstunden)* (1821; 14,387–401); *Recension von M. Bonald: Recherches philosophique sur les prémiers objets des coinnoissances morales* (1825; 5,43–120); *Recension der Schrift: Essai sur l'indifférence en matière de Réligion, par M. l'Abbé F. de la Mennais,* (1826; 5,121–246); *Über die Zeitschrift Avenir und ihre Principien* (1831; 6,29–44); *Über de la Mennais. Paroles d'un Croyant* (1834; 6,109–24); *Rückblick auf de la Mennais in Bezug auf die Widersetzlichkeit das katholischen Clerus in Preussen gegen die Regierung* (1838; 5,383–90).

34 J. SAUTER (Ed.): *Franz von Baaders Schriften zur Gesellschaftsphilosophie*, p. 624.

35 H. GRASSL (Ed.): *Franz von Baader. Über Liebe, Ehe und Kunst*, pp. 54ff. and J. SAUTER (Ed.): *Franz von Baaders Schriften zur Gesellschaftsphilosophie*, pp. 624ff. Both of these sources supply details about the impression made by Baader on some of the persons named in the text.

36 J. SAUTER (Ed.): *Franz von Baaders Schriften zur Gesellschaftsphilosophie*, p. 620.

himself from *Eos*, and he began to look for a foreign periodical with similar aims (15,455). Bavarian Liberals had managed to have *Eos* suppressed.[37]

In 1835, Baader wrote an important essay concerning the social problem and how the exploitation of the proletariat posed a special danger.[38] The full title of the article reads: *Über das dermalige Missverhältniss der Vermögenslosen oder Proletairs zu den Vermögen besitzenden Classen der Societät in Betreff ihres Auskommens sowohl in materieller als intellectueller Hinsicht aus dem Standpuncte des Rechts betrachtet* (6,125–44). It is noteworthy that Baader is the first writer to introduce the word "proletariat", in the socialist sense, into Germany. It is also noteworthy that Baader favors justice and law as appropriate means for addressing the social problem; he rejects sporadic charitable gestures as totally inadequate. Finally, Baader stresses the spiritual as well as the material aspects of the social problem.[39] He shows clearly in this essay that the real danger threatening Europe was the social problem, not political problems. Indeed, he anticipated in remarkable detail the type of systematic analysis that was to make Karl Marx so renowned just before mid-century. Their suggested solutions to social inequity were, of course, worlds apart.[40]

Baader's mature life was full of grand hopes and disappointments, but all of his major projects failed.[41] In 1835, he sustained two heavy personal losses when both his wife Francisca and his brother Joseph died; in 1838, his brother Clemens also died. Because of continuing financial pressures, he had difficulties managing and maintaining his home in Schwabing, and eventually had to sell it. His letters during the last years of his life find him at many different addresses.[42] The increasing loneliness of these years was due, in part, to his alienation from many former friends, most notably from Görres. This unfortunate estrangement was caused, in large part, by Baader's opposition to the papacy. In 1836, Baader wrote to Hoffman that Görres's large work on mysticism was "not without heretical ideas" (15,548). Görres, for his part, responded:

> That Baader is a great, incisive, and penetrating mind, to whom science is indebted for many fruitful and happy insights, no one will deny. As far as dogma is concerned, the Church obviously has nothing to learn from him . . . (15,ivff.)

37 J. SAUTER (Ed.): *Franz von Baaders Schriften zur Gesellschaftsphilosophie*, pp. 621–22.
38 Regarding this essay, see especially E. BENZ: "Franz von Baaders Gedanken über den 'Proletair' ", *Zeitschrift für Religions- und Geistesgeschichte* (1948).
39 E. BENZ: "Franz von Baaders Gedanken über den 'Proletair' ", p. 100.
40 E. BENZ: "Franz von Baaders Gedanken über den 'Proletair' ", pp. 117ff. Benz makes an extended comparison of Marx and Baader. It is of some interest to note that Baader, in his essay, makes it the special duty of the priest in society to care for the poor classes, a notion that in some ways anticipates the "priest-worker" movement in France following World War II.
41 Hans Grassl and Johannes Sauter speak often of this aspect of Baader's life.
42 See E. SUSINI (Ed.): *Lettres inédites*, on this subject.

Late in his life, Baader found a measure of consolation in an unusual marriage to Marie Robel – unusual because the seventy-four-year-old philosopher had fallen in love with a woman half a century his junior.[43] (They were married on December 29, 1839.). This marriage incurred the displeasure of his daughter Julie and probably led to their subsequent estrangement.[44]

In the polemical ferment that followed the "Cologne Troubles" of 1837,[45] Baader expressed certain views about the nature of the Church that led some people to believe that he had left Catholicism. He eventually took direct action against this rumor by writing a two-page rebuttal: *Zurückweisung der von dem Univers wider mich erhobenen Anklage eines Abfalls von der katholischen Kirche* (1839; 5,405–08). Two main points were at issue: (1) Baader's defense of a collegial principle as the final authority in the visible structure of the Church; and (2) his position that the papacy was an historical accretion, one that did not belong to the essential constitution of the Church. His essays on these themes include: *Über das Kirchenvorsteheramt auf Veranlassung der kirchlichen Wirren in der preussischen Rheinprovinz* (1838; 5,399–404); *Über die Trennbarkeit oder Untrennbarkeit des Pabstthums oder des Primats vom Katholicismus* (1838; 5,369–82); *Über die Thunlichkeit oder Nichtthunlichkeit einer Emancipation des Katholicismus von der Römischen Dictatur in Bezug auf Religionswissenschaft* (1839; 10,53–88); *Über die römische und russische Kirche* (1839; 5,391–98); and *Über den morgenländischen und den abendländischen Katholicismus* (1840; 10,89–254). This last essay pleads, once again, for a reunion of the churches through the mediation of the Russian Orthodox Church. Baader never lost hope in the dream of Leibniz and Novalis that one day all of Europe might once again be united in the Christian faith. He considered the papacy a major obstacle to such a hope.[46]

43 See Baader's letters to her: BAADER: *Sämtliche Werke* 15,622–30 as well as 15,120, 125, 128. See also E. SUSINI (Ed.): *Lettres inédites* 3, index, p. 592, and 4, introduction, pp. 7ff.

44 E. SUSINI (Ed.): *Lettres inédites* 4,9ff.

45 The "Cologne Troubles" concerned the dispute between Archbishop von Droste-Vischering of Cologne and the Prussian government over the issue of mixed marriages. See F. SCHNABEL: *Deutsche Geschichte im 19en. Jahrhundert*, volume 4, pp. 106–164.

46 Baader scholars have interpreted his views on ecclesiastical authority variously. E. K. WINTER: "Anton Günther. Ein Beitrag zur Romantikforschung", *Zeitschrift für die gesamte Staatswissenschaft*, 88, p. 327 scores Johannes Sauter and Christoph Schlüter (an editor of volume 14 of BAADER: *Sämtliche Werke*) for underplaying Baader's opposition to the papacy. E. GAUGLER: "Franz von Baader's Kampf gegen die Alleinherrschaft des Papstes in der katholischen Kirche", *Internationale kirchliche Zeitschrift*, 7 (1917) judges that Baader fought an honest fight against the papacy on principle. The message of his struggle was clear, whatever one may wish to make of the "retraction of his errors" just before he died (p. 269). Martin Deutinger takes the view that Baader's feud with the papacy was not consistent with his own earlier thought. (See H. FELS: *Martin Deutinger. Auswahl seiner Schriften*, pp. 217ff.; see also note 18 above). Gerd-Klaus Kaltenbrunner sees Baader as one of a long and

77

It seems fitting that Baader's final words were devoted to reaffirming his lifelong purpose: to re-Christianize all areas of life and knowledge, especially by bringing faith and reason into harmony, and to challenge the spirit of rationalism, the intellectual current which he regarded as the special enemy of this program in modern times. His last essay, *Über die Nothwendigkeit einer Revision der Wissenschaft natürlicher, menschlicher und göttlicher Dinge, in Bezug auf die sich in ihr noch mehr oder minder geltend machenden Cartesischen und Spinozistischen Philosopheme* (1841; 10,255–82), sums up a great deal of his life's striving.

Before he died, on May 23, 1841, Baader received the customary last rites and sacraments of the Catholic Church at his home in Munich, on Dachauerstrasse. Joseph Görres was among the few mourners who attended his funeral. Baader is buried in the South Cemetery in Munich, where many leading figures in Bavarian and German history are interred. He found a place in the Bavarian Hall of Fame and the Valhalla.

Baader's System

Franz von Baader lived in an age of great systematic philosophers, and he knew many of the great systematizers personally. As a thinker, he was rated with the best of them by his contemporaries, yet he was notoriously unsystematic – both in his writing and in his lectures. Paradoxically, no one has ever insisted more strenuously on the unity of all truth and all being than Baader. Josef Siegl writes that "Baader's entire philosophy of life is dominated by the organic idea".[47] Baader was personally convinced that philosophy must be a systematic body of truth, an organic whole; thus, thesis number fifty-three of *Vorlesungen über religiöse Philosophie im Gegensatz der irreligiösen älterer und neuerer Zeit* reads:

Systematic knowledge, which alone can be termed philosophical, is related to a conceptless aggregate of knowledge (which is often also called learned knowledge) as organic knowledge is related to inorganic (1,302; see also 5,249).

distinguished line of "outsiders" within the Catholic Church who have been persecuted because of their "too advanced" thinking (See G.-K. KALTENBRUNNER [Ed.]: *Franz von Baader. Sätze aus der erotischen Philosophie und andere Schriften*, Frankfurt [Insel] 1966, pp. 23ff.; and G.-K. KALTENBRUNNER: "Sozialrevolutionär, Politiker und Laientheologe. Zum 200. Geburtstag Franz von Baaders", *Zeitwende*, new series 9 [1965], pp. 157ff.) Friedrich Heer's judgment tends in the same direction, but is not so forcefully stated. (See F. HEER: *Europa Mutter der Revolutionen*, pp. 578ff.) Franz Hoffmann says that Baader's rejection of papal primacy goes back at least to 1816 (F. HOFFMAN [Ed.]: *Franz von Baader. Sämtliche Werke* 15,123). For Sauter's view, see J. SAUTER (Ed.): *Franz von Baaders Schriften zur Gesellschaftsphilosophie*, p. 630.

47 J. SIEGL: *Franz von Baader, ein Bild seines Lebens und Wirkens*, p. 23.

Ironically, Baader's practice is almost diametrically opposed to this thesis. His work consists, for the most part, of small essays, most occasional in character, scattered over a span of half a century. Many are merely collections of aphorisms. Even in his larger works, the subjects addressed are held together by little more than a common title and physical juxtaposition, not by a single purpose or a systematic methodology. So many parentheses and footnotes appear in a single sentence that the whole looks like a skein of asides, tangents and afterthoughts. Furthermore, the contents of his essays often bear little resemblance to their titles. In a sense, Baader's works are collections of fragments; he never really wrote a book.

Baader's way of understanding things did not possess the serene quality of a steady light beam; instead, thoughts came to him like lightning bolts (15,459) – "the lightning flash is father to the quiet light".[48] The "rhapsodizing" character of his thought, in a phrase coined by Johannes Sauter, was the probable cause of the near oblivion to which Baader was relegated for many years.[49] Baader was fully aware of this apparent "shortcoming" and responded to his critics by noting that "[n]othing would be more foolish or more lacking in understanding than to reprove a seed-peddler for selling only seeds and not grown-up plants" (2,238). *Fermenta Cognitionis*, one of his major works, might with justice be taken as a description of his entire output. Since Baader liked to express his ideas in paradoxical form, with a generous admixture of symbolic and esoteric language drawn from the Bible, the Cabbala, alchemy, and the mystics, one can appreciate that the first challenge faced by any Baader scholar is to seek order in what appears to be chaos.[50]

---

48 See Baader's essay of 1815, *Über den Blitz als Vater des Lichtes* (2,27–46).
49 J. SAUTER: *Baader und Kant*, p. 245; J. SAUTER (Ed.): *Franz von Baaders Schriften zur Gesellschaftsphilosophie*, p. 615.
50 E. WINTER: "Neues über Baader, " p. 433, notes:

It is not accidental, nor is it simply due to unfavorable circumstances, that Baader's speculation appears so fragmented and incomplete; it is due to his very nature that his speculation could never be completed. Then, too, Baader is constantly delving into abysses of magic and theosophy where we could never completely follow him. That is why his language is difficult and at times formless. That is why it could happen that Baader, who stood between the various directions and inwardly overcame them all, could fall into oblivion after his death, although the most profound of his contemporaries universally esteemed him.

Baader's stance "between the various directions", in the hope of synthesizing them all, led to his being "too mystical for critical philosophers, too critical for positive philosophers, too liberal for conservative churchmen, and too church-bound for freethinkers – and so he fell everywhere between the well-known two stools" (J. SAUTER: *Baader und Kant*, p. 217).

Unity and coherence may indeed be found in Baader's overall work; but they are not self-evident, and they must be drawn out of the materials themselves. It is undoubtedly easier for us today to identify this unity and coherence than it was for his contemporaries; they did not possess the *Sämtliche Werke*, and, consequently, were not able to benefit from the scholarly apparatus provided by its editors; nor could they profit from the rigorous efforts of later Baader scholars. When, however, the countless fragments are put in order, and when they are allowed to assert themselves in their proper context, a coherent whole can indeed be discerned.

In Baader's later years, when friends and students asked him to systematize his thought, he responded by claiming that he already had a system (in content) and that it was premature to systematize it (in form). Thus he maintains:

Although I have not put forth my ideas numbered in rank and file order, I have, nevertheless, produced a system, for I always follow the same path in philosophy, though it is an unusual one, to be sure. (9,13)

Under these circumstances, the consistency and virtual freedom from contradiction which can be found in Baader's work is remarkable, and the demand that every science must be organic in structure was indeed fulfilled to his satisfaction. The great synthesizing element in his thought is the principle of *centrality*, a principle that gives organic unity to all of its peripheral entities. True knowledge is best conceived not as a series of concepts but as a circle: it makes no difference where one chooses to begin, so long as one maintains unbroken reference to the Center; this reference alone makes knowledge systematic. Thus, Baader concludes his *Vorlesungen über Societätsphilosophie* with the following statement:

True gnosis is a circle, which one does not really grasp little by little but rather all at once. Here, one thing always leads to every other, and whoever has understood one thing well will soon have grasped the whole. There is no cause for wonder, then, when, in part, one concept constantly refers back to another and also when, while holding on to one concept, we have to anticipate others. For it is precisely therein that the systematic character of gnosis manifests itself, since every single concept leads to and points to the Center and the Center, in turn, to all other concepts. (14,160; see also 8,11 and 15,160)

For Baader, the summit of disorder and chaos occurs when a being is "center-empty" (*zentrumleer*), i.e., devoid of proper relationship to its Center. (See, for example, 3,345; 7,380 fn.; 12,320; and *passim*.) Aligning facts seriatim produces an aggregate, but not a system (1,153ff.; see also 1,319; 7,277; 8,197). Baader's own work, in all its variety, satisfies his demand for organic interconnectedness.

Baader sometimes asserted that it was premature to attempt formal systematization in philosophy. Indeed, "this is the error of our present science, that it wants to systematize everything; in that way, the spirit is killed" (15,140). Baader wanted to concentrate his full energy on research, on uncovering the new and unexplored. Once one adopts a formal system, Baader contended, the disadvantages inherent in systematization come with it: difficulties and objections are rarely given their full due; problems are minimized; the system begins to count more than the truth it is supposed to contain and manifest; form becomes formalism. Baader did not want to be locked up in a system as in a fortress; he wished to be as free as possible to expand and learn.

But all of Baader's excuses are not sufficient to dispel the charge that the formally unsystematic character of his work is its chief weakness. His arguments against systems are, in fact, only arguments against bad systems. They do not compensate for the lack of scholarly discipline and good order in his work.[51]

Baader conceives of philosophy – "the love of wisdom" – in its nominal definition: quite literally as the pursuit of objectively existing divine wisdom or *Sophia*. This means, of course, that philosophy has essentially religious significance (1,155; 1,169).[52] Such a point of view is crucial for understanding Baader. It does not mean, however, that philosophy is the same as knowledge about God and nothing else. In fact, one may never separate knowledge about God from knowledge about the world (1,323). For "the problem of philosophy

---

51 These strictures against Baader are valid, despite the pleas of friends like Ringseis (E. RINGSEIS [Ed.]: *Erinnerungen des Dr. J. N. Ringseis*, volume 1, p. 305):

It may be that his very richness, the constant boiling over of the most profound far-reaching ideas, proved a hindrance to him in forming a rounded-out system, although he did think systematically; indeed, his thoughts flowed from the fullness of the whole (*aus dem Ganzen und Vollen*).

or F. HOFFMANN (Ed.): *Franz von Baader. Sämtliche Werke* (15,109):

One felt indeed that Baader was constantly giving only fragments from a great whole; one could not doubt that this whole was present in his comprehensive inner self, but only whether it would be possible for him, at his advanced age, to present this whole in a sufficiently developed state.

Nor is Baader vindicated by Eduard Winter's reference to Baader's "richness of thought that bursts all forms" (E. WINTER: "Neues über Baader," p. 433), or Max Pulver's enthusiasm for the dynamism of Baader's thought (M. PULVER [Ed.]: *Schriften Franz von Baaders*, pp. v–xv); or O. GRÜNDLER: "Franz von Baader", *Hochland* 21 (1923–24), pp. 149ff.

52 In a commentary on one of Böhme's writings, Baader speaks of a kind of "counter-philosophy": "Scripture contrasts this *philosophia* to *philomoria* (love of ignorance, stupidity, and the like)" (*Sämtliche Werke* 13,323). Baader and Böhme tend strongly to see things only in conjunction with their opposites.

is none other than exposition of the law of manifestation of what exists, in all its phases, both in normality and in abnormality" (10,273). The key figure in Baader's scheme of reality, the solution to every puzzle and the crossroads of every level of being, is man himself (1,57). Baader, therefore, defends the necessity of adopting an anthropomorphic standpoint in religion (philosophy) (8,225; 8,265-67). Philosophy has three objects of study: God, mind, and nature (5,252); in considering them,

one should neither separate nor confuse with one another what God has joined together yet distinguished: namely, the external and the internal, history and the internal life of the spirit, nature and mind; one should believe neither in Godless nature nor in God divorced from nature . . . (7,38)

It is, in fact, impossible to keep Baader's positions in one branch of his philosophy from spilling over into others: material dealing with almost any major theme can be found in any volume of the *Sämtliche Werke*, although the chief editor tried to arrange the volumes topically. J. Sauter explains why:

Characteristic of [Baader,] the great cultural and intellectual synthesizer, is his two-fold demand: (1) the three areas of research [nature, man, and God] must be treated with a constant eye on all three; otherwise, no adequate essential analysis is possible (1,154); (2) philosophy does not take a place alongside positive sciences; it must, instead, penetrate them all, because that is the only way to achieve an "original standpoint". (8,215)[53]

The remainder of this chapter will be devoted to clarifying the main principles that govern Baader's thought; it is not meant to be a survey or summary of his thought as a whole.[54] Four categories will be considered: (1) knowledge, faith, and revelation; (2) God; (3) nature; (4) man. The first category will deal mainly with his theory of knowledge, a category which "contains basically Baader's whole metaphysics";[55] most of Baader's general principles find expression here. The categories of God, nature, and man correspond to the three objects of philosophy recognized by Baader (8,9ff., 225; 13,113).

---

53 J SAUTER: *Baader und Kant*, pp. 39ff.
54 Baader's work is too far-ranging and diffuse, too abstruse and problematic, to allow for a genuine summary of his thought in brief compass. The following pages simply indicate the directions Baader took in philosophizing about reason, faith, God, nature, and man. Comprehensive studies include: J. SAUTER: *Baader und Kant*; E. SUSINI: *Franz von Baader et le romantisme mystique. La philosophie de Franz von Baader;* and D. BAUMGARDT: *Franz von Baader und die philosophische Romantik.*
55 See O. GRÜNDLER: "Franz von Baader", p. 152; J. SAUTER (Ed.): *Franz von Baaders Schriften zur Gesellschaftsphilosophie*, p. 704.

1. Knowledge, Faith, and Revelation

Baader does not attempt to supply anything like "first elements" of philosophy; he presupposes them "as the philologist presupposes grammatical acquaintance with languages on the part of his students" (8,215). Philosophy must aim first of all to "seek out and prove the means and conditions under which a man may attain to free use of his capacity for learning" (8,324). The cardinal principle in Baader's epistemology and metaphysics is this:

Instead of saying with Descartes: I think, therefore I am, a man should say: I am thought, therefore I think, or I am willed (loved), therefore I am. (8,339; see also 1,349; 9,112, 302; 12,238, 376; 15,612, 631; *Lettres inédites* 4,328ff.)

Baader's *cogitor (a Deo), ergo cogito, ergo sum* was a counter-blast aimed not only against the subjectivism of the Cartesian *Cogito* but also against that of Kant's critical philosophy and Fichte's metaphysics of the Ego; it insisted on an *objective* first principle, a ground for all of man's knowing, loving, and doing. Only because I am known, loved, and illumined by God can I know, love, or give light. Baader is insisting on identity between ground of existence and ground of knowledge. To locate either in man, in an ultimate sense, is to deify him (9,292). "Finite mind, with its partial vision, cannot see except by being taken up into a central or universal eye" (1,366). In Baader's view, one knows oneself in proportion to how one knows God; the same holds for love. Descartes's *Cogito* puts what is really "secondary thinking" or derivative thinking (*Nachdenken*) in place of "original thinking" or primordial thinking (*Urdenken*) and, thereby, opens the road to atheism (1,370). Baader insists that participation in divine knowing and loving does not make a man a "part" of God at all (1,122ff.; 2,399; 9,50; 12,205; *passim*). Baader's principle attempts to reunite ontology and epistemology, to overcome solipsism and subjectivism as well as absolute human autonomy and deification of reason. (See 8,202ff.; 9,101ff., 111ff., 292; and *passim*.)[56]

Baader seems to have felt a constant internal pressure to *synthesize*: to reconcile Platonic idealism with Aristotelian realism in a higher synthesis was a cen-

---

56 Knowledge and existence are inseparable from one another (12,85). To talk as though knowledge were a purely human activity without a ground in God is to talk as though existence were also self-given by man and not grounded in God. Thus, Baader sees knowing as *Mitwissen* or *Gewissen* or *conscientia*: i.e., knowing in union with, and in imitation of, God's knowledge (*Sämtliche Werke* 1,256; 5,378; 8,360; 14,76, etc.). For criticism of Baader's one-sided emphasis on the objective principle of knowledge, see M. DEUTINGER: *Das Prinzip der neueren Philosophie*, Regensburg (Drews, Arthur) 1857, pp. 337–70, especially p. 345. Deutinger's two principal objections to Baader's philosophy are precisely those just mentioned, in addition to its lack of systematic form.

tral goal of his philosophy. (See, for example: 3,365; 4,280; 7,262; 8,224; 9,124 and *passim.*) Indeed, his philosophy has been called "ideal realism".[57] Baader's "higher realism" was closely linked to his view that "a fully existent or formed being cannot subsist without both internal and external grounding" (8,319; see also 4,260 fn.). Neither inner nor outer exists except in reference to a middle which effects continual equilibrium between them; that middle is the idea or spirit (13,122).[58]

Baader insisted on both internal and external authority or grounding in all areas affecting knowledge and faith: faith in God is backed by conscience (1,8) and the witness of nature (6,21); the church is both internal and external; art links the spiritual and material; "religion knows of no spiritualization of the corporeal that is not at the same time a corporealization of the spiritual" (4,339); "every living being is, as one, at the same time many" (1,196). In short, Baader is constitutionally opposed to "either-or" types of solutions or any kind of abstraction.[59] One-sidedness was his *bête noire.* His intellectual foes were "the heartless and the soul-less and the head-less, those who want speculation without empirical ground and basis for it, and, finally, those who want the latter without the former" (8,217; see also 11,89; 15,203). Speculation and empiricism need each other; otherwise, both are abstractions (1,398 fn.). Because Baader believed in God as common Center of all things, immediately present to them all, he believed that ultimately unity exists behind all multiplicity and that truth in one sphere cannot contradict truth in any other (1,145ff.).

Knowledge and faith are distinct, but they must not be separated from one another; thus, Baader considered himself a "religious philosopher". "A man cannot exist without faith, nor can he exist without knowledge or without authority" (8,42); religious dogma is the "original pattern for knowledge" (4,261). Hence, both clergy and laity should study theology (6,79; 8,54). Such a posi-

---

57 H. GRASSL (Ed.): *Franz von Baader. Über Liebe, Ehe und Kunst,* p. 25; see also J. SAUTER: *Baader und Kant,* p. x; F. HOFFMANN: *Vorhalle zur spekulativen Lehre Franz Baaders,* Aschaffenburg (Theodor Pergay) 1836, pp. 1–45. Compare: E. SUSINI (Ed.): *Lettres inédites* 2,27, number 15, where the lover is called a "practical idealist".

58 A. DREWS: *Die deutsche Spekulation seit Kant,* Leipzig (Gustav Fock) 1895, p. 306. See also F. KÜMMEL: *Über den Begriff der Zeit,* Tübingen (Max Niemeyer) 1962, pp. 92ff.; 97ff.

59 It is impossible to read very much of Baader without becoming aware of his impelling Romantic urge to synthesize and unify, to put the abstraction to death. Thus, we find him constantly striving to find the "higher unity", which will reconcile the ideal and the real, the one and the many, subject and object, inner and outer, body and soul, mind and nature, knowing and willing, the rational and the empirical, and many other dichotomies.

tion presupposes that man can actually learn something in the area of religion; here, Baader disputes Hegel's stand that the object of religion is unknowable:

As far as the mysteries of religion are concerned, they are by no means absolutely incapable of investigation but only relatively ("Do what I tell you and in that way you shall learn that my teaching is from God."). (2,327–28)[60]

There are limits to human knowledge, not only in an upward sense but also in a downward sense; the evil of excess is possible in both directions (8,237). But, the limits of human knowledge are certainly not to be drawn where Kant draws them, for, in fact, he denies all real knowledge:

Whoever would maintain with Haller and Kant that we are simply unable to know anything in itself (*Ding an sich*) is saying that we can know no thing (or no person) in itself (*in sich*): i.e. as it (or he) is – which is fundamentally the same as saying that we do not know anything at all. (4,385)

Baader resolves many of the classic dualisms by employing the principle of a "higher third". He finds application for this approach in his theory of knowledge too. Thus, understanding is the "higher third" that mediates between reason and the senses (4,65). Similarly, the "higher third" mediates between feeling and imagination:

. . . there is no contradiction when one person says: the concept comes into being only through annulment (*Aufhebung*) of feeling and imagination, and another person says: this concept stays alive only by means of continual nourishment from feeling and imagination; however, one must not confuse feeling and imagination previous to and apart from the concept with their state after and inside of the concept produced. (2,141; see also 2,240)[61]

---

60 Baader's citation is apparently from John 7,17: "If anyone desires to do his will, he will know of the teaching, whether it is from God or whether I speak on my own authority". Baader often seems to cite from memory, and he frequently recollects only the idea, not the verbatim text.

61 The principle of sublation (*Aufhebung*), to which Baader appeals here, is the same principle used by Hegel to describe the dynamics of the dialectic: antithesis between two opposite factors leads to interaction between them, which results in a synthesis that is specifically different from the sum of the two factors in their separated state – the dynamism of each having modified the other. Sublation involved at once annulment, preservation, and elevation: *annulment* of the false claim of a particular thing to be complete in its own right; *preservation* of the positive truth and dynamism of each of the factors in opposition; *elevation* (sublimation) of each of these factors through their mutual interpenetration into the completeness and higher unity of the synthesis. See J. COLLINS: *A History of Modern European Philosophy*, Milwaukee (Bruce) 1954, p. 629. Although Baader's proclivity for dialectical thinking was largely an innate disposition that was only deepened by contact with Böhme's thought, he does not deny Hegel the credit of working out the idea of sublation as one of the great triumphs of modern

Baader regarded knowledge as intimately connected with life itself. In his review of Lamennais's *Essai sur l'indifférence en matière de réligion,* for example, he cites with approval Lamennais's view that instinct for learning is itself merely "an expression of the instinct or demand for existence, because knowledge of an existing thing gives us a share in the being of the thing known, or because we cannot share in any kind of being without at the same time sharing in knowledge of that being". To Baader, this passage suggests Christ's words: "This is eternal life, that they may know you and him whom you have sent" (5,209–10; John 17,3). In a letter to Jacobi, Baader says: "There is no such thing as idle learning. At least I know no other than this: 'Adam knew his wife and she conceived' or: 'This is eternal life, that they may know you' " (15,204). Instinct for learning is one with instinct for creativity and procreation; its object is nothing other than "generation, giving birth, expression and representation of a word, a name, an image" (*Über die Analogie des Erkenntniss–und des Zeugungs-triebes,* 1,43). It is not reason or understanding alone that determines knowledge for man; the whole man knows – as reasoning, as feeling, as intuiting, as willing.[62] The basic distinction to be made in the kinds of knowledge that exist is that between God's primordial, fundamental, and all-encompassing knowledge, on the one hand, and man's non-primitive, derived, and limited knowledge, on the other. Man's knowledge includes the natural kind, that which obtains when he is in possession of his senses, and various unnatural kinds, such as ecstasy or trance (1,265ff.).

Baader's theory of *revelation* or manifestation also bears on his theory of knowledge inasmuch as knowledge depends on what is revealed and who does the revealing; this, in turn, depends on the levels of being that are involved: i.e., God, man, and nature. Thus, Baader views the whole range of existing things in this fashion:

. . . every being or existing thing falls into a threefold category, namely: (a) as a knowing, willing, and acting being that is not known, willed, or acted upon by some other (prior or higher) thing; or (b) as a being that is known, willed, and acted upon by another (higher) being, but that itself knows, wills, and acts; or finally (c) as an existing thing that is merely known, willed, and acted upon, without itself knowing, willing or acting. Under the first heading, falls the concept of God; under the second, that of mind, to the extent that one distinguishes mind from God; and finally, under the third, that of non-intelligent self-less nature. (5,252)[63]

    philosophy (*Sämtliche Werke* 2,141ff.; 8,364); he did not, however, accept Hegel's dialectic without reservation. (See J. SAUTER: *Baader und Kant,* pp. 559ff.).

62 See J. SAUTER: *Baader und Kant,* pp. 71–142, especially pp. 131ff.; and J. SAUTER (Ed.): *Franz von Baaders Schriften zur Gesellschaftsphilosophie,* p. 708.

63 Baader finds a parallel division in John Scotus Erigena's triad: *natura creans nec creata; natura creata et creans; natura creata nec creans;* in Baader's terms, God, mind, and nature

In God, man, and nature we thus have the framework for a theory of revelation, the three kinds of revelation corresponding to these three categories (2,315). The principal revelation about God is his independence from all creatures (13,165, 191). Hegel is scored in this connection for making God depend on creation. Man, the image of God (*microtheos* rather than *microcosmos*), also reflects God as Revealer. It is especially through man that we are to explain everything else in the world, in accordance with St. Martin's axiom: "explain things through man, not man through things".[64] Difference in function corresponds to difference in being, so that: (1) God is the *principle* of revelation; (2) man is the *organ* of revelation; (3) nature is the *instrument* of revelation (4,81; 7,90ff.). Baader often uses the triad of principle, organ, and instrument in place of God, man, and nature. A common error is to confuse the role of organ with that of instrument, thus reducing the three kinds of being, function, and revelation to just two (10,121, 138ff.).

The concept of *polarity* is connected with that of ground and cause in Baader's thought. The ground, or sufficient reason which a cause presupposes, must be distinguished from the cause itself (3,339ff.). The ground is the "middle" or center for every action (2,500ff.; 8,178–84, 278; 9,305 and *passim*). The relevance of this distinction to revelation is that:

a cause (as producing) is able to express (really externalize) itself only through its ground . . . In those primitive concepts of cause and ground we have thus a primitive dualism without which in fact we are unable to declare anything . . . (5,11)

The fact is that "that which reveals itself always differentiates and sets apart something in itself in order to reveal itself in and through that" (9,310). This notion of differentiating and setting apart is of central significance for both

(13,113). Hegel's division of reality into mind and nature is inadequate (BAADER: *Sämtliche Werke* 10,185 fn.; 14,119). The three realms are distinct but must not be separated:

One who seeks in nature for nature but not for mind, and one who seeks in mind only the latter and not God, or one who seeks for mind outside of and apart from nature, or for God without and apart from mind – will find neither nature, nor mind, nor God, but will instead lose all three. (14,316 fn.)

Nature's goal is to rise to the level of mind; mind's object is to rise to the level of God. The process does not involve annihilation of the lower entity, but sublation of the lower into the higher, so that the lower does not lose its identity (6,80). Hegel is the usual scapegoat when Baader requires an example of confused thinking in this matter. (See, for example, BAADER: *Sämtliche Werke* 10,118; 12,226, 230, 447; 13,209 and *passim*.)

64   See above, Introduction.

Jacob Böhme and Baader: a thing can be known only in conjunction with its opposite; every existing thing consists essentially in polarity (9,214).[65] Thus, the paradoxical law of manifestation "consists in the fact that every manifestation is conditioned and mediated by occultation (sublation [*Aufhebung*]) . . . " (4,227; 7,104). Baader adopts Böhme's view that "all things (i.e., purely temporal ones) consist in and pass away in yes and no" (9,189). Affirmation and negation are but two sides of every unity: "J. Böhme says in his last writing . . . that affirmation without negation is not possible, nor is negation without affirmation. 'In yes and no consists the life of all things' " (13,80). Thus, there is no yes without a no, no light without darkness, no one without an other – this is basic.

It is clear that Baader exhibits a predilection for triadic patterns: God, mind, nature; principle, organ, instrument; thesis, antithesis, synthesis; Father, Son, Spirit – and there are still more. In this tendency, Baader shows his affinity with Romanticism and German Idealism; trinities of various descriptions characterized the thinking of the age as a whole.[66] Baader's exposure to Paracelsus, St. Martin, and Böhme resulted, however, in a certain "twist" being given to his understanding of triad: a complete triad is, in fact, not simply a trinity but a quaternity. Resolution of this apparent contradiction lies in the fact that the fourth element is not an element on the level of the first three; it is, rather, a ground for the other three, the basis of the triad's unity (2,243). One model can be found in Paracelsus's affirmation that three elements – mercury, sulphur, and salt – are all made living unities by means of a fourth element, air (8,252; 9,127; 15,190). The supreme analogate, however, is the divine trinity of Persons in a single nature. Baader makes an axiom from St. Martin his own: *Quand on est à trois, on est à quâtre, c.a.d. à un*; in other words, trinity reduces duality to unity – it overcomes duality. (See 1,205; 2,105; 7,159; 12,505; 15,447.) Whereas two lines do not suffice to form an enclosed figure, three lines do, as in a triangle. The fourth element, the enclosed figure, thus constitutes the unity of the triad. Baader's diagrammatic illustration of the whole consists of a triangle with a dot in the center.[67]

---

65 On the polarity of all existing things, see Chapter 4. Although preoccupation with polarity was a key Romantic characteristic, Baader did not derive his position from the Romantics; indeed, the influence was all the other way – if anything – since Baader's earliest writings provide clear evidence of his conviction about the polar makeup of all reality.

66 Thus Hegel posited a trilogy of *Sein, Nichtsein,* and *Dasein,* whereas Schelling had a trilogy of *Seinkönnen, Sein,* and *Sein des Seinkönnens.* (On Baader's opposition to these, see *Sämtliche Werke* 2,348; 3,225, 339ff.; 9,34, 184ff.; 13,172, 194). The strong impact Böhme's dialectical thought had on the Romantics and German Idealists led to widespread preoccupation with triadic patterns such as God, mind, and nature; or soul, mind, and body.

67 Many examples of this quaternary pattern can be found in Baader's writings:

It is vital to note that Baader's use of the trinitarian analogy is based, in the first instance, on a trinity and a "middle" or unity that is *given* and that serves as model for all creatures. Schelling and Hegel, on the contrary, begin with a dualism of opposition (an antithesis), which only *becomes* what in Baader's position is already there from the start. Consequently, the *priority of actual existence* before development is lost for Schelling and Hegel. Nor is that all. Since God's existence is swallowed up in pantheistic development, the entelechy of creatures perishes in the process: the synthesis produced through every antithesis becomes, in turn, part of another antithesis and so on forever.[68]

The problem of *how* man knows God did not bother Baader much at all. Man's conscience gives him immediate knowledge of God; with Kant, he recognizes God "in the quiet rustlings and whisperings of conscience" (1,8; see also 6,294). As for the traditional "proofs" of God's existence, Baader took the position that it is impossible to prove the existence of God through something that is not God (2,499); in fact, "all so-called proofs of God that presuppose such abstract self-consciousness on man's part stem from a denial of God and lead logically back to the same" (9,34).[69] Baader does allow an outer witness to God – in nature – in addition to the witness of conscience (15,455ff). In any case, mere knowledge of God's existence is not the main thing, because "even

Under the term "deed" we understand sometimes the act of doing and sometimes the thing done, which latter however always presupposes triplicity, inasmuch as undetermined (determining) existence (as causality and *concipiens*) and determined existence (as ground or *conceptum*) enter together into unfolding (*explicans*) existence, but thus all three result in the deed as the revealed thing (*explicatum*). (9,180)

Similarly, there are four elements in the production of a word:

Every power is at rest only when it is freely unfolding itself – expressing itself, or in operation – and it works only as resting. This resting or self-grounding (*Sichbegründen*), accordingly, conditions self-expression (*Sichaussprechen*); thus, one has the quaternary [pattern] of speaker, ground for speaking, act of speaking, and spoken word; this quaternary (obviously not a square, but rather a triangle with a dot at its center) in no wise annuls the triad; in fact, it alone establishes it. One is best instructed in these matters by J. Böhme . . .(2,43 fn.). For other examples, see: BAADER: *Sämtliche Werke* 2,46, 195, 232; 3,267; 4,30, 254; 8,64ff.; 10,67; 12,242, 243, 344; 13,201; 14,35.)

68 See H. GRASSL (Ed.): *Franz von Baader. Über Liebe, Ehe und Kunst*, pp. 23ff.
69 The witness of conscience is more than adequate "proof" of God's existence (*Sämtliche Werke* 6,294); it involves absolute certainty of my being known by God (1,8ff.). But between knowledge of God and belief in him, another thing is needed: namely, cooperation of will. As Augustine said: *Nemo credit nisi volens* (No one believes unless he is willing); Thomas Aquinas adds: *Nihil aliud est illuminari quam luci subjici* (To be illumined is nothing other than to be subjected to the light). (See 1,238-241.)

the devils believe and tremble" (James 2,19); what counts is to *believe in* God: i.e., to bind oneself freely to God (*nemo credit nisi volens*) (8,23).

A final major principle of revelation deals with the mode of God's presence in a region or in a person; this is affected, in turn, by the status of that region or person vis-à-vis time and eternity.[70] Heaven, the "good eternity", has three temporal dimensions – past, present, and future; earth (time) has but two – past and future, but no present; hell, the "bad eternity", has only one – the past (2,27). The relationship of God to each region is expressed in one of Baader's favorite distinctions: *Inwohnung* ("in-dwelling"), *Beiwohnung* ("by-dwelling"), and *Durchwohnung* ("through-dwelling"). Analogies with the distinction among principle, organ, and instrument suggest themselves. God's presence through *Inwohnung* is presence as love, the kind most appropriate to the God who is love; his presence through *Beiwohnung* obtains when an intelligent agent cooperates freely with God and acts as God's organ; his presence through *Durchwohnung* is presence through power alone: God deals with inanimate nature – and ultimately with free agents who resist him – through his power: i.e., he treats them as instruments (1,283ff.; 2,38; 4,348; 5,355; 8,317; 9,171ff.; 10,294; 14,77ff., 120 and *passim*).

These distinctions shed light on many of Baader's statements: e.g. "a good person and an evil one will do different things, but both do what God wills" (12,211); and "God makes people good or evil, as they wish, for doing is determined by willing" (13,295). Baader says, in effect, that God offers himself in love to everyone, but love cannot be forced on anyone; although love may be refused, God's presence through power cannot, for nothing can exist apart from him. In an analogous vein, Baader cites Angelus Silesius: "God is master to the servant, he is Father to his child, and he is bridegroom when he finds his bride, Sophia" (8,317).

The fact of revelation does not justify pantheism, for the unity of God's essence is indissoluble and non-transferable (14,132). For Baader, God is not some sort of abstract principle but rather a *personal* being; and the hallmark of personality is incommunicability. God is not "a part of the world" nor is the world a "part of God". God is both above the world and within the world (3,382;

---

70 Baader's theory of time and eternity is one of the more complex parts of his thought. His essays on the theme include: *Über den Begriff der Zeit/Sur la notion du tems* [sic] (1818; 2,47–94, in both French and German); *Elementarbegriffe über die Zeit als Einleitung zur Philosophie der Societät und der Geschichte* (1831; 14,29–54); *Über den Begriff der Zeit und die vermittelnde Function der Form oder des Maasses* (1833; 2,517–34); *Über zeitliches und ewiges Leben und die Beziehung zwischen diesem und jenem* (1836; 4,285–94). See F. KÜMMEL: *Über den Begriff der Zeit*, pp. 87–121; J. SAUTER: *Baader und Kant*, pp. 57–70; E. SUSINI: *Franz von Baader et le romantisme mystique*, volume 2, pp. 406–17.

13,319). In other words, he is both transcendent and immanent.[71] God has "externality" about him (8,315), but this is *immanent* in him:

This is precisely J. Böhme's great merit – that he conceives this innerness and outerness of God in immanent fashion and does not immediately conceive of the outerness of God's existence as creaturely existence, as the pantheists do, to whom God, as soon as he wishes to be or should be a really existing being, immediately takes leave of himself and steps into or falls into creation. The God of these philosophers is a centaur or hybrid being, consisting of a center that is divine and a periphery that is creaturely or non-divine . . . (13,168; see also 8,78)

What is "external" about God is antecedent to and independent of any reference to the world (13,191).

2. God

Much of the preceding has already dealt with God.[72] Far from excepting God from the range or application of his principles, Baader follows Böhme in making God the very paradigm of the principles governing all of reality. So we find that the distinction between ground and cause is found in God (2,154 fn.). Even the triad of principle, organ, and instrument finds its parallel in God as will, wisdom, and (eternal) nature – distinctions that are valid even prior to the creation of the world (2,247). The trinity of will, wisdom, and eternal nature in God is not the same as the trinity of Father, Son, and Spirit; indeed, it precedes the latter logically (not temporally);[73] all life and revelation, at any level, con-

---

71 Baader insists often on the indissolubility and absolutely pure (unmixed with creation) character of God's being (*Sämtliche Werke* 2,456; 12,169, 173; 13,132;); God is complete in himself and needs no course of development to full perfection (9,103); we must completely reject Spinoza's substance-pantheism (1,4; 2,210, 254, 399ff.). On the other hand, Baader finds likeness to God's being in all of nature: God not only transcends nature, but is also immanent in it; in a sense, he is not only center but also periphery (4,297; 12,304ff.; 13,191). *Deus est sphaera cujus centrum ubique, circumferentia nusquam* (2,390; 13,69).

72 A great deal of overlapping is unavoidable, for it is implicit in the character of Baader's thought that no area of being may be treated in isolation, as a purely quantitative entity; there is throughgoing interpenetration (yet distinction) of all areas of reality.

73 Traditional understanding of the trinity Father, Son, and Holy Spirit says that the Father generates the Son through his own self-knowledge: i.e., the Father's knowledge of himself is the second Person of the trinity, the Son. Father and Son know and love each other; their love for each other is the Holy Spirit, who thus proceeds (is "breathed forth") from the Father and Son. This internal dynamism of the trinity is eternal. The trinity of will, wisdom, and eternal nature governs all dynamisms, including the knowing and loving that is the essence of the trinity of Father, Son, and Spirit.

form to its pattern (2,247). There is an "inner" and "outer" as well as process in God too, but these terms may not be used of God and creatures univocally.[74]

Most of Baader's statements about God have to do with unfolding the implications of the two trinities: will, wisdom, nature; and Father, Son, Spirit. It is not necessary for God to run through either a logical or historical course in order to be "completed"; process in God is eternal and without any connection to creation (8,88). God's life is complete in itself; it is movement "in a circle", as much regression as it is progression (13,166).

In the trinity will, wisdom, and nature in God, the analogy with principle, organ, and instrument is clear. Baader and Böhme both follow a voluntarist metaphysic: i.e., they recognize *will* as the first positive principle. God is truth, justice, mercy, and many other things, but most of all he is pure will: it is the will of God that dissipates the indeterminate nothingness of the "Un-ground" (*Ungrund*).[75] Wisdom, the Heavenly Sophia, is the formative idea, the co-operator or organ of God *par excellence* (2,288); it is God's organ and mirror, the image of the whole Godhead (2,247; 7,105).[76] The eternal nature of God is the productive power of God, which flows immediately from his nature. Like Sophia (God's wisdom), the eternal nature of God has no distinct personality of its own; it takes on characteristics of personality only when it operates on objects outside the Godhead (7,34 fn.; 8,78). Indeed, the eternal nature of God has no proper activity of its own, but acts as an instrument of Sophia, the organ of the Godhead (2,47).[77] Baader held that only the acceptance of Böhme's positions concerning the role of Sophia and the eternal nature in God could effectively dispose of the threat of various kinds of dualism in God (3,420ff.; 13,245ff.; 15,651).

Baader was quite dissatisfied with the usual run of explanations about the trinity in God. (See, for example, 2,338ff.; 10,14 fn.) He was particularly aroused

---

74 "Inner" and "outer" have to be defined according to "the three moments of existence and of activity that Böhme distinguished: (1) still, unrevealed or magical existence, as indifference or non-separation of that existence into innerness and outerness; (2) existence distinguished into innerness and outerness; (3) concrete existence and activity that consists in conjunction of the two" (*Sämtliche Werke* 7,298–99 fn.; see also 13,168). All process in God is eternal (8,88).

75 On the *Ungrund*, see Chapter 2. According to J. Böhme, will is "the causality that established itself in revelation and is made independent through it", a notion that Baader calls "the hardest concept in philosophy" (3,388).

76 On Sophia or Heavenly Wisdom, see Chapter 3.

77 Both Sophia and God's eternal nature act in the name of the three persons of the trinity, not just one or two of them. God's wisdom and power belong to the whole Godhead. Baader and Böhme thus avoided conflict with the ancient axiom of trinitarian theology: *Omnia opera ad extra communia sunt tribus personis.*

by Schelling and Hegel for their failure to maintain the key distinction between all production or generation of a created sort and that which takes place
in God himself (2,526; 7,162). One approach used by Baader to illustrate relations among the members of the divine trinity is to employ the category of
work or activity:

We have to consider . . . three producers and three products or effects. The Father, as first
producer who is himself unproduced (*ageneitos*), produces in himself the Son, as first product and second producer, with whom the Father produces the Spirit, as second product and
third producer; the Spirit (together with the Father and the Son) produces Sophia as image
of the trinity (although this image represents the Son in a special way) and as third product,
which, however, is not itself a producer (Person), just as the Father is a producer, but is not
produced . . . (2,530; see also 1,299; 13,190 and *passim*.)[78]

Sophia does not lend actual unity to the trinity except as mediated through the
divine nature:

In this deepest mystery of the Godhead, the holy trinity is, according to J. Böhme, only in
potency or essential; only through the medium of the eternal nature (desire) does it become
actual in a personal way (*in essentia unitas, in personis proprietas*). (2,305)[79]

Baader ascribes the divinity of the trinity to the Father, its personality to the
Son, and its spirituality to the Spirit (3,326 fn.).

One reason why Baader considered speculation on the trinity to be of such
importance is that he regarded the trinity as the model for all thought.[80] He
even recognizes some presentiments of trinitarian doctrine in Plato (1,221). In
his own speculation about the trinity, Baader was guided by official Church
definitions (7,166) as well as by Thomas Aquinas (14,197ff.). The latter won

---

78 The words "produce" and "product", in this and similar texts dealing with the trinity,
    are used analogically of course. Exclusion of all temporal sequences and causal depen-
    dencies in these trinitarian relations is taken for granted.
79 Baader's allusion in the phrases *in essentia unitas, in personis proprietas*, is to the Preface
    of the Holy Trinity, a part of the liturgy of the Catholic Mass for most Sundays of the
    year. Baader rejects "that double error of several thousand years duration" wherein
    theologians have thought that God's personality could be saved only at the cost of his
    nature (*Natürlichkeit*) or vice versa (*Sämtliche Werke* 8,274).
80 Now, if these theologians try to turn the doctrine of the trinity into a mystery inaccessible to all
    understanding, one about which we simply cannot think at all, one about which all thinking
    should instead simply cease and remain *ex officio* eliminated, well, another theologian (Leopold
    Schmid) has just recently asserted to the contrary, and rightly so, that it is precisely from this
    primitive thought alone, i.e., from recognition of this self-manifestation . . . that all thinking (all
    knowledge of self and others) can proceed and begin (*Sämtliche Werke* 4,314–15).

Baader's particular approval because he recognized a motherly as well as a fatherly principle in the Godhead (14,201ff.; see also 10,15). As always, though, it was Jacob Böhme who remained his chief guide on matters pertaining to the trinity. Baader's close reliance on Böhme's symbolic and mystical speculation makes his thought about the trinity extremely abstruse and difficult.[81]

3. Nature

Just as Baader's theology is really a theosophy, so also is his philosophy of nature a "physiosophy" or a "cosmosophy".[82] Baader, in fact, is the first of the Romantics to use the expression "world-soul" (*Weltseele*), anticipating even Schelling's essay *Über die Weltseele* of 1798 (3,30, 226). His earliest writings reveal a genuine horror for the idea of a *mundus machinalis* and a genuine commitment to a *mundus vitalis*. The grossest of modern errors, he argued, are attributable to a *Weltanschauung* centered on a *Dieu-machine, nature-machine, homme-machine,* and *état-machine.* (See 4,301; 11,392.) Nature is a dynamic reality, a vital force (*Kraft, Physis*), not a product (2,378). (On this point, Baader sides with Schelling against Hegel.) Mind so interpenetrates nature that we cannot view the latter solely as dead matter (7,262); an organism is much more than simply a "cadaver plus life", as though life were but an afterthought superimposed on an inert mass (15,619). Thus, nature has a spiritual principle in it as well as a material one (4,350). The general rule for Baader and Böhme is that we must not confuse mind and material nature, but neither should we separate them (2,377; 5,18, 228, 251); "there is no spirit that is not an esprit de corps" (12,46). Baader defends the importance of a close union between mind and nature, particularly in *Über die Begründung der Ethik durch die Physik* and in his rebuttal to a review of this essay (5,1–42). He finds evidence of a constant interchange between the realms of the material and non-material in such processes as combustion, assimilation of food, and procreation (e.g., 4,317; 7,254, 383). There is, in fact, no way of understanding what a physical "element" is in a mechanical sense; it is, rather, an elemental force (*Grundkraft*), not a static

81 F. HOFFMAN: *Vorhalle zur spekulativen Lehre Franz Baaders*, especially pp. 126–56, is a helpful guide in the shadow-world of Baader's speculation about the trinity.
82 Baader uses all three terms (theosophy, physiosophy, cosmosophy) at 1,323 of the *Sämtliche Werke*. Theosophy differs from philosophy inasmuch as it begins with God and from there draws conclusions about the world; generally, it is pantheistic, seeing the world as a process within God himself. It differs from theology inasmuch as it alleges, generally, that God and the contents of revelation are not matters about which to speculate intellectually. (See "Theosophie", *Lexikon für Theologie und Kirche*, volume 10, p. 95.) Inasmuch as he rejects pantheism absolutely and insists on deriving the full measure of good that one can glean from speculation, Baader is unusual as a theosophist.

particle (3,214).[83] One of the reasons why the Romantics and the German Idealists were so interested in parapsychological phenomena in the early nineteenth century was their conviction that spirit and nature were fundamentally interdependent.[84]

Part and parcel of Baader's position concerning the dynamic character of nature and the interpenetration of spirit and matter was his rejection of mechanistic atomism. Organic unity differs from mere aggregation (3,233). The essay *Über das pythagoräische Quadrat in der Natur oder die vier Weltgegenden* (1798; 3,247–68) presents – for the first time in explicit terms – Baader's symbolization of life as *circulus vitae*, an organic unity of center and members. Even his first work, *Vom Wärmestoff, seiner Vertheilung, Bindung und Entbindung, vorzüglich beim Brennen der Körper* (1786), presupposes a similar orientation. In the battle against a mechanistic view of nature, a battle in which Baader was joined early by Novalis, Friedrich Schlegel, and Schelling, it should be noted that Baader had already published four essays addressing the subject before the appearance of Schelling's *Weltseele*.[85] Baader was the real pace-setter in introducing the Romantic view of nature.

Baader held a creational view regarding the origin of the natural world.[86] The expression "*creatio ex nihilo*" indicates that God's action in creating the world represents the apex of spontaneity; it was from the totality of his own fullness that God created, not (*per absurdum*) out of "nothing" as a kind of *materia prima* (3,241 fn.; see also 2,229). Visible creation tells us something about its invisible Creator (2,229). "Creation out of nothing is a production, not an eduction or an emanation" (1,205). It is creation that gives every created being its proper niche in the whole, in its "true region, form, place, mother, or home" (14,92), for God's creation is a system, not a hodgepodge (9,24). Baader finds an analogy for creation out of nothing in the process by means of

---

83 Baader's notions about physical elements are mostly borrowed from Paracelsus. (See above.) Both men regard salt, sulphur, and mercury as dynamic physical forces; see *Sämtliche Werke* 3,206ff.; 4,146; 8,252; 9,204 fn. On love as one of Böhme's "natural forms" [*Naturgestalten*], see 13,84, 106, 112, 118, 141. See also 14,423.

84 On this point, see J. SAUTER (Ed.): *Franz von Baaders Schriften zur Gesellschaftsphilosophie*, pp. 715ff.

85 Those essays are: *Vom Wärmestoff, seiner Vertheilung, Bindung und Entbindung, vorzüglich beim Brennen der Körper* (1786; 3,1–180); *Ideen über Festigkeit und Flüssigkeit zur Prüfung der physikalischen Grundsätze des Herrn Lavoisier* (1792; 3,181–202); *Beiträge zur Elementar-Physiologie* (1797; 3,203–46); *Über das pythagoräische Quadrat in der Natur oder die vier Weltgegenden* (completed, 1797; published, 1798; 3,247–68). For Baader's influence on Schelling, Novalis, and Friedrich Schlegel in the sphere of the philosophy of nature, see J. SAUTER (Ed.): *Franz von Baaders Schriften zur Gesellschaftsphilosophie*, pp. 730ff.

86 For Baader's position on creation, see Chapter 2.

which an intelligent being comes actually to will and desire something that, previous to that desire, exists only in a "magical" or potential condition and, in consequence of that desire, is actualized.[87]

We have seen that mind and matter are closely linked in Baader's view. This union of mind and matter led to dramatic consequences in nature when man and the angels fell from God's favor. The chief result of the sin of the spirit in nature was its materialization. The material character of nature was not its original state, but rather a punishment for sin and a barrier to further sin, because all matter confines and limits. (See, for example, 2,489ff.; 4,345; 9,87; 13,121) Baader supposes some kind of primordial deterioration of nature, an idea hinted at in the myths of all nations. He believes that this world catastrophe occurred before the beginning of recorded history and was the consequence of sin (2,295; 5,256; 7,294; 8,151; 9,53, 79ff., 113, 151, etc.). Natural catastrophes are but echoes of the original one (7,331); even the animal and plant worlds preserve vestiges of an earlier struggle (14,465ff.).[88] Because of sin, order in the universe now is largely external and forced (*gleichsam polizeilich*) (8,152). It is man's vocation (led by Christ) to restore the universe to its pristine harmony and perfection (4,279ff., 339; 15,549 and *passim*). One should avoid the extremes of denying the permanence of the present world, as some mystics do, and of maintaining the absolute permanence of our present corruptible matter. In the end,

---

87 When a thought rises up within us, it appears to us at first like the shadow of a yet unborn child, only "magical". Its content (*Fülle*) is still without its own proper life. Only desire and will make possible the transition from potential to actual existence. That quiescent magical thought already brings something along with it — it manifests itself as a potency that stimulates our will as quiet lust — and with that we have expressed the open secret of all activity. The law of transition from potential to actual being is a general one. This transition from desire and lust to action deserves careful attention. Everywhere the transition proceeds through lust to inflamed desire. If people had taken thorough account of this transition of purely magical thought through desire in theology, they would not have had to break their heads over creation out of nothing . . . (*Sämtliche Werke* 8,79–80)

Inasmuch as creation and every act of production follows the pattern just described, divine Wisdom (Sophia) must also separate itself into lust and desire in order to evoke God's creative act (2,255–56).

88 It is not only the fall of spirits before man that has had such baneful influence on the present state of the world; man's fall also contributed its share (*Sämtliche Werke* 2,376). Through his sin, man earned a kind of curse, not only for himself but for the world.

Man perceives through all the beauties of nature, now softly and now more loudly, her melancholy lament over the widow's veil she must wear through the fault of man. (2,120)

If we have not lost capacity to wonder, it can serve as a bridge for us to arrive at some notion of what pristine purity of nature was like before the fall. (4,49ff)

all matter will be spiritualized again as Christ's body was glorified after his death (3,352).

Baader finds a close connection among the concepts of earth, culture, and cult; one needs to understand each properly if one is to understand sacrificial worship correctly (3,314ff.; 7,305; 12,212). Man serves nature now through his work; if he rectifies his relationship to God, however, he will be freed from that service – though in a sense different from that intended by Bacon (9,63). Man should not cut himself off from nature, but he should be free from being dominated by it: *naturfrei* but not *naturlos* (7,31, 38, 85, etc.).

Baader preferred his highly symbolic view of the world to Newtonian astronomy. He rejected Newton's theory of attraction and repulsion as well as his theory of gravity and of planetary orbits. (See 2,61; 3,292ff., 320)[89] Baader was convinced that the sun regulated the paths of other heavenly bodies. Both sun and earth are unique in their kind, not simply two more among a host of similar bodies (3,313; 4,379).

Ultimately, one must understand Baader's philosophy of nature against the background of his two major philosophical preoccupations: to reconcile idealism with realism; and to reconcile faith with reason. The whole universe is a poem, man the original poet (3,245); man's whole vocation is to discover the divine in nature (4,215; 11,156).

No genuine adept of nature has missed the great truth that every spiritual entity has its symbol in the material world here below and that as a result the whole of nature lies before our eyes as a hieroglyphic. (12,172; see also 1,130; 11,149)

4. Man

Man is the keystone figure in Baader's scheme of thought, at once *microcosmos* and *microtheos* (11,78; 12,205). In the mind of God, man is the apex of creation, the "final creation" – *Schlussgeschöpf* (4, 431; 12,97). Like Aristotle's "final cause", he was first in intention and last in execution. Although man mirrors the universe and God, he is an essential unity:

. . . one must above all guard against the usual erroneous notion . . . according to which man considers himself a closed figure or a triangle without a center and, consequently, fails to see

89 Baader rejected all forms of atomism, Leibniz's idealistic atomism as well as ancient materialistic atomisms (*Sämtliche Werke* 2,165); Herbart may be classed with Leibniz on this point (2,lxxvii). Descartes has aided the cause of mechanism and materialism in the philosophy of nature through his "spirit-less conception of nature and his nature-less conception of spirit" (5,6). For Baader, it is one thing to understand the laws of matter, but it is something else to understand nature.

that it is one and the same individual being who, as man in the normal integrity of his existence, exists as body, soul, and mind simultaneously. From which it follows that true and complete man, in his integrity, is neither soul alone, nor mind alone, nor body alone, but only all three at the same time . . . (4,153; 8,148–49)

Thus, soul, mind, and body are not "component parts" in man but organs or attributes of one unitary person, the ultimate center of attribution and reference. (See 3,214ff.; 4,241; 8,252ff., etc.) Among these three attributes of man, mind holds highest dignity because it is the "higher third", that which links the other two: "It is, therefore, not the soul that mediates the higher mind (idea) with the body, but, rather, it is the mind that is the middle for both . . . " (4,373–74; see also 2,240 fn.; 8,91 fn.). Man's body is created, his soul is "breathed into" him (eingeblasen), and his mind (the "light image") is directly born of God (2,92 fn.). Separation of body and soul principles at death is only temporary (4,272ff.; 10,228ff.).[90] Baader vigorously rejects the extremes of materialism and "spiritualism". Thus, "it is sheer pride to wish to be without a body (nature). In this sense, it was the first arrogant spirit who was also the first supernaturalist . . . If one could make God natureless (naturlos) and nature Godless, both of them would disappear . . . " (2,15). Without the resurrection of the body after death, man would be forever incomplete (8,368). However, in the resurrection, the whole natural man will be "spiritualized" (vergeistigt): the soul will be a life-giving spirit (spiritus vivificans) and the body will be a "spiritual body" (corpus spiritale) (4,344–49; see also 13,294). Neither the physical nor the spiritual may be sacrificed: "just as man's body (as matter) is not such if it is not spiritualized body, so is the spirit of man not such if it is not embodied spirit" (10,69ff.). "Religion knows of no spiritualization of the bodily . . . that is not at the same time embodiment of the spiritual" (4,339).

A substantial part of Baader's philosophical anthropology is implicated in his view that man is made in the image of God and that man was originally, and still is by vocation, an androgynous being.[91] Man is mediator between God and the world (2,35). Through the presence of the Heavenly Sophia in him, he is God's very image (2,209; 4,311, 351ff.; 9,167, etc.). This condition is at once a free gift of God to man (Gabe) and a challenge to conform his life and love to establishing that image in himself (Aufgabe) (4,214). Man was originally like the sun of the world:

---

90 One of the results of the fall of man is that a certain degree of composition has entered into his makeup, a certain lack of unity and simplicity to which death and lesser forms of decomposition in human life bear witness (Sämtliche Werke 8,254).

91 On man as the image of God and on androgyny see Chapters 3 and 4.

Man stands in a like category with the sun. The sun strikes deeper root than all other creatures. Only when God finds himself in man, reflects himself in him, can nature celebrate its sabbath. (8,59; see also 5,32)[92]

Sophia, the image of the trinity, enables man to be spiritually creative and fruitful for the whole universe (2,418; 10,9); like Sophia and Christ, man is the "representative and organ" of God in the universe (7,295). The limitations inherent in a single and incomplete sexual endowment for each human being now were not present from the beginning: man was originally integral, possessing the fullness of humanity within himself as an individual – including even the procreative capacity which now requires two distinct sexes.[93] The state of disintegration now existing is the result of sin.

Even without a fall of man, God would have become incarnate (2, 64; 4,333); in view of this sin, however, God's loving condescension is all the greater in becoming incarnate (2,58, 159).[94] A kind of intellectual-spiritual incarnation was going on among the Jews even before the historical physical incarnation in Christ (7,289); the incarnation will continue to the end of the world (7,304 fn.). The incarnation of God's Son and his sacrificial death had a profound ethical effect, as the shedding of blood always does (*Vorlesungen über eine künftige Theorie des Opfers oder des Cultus*, 7,271–416). Intimately linked to Christ's incarnation and death is the Christian's rebirth – Christ "takes form in His disciples" (5,90); indeed, "the basic concept of Christianity . . . is that of complete transformation and restoration (rebirth) of man in soul and body . . . " (8,46, 157).

One of Baader's chief complaints against Kant was that his ethics, based as it is on an analysis of the "moral law", was one-sided and powerless; all it does is tell man that his life is out of order (1,55; see also 5,1ff.). But "remorse of conscience (or the moral imperative), as such, has no power to make the sinner better . . . " (4,170). Speaking of good or evil makes little sense to Baader except in the context of man's vocation of establishing God's image within himself

---

92 The sun is one of Baader's favorite symbols, and it is one which he uses to describe not only man's role in the world, but especially the role of Sophia and of Christ. On Baader's use of symbols, see J. SAUTER: "Der Symbolismus bei Baader", *Blätter für deutsche Philosophie*, 1 (1928), pp. 348–66.

93 See Chapter 4. The procreation referred to here is not numerical procreation. (See BAADER: *Sämtliche Werke* 2,315ff.; 7,223ff.; 9,209ff., 221ff.)

94 If man had not fallen, the incarnation of God's Son would have involved assuming the role of organ on his part (though he would not cease to be a principle too). But given the fall, God's Son had to become not only organ but even instrument "because it was not only that the organ had dared to elevate itself to the level of principle, but also that the instrument rebelled against the organ and climbed to its level . . . " (BAADER: *Sämtliche Werke* 2,159; see also 2,472ff.).

(2,281, 346ff.; 8,46; 10,32); he rejects all moralities that have no place for a redeemer (2,25; 4,67 and *passim*). In place of Kant's powerless categorical imperative, Baader postulates faith in a personal God: "The pertinent question with regard to faith is not what a man believes but in whom he has faith" (5,221 fn.).[95] Faith affects one's knowing, willing, and acting – the theory and practice of life – and is, in turn, affected by them (1,103ff.; 5,251). Faith is willing obedience to higher command, "taking to one's heart or inwardly incorporating" the one in whom one believes; "no one believes unless he is willing" (1,133; 4,310; 8,28 fn.; 9,96, 104 and *passim*). Prayer is vital: it is the expression of faith and fosters greater faith.[96] The sacraments too, especially the Eucharist, play an important role in joining the whole man to God in worship.[97]

The human race as a whole goes through five stages of existence, "a cycle through which man runs: from the first androgynous condition to that of sexual differentiation in paradise, from that into an earthly-animal condition, and from

95 Baader very insightfully maintains that everyone has a faith of some kind:

Theologians and philosophers are in error when they think that intelligent disbelief is the opposite of ignorant faith, because a person acquires the power to disbelieve in A only by means of belief in B. Thus, you can say to a man: Show me what you do not believe in, and I will show you what you do believe in; and you can say to him: Show me the power against which you are rebelling, and I will show you the one to which you are submitting yourself . . . " (*Sämtliche Werke* 6,66 fn.)

96 Baader's standpoint is that of the "priority of the optative" (*Sämtliche Werke* 15,168; see also 8,205 fn.). Prayer and faith are not self-made or man-made constructs, but rather gifts of God and challenges to man's response (*Gegeben und Aufgegeben*).

It is the same power that both solicits and accomplishes faith within me. "Pray in my name, so shall you receive." People have believed rather generally up to this point that prayer is a subjective personal construct, so that every whim and caprice of prayer should be heard. But hearing is promised only to the objective prayer that is prayed in Christ's name, and it is a duty to suppress the purely subjective. The same God who prays in me will also hear himself in me . . . (8,28–29 fn.; see also 2,512 and *passim*)

Baader's views on prayer are utterly opposed to the Kantian view as expressed, for example, in *Religion Within the Limits of Reason Alone* New York (Harper Torchbook) 1960, pp. 181ff. See also 14,487 fn.

97 Whereas faith begins within man and works outwardly, sacraments begin outside man and work inwardly. Sacraments indicate need for a higher physics as ground for true ethics. (See *Über die Begründung der Ethik durch die Physik*, 1813; 5,1–34.) Baader is at one with Christian tradition in recognizing the Eucharist as the focal point of all the sacraments, but his adherence to such Böhmean and Paracelsian notions as that of "tincture" as well as his own mystical theory of "alimentation" make his position quite unusual. See, for example, his essays *Über Alimentation und Beiwohnung* (1838; 14,459–88); *Alle Menschen sind im seelischen, guten oder schlimmen, Sinn unter sich: Anthropophagen* (1834; 4,221–42); and *Sur l'Eucharistie* and *Über das heilige Abendmahl* (1815; 7,1–28). On "tincture", see *Sämtliche Werke* 13,82.

this latter (via death) back to the first androgynous situation" (8,278 fn.). The five kinds of relationships man has are to God, to himself, to other men, to other intelligent beings, and to the nonintelligent world (8,311ff.). His powers of communication with other levels of reality are far wider than he generally thinks (1,192ff.; 2,211). Indeed, man is the bridge between the intelligent and non-intelligent worlds, between heaven and earth, mind and nature, God and creation (2,194, 464; 4,299, 311, etc.). Man will never be an angel, but his destiny exceeds that of the angels (3,313ff.). The destiny of earth as a whole is bound up with man's destiny.[98]

In a manner reminiscent of the method adopted by Joachim of Flora to catgorize the ages of the Father, Son, and Holy Spirit in history, Baader divides world history into the ages of creation, incarnation (beginning with the fall of man), and resurrection (beginning with Christ's ascension into heaven); these periods, too, may be styled the ages of the Father, Son, and Holy Spirit (2,419). Likewise, one may see a foreshadowing of world history in the patriarchal, Mosaic, and prophetic epochs of Old Testament history; they correspond to the natural, spiritual, and divine stages of revelation (7,311ff.).

Baader's social philosophy is clearly built on the organic model.[99] He holds that society, in its deepest sense, represents a "primitive and radical link be-

---

98 One has good reason to believe, however, that this help for man extends also to other intelligent beings. This is something that is of a piece with that great and still hidden mystery of the solid bond of man with the earth and the harmonious agreement of both in the universe: of the first, that is, in an intellectual sense; of the latter in a physical sense . . . (BAADER: *Sämtliche Werke* 4,409; see also 2,29; 3,314; 9,344ff.).

99 Franz von Baader's social philosophy is perhaps the most important part of his work; certainly it is the best known. The chief sources for this aspect of his thought are: J. SAUTER (Ed.): *Franz von Baaders Schriften zur Gesellschaftsphilosophie*; J. SAUTER: *Baader und Kant*; J. SAUTER: *Die Sozialphilosophie Franz von Baaders*, Munich (doctoral dissertation) 1926; J. SAUTER: "Franz von Baaders romantische Socialphilosophie", *Zeitschrift für die gesamte Staatswissenschaft*; H. REICHEL: "Die Sozietätsphilosophie Franz von Baaders", *Zeitschrift für die gesamte Staatswissenschaft* 57 (Tübingen, 1901); H. GRASSL (Ed.): *Franz von Baader. Gesellschaftslehre*, Munich (Kösel) 1957; H. A. FISCHER-BARNICOL (Ed.): *Franz von Baader: Vom Sinn der Gesellschaft. Schriften zur Sozialphilosophie* Cologne (Hegener) 1966; J. BAXA: *Einführung in die romantische Staatswissenschaft*, Jena (G. Fischer) 1923, pp. 158ff.); F. HOFFMANN (Ed.): *Grundzüge der Sozietätsphilosophie Franz von Baaders*, Würzburg (Hellerau) 1865; L. LÖWENTHAL: *Die Sozietätsphilosphie Franz von Baaders*, Frankfurt (doctoral dissertation) 1923; K. SPRENG: *Studien zur Entstehung sozialpolitischer Ideen in Deutschland auf Grund der Schriften Franz von Baaders und Franz Joseph von Buss*, Giessen (doctoral dissertation) 1932; K. SPRENG (Ed.): *Franz von Baader. Gedanken über den Staat und Gesellschaft, Revolution und Reform (1831). Über das dermalige Missverhältnis der vermögenslosen oder Proletairs zu den Vermögensbesitzenden Klassen* . . . Darmstadt (Wissenschaftliche Buchgesellschaft) 1968; D. BAUMGARDT: *Franz von Baader und die philosophische Romantik*, Halle/Saale (Max Niemeyer) 1927, pp. 368ff. Many other entries in the bibliography bear on the subject.

tween God and man" (5,244). In establishing an organic bond between himself and God, man also lays the basis for organic unity between himself and other men and nature (8,73). For the "indwelling of the Center" enables all members to be properly grounded in their own "middle" (8,240). Baader finds the "quintessence of my philosophy" embodied in the following statement: "How a man is related to God determines how he is related to himself, to other men, to his own nature, and to the rest of nature" (15,469). It is only in the context of proper relationships to God and to other men that man can be free and productive (6,65, 80, 86). The principle of productivity *par excellence* is love, because love is the sole principle that can free man from the negative burden of himself, of other men, of nature, and of God. The love that Christianity teaches is this love; therefore, "religion alone is the ground for society" (6,41; see also 5,258).[100] The contrast between this point of view and rationalist-utilitarian social-contract theories could not be more stark![101]

Since every organism is hierarchically structured according to the number of functions engaged in by its components, inequality or dissimilarity is an invariable concomitant of the organic idea. In the societal organism, it is love that associates unequals with equals in humility and nobility (6,232). Inequality of place and function in society also justifies the need for authority (1, 138; 6,115). Developing (see 6,127) or unfolding, processes that preserve the past as they build the future, are further concomitants of the organic idea.[102] As Baader's essay *Über den Evolutionismus und Revolutionismus oder die posit. und negat. Evolution des Lebens überhaupt und des socialen Lebens insbesondere* (6,73–108) argues, stagnation and revolution are extremes to be avoided; neither contributes to progress and growth. The first denies life's basic law of development; the second wrenches one violently away from the matrix of the past. Generally, such wrenching results from continued frustration of proper evolution. Truth stands in the middle:

---

100 Because of the inseparable relationship between love and religion in Baader's thought, this theme will be revisited often during the course of this study

101 . . . and because no man can have the right on his own to give orders to his equal and no one is obliged to obey his equal, so it is also true that men are not able of themselves to unite or form a society; only their association with God was able and is able to establish such union among them. (BAADER: *Sämtliche Werke* 5,166; see also 14,128)

Thus, state and society – first and foremost – form a kind of "divine contract".

102 Baader fought both the "Jacobins" (i.e., radicals in general) and reactionaries but, as Baumgardt notes, he was himself probably "a few degrees" closer to the reactionaries than to the Jacobins: D. BAUMGARDT: *Franz von Baader und die philosophische Romantik*, p. 384. See H. SEDLMAYR: "Erneuerung als konservatives Prinzip bei Franz von Baader", *Studium Generale. Zeitschrift für die Einheit der Wissenschaften im Zusammenhang ihrer Begriffsbildungen und Forschungsmethoden*, 15 (1962), pp. 264–71.

Only that folk (this holds for the individual person too) which holds its own past together as it guides it [i.e. its past] toward the future, uniting one with the other, lives integrally and prudently in the present in stable fashion; for it is only in this union or concretion that the old renews itself and the new gains strength. In this sense, Cicero once remarked that an individual man (as well as a people) who tries to break loose from his history becomes and remains a child. (6,70 fn.; see also 6,73ff.)

Hence, free and productive society can only be an organism, not an "association" (6,78) or a "mechanism" (14,466). Baader's sociological universalism corresponds with his theocentric philosophy as a whole: give-and-take between God and man conditions give-and-take among all men and with nature.

When Baader speaks of society in general, his perspective is that of Edmund Burke: i.e., society is an organic unity linking all persons who have died, who are living, and who are yet to live (5,269; 6,70; 8,219; 14,53). The state is not synonymous with society; it is, rather, the third moment in a process of development. Baader follows St. Martin in distinguishing

natural society, civil society, and political society as three moments which mark the formation of society; indeed, civil society (the declaration of law) does not come into being until the dogma of love and harmony (natural society) is attacked. Likewise, failing to heed the law or transgressing it calls forth power that will maintain and vindicate it; at this point, political society comes into being. This is a gradation that is valid for every society (civil or religious) . . . (2,213; see also 5,74, 297)[103]

Further development of society has led to its present division into church, state, and universities. Baader believed that relationships among these three groups left a great deal to be desired. His main belief in this area was that church, state, and the academic sector of society must be free from mutual interference. On the other hand, they must work together for the good of society. Priests, monarchs, and scholars should be a blessing to the world instead of being the degenerate clergy (*Pfaffen*), tyrants, and sophists, which they so often are (1,150; 6,65; 9,29 and *passim*).

The state is an organism, just as society as a whole is an organism. Its living cells are human families (5,98; 12,139ff.). For both, God is origin and guarantor of stability (5,99). Because the state, under God, has the duty to see to the lawful security, culture, and economic prosperity of its citizens, Baader defended active state economic and social policy against *laissez faire* economics

---

103 Elsewhere, Baader refers to the same division in slightly different terminology: religious society denotes indwelling (*Inwohnung*) of the associative principle (love); political society denotes "by-dwelling" (*Beiwohnung*); police society denotes "through-dwelling" (*Durchwohnung*) (*Sämtliche Werke* 3,297). On the distinction between *Inwohnung*, *Beiwohnung*, and *Durchwohnung* see above.

and governmental unconcern about the plight of society's disadvantaged. This does not mean that he proposed a classless society. On the contrary, he was an energetic defender of aristocratic elements in society, most especially of guilds, corporations, and other associations for mutual benefit (2,289; 5,276ff., 290 and *passim*). Without the power of corporations, individuals would be defenseless against the despotism of a central power (5,290). Functions of central government could be simplified, extension of credit would be facilitated, and the honor of individuals would be more solidly grounded, if men had their roots in corporations and guilds (5,290). The church (without a monarchical pope) is also built on the corporative or guild principle (15,603, 615, 652); indeed, Christianity itself is a guild (2,215). A democracy that tried to destroy all classes would be nothing more than "despotism from below", which is as reprehensible as tyranny from above (6,88). For Baader, "the ruler of the state represents the unity of the state, but is not the principle of that unity"; he does not own the state as his property, but rather ruler and ruled exist "by the grace of God" (6,86–87).

Baader's theory of law and of property is as theocentric as the rest of his thought. When he speaks of a "natural law", he means something very different than the Enlightenment meant when it invoked that term. In particular, it has nothing to do with "the fundamentally false principle of the absolute autonomous use of reason" (5,194). Laws which govern anything flow from the inner constitution of that thing, including immediate reference to the Ground of its being, God Himself. Thus, law rests on ontology; right order is a function of proper relationship between center and periphery. (See 5,166; 6,326ff.) Establishment of positive law by the state must take account of the divine basis of law (5,166), which means, for example, that no rule of justice can be based on injustice, regardless of precedents. (See 6,68.) Law develops, of course, since the society with which it deals is in constant process, but it remains firmly fixed in its origins and authority: i.e., in God.

Christianity "has completely destroyed the pagan concept or opinion of absolute property" (6,95). Baader shares Thomas Aquinas's view that possession of property is something entrusted to man by God for his use. Thus:

The Christian cannot say: this property, this right, this office is mine, and I can do what I want with what is mine; the reason is that those things are, in fact, gifts of God and tasks too (*Gottes Gaben und Aufgaben*), so that he can do with those things only what God wills. Thus, for every truly Christian folk, all possession is administrative possession (*Amtsbesitz*) and all enjoyment is delegated (*Amtsgenuss*). (6,95)

Baader defended the right to private property; in fact, a blow at *anyone's* property was an attack on *everyone's* property because the lives and property of men in all nations are organically linked (5,249). What makes property so important is that the lives and personalities of people are so intimately involved in it; this is particularly true of ties to the land, the basis of culture. (See 5,283, 310, 312; *Lettres inédites* 4,204, 220.) A certain amount of property is essential if one is to be a citizen in the full sense of the word, because ownership of property entails supporting the state (5,285). A modern economic-social development that disturbed Baader a great deal was the tendency to convert more and more wealth from immovable property into fluid capital and to look for economic security and soundness preponderantly in the area of finance (6,65; 7,338). Even the use of money presupposes faith in other men: "Without faith there is no credit (*Ohne Credo gibt es keinen Credit*)" (2,181).[104]

It is remarkable that the large and fragmentary body of writing which Baader produced over the course of more than five decades should exhibit such thoroughgoing inner coherence and interconnectedness. There is no major part of Baader's work that is not integrally connected with every other major part. Indeed, Baader's thought is extraordinarily free from self-contradiction. In the character and style of his thought, Baader showed himself to be a genuine Romantic and mystic – he seemed to think "from the inside out". More than anything else, it was his closeness to the idea of the center that kept his thought so unified and organic. Whether one agrees or disagrees with Baader's *Weltanschauung*, it is possible to accept Ringseis's judgment that "he did think systematically, because his thought flowed from the fullness of the whole".[105]

104 In supplying this sketch of Baader's thought, I have been guided, in part, by the general outline suggested in J. E. ERDMANN: *Die Entwicklung der deutschen Spekulation seit Kant* and that followed by A. LUTTERBECK in his précis found in volume 16 of BAADER: *Sämtliche Werke* (pp. 26-50).
105 See note 51 above.

Chapter 2
God Is Love

> My dear people, let us love one another, since love comes from God. And everyone who loves is begotten by God and knows God. Anyone who fails to love can never have known God, because God is love.
>
> I John 4,7–8

St. John's statement that "God is love" expresses Franz von Baader's most fundamental conviction on the subject. But the very notion of God, in the Christian tradition and therefore in Baader's mind, is that of a Being who defies adequate definition. Mankind, with its limited intelligence and power, is, consequently, unable to cope comprehensively with the concept of God. The very terms used to talk about God do not apply univocally, only analogically. God is described as inscrutable mystery, ineffable fullness of being, boundless life, infinite power, and immense richness – all standard locutions which are *negative* in form and drawn from negative theology. None is adequate. For the mystically-oriented Baader, as for the mystical apostle St. John, the most important thing to be said about God is that he is love. In a sense, of course, this is but to cover one mystery with another. Yet, everyone knows something of love, and the experience of religious mystics suggests that love has something more vital to say about the mystery of ultimate reality than anything else can. For them, love and the absolute fuse into a single identity. There are many kinds of love and many degrees of participation in it, but only God is love: all love begins and ends in Him, and there is no love apart from Him. To "begin at the beginning" is, for Baader, to begin with God: i.e., with love.

God Is Love: The Love-Center

Like most people of mystical bent in the western world, Franz von Baader was a devoted student of the Bible. He did not read it for entertainment or even for edification; rather, he studied it as a repository of essential truth about God, about man, about the world, and about himself. It was his daily bread. This is evident from the first pages of his *Tagebücher* through the last pages of his final essays. It is not surprising, then, that Baader took John's proclamation that God is love at face-value and made it the foundation of his entire philosophical-theological *Weltanschauung.* The following passage, one of Baader's many explicit declarations of the central truth that God is love, illustrates the point:

> To the extent that the creature has conformed himself to divine selfgrounding, he is united to God and made a participant in his love. God is love. The philosophy of love, therefore, must be the central doctrine. (8,187, number 40)[1]

Love is "the essential and universal character of God" (12,255). "God himself lives eternally only because he loves eternally" (10,344). Since love is God's very nature, and every being necessarily functions according to its nature, we are faced with the paradox of a God who cannot not love, yet who acts in an eminently free manner in loving – a reconciliation of the opposites embodied in necessity and freedom (12,430ff.). The mystery of love is one with the mystery of life itself (8,162; 14,124).[2] "Love is the specifically organizing and organic principle that holds together the manifold or fullness in unity and imparts unity to that fullness" (14,85, 145). This, in fact, is the function of life itself: harmonious interpenetration of rest and movement, of freedom and determination, of spirit and nature, of the one and the many. Thus, in Baader's scheme of reality, the ultimate formula is: God=life=love. The terms may be freely interchanged. Logical positivists may well find this kind of language and reflection annoying. But the only way to avoid it, Baader would say, is to restrict one's inquiries solely to natural scientific and/or logical problems, which,

---

1   Baader says explicitly that God is love in the following texts: BAADER: *Sämtliche Werke* 1,61; 2,90, 231, 455; 3,386; 4,186, 408; 5,117 fn. 2 (ed.), 264, 273; 6,14, 306; 7,333, 334; 8,264; 9,115, 202, 270 fn., 335, 356; 10,326, 344; 12,276, 286, 289, 332, 339, 398, 431, 535 (ed.); 13,62, 69, 96; 14,107, 252, 408; 15,462; E. SUSINI (Ed.): *Lettres inédites* 1,159. Other texts simply speak of God as loving (13,109, 180; 14,113, 201) or as always loving (7,283; 12,173; 13,282) or as loving all things (12,200, 208). Baader speaks of eternal love in God (13,321), God's "love-game" (*Liebesspiel*) (13,269), and God's spirit of love (13,138). God is love and man is not (14,206), but God's love is in man (12,205). Since love and goodness belong so intimately together (11,180; 14,398), love of virtue is equivalent to love of God (E. SUSINI [Ed.]: *Lettres inédites* 1,181). It is God's love that causes our goodness (14,345). He also repels evil through love (13,63). He loves everything all at once (14,209). His will is his love (14,200). Love of God is not proved or disproved, any more than God's existence is proved or disproved. Love and existence are simply experienced (E. SUSINI [Ed.]: *Lettres inédites* 1,160; 4,219).
2   Baader also identifies loving with living in the following passages: *Sämtliche Werke* 7,389; 12,216; 13,63, 390; E. SUSINI (Ed.): *Lettres inédites* 1,159.

in fact, is what is often done. For the mystics, that would be to consign oneself only to a part of reality, and the most superficial part at that. For the mystically-oriented Baader, the best statement about ultimate reality remains: God is love.[3] It is not simply that the Bible has consecrated this usage, for it also often speaks of "the living God". Baader's own personal proclivity tends in the direction of stressing love above all else. Thus, he writes in his commentary on St. Martin:

Everything is feeling (*Alles ist Affect*). Love is God; hate does not exist, but only strives to exist. Our existence consists solely in feeling (*im Affect*); (voluntary) feeling is existence. It is wrong that so many theologians miss the identity of the ground for feeling, affection, and will. (12,332) What we do not desire, love, or hate – what does not affect (touch) us – that is nothing for us. Our whole existence is in affection . . . *Anima est ubi amat* (12,341). Feeling is higher (deeper, more inward) and more external than knowing. (12,467)

The voluntarist basis of Baader's thought was not all pervasive or exclusive, despite the sweeping character of the statements just cited. The voluntarist *a priori* is accompanied by an intellectualist *a priori*, the former having primacy over the latter.

---

3   On occasion, Baader also identifies love and warmth, or at least closely links them. See, for example, BAADER: *Sämtliche Werke* 2,109; 3,35, 38; 7,333; 9,246; 10,4, 5; 12,237. A passage in *Vom Wärmestoff* states that "love is the universal bond that joins and meshes everything in the universe" (3,33). In the discussion which follows this statement, Baader identifies love as the great principle of unification on all levels in the universe. Love is a force that unites *per se*: 3,402; 6,19, 20; 12,273; 13,121, 300, 306; 14,267, 311. Love and religion unite and divide (14,433). Love unites and distinguishes (1,232; 14,397). Knowledge divides, love unites (14,205). In particular, it is love that reconciles or unites the one and the many (13,79 fns. 1 and 2). Many of Baader's symbols are adopted from Jacob Böhme. And along with the symbols, came a tendency to see every entity in combination with its opposite or with a complementary aspect of that entity. Thus, Jacob Böhme (and Baader) regularly combine the notions of love with anger or fury or power. In Baader's writings, examples of this kind are frequently found: for example, a combination of God's love with anger in 13,321, 322, 325, 339, 358, 370, 380, 385, 386; 14,102; E. SUSINI (Ed.): *Lettres inédites* 4,86 fn. The most favored of all symbols, for both Böhme and Baader, was that of fire (often combined with light). The fire-symbol is also juxtaposed with both love and anger: e.g., "The expiatory sacrifice can be effective only in igniting the fire of divine anger (*Zornfeuer*), but this latter must itself be ignited by love . . . in order that anger-fire may be transformed through burning away of evil . . . into the fire of love (*Liebesfeuer*)" (10,349). Texts that deal with the themes of fire and anger in combination with love include: 2,31, 36fn., 252, 254, 300; 5,230; 8,185; 9,314, 320, 323 fn. 3, 420 fn.; 10,313, 330; 13,62, 63fn., 66, 79, 86, 88, 111, 119, 129, 260, 261, 263, 294, 306, 307, 339, 341, 345, 346, 352, 355, 370; 14,484, 486. When Baader wants a symbol for love that emphasizes its mildness and soothing quality, he uses water. Thus, in the following passages love is represented as water (here in contrast to fire): 13,84, 94, 112, 264, 346.

A third major influence (not independent of the first two) that led Baader to emphasize love and will more than anything else was his adherence to Jacob Böhme's mystical metaphysics. In its deepest roots, Böhme's metaphysics is voluntarist, not intellectualist. The first positive principle for Böhme and Baader is will. Since neither can conceive of anything except in conjunction with its opposite, their postulate of primordial will as first among all positive principles is accompanied by the postulate of an "Unground" (*Ungrund*). The "Unground" is original freedom, freedom that does not originate in reason but in primordial nothingness: "freedom in darkness" and irrational chaos, which is the necessary background and presupposition for the light that is God. Baader considers the "Unground" or Nothing the negative basis of will, which is the first positive principle, the ground of all else (2,3; 9,210; 13,358–62, 385).[4]

On the basis of these considerations, Baader finds it better to say of God that he is love than to say, for example, that he is justice, or truth, or the Great Geometer. "Love is grounded more deeply than justice, says J. Böhme" (14,359, 395), though the separation of the two is possible only through a creature's fault (12,437).[5] In *Fermenta Cognitionis* (2,455), Baader says that God *is* reason and God *is* love; likewise, in *Socialphilosophische Aphorismen aus verschiedenen Zeitblättern:* "Only God is love as a substantive, just as only he is reason or the light of reason, whereas this love and reason in man (in the creature) applies only as an adjective" (5,273; see also 1,121ff.). God is reason and love essentially, whereas man only shares in reason and love. As for Baader's calling God both reason and love, Johannes Sauter explains:

. . . there is no contradiction here with respect to the "religious erotic", but rather a double intentionality very similar to that in Augustine and Clement of Alexandria. For both of these philosophers, God is entitatively "the" truth and with that they remain basically within the bounds of Platonism. It is only that they emphasize the idea of love in ever-increasing measure within those boundaries. To them, love is no longer a simple characteristic, the upswing toward truth; rather, it is truth itself, penetrated by love, so that it is in loving as such that God is made manifest as truth.[6]

4   For a very illuminating essay on a most difficult problem, see: N. BERDYAEV: "Unground and Freedom", introduction to: J. BÖHME: Six Theosophic Points, Ann Arbor, Michigan (University of Michigan Press) 1958. In this essay, Berdyaev remarks that Schelling comes close to Böhme's idea of the Unground when he writes that "every birth is a birth that draws from obscurity to bring into light". Berdyaev gives credit to Schelling who "first in German philosophy, develops the voluntarism of Böhme". He continues with some of Schelling's ideas and then concludes: "All this, of course, is Böhme. Yet closer to Böhme, and more kindred to his genius, seems to us Franz von Baader, the mind least corrupted by the idealist's break with being, who led Schelling to Böhme. . . Baader justifies Böhme's concept of God . . . " (p. xxviii).
5   On justice and love see also BAADER: Sämtliche Werke 11,281; 13,314; 14,395; E. SUSINI (Ed.): Lettres inédites 1,268.
6   J. SAUTER: Baader und Kant, p. 453 fn.

Thus, Baader calls his philosophy "a philosophy of love" (8,187, *Lettres inédites* 4,206) or "erotic philosophy" (4,163, 179), "because the highest object it considers, namely the absolute ground of being, is substantial love".[7] "The real riddle of philosophy, which philosophical philistines have left unsolved, is that of generative and creative love" (10,29 fn. 2).

Baader had a compulsion to unify and synthesize, to reconcile the many with the one.[8] The principle of participation by the many in the unity of a prime analogate is congenial to his style of thinking. Strongly reminiscent of Plato's theory of substantial forms or ideas that are "originals" – timeless and absolutely perfect – of which there are only "copies" in the world of space and time, Baader's notion of participation is a controlling idea in all his thought. If God is substantial love, then his creatures share in love only through him. Therefore, "love is divine in all its forms" (9,212). "Every true love is born of God" (12,242). Love is "a foreign guest, not at home in this world" (10,117); hence, two people "can love one another only to the extent that God's love dwells in each of them" (10,287; see also 9,269-70, 269 fn. 2; 13,329). "Godless=loveless; loveless=Godless" (9,359 fn.).[9]

Baader did not restrict the principle of participation to love; it applied also to knowledge and speech. His chief epistemological principle, *Cogitor, ergo sum*, is a case in point. "It is God's thought that is the *a priori* of all *a prioris* and, therefore, simply 'the category.' "[10] An important consideration, however, is that Baader does not hermetically seal off knowledge from love. The *whole man* knows; emotions and feeling, not just intellect, play a role in knowledge. There is an "emotional *a priori*" in Baader's epistemology as well as a purely intellec-

---

7 J. SAUTER: *Baader und Kant*, p. 449.
8 P. KLUCKHOHN: *Die deutsche Romantik*, p. 97, notes: "What Romantics found so captivating in Baader, more than his individual views, was the whole of his intellectual personality which, despite its manifold dimensions, he reduced to living unity. Baader does not simply know; he is, instead, a 'living, constantly active and yet complete personality of knowing', said Schelling of him. To see everything in its setting, to reduce it to final unity – that was his 'spellbinding magic'. Like Schelling, he strove for a cyclical philosophy in which every concept must be referred to the center. He showed this synthetic tendency even in his earliest writings . . . "
9 Baader either argues for, or alludes to, his claim that all love comes into being only through God in the following texts: BAADER: *Sämtliche Werke* 7,357 fn. 3, 362; 9,297, 356; 10,93, 101, 235 fn.; 12,230; 13,241, 284. Hence, love is *deodata* (=given by God) (15,627). Loving God is loving "the whole", therefore, everything besides God too (14,453). Just as the Bible says: "Seek first the kingdom of God and his justice" (Matthew 6,33), so Baader suggests that one "seek first God's love" (1, 397; 8,117, 160) and all else will be added. For God, as "idea" or "original", is the vowel, and every creature is but a consonant (1,230; 15,628).
10 J. SAUTER: *Baader und Kant*, p. 75.

tual one.[11] Indeed, Baader himself links the two: "Instead of saying with Descartes: I think, therefore I am, a man should say: I am thought, therefore I think, or: I am willed (loved), therefore I am" (8,339ff.). In fact, how one feels deeply affects how one knows.

I know something that I love (or hate) in a different way than something that I do not love (or hate) or that does not affect my soul and, consequently, does not affect me in my wholeness (*Ganzheit*) (1,106). The spirit of God or the spirit of knowledge rises and falls only in love; thus, whoever extinguishes this love is a true obscurantist. (1,157 fn.)

Depth of soul goes parallel with depth of mind. The more superficial one's feeling is, the more superficial one's speculation is (8,187). All knowledge arises in feeling and returns to feeling. Love generates knowledge and knowledge love. The word is the hymn of love. (12,416)

To know the truth, and to love it, and to do it are one and the same thing. (11,281)

For it is only in that reunion of affection with knowledge that love lives, as it were, in its own proper element . . . (10,281). As being, love is already the identity of thinking and willing. (14,428)

Thus, Baader holds that knowledge is inseparable from feeling or from loving, and that both knowledge and love are grounded in God.[12] His justification for using the principle of participation is not an appeal to Plato but rather the following:

When one thing divides itself into two, each of them is an other. The first, the one, the single, and the absolute (totality) are synonymous. Therefore, everything that comes after the first thing exists only in relationship to it.*
    *[Footnote]: Consequently, we can understand nothing about the essence of anything that follows the first thing, so long as we think of it without reference to the first thing. This must be as valid for the smallest speck of dust as it is for man and for every intelligent being. Therefore, a man cannot even really know himself apart from his relationship to God. It is from this, too, that the truth of the principle *Cogitor (a Deo cogitante), ergo sum, ergo sum cogitans* (I am thought [by a thinking God], therefore I am, therefore I think) flows. (12,376)

---

11 J. SAUTER: *Baader und Kant*, pp. 131ff.
12 Additional texts dealing with the effect of love on knowledge include: BAADER: *Sämtliche Werke* 1,39, 108, 109; 8,230; 9,11–12 fn., 47; 12,227, 412; 14,203, 415; 15,454; E. SUSINI (Ed.): *Lettres inédites* 1,159. See also: J. SAUTER: *Baader und Kant*, pp. 133 fn., 165; O. GRÜNDLER: "Franz von Baader", p. 151. Texts dealing in various ways with mutual relationships of knowledge and love include: *Sämtliche Werke* 2, 458; 9,80, 161, 164; 11,255; 12,237, 347; 14,244, 428, 457; E. SUSINI (Ed.): *Lettres inédites* 1,160. Love, intuition, and action belong together in God (14,32). Light and love belong together, as do their opposites: darkness and anger. There is no such thing as "blind" love. Thus, Baader mentions light and love together in: *Sämtliche Werke* 7,21, 371 fn.; 8,185; 9,11–12 fn., 47, 164, 241, 246, 323 fn.; 10,4, 242, 271, 316, 326, 328; 11,78; 12,237; 13,66, 117, 118, 147, 347, 352, 358, 386; 14,220, 457, 484, 486.

Therefore, "self-love is only striving (*conamen*): true self-love and love of God exist only simultaneously" (14,404); hatred of God is hatred of self (12,383); love leads to God (12,417).

To this point, the relationship of God (as First Knower, First Lover, and First Speaker) to his creatures (who are "secondary" and "imitative" knowers, lovers, and speakers) has been explained by the "principle of participation". But, in fact, Baader rarely speaks of "participation". He speaks very often, however, of "center" and "periphery" to convey his thought in this area. The word "center" does not refer to the midpoint of a geometrical circle but rather to the "mid-point" of an organism, a kind of "ground of being" for it: "the center for J. Böhme is always a circle, a setting, a ground" (2,164 fn.). In *Speculative Dogmatik* Baader explains the ancient dictum: *Deus est sphaera, cujus centrum ubique, circumferentia nusquam* thus:

One of the most common and false interpretations of this expression stems from superficial consideration of the geometrical figure (of the circle or the sphere), according to which one imagines God (the middle-point) as surrounded by (locked in by) the world (creation), just as though the former, as center, and the latter, as periphery, were simply two constituent elements of one and the same X. One could hardly say anything about the nature of such a thing, such a *je ne sai [sic] quoi* or Spinozistic indifference, since it would be neither God nor creature. In such a case, there could be no question of a super-worldly or world-free God; in fact, God would really consist of something that is made a center simply by the world and by creation, whereas it is God who takes the latter into his own center, because all things are immanent in God . . . (8,238)

Baader's glosses on St. Martin refer to the center as the *principe d'être* (principle of being) and "the productive center", a principle that is immediately applicable to the essence of every existing thing (12,320). It is, thus, "erroneous to conceive the idea of the center as if it were contracted within the sphere to one single point (the middle-point) and not to think of it as present in every single point of its totality, both as filling it and as containing it" (7,380 fn.). "Every center is also a periphery-point" (12,211). The center is not a mathematical point, but the "productive inner One in contrast to the external, phenomenal Many" (3,257).[13] Baader's concept of the center is similar to St. Paul's notion of God, in whom "we live and move and exist" (Acts, 17,28), a kind of immediate presence "from the inside".[14]

13   The index volume of BAADER: *Sämtliche Werke* offers numerous references to the concept of center. See also: J. SAUTER (Ed.): *Franz von Baaders Schriften zur Gesellschaftsphilosophie*, pp. 664ff.
14   Texts in which Baader speaks of God as "love-Center" with respect to members or "periphery" to whom he imparts love may be found in BAADER: *Sämtliche Werke* 6,14, 307; 7,112, 284 fn. 2; 9,202; 13,193; 14,79. See also: F. BÜCHLER: *Die geistigen Wurzeln*

In Baader's scheme, then, God is Center for all created things: whatever the latter have, they have by way of participating in God's being. The *a priori* function of God in human knowledge is particularly stressed in the *Cogitor* axiom; his *a priori* function in love is also expressed in the same axiom[15] as well as in the explicit statement that "love, as supernatural, is a miracle (*Wunder*) to nature and creation and is, therefore, an *a priori* to them" (9,288). Knowledge and love are, thus, the two primary categories but, as intimated earlier, they are not paired as equals: for "the heart stands higher than thought", and "love is the source of all perfection" (12,212). Baader expressly asserts the primacy of love over knowledge in a gloss on St. Martin:

Love (in God) gives form to knowledge, for she is the formative element. The statement that love has brought forth knowledge and not knowledge love is intended to show the superiority of feeling as *force* over knowledge as *resistance*. Therefore, where you find true knowledge, love is also there. (12,227)[16]

J. Sauter explains Baader's position as follows:

Baader calls his philosophy "erotic", because its highest object – namely the absolute ground of being – is substantial love; and furthermore, because this love mediates transition from the absolute to the relative, while preserving individuals in their continued being, it is the *raison d'être (ratio essendi)* in an all-inclusive sense; it is also the essential form for knowledge (*ratio cognoscendi*).[17]

Baader approves Plato's assertion that "only love is able to make man divine (make a creature share in the divine nature) and to elevate him out of and above himself", but he adds: "this statement really only expresses a law of all life" (1,59). With Plato and Aristotle, Baader sees Eros as the mysterious power to transcend limitations of self and achieve union with the divine.

Eros is, therefore, the basic norm for all values – from life values to the highest ideal values; one may not restrict it, then, to "love of life" (*Vitalliebe*) or to sexual love or to "intellectual" love; for, in every case, the basic concept of participation of the nucleus (*des Kerns*) of a finite person in the essential Being would be excluded.[18]

    der heiligen Allianz, Freiburg im Breisgau (doctoral dissertation) 1929, especially pp. 53–55 and 78–79. See Chapter 6, proposition 30 below.

15 The longer version of the *Cogitor*: i.e., "Ich werde gedacht, darum denke ich, oder: ich werde gewollt (geliebt), darum bin ich" (*Sämtliche Werke* 8,339 fn. 1).

16 In the passage cited, the words *force* and *resistance* appear in italics and in that spelling. Since it is a commentary on a text of St. Martin, presumably Baader intended to use the French words *force* and *résistance* rather than the English words "force" and "resistance". In citing French, he sometimes omits accent markings.

17 J. SAUTER: *Baader und Kant*, p. 449.

18 J. SAUTER: *Baader und Kant*, p. 449.

Almost all that has been said thus far has had to do with God as love *in se*, or with God's imparting that love to his creatures through participation: i.e., with love in the "vertical" sense. But in Baader's thought, God is also immediately implicated in love that exists between people: i.e., with love in the "horizontal" sense:

Just as all beings . . . stand in unalterable relationship to God, and these relationships are constitutive – i.e., a ground of being for them – the same thing holds for their relationships with one another. For these secondary relationships are merely consequences of that primary relationship and are mediated through it, just as the relationship of periphery-points to one another [is mediated] through the relationship of the latter to their common center. Brotherly love and love of neighbor, is, therefore . . . as Holy Scripture says, grounded in love of God, just as hatred of neighbor is grounded in hatred of God. For I have power to unite myself truly to another person only if I first unite myself immediately with God, and, in like manner, I can break completely with my neighbor only if I fall away from or turn away from God. (5,230)[19]

Thus, it is "precisely because a man is aware of being loved by God that he himself gains power not only to love God in return (*Anteros*) but also to love himself, other people, and the world . . . " (8,230). A declaration of independence from God – i.e., egocentrism – is nothing but a lie, and that is why "when the mystic says that I should love myself and my neighbor only in God, this is evidence of the fact that true love of self goes toward another (my being in God), just as false love of self goes to untrue, illegitimate existence" (2,180).[20] God's substantial love is not regarded as "totally other": i. e., as transcendent love, which stands opposed to created love as a foreign category. On the contrary, they are organically linked. Thus, Baader cites Meister Eckehart engaged with an unspecified group of mystics:

19 The footnote to this text reads: "A French writer says: 'Parceque l'unité parfaite ne se trouve que dans la jonction individuelle avec Dieu, et que ce n'est qua'après [*sic*] qu'elle est faite, que nous nous trouvons naturellement les frères, les uns des autres'. ('Because perfect unity is found only in individual union with God, it is only after this [unity] has been accomplished that we truly realize we are each other's brothers.') But one must not take this "only after" (*n'a que après*) in a narrow sense, because love and hatred of God and love and hatred of man or men are always simultaneous . . . Hence, the same Scripture says: if you do not love your brother whom you see, how can you love God whom you do not see? One could apply this scriptural text to authority and say: if you do not obey your visible sovereign, how can you obey an invisible one? Moreover, since love of God is active in worship, neglect of worship must also extinguish the love of people" (5,230).
20 On types of true and false love, see BAADER: *Sämtliche Werke* 9,12 fn.; 12,225, 279. On abstract and incomplete love, see 4,292. Baader pairs love and truth against hatred and lies in 14,425, 426. "All harmony and love that is not grounded in truth is really only false harmony and love, which we must, therefore, sacrifice without hesitation for true harmony's sake" (7,217; see also 5,223; 12,270).

It is not that you know, love, and need different things in and apart from God – i.e., in eternity and in time – but rather that you know, love, and need the same things in a different way. If you leave creatures where they are divided, fragmented, incomplete, and in tension, you take them and find them again where they are united and perfect (in God). It is, therefore, a false and misleading idea, held by a number of ascetics, to be told that loving God the Creator contradicts love of creatures, as though we should see God as simply one object *alongside of* creatures as other objects, etc. But religion commands us expressly to love creatures in the Creator, not apart from him or even against him. (5,263; see also 2,180, 181)[21]

The concept of God as substantial love in his own right and as "love-Center" with respect to his creation removed Baader *toto caelo* from Kant on this point. Baader had no use for Kant's reduction of love to mere selfish inclination. Thus, he writes in section 19 of the first book of *Fermenta Cognitionis*:

It is generally conceded that love does not seek its own and that one does not love a person whom one does not trust farther than one can see him. But there have been and are writers who make an exception to this in the case of love of God and faith in him, seriously maintaining that one ought to be obliged to trust and believe in God only to the extent that one can see or observe him in his activity. Kant, for example, does not reason much better about love than a blind man does about color when he (following Spinoza's definition: *Ideo bonum quia appetimus*) defines love as inclination we have toward whatever brings us advantage . . .[22] Love is love only because it is not bound by need or desire or nature. (It is not, therefore, unnatural, however). One can see this in the consecration of sexual desire (which is of itself the zenith of passionate self-seeking, thus complete lovelessness) through love in marriage. (2,178–79)[23]

21 "We love each other as ourselves, because we love God above all" (15,155). On brotherly love, see BAADER: *Sämtliche Werke* 7,239, 362, 413, 415; 11,180. See also J. SAUTER: "Franz von Baaders romantische Sozialphilosophie", *Zeitschrift für die gesamte Staatswissenschaft*, p. 477. Baader enjoins on everyone the love of God and neighbor (14,314; E. SUSINI (Ed.): *Lettres inédites* 1,189), of the sinner (*Sämtliche Werke* 4,408), of everyone (11,281).

22 Hoffmann cites the larger passage from Kant's *Werke* (von Hartenstein edition, volume IV, p. 18): "Likewise, I can have no respect for inclination in general, whether it be my own or someone else's; the most I can do is sanction it in the first case and love it sometimes in the second case: i.e., see it as something favorable to my own advantage" (2,179 fn. 2). Hoffmann also supplies the context for the reference to Spinoza: "Constat itaque ex his omnibus, nihil nos conari, velle, appetere, neque cupere, quia id bonum esse judicamus; sed contra nos propterea, aliquid bonum esse, judicare, quia id conamur, volumus, appetimus, atque cupimus (It is clear from all this that we do not strive for, will, seek, or desire anything because we judge it to be good; on the contrary, we judge something to be good because we strive for, will, seek, and desire it.)". Hoffmann cited this passage from H. E. G. PAULUS (Ed.): *B. de Spinoza opera quae supersunt omnia*, Jena 1803, volume I, p. 141.

23 Baader's note on this text reads: "The ideal in animal copulation (so-called love) is unfolding the eternal race in the decline of the individual; but the ideal of human love is unfolding the eternal race in the uniqueness of the person, so that it is precisely this person who is posited in accordance with his eternal uniqueness (as a member of the

Baader voices a similar complaint against Kant in number six of the *Socialphilosophische Aphorismen aus verschiedenen Zeitblättern:*

The same German philosopher of whom we spoke deduced even love from a conviction of net advantage that the loved person provides us or leads us to hope that he will. Just as he was infected with the peculiar idiosyncrasy of being unable to tolerate any public (social) prayer, he declared *ex cathedra* that prayer is pure fetishism. His God (the deaf and dumb law) was no less impersonal and inhuman than Spinoza's God. We have him to thank particularly for the purism of the new morality, which has removed every personal relationship of man to God and, consequently, all feeling from this morality. (5,282)

Here we find Baader emphasizing the point that he and Kant had vastly different conceptions of what the ultimate or the absolute is, or – in the language of religion – what God is. This made literally "all the difference in the world", as J. Sauter points out:

Baader believed that he was achieving a profound turning-point in German idealism – similar to Augustine at the beginning of medieval idealism – and indeed for this reason: that the fundamental form of our participation in the ultimate world-ground is governed by the latter's essential content. If it is, for example, a Categorical Ought – as in the case of Kant and Fichte – then our maximum participation in ultimate being can, in the nature of the case, only be sharing in that Ought (*Mit-sollen*). If it is primordial Thinking – then sharing in that (*Mit-denken*). But if it is primordial love – then sharing in love (*Mit-lieben*). And this love is then – even if one does not allow a primacy of love – ontologically and noetically a power that is independent of the rational act of knowing. One who is touched by Eros has no doubt of the fact that he is closer to the world-mystery when he is in this state than in any other state of exaltation.[24]

It is thus apparent that Baader's affirmation of a God who is quintessentially substantial love placed him in a totally different intellectual-spiritual milieu than the one Kant and the German Idealists occupied.[25]

In some aspects of his thought, Baader's mystical-theosophical cast of mind moved him well along the road to pantheism. His "principle of the center",

---

whole). This unique element thus stands for everything in the eyes of his lover. Here we have a case of the Whole (God) shining through in the transfigured uniqueness of the person" (2,179 fn. 3). See also Chapter 4 below.

24   J. SAUTER: *Baader und Kant*, pp. 450–51. In a footnote on p. 451, Sauter says: "The idea of absolute existence is for [Augustine] creative love and at the same time an all-merciful drive toward communication of self. This intellectual shift from pure existence to substantial love has been worked out especially by Ernst Troeltsch in *Augustin, die christliche Antike und das Mittelalter*, 1915, 86ff".

25   On the contrast between Baader's and Kant's notions of love, see J. SAUTER: *Baader und Kant*, pp. 131–43, 449–66. In addition to these major discussions of the theme, see also pp. 33, 133, 136, 165, 199, 239, 256, 263, 339, 351, 407, 410, 473, 479, 551 fn., 554, 559, 581. For the ways in which Baader differs from Kant about love, see BAADER: *Sämtliche Werke* 5,17 fn., 117 fn., 264, 282; 9,361; 11,184; 12,431 fn.; 14,408.

and of participation in it by all else, particularly lends itself to pantheistic interpretation. He was, of course, very much aware of this danger and often took pains to dissociate himself explicitly from pantheism. An example, drawn from his glosses on St. Martin's *Tableau Naturel des Rapports qui existent entre Dieu, l'Homme et l'Univers*, clearly makes the point. In a section dealing with concepts of production, action/passion, and reciprocity, Baader says:

> The more intense the feeling of union between action and reaction (the more inward their union), the more inward is the bond that links product with producer. The more closely united the factors of production are, the more intense is their feeling (affect) and the closer is their union with the product. In the love of God for man also, there is most intimate union together with highest distinction. But distinction, in this case, has to do with essence, whereas union has to do with action. (12,186)

Creatures cannot love apart from God (15,155), but their love is not simply a "mode" of God's love, any more than they are simply "modes" of God's being.

In summary, Baader's natural tendency toward mysticism, cultivated by extensive and intensive grounding in the Bible and in Böhme's theosophy, led him to conclude that love is a more adequate description of God than life, or thought, or justice, or any other attribute. He linked love with knowledge and with life very closely, but love was always accorded first place. God is First Knower, First Speaker, and most properly First Lover. All other love is simply participation in the subsistent love of the divine "love-Center". Here, we see a fundamental difference in the respective worldviews of Kant and Baader especially, although Baader's "God is love" postulate separated him from the whole German Idealist school as well. He also took great pains to dissociate himself from the pantheism of Spinoza, Schelling, and Hegel.

God Is Love: Creation and Redemption

The final entry in Baader's *Tagebücher* for 1788 reads: "I am a free creature of a free (God), a living creature of a living (God), a loving creature of a loving God" (11,176). In retrospect, this remarkable statement is much more than a youthful manifesto; its credo permeated Baader's entire life and outlook. In a footnote to this very passage, Franz Hoffmann, the diary's editor, notes in part: ". . . Baader's developed system is nothing other than the mature development of the basic thought of his early youth, which sprang from his own most personal nature". And it is, in fact, true that the great themes of freedom, life, and love serve as *Leitmotives,* not only in the diary he wrote as a young man but throughout his entire life as well. Just as truly, the conviction and awareness never left him that he was free, living, and loving only as God's creature.

Baader's theory of *creation* is fully consonant with his view that love is "God of God", a kind of "absolute within the absolute". "Love is creative, it alone is productive" (12,452). No love is idle or fruitless, but instead is universal activity" (12,285). Love is "radical power" (12,259). "Of course, only love is creative, since the light merely illumines the thing created and the word is only the organ of creation" (10,316). Baader speaks of the "mystery of creative love" (*Lettres inédites* 4,335; see also *Sämtliche Werke* 14,479) in much the same way as Thomas Aquinas repeats: *Bonum est diffusivum sui* (Good is diffusive of itself). (See 12,395; see also 14,202.) But Baader specifies that the good that diffuses itself is love. It is the very nature of love to create.[26]

Some of Baader's statements seem to preclude the possibility of saying anything further about creation. Thus, he cites Jacob Böhme to the effect that God's creative act cannot be investigated (13,250; see also 7,267ff.). He says that any attempt to conceptualize the divine act of creation is equivalent to an attempt, on the part of a creature, "to ascend back into God" (8,286). We cannot comprehend creation in conceptual terms (7,267 fn.). The divine act of creation and the conservation of finite beings in existence is a knowledge-boundary for every created being (5,26). "This eternal mystery of the How of our coming to be and our continuing to be is precisely the basis of our wonder in the face of God and of our reverential subordination of self to him as our creator and preserver . . . " (2,352). And so on in the same vein.[27] But after closing the front door on research into the problem of creation, Baader proceeds to find a back door. In the essay *Über die Begründung der Ethik durch die Physik,* he states at one point that "every speculative attempt at reconstructing (explaining) this primordial act of creation must fail" (5,13); but, he adds a little further on: "Even though this primitive act of creation itself needs no further construction, and is incapable of any, it, nevertheless, can be and needs to be dealt with in descriptive fashion . . . " (5,14). He then proceeds to talk about it.

Baader's theory of creation as a whole is not of principal concern here. What is relevant to our purpose, however, is the motivation for creation. Klaus

---

26 Baader frequently combines the adjectives *produktiv* with love and *destruktiv* with hate, as though to say that love is intrinsically productive or creative and hate is the opposite. See BAADER: *Sämtliche Werke* 2,40, 209 fn., 228, 472, 502; 4,106; 5,223, 258; 6,13ff., 84; 8,280; 9,47, 297; 12,259, 273, 274, 276, 467, 498; 13,79 fn. 2, 83; 15,469. Love is something that tends to "spread" (6,30; 15,628). Hence, creation and love belong together (13,146 fn.; 14,107, 119). Love is an active force: 10,326; 12,194. Other passages in which Baader directly contrasts love and hate include: 9,201, 243, 296 fn. 4, 297, 374; 10,93, 242, 271, 339; 12,284; 14,316, 357, 411, 428, 457.

27 It may be noted here that Schelling also considered the basic motive of creation to be love. See J. SAUTER: *Baader und Kant,* p. 199 fn.

Hemmerle deals briefly with this point.[28] He explains Baader's position as follows: although we know nothing about the manner of creation, the very fact of creation tells us something about the motive for it. It would be to deny God's absolute freedom if one chose to treat the divine decision to create a world as "accidental". Treating God's decision as mere whim or arbitrariness is the same as making it purely fortuitous. It would be the same as "shutting God up within himself" again if one were to fail to see the motive that prompted God's creative action. "And that is why Baader never grows weary of referring to the love of God as that which prompted his absolute superfluity to overflow into the superfluous (. . . *seinen unbedingten Überfluss ins Überflüssige hinein* . . .)".[29] In more pedestrian language, this tells us that God created out of love. Hemmerle reminds us of Baader's passionate insistence on the complete freedom with which God created: He did not create out of necessity or need, nor did he do so accidentally. This can only mean that he created out of love, out of the superabundant freedom which he "is" – "for what is love, if it is not the perceived identity of completeness within oneself with openness above and beyond oneself?"[30] Hemmerle concludes his study of Baader's theory of creation with this brief and tightly reasoned paragraph:

God did not *have to* create because he is God, but God *can* create because he is God, and so he also *does create* because he is God. It is precisely in the underivable, the unowed, that the essential manifests itself: what God is in himself, what he "necessarily" is. That in which the "superfluity" (which God "necessarily" is) shows itself to be such, is necessarily *not* necessary. Using this kind of dialectic, Baader answers the question about the *motive* of creation with "the indicative", with the statement "that fullness or totality of this sort does not jealously shut itself up, but instead moves to action, freely extending itself, spreading itself, stretching out its being to another, thereby encompassing this other within itself".[31]

28 K. HEMMERLE: *Franz von Baaders philosophischer Gedanke der Schöpfung*, Freiburg/Munich (Karl Alber) 1963, p. 144.
29 K. HEMMERLE: *Franz von Baaders philosophischer Gedanke der Schöpfung*, p. 144.
30 K. HEMMERLE: *Franz von Baaders philosophischer Gedanke der Schöpfung*, p. 144: "Denn was ist Liebe anderes als die ergriffene Identität der Geschlossenheit in sich selbst mit der Offenheit über sich selbst hinaus?" See BAADER: *Sämtliche Werke* 8,82.
31 K. HEMMERLE: *Franz von Baaders philosophischer Gedanke der Schöpfung*, p. 144: "Gott *müsste* nicht schaffen, weil er Gott ist, aber Gott *kann* schaffen, weil er Gott ist, und so *schafft* er auch, weil er Gott ist. Gerade im Unableitbaren, Ungeschuldeten offenbart sich das Wesentliche: das, was Gott aus sich selbst, was er 'notwendig' ist. Das, worin der 'Überfluss', der Gott 'notwendig' ist, sich als solcher zeigt, ist notwendigerweise *nicht* notwendig. Aus dieser Dialektik her antwortet Baader auf die Frage nach dem *Motiv* der Schöpfung mit dem 'Indikativ', mit der Feststellung, 'dass eine solche Fülle oder Totalität sich nicht neidisch verschliesst, sondern in eine factio über- und ausgeht, sich frei ausbreitend, gemeinsamend, ihr Sein über anderes ausdehnend, und dieses

It should be noticed that Hemmerle's citation from Baader refers to God as "fullness or totality". This expression and this way of viewing God is a highly significant one in Baader's whole system, not because of any possible pantheism – we have ruled this out in Baader – but because it tells us something about God or love as he understands them. To say that God is substantial love is to say that he is superabundant being, overflowing richness, infinite life, unbounded totality, alpha and omega, unimaginable and inconceivable superfluity.[32] God's very fullness is a kind of "sufficient reason" for creation. The reference from Hemmerle was picked at random; it can be supplemented and complemented by many others. For example, in speaking of various erroneous notions of God's activity in creation (especially Hegel's), Baader says:

. . . one can see already from what has been said that the concept of God as one who is his own ground absolutely has remained so lifeless partly because people have mistaken this inner and outer grounding in God, and partly because they have not posited this latter (grounding) in God himself independently from creation, so that God *had to* create in order to actualize his existence fully. Thus, the creator would have been dearth and poverty of need, instead of richness of love. (3,340; see also 9,334)

Baader will have nothing to do with a "minimum God" of the Hegelian sort, a God who needs a changing and imperfect world and the medium of man's always limited intelligence to realize his own completeness (12,226, 230). He would certainly have agreed with Ruskin's position that "he who gives God a second place gives him no place at all", because God is not simply one – even the greatest one – in a row of essentially comparable magnitudes, differing only in degree from one another. For Baader, the principle always remains:

Andere in sich hiemit befassend' ". The quotation from Baader is from 1,214. The italics are Hemmerle's. On the paradox of God's love being necessary but not forced, see: 12,430ff.

32 Sauter says in this connection (J. SAUTER: *Baader und Kant*, p. 452 fn.): "In a very similar way, Thomas calls ontological goodness diffusive of itself. Primum bonum habet diffusionem secundum intellectum, cujus est secundum aliquam causam certam profluere in causata; aliquis certus modus adhibetur bonorum effluxui a primo bono, a quo omnia alia bona participant virtutem diffusivam (The first good diffuses itself according to intellect, whose characteristic it is to flow into its effects according to a certain fixed cause. A certain fixed mode is adhered to in the flow of good things from the first good, from which all other goods share the power of diffusion.) (*S. Th.* 1,2; q. 1, a.4 ad 1). In accordance with the same metaphysics of love, Plato considers love the daughter of superfluity (*Überflusses*); the act of love itself is thus a kind of marriage between richness and poverty, something of which Baader completely approves (9,189; 10,4) . . . " On the link between love and richness in Baader's work, see BAADER: *Sämtliche Werke* 5,17, 19; 6,84, 307; 8,160, 222; 9,57, 243; 10,117, 339.

Only what is perfect in itself, free from every other thing, needing nothing, in the fullness and richness of all being – only that can give. Jacobi says very beautifully: superabundance has found poverty [no quotation marks in text]. But one could also say that poverty brings super-abundance to itself (*zu sich selber bringt*). It is clear, here also, that it is absurd to seek a non-intelligent cause for the world. For only the subjective-objective is capable of that sufficiency of love. (8,82–83)

A different but complementary approach to the same theme is found in Baader's eighth lecture on Böhme's *Mysterium Magnum.*

The God who is fully free and independent in his own being hides creation's dependence on him from it in order that worship of him may be free worship, not servile worship, forced by necessity. This free relationship between creature and creator would not take place . . . if it were only need and lack of integral existence that linked the two to each other. In that case also, no free love of God for his creature would be possible, because it is only the rich, whole, self-sufficient soul that can love, whereas the poor, halved, incomplete, and needy soul can only desire.

"Rightly said, Schlosser, one loves what one has; one desires what one does not have. Only the rich soul loves, only the poor one desires."[33]

To ascribe the origin and preservation of creation to any other cause than to the love of God is the same as denying God, and if that doctrine – and only that doctrine – is heretical which denies this love, then one must reject all these philosophies as God-denying and heretical. (13,195)

In the following passage, drawn from the foreword to the second volume of Baader's collected writings (1832), Hegel is again the main target for Baader's barbs:

As far as the pantheistic confusion of God with creation (which we have censured above) is concerned, it would, of course, be a totally false statement, contrary to all religion, to maintain that God (World-Spirit, as Hegel calls him . . . contrary to scriptural usage) acquires content only through creatures, and that the One who determines all things first finds his own determination and fulfillment through his act of creation – in other words, that God achieves reality only from something that is not God, but that transforms itself into the real God . . . Finally, it would be no less erroneous not to recognize the free and, so to speak, artistic production of created being as that of likeness and image (which is, therefore, not to be confused with the original): i.e., as poetry, as invention, and as free projection of creative love . . . (1,396)

Thus, love is fullness of being, overflowing richness, the mystery that reconciles the one and the many. (See 1,231; 13,79 fns. 1 and 2; 14,149.)

33 Baader does not identify the source of the couplet which he cites: "Recht gesagt, Schlosser, man liebt, was man hat; man begehrt, was man nicht hat. Nur das reiche Gemüth liebt, nur das arme begehrt".

As noted earlier, Baader seems, on the one hand, to exclude the possibility of our saying anything at all about God's creative act; on the other, a sizable portion of his own work deals with the subject. Specifically, he seems quite convinced that at least the motive of creation is quite clear. Is there a contradiction here? It seems not. For, in saying that God is substantial love and that creation is motivated by love, Baader is not "explaining" either God or creation. To say that God is substantial love is to say that he is unfathomable mystery, infinite fullness and richness which is not amenable to conceptual characterization. In speaking of mysteries of this sort, what one *does* say about them merely expresses the fact that *words fail* and explanations falter: the greater the mystery, the greater the abyss of incomprehension. Baader's view merely reflects – at a deeper level – the meaning behind such commonplace statements as "*I can't tell you* how much I love you", or "*I can't tell you* how sorry I am that your mother died", or "*I can't tell you* how much my faith means to me". Baader shows that he means to go beyond such commonplace utterances when he quotes the theologian Marheinecke and comments on his statement:

"In finite things", says Professor Marheinecke . . . "wonder diminishes as a matter of course as deeper understanding increases; but in the case of God, a source of knowledge is opened up to the mind from which ever-increasing wonder arises in and with growing knowledge". The expression *nil admirari* can, consequently, mean only that the wise man should not wonder at anything, except to wonder at the One alone. But one cannot ascribe wisdom to the cessation of all wonder, which would, otherwise, give the stupid (and precisely therefore non-wondering) brute animals a rank higher than ours. (1,235)

In other words, someone who knows nothing or very little about the meaning of a mystery is able to express and feel far less wonder over it than someone who has contemplated it and meditated about it intensely for a lifetime. The great philosopher wonders about the one and the many, stability and change, and the mystery of "self", while the average man has no notion that there is even a problem in these areas. The high school or college student knows "all about" chemistry, physics, or religion, while seasoned chemists, physicists, and theologians grow ever more humble as the scope of their ignorance becomes apparent to them. William Blake's intuition of "a world in a grain of sand and a heaven in a wild flower" may be relatively meaningless for most people, but not because they understand the matter so much better than Blake. In having recourse to mystery, Baader, of course, faces the same kind of problem that Plato faced in trying to talk about the Good, or, that negative theology and mysticism face in trying to talk about God, or, indeed that anyone faces in addressing ultimate questions. For Baader, the ultimate mystery is that God is love and creates out of love. Everything else follows from that.

We have spoken about Baader's views concerning God's love and creation. He also had a good deal to say about God's love and *redemption*. Redemption presupposes, of course, that man is in a fallen state, and that the human condition is not a *res integra* as Baader says so often. The problem of man's "fallen nature" shall be considered more fully later.[34] For the moment, it suffices to point out that Baader viewed man's "fallen state" as a necessary presupposition for any Christian philosopher (8,38, 46ff.). The fallen state of man indicates that at some point he was tested by God and found wanting. According to Baader, temptation or testing plays a very significant role in all love; without it, love tends to remain superficial. Love may seem easy and enticing when no differences between lovers have asserted themselves. True love, however, is love that has faced up to differences, in their full extent and intensity, and has overcome them.[35] In the case of man's love for God, man failed, at the start, to make the sacrifice necessary to maintain his love; the "possibility for difference, for fragmentation or for a dying off of the relationship" (4,166) became a reality – real difference, diremption, the death of love.

As substantial love, God takes the initiative in setting things right again: "Thus, only God himself can redeem, because only he can unite me with my root (*Wurzel*) again" (12,226). Baader speaks of "saving love" (4,199, 282; 13,127), since "love transforms crime into infirmity" (*Liebe wandelt Verbrechen in Gebrechen*) (12,226). This striking turn of phrase expresses the mystic's view that one who judges another with love will not regard his subject so much as a criminal, but as a person suffering from some disability or weakness. Thus, God did not simply condemn mankind once and for all after man's fall from grace; instead, he reached even more profoundly into his infinite love and sent man a redeemer, not only to make good what was lost but to exceed it. God seemed to pay more attention to man's weakness than he did to his guilt. "The fall of man directly affected the heart of God, whereas Lucifer's fall did not" (12,281). Out of compassion for man's weakness, God sent his saving love: "Love was and is with God, as St. John says, as he created the world and man, but when man fell, this love went forth from God and came into the world as his redeeming Word" (4,199–200). Thus, "out of love for his creation, God entered history (14,111), an action that, "as an act of sav-

---

34 On the fall of man through sin, see: H. SPRECKELMEYER: *Die philosophische Deutung des Sündenfalls bei Franz von Baader,* in: *Abhandlungen zur Philosophie und Psychologie der Religion,* volume 43/44, Würzburg 1938; H. WIMMERSHOF: *Die Lehre vom Sündenfall in der Philosophie Schellings, Baaders und Friedrich Schlegels,* Freiburg (doctoral dissertation) 1943; E. SUSINI: *Franz von Baader et le romantisme mystique,* volume 3, pp. 405ff. See also Chapter 4.

35 For fuller development of this theme, see Chapter 5, Proposition 1ff. below.

ing and restorative love is the absolutely greatest miracle, a greater one than the act of creation itself" (4,282). It is worth noticing that Baader sees Christ as incarnate love, the "ray of divine love" (4,200), whose religion of love was to save man from his fallen state. Baader identifies Christ, the fullest revelation of the Father, with love; this makes it possible to interchange Christ with love in locating his central idea.[36]

A rather unexpected aspect of Baader's position on reconciliation between God and man is that he considers the restored love bond in no way inferior to love in the as yet "untested stage". Indeed, he asserts the opposite: reunion effects an even closer (and, to that extent, superior) love than that which existed previously. This is a rule that applies not only to reconciliation with God in redemption, but to all love: *restored love is deeper than untested love.* The reason is that forgiveness and reconciliation call for a more profound plumbing of the depths of one's soul than initial, untested love-experience requires. Reconciliation demands denying selfishness to a degree unknown to and not demanded of the light-hearted enthusiasm of newborn love. Thus, "one could say to every person who has honestly and sincerely effected the process of reconciliation: you are not far from the kingdom of God!" (4,200).[37]

The ability to forgive is a mark of love's special richness; thus, God is the most perfect forgiver. Baader could not say this more clearly than he does in proposition eight of the *Sätze aus der erotischen Philosophie*:

When it is said, and rightly so, that love is closely related to sympathy, or when Plato calls it the daughter of superfluity and of poverty, one can also interpret this to mean that love is the daughter of forgiveness and repentance: i.e., of reconciliation, for only the rich soul forgives and only the poor soul needs forgiveness. But we are unable to forgive and to repent within the limits of our natural selfhood and isolation; we can do that only by virtue of that love which penetrates these limits and over-reaches them: i.e., the love of God, who is love. (4,170; see also 2,352)

Once again, what holds true between God and man also holds true of men among themselves: it is only a "higher, mediating action" that "gives to one

---

36 Baader equates Jesus with love in the following texts: BAADER: *Sämtliche Werke* 2,311; 4,106, 213, 238; 8,152, 156; 10,125, 317; 12,225, 279, 283, 360; 13,267, 367. Christ is the "loving Central Soul" (*liebende Centralseele*) (E. SUSINI [Ed.]: *Lettres inédites* 1,423). The expressions "love, sun, and Christ" belong together (10,330); one can also say that Christ is freedom, truth, and love (E. SUSINI [Ed.]: *Lettres inédites* 1,163; see also, 162). Christianity is a religion of love (10,189, 195). Love makes a kind of heaven on earth (E. SUSINI [Ed.]: *Lettres inédites* 1,161; 2,27 number 18).

37 On this point, see especially *Sätze aus der erotischen Philosophie*, proposition 6; and Chapter 5 below. On reconciliation and love, see further BAADER: *Sämtliche Werke* 2,461; 4,234, 267; 5,311; 7,345; 8,262; 9,246, 314, 397; 10,39; 12,521. See also H. GRASSL (Ed.): *Franz von Baader. Über Liebe, Ehe und Kunst,* pp. 95–100.

person the richness to forgive and to the other the power to be humble, and we must, therefore, conceive of every true act of reconciliation as a religious act that manifests this higher, mediating action" (4,171).

The manner in which God redeemed fallen man provides still another indication that his action was preeminently an act of love.

Man wished to be man without God, says St. Martin, but God did not wish to be God without man. To create nature and man, God had only to let his power and glory freely go, to give them free rein, as it were; but, in order to redeem fallen man, it was almost as though he had to do violence to himself. He had to divest himself of his glory so that we might be able to grasp and bear him and his help in our weakness and corruption. Only love conceives of such sacrifice; only love is able to make such sacrifice. (4,183)

Throughout the whole history of man's relationship to God, God takes the initiative in love: he creates in love and restores out of love, presiding over man's history both before he sins and afterward; "in other words, it is the same God who searches for us even when he visits us with trial and testing in time" (14,107). Consequently, man is capable of no love by means of which he might return to God after he has sinned except the love that God enables him to exercise. In short, all human love is only counter-love:

Some people have found the statement very touching and sublime "that man is able to love God even without being loved in return", but this assertion is supported only by overweening pride, for, in fact, even man's love for God is only *Anteros* or love-in-return; hence, man cannot excel God in magnanimity. (8,231 fn.)[38]

To sum up: Love is intrinsically creative; therefore, God who is love is intrinsically creative. Although Baader holds that we cannot investigate the act of creation, we can know something about what motivates it. The notion of love is closely akin to that of superabundant richness of being, totality, fullness. God's fullness and love – not any supposed poverty or incompleteness in him – led him to create. God's love and fullness are an inscrutable mystery: the more one probes, the more one becomes aware of that fact. Man failed the test God imposed on his love, but God had compassion for man: he sent him incarnate love, his Son, to restore what was lost. God's willingness not only to forgive but to give in even greater measure than before is another indication that he is love *par excellence*. Through God's love and forgiveness man can love again and forgive.

---

38   On all human love as "counter-love" (*Gegenliebe*), see BAADER: *Sämtliche Werke* 1,230 fn. 2, 327 fn.; 2,352, 461; 8,230; 10,44; 14,331; E. SUSINI (Ed.): *Lettres inédites* 4,328.

In speaking of God as substantial love, certain qualities of love – i.e., those proper to all types of love – must be identified. Some of these qualities have already been considered: for example, the fact that love is something closely akin to life; that it is inseparable from knowledge; that it is essentially creative; that it is forgiving; and that it gives freely and abundantly. Baader's work points to still other qualities of love that can be detected at its source: i.e., in God.[39]

First, there is a group of texts that treat love as something essentially linked to religion, mystery, wonder, and reverence. Every mystery of religion is "a mystery of love" (7,26). "The mysteries in the world are religion and love" (14,377; see also 15,268). "True love is divine in all its forms" (9,212; see also 1,59; 5,264; 11,255). Sin is lovelessness (6,13, 18, 20), just as "there is no more proven means of preventing immoral excesses than genuine love" (11,194). These are but random and casual utterances[40] about a conviction that Baader discusses more fully elsewhere: for example, in a passage from the *Socialphilosophische Aphorismen aus verschiedenen Zeitblättern:*

It is just because all true love is religious in nature that the worldly-clever and worldly-wise ignore or deny it. These loveless, worldly-clever people think that they are not only more intelligent but also happier than love-filled fools who go out of themselves and who love something or someone other than themselves and who have a different definition of love than Kant does. Kant thought that love of something is grounded in the conviction of some advantage that the object promises us. (5,264)

In fact, however, these worldly-clever people are neither more intelligent nor more happy in their lovelessness than are people who love, even when their love or their good will is misjudged or unrecognized. We do not consider God unwise or unhappy because he gives himself lovingly to all men, yet receives full recognition of his love from only a few of them; and because, as Tauler says, he loves men (his creatures) so madly that he lays it up to their credit and is really thankful to them if they let him love them and, thereby, make them happy. In the same way, no true lover fails to experience a feeling of gratitude toward the object of his love, and, indeed, for no other reason than that he loves it. The only reason why he seeks recognition of his love is that failure to recognize it would hinder and restrict him in his love and expression of thanks. Likewise, a lover asks for respect from one he loves for no other reason than that he is

---

39 Qualities of love to be treated in this section of the chapter, together with qualities of love already addressed, are characteristics of "love at the source": i.e., in God particularly. The treatment is not exhaustive. Indeed, it must be supplemented by material presented in the rest of the study, especially Chapters 5 and 6 below.

40 On the connection between love and faith, see BAADER: *Sämtliche Werke* 9,104, 105 fn., 291, 338 fn.; 12,215. Love is a "divine spark" (11,184). One speaks of the "miracle of love" 7,123; 15,627. Because sin and love are opposites (2,20; 13,305), love is not for the profane (2,44). Love is a mystery (E. SUSINI [Ed.]: *Lettres inédites* 3,450; see also *Sämtliche Werke* 15,626).

unable to love someone who does not respect or honor him . . . The worldly-clever and worldly-wise are no less ignorant about the feeling of wonder than they are about the feeling of love, because both of these affects are inseparable and both are religious in nature. Because a person wonders only at something he does not comprehend – i.e., something he cannot do or imitate himself – the worldly-wise think that a philosopher ought to be ashamed of the religious feeling of wonder, as though it constituted proof of his ignorance; at most, he should wonder at himself and let others wonder at him. But, if expressing wonder at something that merits no wonder passes for a sign of ignorance, one should also consider failure to wonder at something that does merit wonder as no less proof of ignorance. In this sense, a French writer says: "Not to love is the greatest proof of ignorance (*ne pas aimer est la plus grande preuve de l'ignorance*)" . . . The unreasoning animal cannot, and the devil will not, wonder . . . As far as the religious nature of the sentiment of wonder and its connection with the feeling of reverence, of love, and of submission is concerned, we must observe that every object that arouses wonder would arouse only blind stupor and crippling, depressing fear instead of the elevating feeling of wonder if that object did not, in its turn, reach down in love to one who loved it and humbled itself before it and raise that lover . . . up to and into itself. . . (5,264–66).[41]

The regularity with which Baader links wonder and reverence, mystery and godliness, with love constitutes one of the most distinctive features associated with his handling of the theme of love as a whole.[42]

Worship is also a service of love: "Inner worship is the only true kind, and all external worship has significance only to the extent that it serves and advances internal worship" (15,629ff.). Hence, Baader bemoans the fact that "we

41 The "French writer" to whom Baader attributes the statement, "ne pas aimer est la plus grande preuve de l'ignorance", is, of course, Louis Claude de St. Martin. In commenting on a work of St. Martin, Baader writes: "When one sees how even philosophers of the stature of Kant and Hegel would like to exclude all feeling from science, it is no wonder that Saint-Martin looks for the reason why the wise of this world (in human science) do not attain the lofty goal of knowledge precisely inasmuch as they have no yearning [*Sehnen*]: i.e., no love. He thinks that they do not love because they do not know, because not loving is the greatest proof of ignorance" (12,365ff.). Similarly, Baader prefaces his essay *Sur l'Eucharistie*, in part, with the words: "With many religious people, one encounters the prejudice that science is something pernicious to both faith and love, despite the fact that not loving and not believing are the greatest proof of ignorance . . . " (7,3). On the same idea, see BAADER: *Sämtliche Werke* 5,255; 6,300; 9,164; E. SUSINI (Ed.): *Lettres inédites* 4,122. Baader goes so far as to equate lovelessness with idiocy (5,200).

42 The combination "wonder, respect, love" occurs many times in Baader's writings. "We do not hate or love what is despicable" (14,409). "When we begin to grasp in conceptual fashion, we cease to wonder, to love, to create" (12,463). Apart from frequent references to wonder and love that occur in 4,163–200 (and Chapters 5 and 6 below), these ideas appear together in the following places: BAADER: *Sämtliche Werke* 1,54, number 19; 2,14, 324, 337, 531-32; 3,390; 4,158; 6,38, 299, 300, 321; 8,49, 172, 237; 9,107, 164, 274, 358, 359 fn.; 10,16 fn.; 12,235, 267, 270, 272, 279, 280, 290, 292, 384, 430, 459, 460, 461, 465, 467; 13,314; 14,32, 429, 447; 15,408.

see most men behave themselves as though external worship of God were the all-important thing and as if they could dispense with internal worship – that of the heart" (15,629ff.). We should not take capacity for true worship for granted any more than capacity for true wonder or reverence:

Most people think that it is purely a matter of their whim and fancy to refuse to wonder at something truly worthy of wonder, to refuse to love something worthy of love, and to refuse to believe in something worthy of belief, and, therefore, also to refuse to serve their proper master. These people generally find out only too late that by doing so they have lost their freedom and have fallen subject to necessity, that they expend their wonder on something that is not worth wondering at, that they love something not worth loving, that they believe in something not worth believing in, and that they are forced to serve one who merits no service. (4,183; see also 5,125; 10,281)

There is no question here of escaping completely from God and his love, for "the man who loves God as well as the man who hates him unceasingly bear witness to God" – the one through loving worship, the other through cursing and defiance (4,186). There is also such a thing as "potential love" of God toward his creatures (14,102, 114, 115). Where God does not dwell through his love, he does so through his power.[43]

Baader sees all love, but most especially God's love for man, as action involving ascent and descent. His much-used axiom in this connection is: *Amor descendit ut elevet* – "Love descends in order to raise up". Here is another instance of Baader's seeing something only in connection with its polar opposite, just as he considers the Ground of Being only against the backdrop of the "Unground", light in contrast with darkness, affirmation as the antithesis of negation, etc.[44] "In yes and no consists the life of all things" (13,80). This is valid for love too:

There is no descent without elevation, and if anything descends from the height, something has to ascend from the depths to meet it . . . One says, in fact: *l'amour descend,* but one should say:

43 "Just as all things exist in God, the all-encompassing highest Being – i.e., in his power – so some of them exist, at the same time, in his love (he dwells 'in' these); other beings do not (he, therefore, only dwells 'through' or penetrates 'through' them (*die Er darum bloss durchwohnt oder durchdringt*), whether it be because they are naturally incapable of such indwelling or because they have lost it" (1,284). Baader makes, or alludes to, the same distinction in the following places: BAADER: *Sämtliche Werke* 2,38, 106; 3,296; 4,125 fn.; 6,296; 8,187 number 40, 343; 9,171, 242, 264 fn. 2, 291; 12,415, 417 fn. 2; 14,106.
44 See, for example, Hans Reichel's treatment of such polarities as rest and movement, freedom and determination, mind and nature, and unity and multiplicity in Baader's thought: H. REICHEL: "Die Sozietätsphilosophie Franz von Baaders", *Zeitschrift für die gesamte Staatswissenschaft*, pp. 199ff.

l'amour descend en élevant et éleve en descendant, comme elle donne en prenant, et prend en donnant (love descends as it elevates and elevates as it descends, just as it gives in taking and takes in giving). (15,486)

God always takes the initiative in love with respect to man. He condescends to offer his love and elevates its recipient. "We should not forget that love descends, or that love of the higher by the lower is only love that reacts (*Anteros*) to love that has stooped down to it . . . " (1,326). The descent-ascent motif in God's love for creatures holds just as truly before the fall of man as after it (14,107). In fact, it holds true for all love.[45]

Nobility and humility are two additional qualities that characterize all love.[46] They always appear in combination, like two sides of a single object, never separately. If love dies or weakens, the opposite qualities of baseness and pride immediately appear; they are just as surely evidence of lovelessness as their opposites are evidence of love. A passage from *Über die Analogie des Erkenntniss- und des Zeugungs-Triebes* states this position plainly:

Love contains two elements, nobility and humility. It is only when love flickers out that these two elements are transformed in and through their separation. They become arrogance and baseness, and we must regard these latter qualities not as components drawn out of love, but as products of its dissolution. Their presence testifies everywhere to the fact of such a past and present process of dissolution. In this two-fold mishap (*Unfall*), lies the key to the present state of nature and of man. (1,48)

In a passage from *Fermenta Cognitionis*, Baader specifies that nobility and humility are transformed into baseness and pride as a result of sin: i.e., in an attempt to "escape from the center" (2,316). To attempt an escape from the center is, in Baader's terms, the same as sin, because the center is love and sin is lovelessness (6,15, 18, 20). One reason why love requires humility is that it involves an act of self-subjection or homage to the beloved. Thus:

He who humbles himself, says Christ, will be exalted, or: we must lower ourselves freely if we wish to be lifted up, just as if we freely seek to exalt ourselves we experience unfree degradation. The artist who lacks the humility to recognize the genius of someone else's artistic work cuts himself off in corresponding degree from the source of his own genius. The spirit of pride is a dark, withered, and unproductive spirit. (5,266; see also 8,294)

---

45   On the theme *Amor descendit ut elevet,* see also BAADER: *Sämtliche Werke* 1,63, 140 fn., 161, 230, 232, 327; 2,43, 57, 80, 117; 6,11; 7,21; 8,175; 9,241, 335; 10,3; 12,465; 14,49, 107, 111, 403, 408, 479; 15,486, 597.

46   On the theme of nobility and humility, see Chapter 6, proposition 6 below. See also BAADER: *Sämtliche Werke* 2,110 on love as voluntary surrender of power, *freiwillige Depotenzirung;* and E. SUSINI (Ed.): *Lettres inédites* 3,450.

Another reason why love requires humility is closely associated with a further characteristic of love: i.e., the fact that love unites. It takes humility to unite, whereas pride is purely divisive. The essay *Vom Geist und Wesen der Dinge* begins with the following explanation:

The old assertion "that only God can unify what is multiple and only a devil can divide what is one" is confirmed by the observation that we can conceive of any act which unites two or more individuals only as an act of subjecting these individuals to some higher entity than themselves. We can conceive of the principle of uniting, then, only as working from the top down (consequently, in every case from within outwards) and as elevating those who are to be united . . . From this, it follows naturally that we can conceive of every act of separating, that works against an act of uniting, as working in an opposite direction: i.e., proceeding from the bottom upwards . . . and as an act of revolt. In other words, no true unification takes place without the spirit of humility, and no division without the spirit of pride and arrogance. (1,59)

Baader here speaks in universal terms. He is not discussing man's relations with God alone, but also relations of people with each other. A person needs humility not only for his spiritual life – union with God – but also for his social life – union with other men. Thus, both religion and society depend on the humility required to unite people with God and with each other in love.

Baader clearly defines the nature of a true social community in his essay *Über die Verbindung der Religion mit der Politik*:

When looked at carefully, however, this practical denial of man . . . coincides with true – i.e., practical – denial of God. As a matter of fact, we can regard the bond of love or unity that unites a plurality of people as members of one and the same community in a free manner (since it does so "from the inside out" – through attraction, not pressure) only as activity of one and the same higher or central being (i.e., God, who is common to them all) who dwells in all these people. It is to God that they have all rightfully submitted themselves (for it is, in fact, right that the lower should serve something truly higher than itself). The only way that an individual member can leave or enter this union, then, is to repudiate his submission to that common higher entity in the former case, or to enter into this submission in the latter case. In the first case, the departing member shuts himself off from the central indwelling of the common God (as the true spirit of community), inasmuch as he wants to make himself equivalent to the center (God). Putting himself, then, in place of God . . . he inwardly denies God . . . Thus, lovelessness=Godlessness, or, God is love! (6,13-14)

What is involved here is a plurality of persons united under a higher principle to which they have submitted themselves. The ultimate paradigm for this situation is to be found in the trinity of persons in God (7,161; 9,413; 10,351).[47]

---

47 In *Bemerkungen über einige antireligiöse Philosopheme unserer Zeit*, Baader cites St. Martin: "Parceque l'unité parfaite ne se trouve que dans notre jonction individuelle avec Dieu, et que ce n'est qu'après qu'elle est faite, que nous nous trouvons naturellement les frères les uns des autres". (See note 19 above.) He then comments in the footnote:

There, perfect freedom, perfect unity, and perfect love coincide. Only in imitation of that perfection can society be rightly ordered:

Because love makes people free from each other and keeps them that way, it does not follow that it cuts them off from one another in any way.[48] Instead, it links them in the most indissoluble way to a common life . . . Love, therefore, manifests itself as the truly organic and organizing principle of life; correspondingly, hate is the inorganic and disorganizing principle. (6,15)

. . . love for others and the will to serve them is the principle of society . . . (*Lettres inédites* 4,220).

Love presupposes freedom and is its highest exercise; hence, freedom is an attribute that must always characterize love. As substantial love, God is also substantial freedom. Paradoxically, he is necessarily absolute freedom and absolute love:

We can maintain, without impropriety, that God finds himself in a state of necessity with respect to his creatures: i.e., he has to love them. He who is love itself cannot turn away from his creatures or abandon them. But how different is this necessity to which love freely submits . . . from that fate to which poets and philosophers have subjected the creator . . . In fact, nothing is nobler than this fatalism of love which, in order to develop its richness, willed to give and allow us the power to respond freely to, or reject, its solicitations. In order to give us free choice, it renounced its own freedom, keeping this to itself in order to receive it back again from us. (6,306ff.)

For Baader, "harmonization of freedom and subordination,[49] of ruling and serving, of knowing and believing" is not possible apart from Christianity (13,329); this is so only because Christianity is the religion of love (6,134).

"One cannot find oneself in the plurality of persons and identity of being in God, yet one can require of love the same unity of being with plurality of persons. 'That they may be one', says Christ, 'as you (Father) and I are one'. Moreover, just as surrender of the finite to the Infinite is the medium of love and harmony of every finite [person] to every other, so is the same thing valid in the area of mutual understanding" (2,459–60). The scriptural reference is to John 17,21: ". . . that all may be one, even as thou, Father, in me and I in thee . . . " See also 14,336 on the personal character of love and 9,404 on the Father's love.

48 Baader often plays on the distinction between the suffixes *frei* and *los*. Something is *frei* of another thing when it is not dominated by that other or swallowed by it. This does not mean that it is *los* (i.e., separated) or cut off from it. A man should try to be *frei* of nature, but not *los* from it. A flower in bloom is *frei* of its stem and roots, but not *los* from them. Baader uses the distinction whenever he wishes to make the point that two things should not be confused, but should also not be separated.

49 On the close connection between love and freedom in Baader's thought, see BAADER: *Sämtliche Werke* 3,297; 5,222, 244, 288, 292, 297, 374; 6,15, 18, 24 fn., 26, 38, 64 fn. 2, 306; 7,333; 8,169, 234, 363; 9,61 fn. 1, 256, 301; 11,260; 12,343; 13,193, 195; 14,456, 479; E. SUSINI (Ed.): *Lettres inédites* 1,325. God's love is not bound (BAADER: *Sämtliche*

In summary, then, love is a reality that has essential ties with religion, wonder, reverence, mystery, and worship – which is natural enough if one begins with the postulate that God is love. The exercise of God's love requires that he condescend and that the subject of his love ascend: *amor descendit ut elevet.* Love combines nobility and humility, whereas lovelessness combines baseness and arrogance. Love essentially unites, which presupposes humility and subjection. Love is also the summit of freedom, the most complete disposition of the totality of oneself.

Add to these qualities of love those noted earlier in this chapter – love's kinship with life, with knowledge, with creativity, with richness, and with forgiveness – and it is readily apparent how Baader can say:

It follows from all this that really nothing is worthy of love except love itself. (4,185)

For only love (like life, which love is) has no Why or Wherefore, nothing that would precede it. Hence, love alone is an absolute end in itself (the end or perfection of all things, as well as their beginning), to which everything else serves as means. It is true to say of it:
> They say love has no law.
> Why not?
> Because love is itself
> The supreme law! (10,345)

Werke 6,323); in fact, no love qua love is bound. See F. HOFFMANN: *Vorhalle zur spekulativen Lehre Franz Baaders,* pp. 23–25; H. TUEBBEN: *Die Freiheitsproblematik Baaders und Deutingers und der deutsche Idealismus,* in: *Abhandlungen zur Philosophie und Psychologie der Religion,* volumes 20/21, Würzburg 1929.

Chapter 3
Image of God and Heavenly Sophia

To this point, the study of Franz von Baader's philosophy of love has been confined to its structural foundation: i.e., to love at its essential source, in God, who is substantial love. God, for Baader, is a living "love-center" to every part of the "love-periphery", any segment of which can love only by participating in him. Given this point of view, how does man come to share in the love that is God? It is clear, on the one hand, that Baader makes God the source of all love; it is equally clear, on the other, that an important part of man's experience has to do with love. What is the bridge that links the two? In what form does God's love come to man? A partial answer has already been suggested: i.e., that the creation and redemption of man are both effects of divine love. The question, then, might be sharpened in the following way: since creation and redemption are both effects of divine love, in what particular form is God's love for man embodied and made manifest? What is there in the essential notion of man that incorporates the quintessence of God's love for him?

Baader formulates his answer in the language of Genesis: "God created man in the image of himself, in the image of God he created him, male and female he created them".[1] The greatest compliment and highest expression of God's love for man was to make man in some way a likeness, a copy, a reflection, a mirror of himself. Baader shared the common theological-philosophical position that every created being reflects the perfection of God in some way, but this general statement has a unique application in the case of man (4,329–30). Man is a crossroads, the meeting-ground not only for all the various levels of being in the universe but also, in a sense, the meeting-ground between God and the whole of creation. Man is not merely *microcosmos*, but he is *microtheos* as well (5,256). This is Baader's controlling anthropological idea. The relevance of this position to the subject of love is apparent: if God is best described as substantial love, and if man is best described as the image of God, then love too must be a reality that lies at the very heart of man's being. In Bader's view,

---

1   Genesis 1,27, *The Jerusalem Bible*, Garden City, New York (Doubleday) 1966.

it is the special function of divine Wisdom, "heavenly Sophia", to establish the presence of God's image in man. Just as Sophia is herself the image of the triune God, it is also her presence that makes God's image reside in man. Thus, two closely-related themes are explored in this chapter: (1) that man is made in God's image; and (2) that the Heavenly Sophia causes this to be so.

The Image of God in Man

In general, Baader adopted his basic views about God, man, and the world early in his life and maintained them, without substantial change, until the end of his life. Central to these views was an intense commitment to the notion that man is made in God's image. In 1786, the very first year of the *Tagebücher*, the twenty-one-year-old Baader refers to "the profoundest mystery in us – we are the image of the eternally creative God" (11,61). A letter from Baader to Johann Michael Sailer, dated May 28, 1786, speaks similarly of "the great mystery . . . that man is the image of the Godhead and a microcosm, a little world similar to the great one" (*Lettres inédites* 1,159). Rather than losing interest in his early convictions about man, Baader devoted much attention – in his later thought – to developing them and their implications.[2]

Although Baader frequently cites biblical passages which refer to man's status as son of God or image of God, his main point of departure is the analogue he sees between God and man and the worker-product model: man is to God what a work or product is to a worker or artist. Thus, in *Vorlesungen über speculative Dogmatik*, Baader says:

Just as we must not identify (confuse) a creature with God, nor identify (confuse) God with a creature, neither should we posit a deistic separation between the two. In this connection – i.e., as far as effective relationship between them is concerned – we have a first fixed point in what we said above about the relationship between a man and his work. For we have seen that it is man's thought (idea) that leaves him (without thereby becoming a "piece" that he loses) and is "spoken into" or "imagined into" his work . . . We find the original for this law of connection between a product and its producer in God, because it is just this uncreated idea,* "spoken into" and dwelling in the creature, that keeps it in effective contact with God . . . In the meantime, you will probably have made the application yourselves from man's products to those of God, since I pointed out to you in the last lecture that the love or free interest that a man derives from his

---

2   Baader concerns himself with this subject in numerous writings. Extended treatments can be found in *Vorlesungen über speculative Dogmatik* (see, for example, BAADER: *Sämtliche Werke* 8,93–105; 9,142ff., 197ff.). For more modern treatments of the topic, see L. SCHEFFCZYK (Ed.): *Der Mensch als Bild Gottes*, Darmstadt (Wissenschaftliche Buchgesellschaft) 1969.

work or product as well as the union he effects with it rests solely on the fact that this product completely corresponds to his idea and returns the same to him in a sensible (sensual or perceptible) way (*sensibilisirt*, [*versinnlicht oder empfindlich*]).

*[footnote] "and God created man in his image. God, therefore, formed man from the slime of the earth and breathed into his face the breath of life". (8,92–93; see also 8,86)

As it stands, the term "image of God" is rather vague and indeterminate. What does Baader understand by it? Normally, one would expect a philosopher to supply a compact and precise definition of such a key term, but Baader provides no such definition. To a large extent, he philosophizes by analogies and their implications, rather than by definitions and their elucidations and implications. The largest part of lecture ten in volume one of *Vorlesungen über speculative Dogmatik* is an *ex professo* treatment of Baader's concept of image in general, including some applications of the term in the expression "image of God". The section entitled "Zur Lehre vom Bilde" begins as follows:

God penetrates all creatures until he comes to rest in man as in his goal and reflects himself in him. Only if God rests in man can nature celebrate its sabbath.[3] The goal of every work of art is to reflect its producer in the product – thus an "indwelling". The artist wants to possess himself in his image. One who denies man – i.e., one who denies the true destiny and dignity of man – is, therefore, the most dangerous enemy of the good. Since God does not manifest himself fully in any other creature except man, nature is Godless if man's vocation is denied; as long as its sun – i .e., man – is eclipsed, nature lies in the shadow. But in order to be able to talk about productions of God, we have to know man's productions first, because man is the mediator between God and nature, even in the case of knowledge. Everything man fashions and produces, he fashions and produces according to his image (thought) and in his image, and his entire production is nothing other than an expression of himself. The question arises now as to what an image is, what a living and corporeal image is, and what a non-living and non-corporeal image is. Here, we have two kinds of image: (1) catoptric or mirror-image in its widest sense; and (2) plastic copy or portrait. Both are non-living and non-corporeal. Mirror-image (e.g., the appearance of a rose in the focus of a concave mirror), shadow, the appearance of a spirit as a non-substantial (*unwesentliches*) image of an absent or dead person . . . may serve as examples of non-corporeal images. In this sense, it says in Acts of the Apostles that the assembled apostles, not believing the maidservant that the imprisoned apostle Peter was physically standing in front of the house, thought that it was not Peter himself but only his spirit [Acts 12,15]. "Spirit", in this case, has a remarkable and different meaning from the usual one (e.g., when it is said: God is a spirit, or man is a spirit). Paracelsus and, following him, Jacob Böhme call spirit in this sense a substanceless or at least departed (absent) manifestation of the *Evestrum*; one can compare the

3   Baader clarifies his notion of "sabbath" in the seventh lecture of the first book of *Vorlesungen über speculative Dogmatik*: "Full indwelling of God in the world through the mediation of man and the reflection (*Reflex*) of God from the world is the concept of the sabbath. This takes place in every production. A work of art is completed if the work reflects back on the artist, and the artist thus "rests" in it. The sabbath of God in the world is the total possibility of manifestation of God in it . . ." (8,62; see also 2,410ff.; 8,176; 9,401).

latter with *Fata Morgana*.[4] Catoptric image is distinguished from portrait because in the former, there is indeed a connection with the original, though not an essential one, whereas in the latter, there seems to be no connection at all. In the catoptric image, form has not posited substance, nor has substance posited form, as is the case in the organic. Catoptric image appears in the focus of a concave mirror as perfect (cubic), but the second image appears only as surface. An uneducated person would have to regard the former as magic. That is why I have associated apparition of spirits with these catoptric images. This is also where apparitions of the still inadequately explained *Fata Morgana* belong. With respect to the apparition of someone absent, I make this observation: everything that is not yet present in a substantial way (*wesenhaft*) in a certain region can appear there only as spirit. Indeed, one can see this in the case of the rising and setting of the sun inasmuch as we see it *there* even before it is above the horizon, but only in figure, and we see it *here* when it is already down, again only in figure. Now, if a portrait – to which we can attribute all writing signs, hieroglyphics, and characters – seems to establish no virtual bond between itself and its óriginal, still the child and the common folk have always believed in an indirect connection of this sort at any rate. This is the basis for venerating saints in their images, amulets, and talismans, along with their characters and signatures. It is the basis for the belief, held by many people, that there is magic in writing (runic writing). There is a deep strain of truth in this faith and superstition. Indeed, superstition comes closer to the truth in this case than total unbelief does. People try to clarify this connection for themselves in two ways: (1) through free or unfree presence of the original (*Durch freie oder unfreie Gegenwart des Originals*) – thus Jehovah says in the Old Testament: here (in Jerusalem) will I set my name [4 Kings 21,4]; and (2) through belief that a living concept of the sign will summon the original. Underlying all religions is this belief: to call out a name is to effect contact with the one whose name is called out. If a clairvoyant is in actual contact with someone, and this latter person loudly calls the former's name from a distance, [the clairvoyant person] feels a disturbance. All this shows that belief in an inner connection of image with original is deeply rooted, about which one can find much in Paracelsus and Helmont. *Imago, magnes* and *magia* are identical. Now, man, as image of God, cannot belong to either one of these two types of images, because even separated from the original he remains a corporeal and living being with his own proper life . . . The theory of images must advance a step if it is going to enlighten us about the relationship between God and man. This relationship is religion itself . . . (8,93–95)[5]

If someone says, then, that man is the image of God (or should be), he does not mean by that of course that man is a dead portrait of God, nor does he mean that man is a catoptric (or mirror) image like a lifeless and non-corporeal figure. Not the first, because [in man's case] the image stands in effective contact with the original and because, as substantial and corporeal, it is also living. Not the second, because it has life and stability apart from the original: i.e., it shows itself

---

4 *Evestrum* is the name given by Jacob Böhme and Paracelsus to the perverted substitute for the Idea of God in man. The word itself means "spirit" or "ghost". Man acquires the *Evestrum* by using his imagination improperly: namely, by lusting after an image other than the image of God (see, for example, BAADER: *Sämtliche Werke* 4,350; 7,371, 373). It can also refer to nonsubstantive presence, as of a "ghost" in the popular sense of the word. (See 8,91, 94.) *Fata Morgana* (morning fates) refers to apparitions of the same kind: i.e., non-substantive, "ghostly" apparitions, as in the citation from the text.
5 For a more up-to-date discussion of the problem connected with names and language, see, for example, G. MARCEL: *Problematic Man*, New York (Herder and Herder) 1967, pp. 47ff.

to be a substantial, not an unsubstantial image. Finally, we must, in all events, distinguish image not only from original, but also from the bearer of the image; we must neither confuse the two nor separate them. Moses, and following him the older theologians and Jacob Böhme, understood the word "create", therefore, to mean actuation of substance (of the creature as bearer of the image, by which, however, they meant no absolute substantiality apart from God), and they distinguished inspiration (*das Inspiriren*) of the image from that. (8,95; see also 13,215ff.)

Baader makes five principal points in this passage.

(1) God "rested" from his creative action once he had made man, the peak of creation, the "final creation" (*Schlussgeschöpf*). Thus, man holds a very special place because of "the totality, superiority, and centrality of man as end-creation, although all creatures are the image of God" (13,275).

(2) Every worker or artist wants to reproduce his own image in his work. The same holds for God: "thus, creation can have no law except one which (in its original) exists in God himself. Therefore, creation – in its origin – can be nothing other than an image of God" (13,91). God, however, manifests himself fully only in man.

(3) Previous theory about the nature of images has proven inadequate to handle the case of living and substantive images. Generally, people have recognized only the mirror-type (catoptric) image (which includes non-bodily presence of spirits) and the portrait-type image (which includes various kinds of language symbols). The latter has been closely associated with religious experience, both in the use of sacred images and in the invocation of sacred personages. People have always recognized some sort of inner connection between image and original.

(4) As God's image, man belongs to neither one of the usual image types. His case is unique: "Man alone has been created in the image and likeness of the creator" (14,439). We need a new concept of image to illustrate and embody the peculiar relationship man bears to his maker since, unlike other images, man is a corporeal and living being who maintains "virtual" contact with the original, yet has his own life and stability as a "substantial image".

(5) The image of God in man is something different from the bearer of that image because the actuation of man's substance in the act of creation was something different from the inspiration of God's image into him. The image of God is, thus, an *intentionality* in man: It is, consequently, possible for man to reject this image and still remain man in some sense. Here, the important point seems to be that God does not create man in his image as a completed datum or a finished product, but as a potentiality, a summons, a challenge. The way God creates man reflects the measure of *freedom* that is essential to man's nature. Thus, even though God creates man in being, man uses both his endowment – a foothold in being – and his capacity to create himself: i.e., to actuate the kind of "image" he wills to actuate. Baader would, accordingly, agree with Sartre's

view that "man creates himself", and with the current popular view that "I can be whatever I want to be" – but not in an absolute sense. In ultimate terms, man is not *from himself* and, therefore, will not serve ultimate truth if he tries to be *for himself*: i.e., pretends to claim absolute freedom for his contingent existence.

Baader's problem is trying to explain or define something for which there is no concrete analogate in man's experience. Analogy attempts to bridge the gap between two things that are essentially different from one another but that bear certain similarities and likenesses to one another. The problem is similar to explaining such terms as "the mystical body" of Christ or "sons of God". A standard book of instructions in the Catholic faith explains the term "mystical body" this way:

> The Church is called the *Mystical Body* of Christ: (a) to distinguish it from the physical body of Christ, his human body, which is present in heaven and in the Eucharist . . . and (b) to express the uniqueness of this second Body of Christ.

> The Church is not a physical body . . . Neither is it *merely* a moral body . . . It is a unique body, having all the elements of a moral body plus a living soul . . .

> The word *Mystical* must not be taken to mean vague, shadowy or unreal. Rather, it means mysterious, something which is real, but beyond the powers of our intellect fully to understand . . .[6]

The similarity between this explanation and the last paragraph of the passage cited from Baader is striking. The emphasis, in both cases, is on *uniqueness*. Ordinary categories do not apply in a univocal sense here. More is really said about what mystical body and image of God are *not* than about what they are. Baader rejects the idea that the term "image of God" means anything like a two-dimensional portrait or any kind of mirror-image, just as the book of instructions denies identity between "mystical" body and physical or moral body. For Baader, the concept "image" touches on the very heart of what man is.[7]

The passage from Baader's "Zur Lehre vom Bilde" (8,93–95) cited above is drawn from the first part of that essay. The remainder (8,96–105), however, is

---

6   See J. KILGALLON and G. WEBER: *Life in Christ. Instructions in the Catholic Faith,* Chicago 1958, pp. 94-95.

7   Baader insists on the living contact between God and man, intimate union but not confusion between the two. An analogy commonly used in patristic literature of the Church to describe man's participation in divine life through grace is apropos here. Man is compared to a piece of iron immersed in a raging fire (which is God): the iron becomes red-hot and suffused with many of the characteristics of the fire, but it does not lose its identity (nor does the fire). For a reference to Böhme's use of this analogy, see J. J. STOUDT: *Sunrise to Eternity. A Study in Jacob Böhme's Life and Thought,* Philadelphia (University of Pennsylvania Press) 1957, pp. 112–13, See BAADER: *Sämtliche Werke* 2,224. Luther used the analogy to describe the Real Presence in Consubstantiation.

too diffuse and lacking in precision to warrant citation. The chief points dealing with the image of God in man may be summarized as follows:

(1) "God desires to possess his likeness – i.e., not simply to see himself in a likeness without feeling (*empfindungslos*) – but also to sense himself in a substantive being" (8,96). There must be real correspondence between a being and its image. The whole mystery of the way in which imagination works is connected with the fact that he whose desire is aroused by imagination is profoundly affected by the thing he desires. It stamps him ("builds its image into him"), working its way into his very nature. Like other mystically oriented thinkers, Baader believed that *a person becomes like that which he seeks after and pursues, loves and serves.* The object of desire deposits a "tincture"[8] or "seed" in the one who desires it. The tincture or seed causes whatever is desired to work its way into the very essence of the one who desires it (8,96; see also 13,221ff.; 15,565).

(2) Man's vocation consists of so controlling the use of imagination and will that he consciously "fixes" and establishes the presence of God's image in him rather than a merely earthly or animal-like image. It was precisely by misusing their *imagination* that Lucifer and Adam fell away from God. Man had to choose one of three possible options open to him: to establish the "light-principle", or the "fiery nature-principle", or the "earthly and temporal principle". (See 14,485–87.) It was "his function, by means of opening up his imagination to the light-principle, to 'fix' (*fixiren*) the light-being and the light-image corresponding to it in himself and then to use that light-principle to subject the other two [principles] to it" (8,100–01).[9]

---

8 In the sixth lecture of *Vorlesungen über J. Böhme's Lehre mit besonderer Beziehung auf dessen Schrift: Von der Gnadenwahl,* Baader gives his most succinct explanation of what "tincture" means: "To 'tincture' signifies the effort to introduce a being's form of life into another mode of existence by opening up the 'tincture' hidden in it. Tincture is, therefore, the living spiritual image (*Geistbild*), which exists midway between purely ideal and real existence. Tincture can be heavenly, earthly, or hellish" (13,82). Baader's use of this alchemistic idea is a complex one, closely connected in his thought with the themes of magic, imagination, images, and the general problem of the interconnectedness of the physical and spiritual worlds. See the many references to it in the index volume of the *Sämtliche Werke,* as well as 14,375ff., 478; 15,15, 277, 566, 567; E. SUSINI (Ed.): *Lettres inédites* 1,477 and *passim.* For an instance of "love-tincture", see BAADER: *Sämtliche Werke* 13,303.

9 Baader held that man always reflects some kind of "image". If he rejects the image of God, there are various forms his degeneration can take, depending on the kinds of objects he "lusts after" or loves. But the summons from God to establish his image never completely leaves a man. "If, then, the image of God in man has actually gone under and is present in him only potentially, and if in its place the image of the external world or even the image of hell is in him, then he is in no better condition than a

(3) Baader distinguishes four postures or attitudes in which a person might find himself with respect to establishing God's image within himself: (a) the state of innocence (or untested possession of God's image); (b) the state of those who successfully overcome the temptation to forfeit God's image for some other; (c) the state of those who have fallen from innocence, but still have a chance to restore God's image in themselves; (d) the state of the devil and the damned. "So we have: the state of innocence, fixed integrity, reparable deformity, and irreparable deformity" (8,98).[10]

(4) Baader stresses again that proper use of imagination is the key to confirming God's image in oneself. "There are, thus, three moments in elaborating an image: first is imagination (spirit-image [*Geistbild*]); second is will-formation (substantive image [*wesenhaftes Bild*]); and third is corporeal formation (corporeal image [*leibliches Bild*])" (8,102; see also 13,68). Baader notes that sin is first in imagination, then in will, then in deed – "Therefore, guard your imagination, for you can more easily win out over sin there" (8,102). Throughout Baader's entire treatment of this subject, he insists that man is not merely an inert and passive subject into which God "pours" his image as one pours water into a glass. Man's own cooperation with one of the possibilities open to him "fixes" an image in him, God's image or any other he prefers in its stead.

Baader's use of terms, as one might expect, is rather loose. Much of what he says about man as image of God is contained in expressions like "child of God" or "son of God". In another passage from *Vorlesungen über speculative Dogmatik*, Baader expressly links notions of divine sonship with man as image of God, at the same time reflecting further on his concept of image in general. He speaks of the creature's obligation to subject his will to the will of the creator. If he fails to do so, he

falls (plunges) into an unreconciled condition (that of established non-integrity), whereby he also suffers loss of his childhood (*Kindschaft*) (as natural pre-disposition for sonship) because, as scripture says: "whoever does not possess the Son, loses the Father also"[11] – or else the creature attains to childhood and sonship again, which scripture calls re-birth in the narrower sense. For

sick man or an *emigré* (with titles but without means) . . ." (2,23; see also 14,485-87). There is always the possibility of a "cure", and the destruction of such alternate images as the "darkness image" (i.e., the satanic image) or the "animal image" and their replacement with the ideal divine "light-image" (2,339ff.).

10 Compare Baader's remark that "the devil is a homicide, because he wants to be a deicide" (14,441).

11 No biblical text says precisely what Baader says; but the equivalent is contained, for example, in a combination of I John 5,12; John 5,23; John 14 and other Johannine texts.

the situation of childhood is the potential image of God and that of sonship the actual image of God. The Redeemer restored the former to us as the *posse filii Dei fieri*, [see John 1,12] so that with his help we should actualize that potentiality – something Adam failed to do. I want to take this opportunity to say something about the notion of image in general. A might produce (posit) its own image B; or, an already existing being not posited by (A) might fashion its own image: in any case, B is always recognized primarily as something different (distinct) from A, or as an "other" (a non-A) which becomes an image or likeness of A, but which, therefore, and to that extent, gives up its independence with respect to A. For an image belongs to that whose image it is, just as substance belongs to its spirit. Just as this latter can effectively be a spirit only in its substance (image), so can it [substance, image] be what it is only by means of its spirit. Hence, the absurdity of depicting substance-less or image-less spirit becomes evident. In this connection, one must observe the difference between the case in which the substratum of image comes from A itself (from its essence) and when it does not. The formative or transformative entry (*der bildende oder umbildende Eingang*) of A into B, and vice-versa, is different in each case. One must, likewise, distinguish consubstantiality (*consubstantialis Patri*, as true *Homousie*[12]) from those beings that issue forth from God and are created by him. If, then, Scripture depicts man (creation) as made in God's image, it expresses, thereby, that this creation, as such, was not yet already this image (as established), but rather that development of life and body should be effected only by means of an act of being born (*Eingeburt*), which occurs subsequent to its own creation. Thus, it is also said of the Son of God that he is begotten, not made. Through the act of birth (which, as has been said, takes place through the creator's entry into the creature), the creature becomes Godlike (*gottig*) (as Eckehart [*sic*] says), but not God, and God becomes creaturelike, but not a creature. If it is said, then, that God created man to his image, this image itself is considered as not created, existing before and in the creation, in union with and in the presence of God, impersonal and lacking a self with respect to God, but possessing a self with respect to creatures. From this, one can see that the status of this image as creature is conditioned by its openness (*offene Gemeinschaft*) to its status on the supernatural plane (before God). In any case, it must be said of any creature that it is destined to be an image of God. This expression, however, is used in Scripture par excellence only for man, because it is in him alone, as final and central creation, that the full image of God (Sophia) could and should become creaturely. Only immediate entry of God into him (and with that his participation in sonship) conditions indirect participation in it on the part of creation as a whole. In this connection, one might take note of the ironically deceptive and satanic twisting of "You shall be the image of God" into "You shall be gods" [Genesis 3,5]: i.e, you shall not belong to God and serve him as his image, but rather you shall be gods unto yourselves and reproduce your own image, not God's. This was also Lucifer's crime, which he wanted to carry out through man in this way. Or, as Christ says in John: you do not wish to bear witness to God's honor and glory and God's name, but rather to your own.[13] But how can our philosophers and theologians give us a clear concept of the image of God, inasmuch as they have never achieved a clear understanding of image (*imago*) and of imagining (*das Imaginiren*) and are still completely ignorant of the elucidations Paracelsus and J. Böhme have provided in this area? (9,197–99)

12   The term "consubstantial" refers to the unity of substance that the Christian Church recognized between Christ and God the Father in the Christological controversies of the fourth century (versus the Arians at the Council of Nicaea in A.D. 325). What Baader calls *Homousie* is French for the original Greek *Homoousia*, meaning "of one substance" or consubstantial.

13   Baader is probably thinking of John 5,23 and 5,44, among other Johannine texts.

Analysis of this passage reveals the following points relevant to Baader's idea of man as image of God.

(1) Man is created with the *possibility* of becoming a "son of God". If he uses the opportunity, he establishes or "fixes" God's image in himself permanently – this is the same as becoming a "son of God" in actuality. (See 4,330ff.)

(2) The word "image" does not denote an external characteristic but an internal reality of spirit (*Geist*), essence (*Wesen*), and body (*Leib*). Although "image belongs to that whose image it is", we must distinguish between the case in which the image proceeds immediately from the essence of God as his consubstantial reflection (the Word proceeding from the Father) and those "images of God" that are also his creations. Of course, there is a major theological point at stake here – namely, that Jesus Christ is the "son of God" or the image of God the Father *by nature or essence*: he cannot be other, for he is, as the Creed says, "consubstantial with the Father". Any other human being may *participate in* God's being as an "image of God", but this does not happen in the same sense and with the same fullness of meaning that it does in the case of Christ.

(3) The image of God is, in itself, not a created thing and not a person. When, however, God imparts this image (Sophia) to man, it exercises a personal function with respect to him. Sophia represents not any one of the three Persons in God but "the absolute Person", as it were: i.e., the deity as such.[14] Although the image of god, as uncreated reflection of the Godhead, is indestructible in itself, God's image in man – since it is rooted in or vested in a free, finite being – may vanish. (See 13,185.)

(4) Every creature is made in God's image, but this is best said of man, the "final creation", who acts as mediator to the rest of creation. This special status of man is due to his being not merely a *microcosmos* but a *microtheos* as well. Because he is a personal being endowed with reason and free will, there are dimensions of infinity and of immeasurable worth about him that place him above the rest of created nature.

(5) Sin consists in refusing to establish God's image in oneself and substituting one's own image in its place: "they would be as gods"! Baader thus describes a person's fundamental religious posture in terms of what image he bears, God's or some other one. Thus, Tauler says: "The soul that wishes to be God's child, and in whom God's Son would be born, should give birth to nothing else . . ." (13,389). In this connection, it is interesting to recall how the

---

14 On the personality or impersonality of Sophia, as Baader may have understood the terms, see the second part of this chapter. For a brief discussion of God's "absolute personality", see F. HOFFMANN: *Vorhalle zur spekulativen Lehre Franz Baaders*, p. 135. There is no question of anything like a "fourth person" to be added to the trinity. (See also BAADER: *Sämtliche Werke* 3,395ff.)

atheist and existentialist Albert Camus conceived man. In a footnote to *Helen's Exile*, man is described as "the only being who can refuse to be what he is". The sporadic and occasional coverage which Baader gives to most of the subjects that interest him, even the major ones, results in primary emphasis being placed on only one or another aspect of the subjects which he addresses. For example, a major facet of Baader's view of man as God's image deals with man's cosmically significant vocation of redeeming nature by exercising his divine sonship:

Now, since man is the final creation for the whole of creation, one in whom the creator *reascendendo* (by reascending) "recapitulates" that creation, as it were, he is also one who alone has been designated for such immediate entry of creator into his creation; he is mediator of that entry: i.e., the sabbath. Hence, an ancient teacher in the Church says that prior to creating man, God could still find no room in the whole of creation for him to penetrate or inhabit. (10,221; see also 4,331; 8,316)

Therefore:

Every anthropological or physiological doctrine is hostile to morality and religion if it fails to recognize or obscures this original vocation of man – [i.e.,] as one who completes and transfigures nature and, thereby, brings blessing on it – and it degrades (that vocation) to a level lower than Paul, for example, conceives it to be. For he [Paul] speaks of the anxious waiting and sighing of creation for revelation of the children of God, through which revelation (i.e., of the image of God in man) creation will be saved from slavery to the idle and temporal (of absence or distance from God [*der Gottesleere, der Gottesferne*] – see, for example, Romans 8, 22ff.). I say that all those anthropologies and physiologies are irreconcilable with religion if they do not recognize this fundamental religious teaching (about man as image of God and about distortion and restoration of the same) and if they do not allow man to appear in the world from the very start as image of God and *microtheos* instead of simply as image of nature or of world *microcosmos*. Deprived of full manifestation of God and, therefore, without God and distant from him (*Gottesleer und Gottesfern*), the world needs such representation of God in any case. (5,255–56)

Baader addresses the issue of image of God in man from another point of view – when he deals with the problem in terms of matter and form, male and female, inner and outer – in a passage which states that man's vocation (to be the image of God) puts him in a position intermediate between "purely divine" and "purely created":

The meaning of the words "form" and "being" in the sentence, *Forma dat esse rei* (Form gives being to a thing), seems to be different than when one understands by "form" the hull (envelope, the outer) and by "being" the inner (in English: matter or substance) and also different than when in coition the male is supposed to deliver the element that supplies the soul, the inner, and the female the element of form, the outer. But people think of content (or substance) only as unstable and dependent, and they say that it achieves stability (existence) only in conjunction with something higher than (within) itself. This union, meanwhile, expresses itself only through its form (image), which (thought of naturally not as something rigid but as function) then mediates between that inner and outer. In this sense, one can now say that all content is fashioned to the image of something higher than itself, just as it says in Scripture that man has been created in God's image. Further: just because form (image, hull) always exists *under* that which resides in it and manifests itself through it (the spirit), this must be valid for the image of God in us too. That image is, thus, at once beneath God (the spirit-God [*dem Geist-Gott*]) and above creature-spirit (*Creatur-Geist*). Hence, when Jacob Böhme designates this superiority and "non-dilutable character" (*Unvermischbarkeit*) of the image of God (the Idea) in man with his creature-spirit by referring to a divine Virgin (who no more intermingles herself with creation than iron all aglow with fire thereby confuses its nature with the fire), he has let himself be guided only by deeply grounded philosophical insight into the connection between the divine and the human (the *Verbum caro factum*). To the extent that the principle giving content to form may be called female, this designation should also be valid for the principle giving content (element) to this divine image. If this principle were now to marry – i.e., mingle with creaturely spirit (the fire-spirit as male) – it would not be able to shape and give rise to the image of God, but only to that of this creature. One can see, then, that in an immediate sense only God (*Dieu-esprit*, not *l'homme esprit*) can exercise a male's (father's) function here, the creaturely spirit only mediately through him . . . which is why the ancients rightly called man "the locus of the divine nuptials (*die Ehestatt Gottes)*". (2,223–24; see also 13,184)

In this passage, Baader does several things:

(1) He makes an explicit transition from his general view that "all content has been fashioned to the image of something higher than itself" to the particular application that man has been fashioned in God's image: i.e., the spirit of God manifests itself in a special way through man.

(2) The special presence of God's spirit in man does not somehow (*per impossibile*) divinize man in the full sense, but it does raise him above the purely created level. God and man exist in intimate union, but we must never confuse them with one another.

(3) Man is related to God as content to form, as female to male; hence, the ancients spoke of a kind of "marriage" between man and God, man being the "locus of the divine nuptials".

Baader speaks of man's position as intermediate between God and the rest of creation; God's image resides in man in an eminent way, and this raises man above the rest of creation. But Baader did not regard this image as something existing outside of man, as a kind of bridge between God and man. On the contrary, God's image in man belongs to man's innermost core (in the sense of the purpose of his being); and this core is love. Baader writes in a commentary on St. Martin:

Thus, St. Paul says: "It is now no longer I that live, but Christ lives in me" [Galatians 2,20]. Although we are talking about the image of God in the text of the passage cited, nevertheless, the image is not the form of the soul, in the sense in which one speaks of the form of a cone or of a cube, but rather it is the life of the soul, the soul of the soul . . . Jesus (the heart of God) entered directly into this image in man's case and became his soul or his heart. Jesus (love) became the Christ, the latter Mary's son. (12,283; see also 12,282)

Here we have hit upon the real heart of the piece: the fact that God, as substantial love, creates man in that essential image. What God "mirrors forth" as his essential image (Sophia) is love itself (12,275–76). "If both God and creation are to exist, the latter can only be his image (in love or in anger)" (12,494). Man's whole vocation is to fix God's image as love in himself by responding to the opportunity to love that God allows him:

There are two scriptural doctrines that are so intimately related to one another that we cannot understand either of them unless we clearly see the mutual relation between them. I mean the doctrine about man as the image of God and the one about man's having been foreknown and foreseen as such (in God's wisdom) in the name of Jesus: i.e. in God's love, not only before man's own creation, but even before that of the world . . . (4,329; see also 14,441)

In a letter to Jacobi (dated June 16, 1805) Baader wrote:

. . . the command: You shall not fashion for yourself . . . any likeness or image is of a piece with the command: You shall make yourself into a likeness or give birth to a likeness in you. But man failed the test and made himself into the image of an animal (*Thierbildniss*); then Love spoke: I will fashion you to my image! (15,200; see also 4,241; 6,306)

Bringing the image of God to realization in individual man is something God accomplishes, but not without man's cooperation. In the eighteenth lecture of the fourth book of *Vorlesungen über speculative Dogmatik*, Baader underlines the fact that it is precisely through love and service that man establishes God's image in himself:

Man was to have fashioned the type of his own proper image from a source that existed within and above him, yet was different from him. But, he was to have modified that type – within, and in accordance with, the form given him, as it were, by that source – so that his image might conform to himself. But man did not do this, inasmuch as he diverted from [that image] the power of his love, with which he should have fructified this form in himself and brought it to realization. Because he transferred his love (desire, *désir*) in that way, he lost it, since the alien form did not allow [his love] to develop into a productive organ and bear fruit, but instead kept it bound up and ensnared in itself. In like manner, we daily lose and squander our heart on things that not only do not return [our hearts] to us but also affect it in a heart-chilling and lethal way.*
*[footnote] "Thus it is", says St. Martin, "that every day we see our love detach itself from us and imprison itself in external objects and regions where we allow it to stray". (9, 142–43)[15]

---

15 The text, as Baader gives it, reads: "C'est ainsi", sagt St. Martin, "que nous voyons tous les jours notre amour se détacher de nous, et s'emprisonner dans les objets et régions externes où nous les [*sic*] laissons s'extraligner".

Hence, man's prerogative of exercising freedom includes also the possibility of *rejecting* God's invitation. God does not deliver completed and established participation in his love and life to man. "The creature as such is not God's image, but it is just the seed thereof that is implanted in man" (12,347). Even this "seed" does not grow in a physical way, following the laws of growth of vegetable plants. It requires *voluntary* nurture and care on man's part so that the final product, establishing God's image in man, is the result of cooperative divine-human effort. The idea is the same as that espoused by Thomas Aquinas when he says that God deals with each of his creatures in accordance with the nature with which he has endowed them. If God creates man with a measure of true spiritual freedom, then God obliges himself, as it were, to respect the intrinsic character of his own gift: he respects man's freedom, even to the point of allowing man to miss his own essential calling and fulfillment.

The relationship Baader envisions here is a kind of "family affair", not simply an affair involving unrelated persons:

Inasmuch as man receives something from God, and God, as it were, reproduces himself (posits his image) in him (as a man), God is father and man is son. But, inasmuch as man (as conceiving mother) accepts and receives this conceived being within himself, God is the son of man. (12,347)

In a similar vein, Baader observes:

There is at the base of that baroque assertion "that after God has made us, we in turn ought to make him" the true idea "that every creature should give birth again to its creator by way of imitation in and through itself, or rather should serve this imitative birth-giving on God's part in and through itself". This is also what the word worship expresses.*
*[footnote] The image of God to which (or to the realization of which) man was created was to be born in man with the help of God; it would thus be son of both God and man. (9,167; see also 14,106, 156)[16]

In all such references to man's duty to cooperate with God, Baader does not, of course, conceive of God and man as two workers on a coordinate scale. For him, God is the one "in whom we live, and move, and have our being" (Acts 17,28), even when man freely cooperates with God. God is the "thought that thinks itself in us", "the prayer that prays in us", and "the love that loves in us". As Hans Grassl explains:

---

16 Baader says elsewhere: "Love is 'born within' a being, and it cannot be 'born away' from it; nevertheless, as a *vita propria*, it is to be distinguished from one to whom it is born. (Liebe ist ein Ingeborenes, nicht Weggebarbäres und doch sich von dem, welchem es eingeboren ist, als *vita propria* Unterscheidendes.)" (12,244; see also 12,480)

. . . man can experience only in virtue of the divine Being (*Seins*) that works in him. Man distinguishes himself from God in order to grasp himself as a self. Here the ontological-teleological thought-structure of this mystic [Baader] manifests itself: everything [man needs] to realize his self is determined by divine Being.

Grassl promptly dismisses any pantheistic interpretation of this statement:

Both Hegel and Schelling reduce God, in pantheistic fashion, to development. Because Baader holds on to the divine existential relationship toward which the creature must realize itself, he preserves the priority of being over development and the task that each individual faces of developing itself in relationship to the whole. Both of these factors are missing in Schelling and Hegel: both of them also link Baader with ancient Christian tradition.[17]

J. E. Erdmann speaks similarly of the fact that "man continues the revelation of God" and that in this regard one can speak of "theogony, or it can be said that God creates in order that he himself may be born again". He notes that "a child of God cannot be created; for that purpose, a creature of God must make himself, insofar as he is reborn".[18]

In all of these passages, Baader is underscoring the need to apply a larger metaphysical principle, one that finds expression in the work of that *philosophe inconnu*, Louis Claude de St. Martin:

"Selon la loi de tout ce qui existe, l'homme ne peut trouver de repos, que dans la génération de sa propre source en lui-même. (According to the law of everything that exists, man can only find rest by generating its own proper source within himself.)" Every existing being attains its sabbath only by regenerating its source (father) within itself. (12,259; see also 4,188)

Hence, "man is a being whose vocation is to propagate God (*Gott fortzusetzen*)" (12,397). Indeed, the rule of life for every being is to "regenerate its generator", according to the ancient dictum: "In nature, every son is destined to regenerate his father" (2,8). The idea of the *circulus vitae* is basically the same as the analagous notion expressed by Kant in the *Critique of Judgment*: "In an organism, a cause produces its effect, and this latter in turn becomes a cause".[19] This is a constitutive law for Baader; hence, he speaks of "the identity of the doctrine of law with that of the image of God" (9,43 fn.1).[20] Thus:

---

17 H. GRASSL: "Eine Philosophie der Liebe", *Hochland*, 1950–51, p. 376. See also K. P. FISCHER: *Zur hundertjährigen Geburtsfeier Franz von Baaders. Versuch einer Charakteristik seiner Theosophie,* pp. 20ff.

18 J. E. ERDMANN: *Die Entwicklung der deutschen Spekulation seit Kant,* Stuttgart 1931, volume 3, p. 313.

19 I. KANT: *Kritik der Urteilskraft.* in: VON HARTENSTEIN (Ed.): *Gesammelte Schriften,* Berlin (W. de Gruyter) 1902–1955, volume 7, p. 242.

20 The matter of "constitutive laws" is addressed in Chapter 6, proposition 10, below.

To restore oneself or to return to one's principle is nothing else than to regain possession of everything required to fulfill one's law. And this law of man is none other than that he should be the speaking and acting image and likeness of God (his "working-model"). (2,170)[21]

The nub of the issue is: in loving, one reflects and "reproduces" the God who is love. The goals one serves and pursues, the ideals to which one dedicates oneself, the things one loves – all of these things indicate the kind of "image" that a man builds within himself. "The direction in which man turned his admiration is the same as the one to which he opened up and gave his love. He squandered his heart's strength (*Herzkraft*) on the earthly, because it produced no rebirth in his heart" (12,280; see also 9,145). "God is born again in likeness (restored and gladdened) in every virtue of the just man (says Meister Eckehart)" (3,245; see also 14,150, 399, 456). For Baader, man actually becomes like that which he loves and serves; it is that from which and for which he lives. (See, for example, 5,265.) "Indeed, what we do not desire, love, or hate, what does not affect (touch) us, is nothing for us. Our whole existence is in feeling" (12,341). Here Baader is at one with Goethe's *Gefühl ist alles.*

Baader explains the dynamics of love and desire in connection with the all-important operation of the imagination, the working of which serves as the key to the whole process of loving and desiring:

The chief law of imagination is the following: Every single being endowed with will finds itself effectively in any region only to the extent that it adopts the image (of that region) into its will . . . Christ referred to this law with his statement: "Where your treasure is, there will your heart also be" [Matthew 6,21]. But, your treasure is where your will – or heart-image (*Willens- oder Herzensgestalt*) dwells, therefore, in that being that dwells in you through this "imaging" (*Inbildung*) . . . Hence, the assertion, *Anima est ubi amat et quamdiu amat* (The soul exists where it loves and as long as it loves). "Only for so long as they loved, did they exist", says the poet: i.e., locality and permanence exist for a willing being only in feeling (*im Affect*), but feeling is based only on image (*imago*). If what you love exists everywhere and always, or if it has been taken up into the Everywhere and Always, you also exist everywhere and always. For love works through imagination and is magic (*denn die Liebe ist imaginirend und Magie*) and, as J. Böhme says, it has the radical power to make itself like what it loves. Christ referred to the same law we are discussing here when he had the coin of the tribute shown to him, because he said: "Give to Caesar, what belongs to Caesar (in virtue of his image) and to God what is God's" [Matthew 22,21]. For God demands from man his image, which he had imbedded in him and which man was supposed to "fix" in his will. (13,221–22; see also 2,339; 3,300ff.; 14,203)[22]

---

21 See also H. GRASSL (Ed.): *Franz von Baader. Gesellschaftslehre*, p. 312, and BAADER: *Sämtliche Werke* 8,188.
22 Baader's citation from the *Quarante Questions sur . . . l'Ame* (French translation of a work by Böhme) supplements this treatment (see also 12,480–81): "Therefore, it is up to the imagination to say what a man will permit to become desire for him – there is

Baader's own version of the "categorical imperative" is the duty of every man to establish God's image in himself through love. Because every act of love involves giving of self to the beloved, a kind of renunciation of self or "losing one's life in order to find it", the same holds true for man's life and love. "The purpose of the original state of personal will (in nature and creation) is, thus, to renounce and elevate itself, which renunciation or transformation in joy is giving birth to the image of God . . ." (14,150).

Subjection, as an integral element of love, plays an important role in Baader's understanding of what it means to establish God's image in oneself. On the one hand, Baader regards that image as the "soul of the soul" (12,283); on the other, man's freedom allows him the possibility of being false to his nature, of refusing God's invitation to establish his image in himself. If God is to confirm his image in man, man has to submit himself to God's presence and action within him. Without that submission, God remains "foreign" to man, not at home in him.

. . . certain mystics rightly insisted that the form in which God comes to dwell immediately as in his "light-body" (*Lichtleib*) in the creature . . . can occur only if the creature subjects himself to this [action]. The [creature] must retreat (keep still) (*zurücktreten [schweigen]*) if the image of God (the Idea) is going to appear, shine forth, and express itself in and through him. You will further understand why J. Böhme maintains that the appearance of this image of God (Sophia or Heavenly Virgin, as he calls it) presupposes separation in man: i.e., self-lowering and hiding, to which corresponds ascending or being lifted up . . . (8,291–92; see also 14,158)

In all of these texts, persistent tension between the natural and the supernatural in man is evident. God is in him, yet above him. For man, God's image is a free gift and an unmerited privilege, but it is also something for which the deepest elements in man's nature call out. Man is God's creature; nevertheless, by virtue of his intelligence and will, he somehow transcends the purely natural and creaturely. Man does not coincide with the rest of creation. His life and meaning cannot be "lumped" together with everything else God made.

the likeness. And it is strictly necessary for a person to fight constantly against worldly reason in flesh and blood (*stets wider die irdische Vernunft in Fleisch und Blut streite*), and to accommodate the spirit of his will to the mercy and love of God and constantly deliver himself over to God's will. He must not esteem earthly property, or lust as his treasure or fix his desire on something that destroys the noble likeness in him. For that is a disturbance (*Turba*) of the likeness of God and introduces animal quality into the likeness. To sum up: Christ says, where your treasure is, there is your heart also. That is the measure by which God will judge what is hidden in mankind and will separate the pure from the impure: what is false he will give over to the fiery host (*Feuerturba*) to devour, and what is holy, since it has entered into God, he will lead into his kingdom".

But, of course, one does not understand the fundamental concept of Christianity about restoring and confirming man as image of God if one does not understand the special and higher significance of man. For, when both intelligent and non-intelligent creatures were fashioned . . . an "end-creation" (*Schluss-geschöpf*) was still lacking: i.e., one that would be not only the image of God as "Super-intelligence" (such as spirits are), or the image of God as "Super-nature" (such as non-intelligent natures are), but that would unite both these representations and manifest itself as the image of the whole God . . . (4,299)

Therefore:

This higher dignity of man, or this coincidence of the concept of image of God with that of participation in sonship of God, marks him out (in relation to other intelligent and non-intelligent beings created before him) as a "final creation", hence, as one who is supposed to bind together the two others indissolubly. . . among themselves and with God. (4,330–31)

"The universe was to be united again with the word and with love (the eternal) through man: i.e. reunion with Sophia" (12,405). Man is thus the meeting-place for all forces and beings, *microcosmos* and *microtheos*. His destiny and calling is to reproduce God: i.e., his "image" within himself. He fulfills this duty directly by offering his love to God in worship and observance of God's will. The same imperative of reproducing love (God's image) is the basis for love of neighbor, because man loves God in his neighbor: ". . . the intelligent personal creature enters into indissoluble union with God only by serving the creaturely manifestation of God or his appearance through (that manifestation) as image of God . . ." (13,229).[23]

Baader's mystical-religious view of man as God's image is his most far-reaching anthropological idea, the one that says the most about what man and his vocation really are. And Baader made the following passage, one which he drew from the writing of Jacob Böhme, his very own.

Hear, my brother: God spoke in Moses: You shall make no likeness of a God for yourself, neither in heaven, nor on earth, nor unto anything (*noch in Etwas*). This is to signify that he is no image and also needs no resting-place, and one should not look for him anywhere in a place, except only in his formed and expressed word, in the image of God: i.e., in man himself. As it is

23   R. JOHANN: *The Meaning of Love. An Essay Towards a Metaphysics of Intersubjectivity*, Glen Rock, New Jersey (Paulist Press) 1966, p. 49 cites P. DE FINANCE to make the complementary point that loving other human beings involves loving God too: "In the abyss of its own irreplaceable subjectivity, each 'unique' reflects Him who leaves no room for a second. But it is in this same abyss that he encounters the other uniques. For this Absolute Subjectivity in which my own participates is that also in which participate the other subjects. And the more each one strives to be himself, the more he advances towards perfect authenticity, the more also he enters with the others into a profound communion, since it is the same Act which acts in all and communicates itself to all".

written: the word is near you, namely in your mouth and in your heart. And the nearest path to God is that the image of God should submerge in itself all patterned images and should abandon all images, disputes, and strifes in itself and despair of its own willing, desiring, and opinionating. It should bury and confide itself in the Eternal One as in the pure and single love of God, which he has brought back to mankind in Christ after the fall of man". (13,70)[24]

Heavenly Sophia[25]

The place that divine Wisdom (Sophia) occupies in Baader's thought is very complex, winding its way tortuously through the arcane, clandestine, and labyrinthine by-ways of his and Böhme's speculation on the nature of the trinitarian God. Happily, it is not necessary to assimilate all of it, even if it were possible to do so. For our purpose, it is sufficient to isolate material relevant to the fundamental role Baader assigns to divine Sophia in making man the image of God and in being the ontological fountainhead of every manifestation of love.

Divine Wisdom (Sophia, the Idea) is, according to Justin, the "thinking power" or *Dynamis logiké* of God (1, 300). It is an "impersonal" attribute of the trinitarian God (2,209, 428 fn.; 4,351, 352 fn.; 10,13, 268).[26] Although Sophia is not a

24 Böhme's rather quaint German (as cited by Baader) reads as follows: "Höre mein Bruder: Gott sprach in Mose: Du sollst dir kein Bildniss machen einiges Gottes, weder im Himmel, auf Erden, noch in Etwas; anzudeuten, dass Er kein Bild sei, auch keine Stätte zu einem Sitze bedürfe und man ihn nirgend an einem Orte suchen solle, als nur in seinem geformten ausgesprochenen Worte, als im Bilde Gottes, nemlich im Menschen selber, wie geschrieben steht: das Wort ist dir nahe, nemlich in deinem Munde und in deinem Herzen. Und ist das der nächste Weg zu Gott, dass das Bild Gottes in sich selber allen eingemodelten Bildern ersinke, und alle Bilder, Disputate und Streite in sich verlasse und an eigenem Wollen, Begehren und Meinen verzage und sich bloss allein in das ewig Eine, als in die lautere einige Liebe Gottes versenke und vertraue, welche er nach des menschen Fall in Christo in die Menschheit hat wieder eingeführt".
25 References to Heavenly Sophia in Baader's works are very numerous. Even the scores of references listed on pp. 525–32 of the index volume (BAADER: *Sämtliche Werke*, volume 16) constitute but a partial listing; the bulk of this material is directly or indirectly connected with the work of Jacob Böhme. E. BENZ: *Adam. Der Mythus vom Urmenschen*, Munich (Otto Wilhelm Barth) 1955, offers a considerable amount of bibliographical information on the subject. Gottfried Arnold, partly for his hymns to Sophia but especially for his systematic work entitled *Das Geheimnis der göttlichen Sophia oder Weisheit*, is of particular importance in the tradition of speculation about Sophia. E. BENZ: *Adam. Der Mythus vom Urmenschen*, p. 123, credits him with having had "the greatest share in collecting and passing on the legacy of Sophia-lore for the whole realm of European mysticism".
26 Though not a person in God, Sophia exercises a personal function with respect to created beings: "just as a messenger has no selfhood in relation to his master, but he does have one in the area in which he acts as representative of his master" (2, 209;

"fourth person" in the trinity, the personal Godhead reveals itself through her. She is the "organ" of God and the formative idea in accordance with which he acts (2,288; 9,24). Sophia is "the mirror and the eye of God or the first idea of God" (15,447), the counterpart to Plato's Idea, the Hebrew Sophia, the Maja of India, and Jacob Böhme's *Magie* (9,182; see also 9,219). Sophia is called "the matrix of all primitive patterns" (4,200) and "heavenly Virgin" (8,91; 13,186); but she is not to be confused with Mary, Christ's mother (15,449). God's power is an instrument of his wisdom (Sophia) (2,247), which mediates all of God's actions. The most important thing about the Sophia of God is that she is the image of the *entire Godhead*, as the Son is the image of the Father (2,247; 7,105).[27] Because Sophia stands on such an exalted level, and is untainted with creatureliness, Böhme and Baader refer to her as "the Virgin", a name they adopted from Apocalypse 14,4 to designate a state of particularly elevated purity and sublimity (8,91; 13,186).[28]

4,311 fn.; 4,351; 10,13, 268). Thus, we find Sophia acting in a personal way in this instance: "For of course man cannot by himself bring the Idea to himself through magic or superstition, but the Idea is able to come to him freely . . ." (4,92 fn.; see also 14,422). See note 14 above.

27 On Sophia as the image of the deity in general, see BAADER: *Sämtliche Werke* 8,176; 13,190; 14,158, 203, 432, 434, 438, 442ff., 444, 447; see also F. HOFFMANN: *Vorhalle zur spekulativen Lehre Franz Baaders*, pp. 134, 137.

28 With respect to the relationship of Sophia to nature, Baader distinguishes three moments: Sophia can stand above nature, or begin to penetrate it, or have actually penetrated it. He calls these three moments magical, lively, and bodily (4,279ff.; 9,24ff.). Seen in reverse perspective – i.e., the relationship of nature to Idea – nature may be outside the Idea, or in the process of being penetrated by it, or, finally, completely penetrated by it and mastered by it. Baader calls these three moments (in Böhme's terms) the phases of darkness, fire, and light (2,226; 4,393). The first and third moments in the process consist of triads: the "darkness triad" and the "light triad", which are connected by fire, the middle moment. Altogether, these two triads plus the middle moment make up the seven natural forms (*Naturgestalten*) (13,84). On this subject, see H. BRINTON: *The Mystic Will*, London (G. Allen and Unwin) 1931, chapter 5, "From Nature to God. The Problem of Evolution", pp. 131–68, and chapter 6, "From God to Nature. The Problem of Emanation", pp. 169–204; A. WHITE and W. P. SWAINSON: *Three Famous Mystics. St. Martin, Jacob Böhme and Swedenborg*, Philadelphia (David McKay) 1940, pp. 99–103. Sophia acts in and through fire or lightning, which effects a radical transformation in the "darkness triad". It becomes the "light triad" or the "water triad", which is characterized by love, joy, and being (*Liebe, Freude und Wesen*). (See also 9,240; 13,84.) Böhme always envisions Sophia's action in nature as "fiery". In changing the forms of condensation, repulsion, and rotation (which mark the "dark" triad) into the forms of love, joy, and being, Sophia's action is a "fiery" one. Disorderly motion of the first triad is replaced by calm and regular motion of the second; hunger and consumption of the first triad give way to fruitfulness and satiety in the second (3,401ff.). Böhme's very difficult nature speculation also echoes in his idea of God. For example: in God

In the context of this study, the first thing to notice is the close connection between wisdom and love postulated by Baader in developing his notion of heavenly Sophia. The same connection is found in the thought of those mystics whose work Baader read and on whom, in part, he based his own thinking. Thus, he cites St. Martin:

God thinks eternally and wills that we also think with him eternally, so that there will be a proper balance. God loves and penetrates eternal wisdom eternally – that wisdom which is the true spirit of things, the law and measure of their existence; and he wills that we also should love that eternal wisdom and penetrate it as he does, etc.

Baader then comments:

Wisdom is the expression of God, according to J. Böhme. The universal spirit is Sophia, just as the mirror of the latter is nature. What is sought after is marriage with primitive thought, which is the primitive spirit (Sophia). To think is to beget the spirit (thought), to love is to enter into and fulfill that thought. The soul loves and thinks its thought. What the spirit (as distinct from God and nature) means, then, is Wisdom as *Esprit des choses*,[29] her measure and her active regularity (*ihr Maass und ihre active Regularität*). We also should love this spirit and penetrate it eternally, in order that we might know God's will (*Verlangen*) and disseminate it.
. . . God eternally loves to realize the fruits of his Wisdom (his Spirit). We too should realize these fruits of the Spirit (Wisdom), which we uncover through our will (*Verlangen*) . . . (12,347–48)

Here, we again encounter the same theme explored in Chapter 2: i.e., the intimate bond between love and knowledge. Popularly, love is said to be blind. Baader's conception, however, by no means excludes understanding and vision; rather, it presupposes them. He would no more want understanding without love than he would want love without understanding. (See 12,416.) In this vein, he notes:

From this relationship of light or concept to feeling, it follows that if someone says that concept destroys feeling, one should understand that the (true) concept, freeing feeling from its limitation and impurity, elevates it to the power of something of general validity. Consequently, annulment (*Aufheben*), in this case, is elevation (*Emporheben*); preservation expresses fulfillment.

there is also a negative triad (the "nature-center"), which always remains closed and hidden, while the positive triad in God (the "life-center") is always open and manifest. Böhme seems to require running contrasts on principle, inasmuch as he recognizes no kind of being without its opposite: manifestation can take place only through hiddenness (2,53 fn.; 2,73 fn.).

29 Baader refers here to the title of the work on which he is commenting: ST. MARTIN: *De l'Esprit des Choses ou Coup-d'Oeil Philosophique sur la Nature des Êtres et sur l'Objet de leur Existence,* Paris 1800. (See also 12,261.)

Thus, Heavenly *Eros* wears no blindfold over her eyes; on the contrary, only earthly *Cupido* does, ambiguous in its origins and saddled from the start with an abhorrence of light (*Photophobie*) . . . (9,11ff; see also 7,414 fn.)

In fact, "the excellence of Heavenly Eros consists in the fact that, whereas [earthly Eros] is blind, she is clairvoyant" (4,178; see also 10,286). Baader regarded separation of "light and love" in man as something foreign to his natural state. One aspect of the original androgynous state from which man fell is precisely the union of light with love:

The concept of the redeemer of man can, therefore, be no other than that of one who, through inner contact, releases him from this division and strain and resolves his tensions in substantial unity (*Einwesigkeit*); inasmuch as he frees man's heart from bonds of darkness and his head from its link with coldness and thus, as Heros and Eros, he at once restores an original androgynous essential unity of love and light in man again. (10,6; see also 4,352ff.; 9,322 fn., 326)

Baader's favorite whipping boys in this connection were Jacobi and Rousseau, for their one-sided overemphasis on feeling, or Descartes and the rationalists generally, for their one-sided stress on reason. (See, for example, 1,90, 166; 2,494; 4,165; 15,643.)

It must be noted that Baader's idea of the heavenly Sophia, though generally uniform and consistent, varies at times, especially with reference to her relationship to Christ. In almost all texts that mention her, Sophia is the image of the entire Godhead. On occasion, however, Baader seems to identify her with Christ, the second person of the trinity, the God-man. For example, among the glosses he wrote on *De trinitate ac mysteriis Christi Alcuini Levitae libri tres,* we find: "In the holy trinity, there is not one substance similar to another, but rather the substance of the Father, the Son, and the Holy Spirit is one and the same"; and then, "in this sense, the Son is not the brightness of the substance [see Hebrews 1,3] as God's [Son] but as the Son of Man or Sophia" (14,436). Shortly thereafter we find the phrase: "Christ, who is the wisdom of God – as son of Man" (14,438). Three pages later, Baader speaks of "Sophia – with her was Mary blessed", which, in the context, could apply either to Christ or to the Holy Spirit or to Sophia as image of the "whole God". Soon thereafter (14,445), Baader cites the following passage from Alcuin: *Nec alius est, per quem omnia creata sunt, alius qui creatus est homo, idem ipse creator et creatura* (It is not one person through whom all things were made and another person who was made man; the same one is creator and creature). Baader adds: "We have, then, identity of creature and creator (i.e., Sophia)".

The discrepancy is perhaps more apparent than real. It must be conceded, first of all, that Baader is rather loose with his use of terms. Nonetheless, the difficulty can be reduced, if not fully resolved, by remembering: (1) that there is a close analogy between the role that the Word, the second person of the trinity, exercises within the trinity itself, and the role that Sophia exercises as representative of the triune God: as the Word is the Father's knowledge and love of himself and − in the person of Christ the perfect revelation of the Father (or of God) − so Sophia is the wisdom and love of the entire triune God; and (2) that in becoming man, the Word took upon himself a role with respect to man which was representative of the whole Godhead: i.e., of Sophia, image of God. As the ancient trinitarian formula has it: *Omnia opera ad extra communia sunt tribus personis* (all activity outside the Godhead is common to the three persons). Thus, Baader writes in a comment on St. Martin:

Spiritual incarnation preceded the real one. At the moment of the fall, Jesus became the Christ − by entering into and marrying Sophia (the primitive image of man). The heart of God assumed the form of man in order to penetrate our altered image spiritually and to restore it. The heart of God was, therefore, conceived in this primitive image of man and incorporated with it in his eternal love or in his eternal wisdom, which is eternally a Virgin, though not a human one. (12,360; see also 7,231)[30]

Because of this union between Christ and Sophia, in the context of the redemptive work of Christ, Baader finds it proper to speak of Sophia as "bride of the Son" and as "man's image and glory" (14,141ff.; see also 1,230; 3,395ff.). In fact, "Sophia's (the image of God's) coming to creaturehood is the goal of creation" (14,445).

A key distinction to be made in connection with this problem (i.e., the relationship between Sophia and Christ) is similar to that which must be made between *Logos enthetos* (posited Word) and *Logos ekthetos* (exposed Word). Baader explains in *Vorlesungen über Societätsphilosophie* (number 14) that *Logos enthetos* is the active element in the trinity and *Logos ekthetos* the reactive element. "The identity of active and reactive elements", i.e., of the Son (with Father and Spirit) with Sophia, "makes up the mystery of self-formative life" (14,140ff.). One of

30 Baader places much stress on the depth of love God manifests in restoring Sophia to man: "When man fell away from God, when, by averting his will from the Idea and failing to enter into it, he failed to establish a bond with the Idea, she departed from him and his heavenly being made in her [likeness] vanished. So there was no other way for him to recover the image of God . . . except through new divine action that was even more profound than the act of creation. It was an action through which the creative Word or Light-principle, which remains eternally in the trinity, once again returned back to her the creaturely being that had faded away and vanished from the Idea . . . In that way, as *Heros* and *Eros*, he wedded creature to Idea indissolubly or sacramentally. J. Böhme is right, then, when he says . . . that this more deeply conceived divine act . . . as an act of saving and restoring love, is the absolutely greatest miracle, one that is even greater than the act of creation itself . . ." (BAADER: *Sämtliche Werke* 9,26; see also 2,104, 224; 3,301ff., 307ff., 378ff.; 4,281–92, 279, 351fn.; 10,6). This is why Baader calls Christ "incarnate love" (4,238).

the *Religionsphilosophische Aphorismen* (number 36) deals *ex professo* with the "relationship of Logos to Sophia in God". In that brief statement, Baader denies tautological identity between *Logos* and *Sophia* and also denies that Sophia constitutes a "fourth person" in the trinity. He speaks here of Sophia or Wisdom as "helper" (*adjutor*) of the creative Word (10,342–43).[31] A short passage in the *Vorlesungen über eine künftige Theorie des Opfers oder des Cultus* (number 2) helps to clarify Baader's position. He recalls the fact that the fall of man

affected God profoundly (*Gott zu Herzen ging*). Thus, at the moment of this fall, in which man fell away from the Idea of God and the natural disposition for reproducing it in him vanished, Jesus (the outlet and activity of the heart of God) entered into the primitive image of man, which existed eternally before God, and became the Christ: i.e., spiritually man.*
*[footnote] *Logos* became *Sophia*. (7,289–90)

Baader scores Tertullian for confusing the eternal birth of Jesus as *Logos enthetos* from the Father with his extra-trinitarian activity as *Logos ekthetos*. (See 1,406.)[32]

The notion of Heavenly Sophia is inseparable in Baader's thought from the idea of man as God's image and from loving activity in every form. Sophia's presence in man implants the divine image. The analogy used is the standard producer-product model:

For, just as man fashions everything he makes (posits) in and according to his idea . . . which he, however, does not create but which is inwardly present to him as uncreated and unborn, so too Scripture says that God created man in and according to his (God's) uncreated image. (9,24)

---

31 In a letter to "Dr. S.", dated May 22, 1830, Baader explains his position on the *Logos enthetos* and *Logos ekthetos* as follows: "Modern theologians have completely ignored the doctrine of *Logos enthetos* and *Logos ekthetos, verbum aeterne genitum* (eternally begotten Word) and *aeterne Sophia factum* (Word eternally made Sophia), and since they no longer understand the latter, they also no longer understand the nexus between *verbum genitum* (begotten Word) and *caro (homo) factum* (the incarnation). Now, since it is common knowledge to theologians that the *caro factio verbi* (incarnation) came about through the whole trinity but, nonetheless, that only the second Person became man, so also they should have known that although the *forma (Idea, Sophia, Logos ekthetos) in Deo a tota sancta trinitate aeterne facta . . . ad solam tamen filii Dei (Logos enthetos, verbum genitum) personam spectat. Nam genitor, genitus et procedens simul aeterne faciunt (non generant, non creant) sophiam, exemplar omnis creaturalis factionis . . .* (the form [*Idea, Sophia, Logos ekthetos*] in God is made eternally by the whole holy trinity . . . but still it refers only to the person of the Son of God [*Logos enthetos*, begotten Word]. For begetter, begotten, and one who proceeds, eternally and simultaneously produce [not generate, or create] Sophia, the pattern for all creaturely producing . . .)" (*Sämtliche Werke* 15,463).
32 The entire subject of *Logos enthetos* and *Logos ekthetos* in Baader's work is extremely complex. See the following texts: BAADER: *Sämtliche Werke* 2,524ff., 528; 3,382, 406ff.; 4,434; 7,235 fn.; 8,79; 9,187; 10,294ff.; 12,167, 291, 311; 13,71, 168; 14,136ff., 140, 146, 442ff.; 15,446.

Baader goes on in this passage to distinguish three moments – magical, animated, and corporeal (*magisch . . . lebhaft . . . leibhaft*) – into which one can differentiate the presence of idea or image, and he applies the distinction to the divine Idea too. He singles out man as one who has the specific function of giving corporate form or dwelling-place to the spirit of God (not the Holy Spirit of the trinity): that is, Sophia. Sophia is called the Virgin, because she does not give birth to anything corporeal (*nichts Fassliches*) (9,26). In confirming God's image within himself, man thus "provides a body" to Sophia.

Now, if this creation was to attain its second or chief goal, i.e., that of serving as workshop of that eternal "embodiment" (*Beleibung*), it required the rising of a second sun, which would mediate it (as the external region) with the divine sun, the rising of a divine star: i.e., the image of God . . . Man was created to this image in order that by uniting himself to it in marriage he might give to it the same qualities of body and life that all of creation in its own way and through mediation of this incarnate image should beget. But, as is well known, man did not fulfill this function. Instead of uniting in marriage with the heavenly Virgin . . . he married the external . . . wife. Therefore, God had to perform this function in, through, and for man, and himself make that image substantive – *verbum caro factum* – in order that the spirit of love (the soul-spirit) (*der Liebe Geist* [*Seelengeist*]) should have a body . . . (2,418)

Both Böhme and Baader speak of the intimate relationship between Sophia (God's image) and man as a marriage bond.[33] Through the incarnate Word of God, the second person of the trinity, say Böhme and Baader, heavenly Wisdom becomes a bride for man: "He [Christ] brought no soul from the holy trinity . . . but rather the heavenly Virgin was the soul in the holy trinity and he brought her along with him to be a bride for our soul . . ." (4,351 fn.; see also 14,446). Christ recouped what was lost when man rejected God's image through his sin:

. . . God (the God-Word, not God's word) brought the uncreated heavenly essence (in Mary's seed) into the vanished human and joined the two together (indissolubly) in the image of God, which took soul and body unto itself from Mary's seed . . . (15,583)

Baader and Böhme use the symbolism of marriage copiously to describe unions of various kinds. For example, they put Sophia in the same relationship to *Logos* that St. Paul (Ephesians 5, 21ff.) puts the Church in relationship to Christ: i.e., a marriage relationship. In the same place, they characterize the disrup-

---

33 Baader also speaks of Sophia as existing in a state of marriage with the trinity: "The Word, which is an inseparable companion of the Principle, is the expressed Word for immanent production, which [Word] as Idea, Sophia, Name, is in a state of marriage with God" (12,357). The German reads: "Das Wort, welches ein unzertrennlicher Gefährte des Princips ist, ist das ausgesprochene Wort zur immanenten Production, welches als Idea, Sophia, Name in der Ehe mit Gott ist".

tion of normal relations between the Idea and God in a creature as "adultery" (3,395 fn.; see also 1,45; 3,301; 10,296). The possibilities are many:

Man can marry in God, with God, through God, without God, and against God. Union without God is purely material. Divine marriage exists to restore the image of God *in solidum* (*solidären*). (12,361; see also 12,360; 14,235)

"Marriage", in these and similar texts, is of course not carnal but spiritual union. In the case of union with Heavenly Sophia, Baader marks the contrast between it and earthly marriage in the following couplet:

Earthly virginity perishes in man's embrace,
Heavenly [virginity] comes to be in heavenly conception. (2,225; 3,303)[34]

Heavenly Sophia is, in fact, neither male nor female (3,303; 9,211 fn.; 12,382).[35] But the separation of sexes in man[36] is directly related to man's separation from, and rejection of, his "heavenly bride", Sophia. Divorce from Sophia drastically altered the kind of "image" that best described man's state:

Separation of the sexes in man (which took place only through his "substantiation" in this lower world . . .) or the appearance of another mate, must be ascribed, then, to man's original adultery, his separation from the inborn (*eingebornen*) image of the Father: i.e., from Christ. Hence, Scripture says that with the complete return to Christ, with full restoration of this image in man as the image of the Virgin (which is neither a male nor a female image), this separation of sexes will cease, because it is precisely the immediate manifestation of this inborn image in a creature that elevates the latter above the region of visible fathers and mothers: i.e., above the region in which this manifestation takes place only mediately. (7,27 fn.)

The "marriage" referred to here is obviously not marriage in the usual everyday sense of the word. One of Baader's clearest statements about the question of "marriage" with Heavenly Sophia occurs in the sixth number of the *Vorlesungen über die Lehre Jacob Böhmes mit besonderer Beziehung auf dessen Schrift: Mysterium Magnum* (13,184ff.). After speaking of the intermediate position (between uncreated and created) in which God's image in man places him, Baader says:

One could say now, entirely in J. Böhme's spirit, that if the creature from its first beginnings (i.e., from nature) has not yet confirmed divine kinship for itself, it gains that [kinship] through

---

34 "Die ird'sche Jungfrauschaft stirbt in des Manns Umfangen,/Die himmlische entsteht im himmlischen Empfangen".
35 This characterization does not always hold true for Baader: e.g., in 12,388 he speaks of Sophia as exercising a male role. This, of course, is an analogical usage, which Baader employs to designate the active and creative role of Sophia with respect to the passive role of nature.
36 Chapter 4 deals with this problem in some detail.

its real marriage with Zeus's daughter, Pallas or the Idea. But it has happened often enough in the past, even among Christian mystics, that confused, awkward, and even unchaste notions of sexual union, in an earthly sense, have been associated with the word "marriage" and have, thereby, distorted this concept (Schwenkfeld, Weigel). J. Böhme was right, then, to use the word "Virgin", because the Idea (as virgin or maid) is and remains untouchable to the man and (as a young man) to the woman. This Virgin, as the Idea, is, in fact, born superior to both man and woman – to him as womanly and to her as manly – and so is not wife to him nor husband to her. Therefore, the Idea's approach, and even more her indwelling, brings it about that maleness in the man (as desire for the woman) and femaleness in the woman (as desire for the man) subside and vanish. The only likeness in which this Idea dwells (hence the true, immortal creature) can thus only be androgynous. The same thing must have been true in the beginning for Adam, as the first man created into and unto the image of God. Hence, the Idea, as uncreated spirit or figure, is not to be confused with the likeness fashioned after her as a creature. So also in the fall of Adam, the Virgin as the Idea departed, but the essential likeness perished. (13,185; see also 3,385 fn.; 14,439)[37]

Baader goes on to describe how Adam squandered divine kinship through his sin and how Christ restored it and brought back departed Sophia to man. He speaks again of the reasons for calling Sophia a virgin and why only Sophia, as God's image, can make man the image of God too. He speaks of the proper "disposition" man needs if he is to profit by the life God offers him. Just as a plant, having the proper fluids within itself, profits by the benevolent effect of sunshine, so the plant, lacking these fluids, will wither up under that same sunshine: blessing for one is destruction for the other. Baader concludes his lecture with a word of praise for the *philosophus teutonicus*: "J. Böhme, who deserves, *par excellence*, the name of 'philosopher', because his philosophy begins, as the word itself says, with the love of the divine Sophia, refers back to her and lives in her" (13,185-87).

The focus of interest, for our purpose, is Sophia's dominant position in Baader's understanding of the dynamics of love and the interrelationships between the sexes. It is Sophia that enables man and woman to achieve the experience of love and wonder together:

We are describing the link between man and woman here as one that effects their completion (*Ergänzung*) in Sophia, therefore, differently than Gichtel describes it.[38] They complement each other, in fact, in their *facultés admirantes and aimantes*, hence, not directly, but only because they unite themselves first to God, each of them for himself . . . Man helps woman to wonder, and

37 See F. HOFFMANN: *Vorhalle zur spekulativen Lehre Franz Baaders*, p. 133, number 9.
38 Johann Georg Gichtel (1638–1710) radically interpreted the myth of androgyny and marriage with Heavenly Sophia. Instead of viewing earthly marriage as an institution in which man and woman complement each other in the higher unity of Sophia, Gichtel considered marriage with Sophia sufficient grounds for excluding all earthly marriages and exacted strict asceticism from his followers. See E. BENZ: *Adam. Der Mythus vom Urmenschen*, pp. 101-20.

woman helps man to love and worship; hence, they complement each other mutually in their powers . . . (12,380)

Thus, no created being can exercise love in his own right or directly toward another created being. In accordance with the principle of participation (or the Center), all love is mediated through Love – i.e., through God, through his Idea: "Wisdom is the mirror of love" (12,382).[39]

Baader identifies Sophia so closely with love that he often speaks of her under the designation *Eros*. (See, for example, 14,234.) The nomenclature is very significant. Sophia is *Eros*, and *Eros* is love. Two of Baader's major essays on love are entitled: *Sätze aus der erotischen Philosophie* (4,163–78) and *Vierzig Sätze aus einer religiösen Erotik* (4,179–200). Baader's whole thought on the subject of love might be styled *Sophia-lehre*. If this appears to overemphasize the purely nominal import of the words unduly, one need only refer to number fourteen of the *Religionsphilosophische Aphorismen*. It is entitled "Schlüssel zum Verständnisse des Mysteriums der Liebe" and is one of Baader's clearest statements on the subject:

J. Böhme has shown that (and how), after man had lusted after the earthly and had become deformed and distorted from his virginal (divine) image into the image of man and woman, the Virgin (Sophia or heavenly humanity), nevertheless, presented herself or appeared like a star shining in the night (an angel or guide) to direct him in and out of his misery (out of an alien land)[40] – back to his lost homeland (Wisdom guides). This Virgin is present in every man's and every woman's soul as such a helper (aide), director, light, and leader. But, if she establishes a liaison in a special and interdependent way in a man's and woman's soul, betrothal and union of true love and marriage take place: although, in consequence of a sidereal phantasmagory (*in Folge einer siderischen Phantasmagorie*), this interdependence and identity of the Virgin (as the same inner helper and angel for both) appears to the male lover under the form of his beloved and to her under the form of her lover. Similarly, this intrusion of the Heavenly Virgin – which, due mostly to the fault (impurity, unfaithfulness, and lack of understanding) of the lovers is not permanently established by them – makes the ecstasy of love and its "magic moment" (*Silberblick*) understandable. The higher, time-transcending goal of love is, therefore, precisely this joint (*solidaire*) restoration (incarnation) in both lovers of that divine or virginal image . . . whereby they are both reborn as children of God. And just as Adam's deformation or distortion in the male and female image took place inwardly first, and then completed itself outwardly in a corporeal way . . . so now restoration of the image of God must first take place inwardly, through re-destruction of that deformation, not in external earthly life. In other words, love should help the man to perfect himself inwardly to the level of the full image of man, overcoming his incompleteness; the same holds for the woman. The upshot of this is that we cannot separate aversion

39   Sophia, as love, has in reality been the focal point of all poetry (8,176).
40   The equating of misery (*Elend*) with alienation (*in der Fremde sein*) is explained in proposition ten of Chapter 6: "The old Germans called being-in-a-foreign-land the same as being-in-misery. One who is in misery is one who has lost his mother and is confronted with an alien or step-mother . . ." (*Vierzig Sätze aus einer religiösen Erotik*, 4,187)

or the cross from the desire to love, for a man must depart with aversion from what he has entered with lust. So also, the still abstract inner manliness and womanliness that selfishly fight against love are the cross that lovers in this world have to help each other carry and tolerate. This process of love being reborn (religion) in two lovers, presented in dramatic fashion and in conflict with its adversary (for the devil is hostile to marriage or love, because he is hostile to rebirth), would, at the same time, offer something at once truer and more poetic than everything that all the poets up to now have been able to offer on the subject of love. For without exception, they have remained completely blind about the mystery of love or have had extremely cloudy vision. (10,304–06; see also 2,315; 3,307; 4,177ff.; 14,159ff.)

Baader's message is clear enough. Particularly important is the point that Sophia's aid is necessary if man is to be complete. The existence of two separate and incomplete sexes is a sign of deformation and incompleteness: "Virginity is integrity (androgyny)" (12,281; see also 3,303 fn.).[41] Baader's discussion of Sophia's activity in human love is not meant as allegory, or poetry, or fantasy, but rather simply as "the facts of the case". Baader says that the extensive passage cited above is "a key to understanding the mystery of love". In *Vom Geist und Wesen der Dinge*, Baader again addresses "the economy of love" and immediately invokes his ideas about Sophia. After making the point that uniting is divine activity and separating is devilish activity, the former requiring humility and the latter pride (1,59), Baader writes:

According to the view of the inner economy of love presented above . . . lovers would be, so to speak, simply visible servants, priests, and agents of a higher *Eros* ("God is love") who makes his presence known invisibly in their midst as soon as they gather in his name. One could rightly say, then, that lovers do not so much love one another mutually, as rather that a Higher Being loves himself in and through them. [This Being] simply dismembers and divides himself, so to speak, in single individuals so as to be able personally to touch, find, and feel himself. So the common notion of love would be erroneous, for it says that in love there is mere exchange of selfhood between lovers, that lover and beloved go out of themselves and into one another. In fact, in that way these lovers would only be exchanging the limitations of their narrow existence, but the two of them would not, as the fact shows, be able to rise above themselves to freer, heavenlike existence. That is possible only through mutual self-discovery and suspension in a higher third [Being]. (1,61; see also 4,165, 170; 5,263ff.)

Hence, two lovers do not love each other directly on a one-to-one basis; their love is not simply a personal or an interpersonal affair. They are, in fact, "in" love: i.e., they are both immersed in a superior presence, the "higher third" who is the Heavenly Virgin, Sophia – God himself. All true love is grounded in the image of God, and that is why it is "a false and misleading notion that several ascetics have maintained when they describe love of God, the Creator,

41   On androgyny, see Chapter 4.

163

as something incompatible with love of creatures, so that one would have to consider God as just one more object of love alongside of creatures" (5,263). The principle of the "higher third" applies, likewise, in the area of giving and receiving. These actions are the essence of love; therefore, they cannot take place directly, but only in virtue of the higher Eros or Sophia:

In mind and in spirit, one possesses and obtains only what one gives. The giver is, therefore, just as obliged to give thanks to the recipient as the latter is to the former: i.e., both thank God who is the same in the giver and the recipient. In this blessed knowledge that it is one and the same [Person] who gives and receives in us, who seeks and finds in us, who listens and who prays in, through, and with us, who is light and eye [to us] – in this blessed knowledge, I say, the abstract, poor I and Thou (or not-I) dissolves itself in the rich and self-sufficient We. (15,476; see also Chapter 6, propositions 3 and 13)

It is an essential part of Baader's thought that there is constitutionally and metaphysically no way in which a creature can escape from God, the source of its being. What Baader says about God's image or Sophia in man is also regulated by that larger principle. He says often, as we have seen, that Sophia "departs" from man because he has rejected her through sin. This means, in fact, that Sophia has departed under the guise of *love*: those who reject God's love are condemned to come under the control of his naked power.[42] Thus, we read:

J. Böhme says that as soon as God's image (Sophia) vanished from man, [she] inserted herself into the light of his life (*selbe sich in seines Lebens Licht einsetzte*), calling out to him and warning him. With that she would become *Nomos* (Law) and remain such until she was brought back again to man by the *Logos*. (14,424)

Baader's understanding of what kind of activity God exercises with relation to the world is consistent with his convictions regarding the nature of God. Since God is love, it is only proper that his image, Heavenly Sophia, should also be

---

42 J. HAMBERGER, editor of the thirteenth volume of BAADER: *Sämtliche Werke*, offers the following comment after the fifteenth lecture of *Aus Privatvorlesungen über Jacob Böhmes Lehre mit besonderer Beziehung auf dessen Schrift: Von der Gnadenwahl*: " . . . The fatalist proves nothing in favor of the existence of fate but only something about the perversity of his heart, to which God cannot reveal himself as a free spirit and as effective love. The atheist proves nothing in favor of the non-existence of God but only something about the depth of confusion of his will and understanding, to which God cannot reveal himself as what he is, as absolute and world-transcending (*weltfreier*) Spirit. The good man experiences God as effective love, the evil man as judge and punisher. God is love in both modes of manifestation, but man is aware of that only in the first case. If he begins to be aware of it or to grasp it in the second mode, he has inwardly already made the first step on his return to God" (13,110 fn.; see also 12,98, 206 on love and punishment).

love, and that man's duty to establish this image in himself should be essentially a labor of love.

Baader's whole conception and emphasis is radically different from that developed and favored, for example, by Kant. Kant's entire ethical scheme enshrined Law and the Categorical Imperative as its centerpiece. For Kant, God was immeasurably distant from the center of action, man's autonomous self; love and prayer found no place at all in his schema. It is no wonder that Baader could not remain a camp-follower of Kant for long. Again, Baader was worlds removed from the machine-God of the deists, not only because mechanistic constructs were so contrary to his proclivity toward the organic in general, but also, and especially, because it was utterly foreign to his experience of a personal God whom he knew as life and love. In his convictions about the nature of God, he was not much closer to the pantheistic nature-God of Schelling, the ever-incomplete idea-God of Hegel, or Fichte's apotheosis of the ego.

The radical differences between Baader's idea of God, and those of these other thinkers, had, of course, profoundly far-reaching consequences in their respective conceptions of the nature of man. Baader was the only major thinker of his time for whom it was literally true that "love is what makes the world go around". For him, it was Love that made the world, Love from which and for which the world was made, and Love that points not only to the source but also to the destiny of man. For man was made in the image of Love.

Chapter 4
Androgyny and Marriage

Mircea Eliade has shown that the concept of "totality" or "coincidence of opposites" embodies a large and varied complex of mystical rites, legends, and beliefs.[1] The phenomena he describes are not only characteristic of Western countries, but of Eastern ones as well. They appear in ancient times and modern times, in primitive societies and sophisticated societies alike. More than 2500 years ago, Heraclitus concluded that "God is day and night, winter and summer, war and peace, satiety and hunger – all the opposites, this is the meaning".[2] Two millennia later, Nicholas of Cusa similarly judged the best description of God to be *coincidentia oppositorum*. In such works as *Mysterium Conjunctionis* and *Psychologie der Übertragung*, Carl Gustave Jung has argued in our own century that totality and unification of opposites is at the heart of all human psychic activity.[3]

Eliade explains that symbols, myths, legends and beliefs reveal man to be profoundly dissatisfied with "the human condition": i.e., with its incompleteness and division, with its partial character and diremption. Man seems to be aware of a deep fissure in himself and the world, not necessarily a "Fall" in the Judaeo-Christian sense, but some kind of fatal disaster that took place in pre-

---

1   M. ELIADE: *Mephistopheles and the Androgyne*, New York (Sheed and Ward) 1965, pp. 78–124.
2   M. ELIADE: *Mephistopheles and the Androgyne*, pp. 78–124
3   C. G. JUNG: *Mysterium Conjunctionis*, in: H. READ, M. FORDHAM, and G. ADLER (Eds.): *The Collected Works of C. G. Jung*, volume 14, New York (H. Wolff) 1963; the volume is subtitled: "An Inquiry into the Separation and Synthesis of Psychic Opposites in Alchemy". Material found on pp. 47, 373ff., 405, and Chapter 5, "Adam and Eve" – plus references to "Christ", "hermaphrodite", "lapis", and "mercurius" which appear throughout the book – are particularly relevant to the subject androgyny. Jung discusses a work by G. KOEPGEN: *Die Gnosis des Christentums*, Salzburg 1939, which posits the androgynous character of Christ and of Christianity. This book received an episcopal *imprimatur*, but it was later placed on the Index. (See C. JUNG: *Mysterium Conjunctionis*, pp. 373ff.)

historical times. Rites and myths reveal "a nostalgia for a lost paradise, a nostalgia for a paradoxical state in which contraries exist side by side without conflict and multiplications form aspects of a mysterious Unity".[4] The "mystery of the Whole" or of totality forms an integral part of the human drama. Man has always tried to overcome the limitations inherent in the human condition by aspiring to become some kind of "total" being. At the same time, he fears losing his identity in some nondescript monadic mass. Before philosophers ever saw fit to frame the problem of the one and the many in conceptual terms, or to concern themselves formally with the problem of "alienation", man felt the issue in his very bones.

Androgyny: Background and Meaning of the Myth in Baader's Work

The myth of androgyny[5] is a myth of integration, one whose object is to recapture a lost primordial totality. The best-known ancient source of this myth is Plato's *Symposium*, a dialogue in which the philosopher describes primeval man as sexually complete (undivided): i.e., androgynous. In the thought of Philo of Alexandria, the neo-Platonists, the neo-Pythagoreans, and various alchemical traditions (see, for example, Hermes Trismegistus), "human perfection is imagined as an unbroken unity".[6] Many passages in the apocryphal writings of the

---

4   M. ELIADE: *Mephistopheles and the Androgyne*, p. 122.
5   The most important studies devoted to Franz von Baader's thought concerning androgyny are: E. BENZ: *Adam. Der Mythus vom Urmenschen*, Munich (Otto Wilhelm Barth) 1955, pp. 209–36; F. GIESE: *Der romantische Charakter*, in: *Die Entwicklung des Androgynenproblems in der Frühromantik*, Langensalza (Wendt and Klauwell) 1919, especially pp. 350–93; H. GRASSL (Ed.): *Franz von Baader. Über Liebe, Ehe und Kunst*, Munich (Kösel) 1953, pp. 232ff. In general, all major studies of Baader's thought include sections on the subject: see, for example, J. SAUTER: *Baader und Kant*, Jena (Gustav Fischer) 1928, pp. 449–66, especially 463ff.; D. BAUMGARDT: *Franz von Baader und die philosophische Romantik*, Halle/Saale (Max Niemeyer) 1927, pp. 295ff., 463ff.; E. SUSINI: *Franz von Baader et le romantisme mystique*, Paris (J. Vrin) 1942, volume 2, pp. 547ff., especially. 567ff. See also H. SPRECKELMEYER: *Die philosophische Deutung des Sündenfalls bei Franz von Baader*, Würzburg 1938, pp. 262ff. A fine study of the general problem is found in M. ELIADE: *Mephistopheles and the Androgyne*, especially pp. 98–111. Among P. KLUCKHOHN'S many valuable contributions to research in the field of German Romanticism, his comprehensive study *Die Auffassung der Liebe in der Literatur des 18. Jahrhunderts und in der deutschen Romantik,* Tübingen (Max Niemeyer) ³1966 is especially noteworthy in this regard; see especially pp. 542–53. See also note 3 above. Additional bibliographical references may be found in several of these works, especially those of ELIADE, KLUCKHOHN, SPRECKELMEYER, and JUNG.
6   M. ELIADE: *Mephistopheles and the Androgyne*, p. 107.

early Christian Church speak of primal man's being "neither male nor female". In addition, a number of *midrashic* texts describe Adam as an androgynous figure, while several Christian Gnostic sects made the androgynous ideal a central doctrine. John Scotus Erigena, following Maximus the Confessor, also affirmed the original androgynous condition of man. Christians who believed this myth made much of St. Paul's statement in Galatians (3,28): "There is neither Jew nor Greek, there is neither bond nor free, there is neither male nor female: for you all are one in Christ Jesus".[7]

The idea of universal non-differentiation of the sexes involves the conception that "perfection – and, therefore, Being – ultimately consists of a unity-totality". This ideal was taken to be so certain that the notion of God, or ultimate reality, was equated with *indivisible totality*. Indeed, there are many cults which recognize gods who are androgynous, a notion "which is explicable if one takes account of the traditional conception that one cannot be anything *par excellence* unless one is at the same time its opposite . . ." Thus, there is a mythical tradition not only of human androgyny but also of divine androgyny.[8]

In the late Renaissance, the myth of androgyny received new emphasis at the hands of Leone Ebreo, a scholar instrumental in mediating cabbalistic lore to the philosophy of the Italian Renaissance. In *Dialoghi d'Amore*, he linked Plato's myth with the biblical story of the Fall of man, an event which he saw as creating a cleavage in primal man. Jacob Böhme (1575–1624) too was a major exponent of the biblical interpretation of the myth. In this regard, and in his entire position on Heavenly Sophia, he was followed by such English Böhmeans as John Pordage and Jane Leade. Böhme also provided a foundation for further development of the myth in the thought of Johann Georg Gichtel (1638–1710) and Gottfried Arnold (1666–1714).[9]

The myth of androgyny spread rapidly in the German states, largely because the *Berleburger Bible* (1726–42) – edited by Johann Heinrich Haug (died 1753) – was widely used by Pietist and Spiritualist Conventicles all over Germanic central Europe. Consequently, it became a chief conduit of the myth to German Romanticism and German Idealism. Friedrich Christoph Oetinger (1702–82) also played a notable role in propagating the myth. As founder of the theosophical branch of Pietism and a rediscoverer of Jacob Böhme, he was instrumental in introducing Böhme's thought into the milieu of German Romanticism and Idealism. Both Schelling and Baader were influenced by him. Next, Michael Hahn (1758–1819) took up the myth of androgyny. Though he

7   M. ELIADE: *Mephistopheles and the Androgyne*, pp. 103ff.
8   M. ELIADE: *Mephistopheles and the Androgyne*, pp. 108ff.
9   E. BENZ: *Adam. Der Mythus vom Urmenschen*, pp. 31ff.

never specifically identified himself with Böhme, still, their ideas are very similar. His views were also close to those of Gichtel: both advocated strict sexual asceticism (including celibacy) and established separatist communities. Emmanuel Swedenborg (1688–1772) and Louis Claude de Saint-Martin (1743–1803) were two foreigners who helped propagate the myth in the German states. Indeed, St. Martin probably had a larger influence on early nineteenth-century German philosophy than any other foreign thinker of the time.[10]

Although the myth of androgyny is a persistent one in human history, it remains largely among the underground streams which meander through the history of ideas. It is perpetually on the verge of being forgotten, yet it never entirely leaves human consciousness. Fritz Giese has shown how the myth experienced a resurgence in German Romanticism, after a period of near-oblivion.[11] Antecedents of this resurgence may be found in literary developments associated with the *Sturm und Drang* movement. In works of Heinse (*Ardinghello*), Brentano (*Godwi*), Herder, Wieland, and Fichte, woman began to assume a position of equal importance with man. As her star rose, polarization between "herself" and "himself" became more manifest.

Winckelmann's work in ancient Greek art, particularly insofar as it dealt with hermaphroditic figures, was another factor. Wilhelm von Humboldt addressed the theme in his youthful *Über die männliche und weibliche Form* (1795), a work that stresses divine androgyny. Friedrich Schlegel's *Über die Diotima* attacked exclusive emphasis on either the masculine or the feminine. Both Schlegel and Schleiermacher did extensive work in establishing a psychology of the sexes, one which identified a new womanly type that was a true counterpart to the male. In addition, some of the better-known Romantic women – e.g. Caroline Schlegel/Schelling, Bettina von Arnim, and Dorothea Schlegel – presented flesh-and-blood examples of the new female ideal.

Another way in which Romanticism attempted to address the differences between the sexes is related to "progress" made in the natural sciences, and in the philosophy of nature, toward the end of the eighteenth century. (Interestingly, mystical ideas have often been associated with advances in philosophy of nature.[12]) Experiments dealing with "animal magnetism" or Galvanism called attention to the fact that positive and negative electrical poles exist in all living things, as well as in metals. For various reasons, neither Schelling nor Novalis (both active in the natural sciences and in philosophy of nature) engaged in

10 On all of these figures, from Ebreo to St. Martin, see: E. BENZ: *Adam. Der Mythus vom Urmenschen.*
11 F. GIESE: *Der romantische Charakter* is the most complete work on the problem of androgyny in early Romanticism.
12 F. GIESE: *Der romantische Charakter*, p. 289.

speculation about the myth of androgyny to any notable extent.[13] Novalis's friend Johann Wilhelm Ritter, on the other hand, outlined an entire philosophy of androgyny in his *Fragmente aus dem Nachlass eines jungen Physikers.* He envisaged future humanity as androgynous, just as Christ was. Eliade notes that Ritter uses alchemical language, "a sign that alchemy was one of the German Romantics' sources for their revival of the myth of the androgyne".[14] Philipp Otto Runge, the Romantic painter, concerned himself to an extent with the myth of androgyny, but his was an "androgyny of death": i.e., a fulfillment that came about only through death.[15]

Questions associated with the relationship of the sexes became something of a Romantic preoccupation, especially in the earlier years. It is easy to see how Paul Kluckhohn could claim that "it was a mystical philosopher who led the Romantic conception of love to its peak – Franz von Baader. One can call him, in fact, the 'philosopher of love' ".[16] In particular, there is no other Romantic figure who developed the myth of androgyny to the extent that Baader did. An important part of Baader's contribution to German Idealism and German Romanticism is connected with it:

Through Franz von Baader, the idea of androgyny became a leading theme of philosophical anthropology and philosophy of religion in German Idealism. All of ancient speculation on androgyny was summed up in Baader. From him, it took effect in universal fashion, not only in German – but also in French, English, and Russian – philosophy of religion, and, thanks to

---

13   F. GIESE: *Der romantische Charakter,* pp. 295ff., explains that Schelling's profound interest in the generic notion of polarity, an interest developed in his philosophy of nature and the organic, led him to view the polarity of sexes as a relatively minor and uninteresting particularization of a law that pervades all of nature. As for Novalis, his "magic idealism" (pp. 308ff.) led to a position in which reality, even personal identities, was so transposed and metamorphosed that total relativism resulted. And the relativism was so total that it even entailed the nullification of sexual differentiation. He began with intense love for Sophie, transferred his love for Sophie to Julie, whom he married. In the process, however, he ceased loving any particular person; rather, he chose to love an "ideal type" of woman who functioned as a symbol of the absolute for him. In light of the relativity of all earthly things, it ceased to matter who or what was the bearer of that symbol. Thus, toward the end of his brief life, Novalis ceased to preoccupy himself seriously with the subject of sexual differentation, though this theme had interested him a great deal earlier in his career. F. GIESE: *Der romantische Charakter,* pp. 308–50, examines the problem of Novalis at some length .

14   M. ELIADE: *Mephistopheles and the Androgyne,* p. 101. See C. G. JUNG: *Mysterium Conjunctionis,* for a thorough treatment of the relationship of alchemy to the myth of androgyny.

15   F. GIESE: *Der romantische Charakter,* p. 358.

16   P. KLUCKHOHN: *Die Auffassung der Liebe in der Literatur des 18. Jahrhunderts und in der deutschen Romantik,* p. 542.

Baader's close relations with Romanticism in Munich, in the great poets of Romanticism. Franz von Baader is the most significant re-discoverer of ancient mystical and theosophical traditions in German intellectual history . . .[17]

Bizarre though the myth of androgyny may seem, there is no doubt that it responds to some deeply felt human need. Nicholas Berdyaev goes so far as to say: "The myth of androgyny is the only great anthropological myth which can serve as a base for an anthropological metaphysics".[18]

A number of Baader scholars have observed that Baader's letter to Jacobi, dated June 16, 1796 (15,165), touches on the theme of sexual androgyny, thus making him the first of the Romantics to take up the motif.[19] It is interesting to note that in a letter to J. M. Sailer, dated March 6, 1787, Baader speaks of man as androgynous, not in a sexual sense, but as a composite being made up of both eternal and temporal elements.[20]

The concept of androgyny is at once an anthropological notion, concerning the combination of male and female characteristics in primal man, and a theological-ontolgical one, concerning man's relationship to God as disclosed by the combination of sexual characteristics in primal man. Two main ideas are embodied in the overall concept: (1) The primordial tension of existence is male-female tension, the tautness between an active and aggressive male spontaneity and a receptive-conserving female reflectiveness. This tension obtains even on the level of mind and spirit, though in a "sublated" sense.[21] (2) The separation of these two complementary principles into a plurality of individual persons is evidence of an essential "fault" in the cosmos as a whole. Baader sees the present state of sexual separation as the most manifest sign of fundamental disorder in the world.[22]

17 E. BENZ: Adam. Der Mythus vom Urmenschen, p. 209.
18 N. BERDYAEV: Von der Bestimmung des Menschen, German translation by I. Schor, Bern-Leipzig 1935, p. 92. E. BENZ: Adam. Der Mythus vom Urmenschen, cites this text immediately after the title-page; H. SPRECKELMEYER: Die philosophische Deutung des Sündenfalls bei Franz von Baader, p. 262 fn., also cites it.
19 See J. SAUTER: Baader und Kant, p. 463; F. GIESE: Der romantische Charakter, p. 364; H. SPRECKELMEYER: Die philosophische Deutung des Sündenfalls bei Franz von Baader, p. 263; D. BAUMGARDT: Franz von Baader und die philosophische Romantik, p. 297. All wrote prior to the publication of E. SUSINI (Ed.): Lettres inédites de Franz von Baader, a work which includes a letter by Baader (December 5, 1796) addressing the subject of androgyny at an earlier date than anyone previously thought.
20 E. SUSINI (Ed.): Lettres inédites 1,178: ". . . man, this androgyne composed of an eternal (abiding) and a temporal (corruptible) nature, at every moment affixes his inner ideal of (non-sensual) truth to passing (sensual) life".
21 On the notion of "sublation", see Chapter 2.
22 The explanation of the term "androgyny" offered in this paragraph is based on K. HEMMERLE: "Franz von Baader", in: Lexikon für Theologie und Kirche, Freiberg (Herder) 1962.

It is of prime importance to note that androgyny is not synonymous with hermaphroditism. The two terms, in fact, are actually opposities:

We see further . . . that all impotence in generation . . . can be caused only by the difference (the non-union or opposition) of the generative powers of the organ. In other words, separation of sexual powers nullifies their productivity. The only way to understand this separation and opposition is to recognize that the principle, having lost its legitimate manifestative organ, has entered into adulterous union with another form . . . In the case of such transformation, *mésalliance*, and inner opposition, only purely external composition of generative powers of the organ can occur – in other words, something one could call hermaphroditism in the narrow sense of the term, *Venus barbata* [bearded Venus] but not true androgyny . . . (9,136)[23]

To Baader, hermaphroditism is "negative androgyny" and "absolute impotence" (14,415), a kind of monstrosity (14,142); such purely external conjunction of male and female characteristics in one individual is nothing less than a freak of nature. Androgyny, on the contrary, is "completeness" of the positive procreative features of both sexes in a single person: "Androgyny consists in identity of the generative and the formative principle or organ" (12,409). Mircea Eliade cites the confusion of the myth of androgyny with hermaphroditism as an example of "the degradation of the symbol", which takes place in connection with "all the great spiritual crises of Europe".[24]

The term androgyny, as applied in Baader's work, is not limited to sexuality alone. It ranges over a much wider sphere, often being used as a simple substitute for the unity of opposites or polarities seen everywhere, a favorite Romantic idea. Baader's essay *Über die Analogie des Erkenntniss- und des Zeugungs-Triebes*, for example, begins as follows:

Regardless of whether I find myself in a position superior to or inferior to what I perceive when I perceive and know, it is still a fact that knowing itself, to the extent that it is accomplished, is by no means indifferent to or independent of feeling. The situation, with regard to knowing, is rather much like the situation with regard to light: the physicist says that to the extent that light is activated, it never does so without change in temperature. It is, then, analogous to the capacity for knowing a bisexual thing that is androgynous in nature. (1,41; see also 1,45; 12,281)[25]

Baader refers to the complementary aspects of faith and reason, as well as those of nobility and humility, as androgynous. (See, for example, 2,340; 5,126 fn.; 9,8.) We have seen earlier that the temporal and the eternal aspect of man's life are androgynous (*Lettres inédites* 1,178). The catholicism of the Christian church is also androgynous (*Lettres inédites* 1,411ff.). With respect to physical

---

23 On this same point, see BAADER: *Sämtliche Werke* 2,314: 3,304; 7,238; 9,211; 10,128; 14:141ff. and *passim*.
24 M. ELIADE: *Mephistopheles and the Androgyne*, p. 100.
25 On the same point, see J. SAUTER: *Baader und Kant*, pp. 80, 133ff.

properties of matter that one usually considers to be opposites – for example, fluid and rigid (solid) – Baader declares:

> The rigid and the fluid have, each of them, the same two factors of a living substance in them: one finds that in every case one of the two factors is predominant and the other recessive . . . On this fact rests the possibility of stimulation of life in the forms of the rigid and the fluid: they need each other's assistance, such that fluid can be activated and supported only in something rigid, and something rigid, likewise, only in something fluid. Who can fail to see here the general law for all partial forces of nature, whose isolated manifestation (as in electricity and sexuality) similarly responds only to that condition. And who can fail to see that the proper bearer of both the one and the other sex is only complete androgyny? (3,273 fn.; see also 14,352)

In a comparable vein, Baader speaks elsewhere of the androgynous character of energy, which combines action and reaction (14,145). For the Romantics generally, the transition from nature to spirit was an easy one. So also for Baader. Immediately after mentioning the "bisexual condition of nature", he goes on to say: "Just as generative and formative powers condition nature, so also do reason and freedom condition personality . . ." (14,421). Spirit itself is androgynous, as explained in the fifth book of *Fermenta Cognitionis*:

> Spirit is everywhere the concept or the middle (center), as Hegel particularly (among the more modern thinkers) has shown. The central, or, if one wishes, androgynous nature of spirit is signified already by its ancient signature, where ♀ designates the female, form-giving factor and ♂ denotes the male, soul-imparting or "filling" life-factor, and + makes their union manifest . . . (2,326; see also 4,194)

Since it is from the sexual sphere that the paradigm for all other uses of the word "androgyny" is taken,[26] it is no surprise to find that Baader considers the process of procreation, as originally constituted, an androgynous one: "The concept of the perfection of the image of God includes androgyny as self-sufficient for generation and birth" (12,480; see also 1,410; 2,271ff.; 12,280, 324; 13,282). The fact that man is no longer androgynous in the procreative-sexual sense is for Baader a clear sign that not all is well with the world as a whole: since man is now "incomplete", the world is also somehow incomplete. The present state of separation of the sexes is a "developmental illness (*Entwicklungskrankheit*)" (14,352). "Separation of the sexes is thus everywhere the mark of purely heteronomous life" (3,275 fn.).[27] No theory of human alienation in the world can point to more palpable evidence for its position than this.

---

26 The word androgyny combines two Greek words *aner* (genitive, *andros*) – i.e., man – and *gyne* – i.e., woman; in other words, it literally means "man-woman".
27 See J. E. ERDMANN: *Die Entwicklung der deutschen Spekulation seit Kant*, volume 3, pp. 221ff.

Highly characteristic of Baader's concept of androgyny, which Giese treats under the heading "religious-philosophical theory of androgyny",[28] is its close connection with his views about man as image of God. The fact is, says Baader, that nearly total ignorance about the "mystery of the differentiation of the sexes in man" is one of the main reasons why people fail to understand scriptural teaching about the image of God in man (2,268). It is only "the entire tincture, androgyny", that is "the sole and immediate dwelling-place and temple of God in man" (15,666; see also 7,27; 10,330; 14,142; *Lettres inédites* 4,247–48).

When speaking of androgyny, Baader generally stresses the (originally) undifferentiated sexual character of man. But this is only one aspect, albeit a major one, of the general principle that life and reality as a whole are androgynous. As already noted, this is not a new idea with the Romantics;[29] but their enthusiastic acceptance of it, and its incorporation into the philosophy of German Idealism, provided a dramatic contrast to static and mechanistic eighteenth-century cosmology and philosophical anthropology. The very wellsprings of Baader's mystical and dynamic intuitions into the nature of reality seem to be tapped in such statements as the following one, drawn from *Über die Analogie des Erkenntniss- und des Zeugungs-Triebes*:

Everything that lives and assumes bodily form results from this androgynous desire, which is the secret, impenetrable, and magical workshop of all life. It is the secret marriage-bed which, if kept pure and undefiled, gives birth to happy and healthy life; whereas, if it is defiled, it gives birth to unhappy and sick life. Every living creature on every level and in every sphere of life is, as the ancients said, both solar and terrestrial, both sidereal and elementary at the same time, and the sacrament of life is offered to them all only under these two forms. (1,46)

The mystery of generation and propagation engaged Baader's attention all his life. Hans Grassl remarks that "the concept of generation was as fundamentally significant for the philosopher Baader as it was for Hamann".[30] As early as December 5, 1796, in a letter to his creditor, von Oppel, Baader wrote: ". . . I reduce everything to nature and art, to generation and formation: i.e., to the double process of the sexual principles" (*Lettres inédites* 1,212). In an admonition that appears in *Vorlesungen über speculative Dogmatik*, Baader appeals to his reader to "get yourself very well acquainted with our notion of the polarity of everything that exists, because without this key nothing is going to make any sense to you" (9,213).[31]

---

28 F. GIESE: *Der romantische Charakter*, p. 350.
29 See, for example, M. ELIADE: *Mephistopheles and the Androgyne*, pp. 98–111 and M. C. D'ARCY: *The Mind and Heart of Love*, New York (Meridian Books) 1955, pp. 220ff.
30 H. GRASSL (Ed.): *Franz von Baader. Über Liebe, Ehe und Kunst*, pp. 14–15.
31 The literature cited above deals with the connection between androgyny and polarity in many places; see, for example, H. SPRECKELMEYER: *Die philosophische Deutung*

So much for the notion of androgyny. As noted above, the heritage of the myth is an ancient one. It is also so widespread that Ernst Benz can declare:

... that the problem of androgynous perfection of man springs up spontaneously over and over again in the realm of mysticism, establishes the fact that we are dealing here with a universal archetype of human intuition that will not be suppressed, but rather reappears in ever new forms.[32]

Benz points out, however, that as far as Western intellectual history is concerned, there are two main starting points for speculation about androgyny: (1) the Platonic myth of primal man; and (2) cabbalistic interpretation of the biblical story of creation.[33] Baader knew both sources. Although he personally received the myth of androgyny principally through Böhme and St. Martin, he was not unaware of Plato's views (2,314; 7,238). As for the Cabbala, Baader wrote to Jacobi, on November 19, 1796, that he had begun to study it and that "the secret of the Cabbala has to do mainly with the relationship between androgynous generation and generation through two separate sexes: i.e., between integral and separated nature" (15,168ff.; see also Lettres inédites 1,212, 301).

In this regard, Baader seems also to have had considerable acquaintance with patristic tradition, and its later medieval development, finding two powerful supporters for his position in Gregory of Nyssa and the later (ninth century) John Scotus Erigena:

About this matter – i.e., about the concept of image of God in man as androgyny (not to be confused with the concept of hermaphroditism) – the older theologians are mostly silent or else in error most of the time. Only Gregory of Nyssa distinguishes a double creation of man, in accordance with the first and second chapters of Genesis: in the first, man was created in God's image; in the second, he was created in the image of man and woman . . . Likewise, Scotus Erigena (De Divisione Naturae) says: "Homo reatu suae praevaricationis obrutus, naturae suae divisionem in masculum et foeminam est passus, et quoniam ille caelestem multiplicationis suae modum observare noluit, in pecorinam corruptibilemque ex masculo et foemina numerositatem justo Judicio redactus est, qua [sic] Divisio in Christo adunationis sumpsit exordium, qui in se humanae naturae restaurationis et futurae resurrectionis Initium praestitit (Brought low by the guilt of his sin, man suffered the division of his nature into masculine and feminine, and because he was unwilling to use the

---

des Sündenfalls bei Franz von Baader, p. 263, or F. GIESE: Der romantische Charakter, p. 373.

32 E. BENZ: Adam. Der Mythus vom Urmenschen, p. 15.

33 E. BENZ: Adam. Der Mythus vom Urmenschen, p. 15. M. ELIADE: Mephistopheles and the Androgyne, p. 103, questions the derivation of the idea of androgyny from the Cabbala, at least as far as Böhme is concerned: "Jacob Böhme probably borrowed the idea of the androgyne not from the Cabbala but from alchemy; indeed, he makes use of alchemical terms".

heavenly mode of propagation, a just judgment reduced him to animal-like and corruptible multiplicity, consisting of male and female. This division began to be healed in Christ, who in his own person accorded human nature the beginning of restoration and of future resurrection)". (10,128; see also 2,317ff.; 7,235 fn.; 14,143, 290)

The notes made by Baader, while studying the works of Thomas Aquinas, contain a repudiation of Augustine's and Thomas's position on the subject; both rejected the notion of androgyny as the condition of primal man. (See 2,318 fn.; 14,290, 294.)[34] Volumes three, twelve, and thirteen of the *Sämtliche Werke* amply show that Baader's main inspiration for the great interest he took in androgyny was Böhme and St. Martin.

Baader held that all of living reality and every active principle is androgynous. He did not make an exception in the case of God. In fact, the strong mystical thrust of his thought and intuition led him to begin serious consideration of any critical theme with God.[35] Actually, he begins with personal experience, the most profound of which he felt to be experience of God: the experience of existential tension toward a personal ground of being, a deeply-felt realization of his own contingency, together with an urgent conviction that ultimately life and reality have an all-encompassing unity and sense that point to their root in God.

Revelation of the mystery of the divine Trinity is, for Baader, revelation of the androgynous nature of God. In the essay *Über den biblischen Begriff von Geist und Wasser, in Bezug auf jenen des Ternars* (10,1ff.), he rejects the view of some theologians and mystics, among them Schwenkfeld, who "have so distorted this concept of the Trinity that they have dragged in the concept of sexual powers, as they are used in creaturely fashion and as powers of reproduction, and have applied that notion directly to God". But, he warns, "one would fall into an opposite error and render the concept of the Trinity completely dead, impotent, and empty . . . if one were completely to bypass the notion of fecundation and fruitfulness, and, consequently, of generation and parturition in connection with it – for even the words Father and Son will not allow that . . ." (See also 14,202, 240, 417.) The key to understanding this problem correctly lies in the idea of androgyny:

---

34 F. HOFFMAN (Ed.): BAADER: *Sämtliche Werke*, volume 2, p. 318 fn. summarizes some of the older (pre-1850) discussion of androgyny as well as some of the pertinent literature on the subject.

35 See, for example, the discussion on the principle of participation in Chapter 1. On the notion of "divine androgyny", see: M. ELIADE: *Mephistopheles and the Androgyne*, pp. 108ff.; F. HOFFMANN: *Vorhalle zur spekulativen Lehre Franz Baaders*, p. 194; J. E. ERDMANN: *Die Entwicklung der deutschen Spekulation seit Kant*, volume 3, p. 324.

It is not to be denied that most people who parrot the words of the dogma about Father and Son do not think of anything at all in connection with those words and pass off this lack of thought for themselves and for others as belief. Or else, they confuse the concept of immanent birth and formation (with which we are dealing here) with one which is emanent and, in fact, creaturely (as reproduction in time and amplification and multiplication on the horizontal plane). Thus, since they lack the concept of androgyny, they understand by the word "Father" nothing more than fecundating, generating potency, as separate and cut off from conceiving and birth-giving potency. The reason is that in the temporal order and in the condition of separation of the sexes both of these potencies appear as really separated and cut off from one another (and are to that extent abstract) . . . (10,7ff.)[36]

Although Baader applies the notion of androgyny even to God, the myth of androgyny is most important and urgent, for him, as an anthropological myth. In addition to treating the myth extensively in a number of places,[37] Baader often touches on it throughout much of his work. Indeed, a great deal of the material is repetitious. The single most important source for Baader's thought on androgyny is his essay (published in 1829) entitled *Bemerkungen über das zweite Capitel der Genesis, besonders in Bezug auf das durch den Fall des Menschen eingetretene Geschlechts-Verhältniss* (7,223–40).

The discrepancies which seem to occur between the first and second chapters of Genesis serve as the point of departure for Baader's study. In the first chapter, man appears as a single individual, and God calls everything he has created "good". But in the second chapter, we learn that Eve is created from the supposedly complete and perfect Adam, and we hear God saying that it is not good for man to be alone (7,225; see also 9,210 fn.; 10,295).[38] The question

36 On the distinction between immanent and emanent birth and formation, see also BAADER: *Sämtliche Werke* 8,317. It will be noticed that Baader sometimes uses the same term, in this case "androgynous", in different senses, even when applying it to one and the same object. For example, we have seen that he has called Sophia androgynous, because it is neither male nor female in itself but comprises fullness of perfection of both sexes (3,303; 13,185). On the other hand, speaking of the same Sophia, Baader writes: "When J. Böhme calls this mirror the virginal matrix, he expresses by that term the original conjunction of virginity and motherhood: i.e., androgyny. This is an idea which, after it has been lost in theology, has maintained itself only in art (as the Madonna). In this connection, Scripture speaks of the single woman who is more fruitful than one who has a husband" (3,385 fn.). There is abundant evidence that "androgyny" was a most flexible term in Baader's usage.

37 The major sources in BAADER: *Sämtliche Werke* include: 3,301–10; 7,223–40; 9,209–21; 10,294ff.; 14,141–43.

38 Here, Baader attached a somewhat lengthy footnote that discusses the use of the plural in reference to Adam and Eve in the second chapter of Genesis. He argues that this usage proves no more against original unity of man than use of the plural *Elohim* argues against unity of God. "That plural will, therefore, rightly be interpreted as referring to two sexual powers or tinctures". Baader also considers the "two Adams" theory, a theory which Cabbalists invented to overcome this difficulty.

then arises: Why was Adam at first by himself, and why did he later require a mate? Baader rejects the suggestion, offered by some writers, that part of the second chapter of Genesis has been interpolated; instead, he finds a clue as to why Adam needed a companion in the text itself. In chapter two of Genesis, it states that Adam found no helpmate for himself when the animals were brought before him so that he could assign them names. Baader states, in bold print:

But recognizing this occasion for the origin of Eve from Adam leads us directly to a second admission: namely, that it was precisely deformation into animal nature and into its two-fold form (for which Adam was to blame on the occasion of the presentation of the animals) that was this occasion. (7,226ff)

Baader explains that man's role as ruler of the animals (Genesis 1,28) was not a status to which he was automatically entitled. First, he must withstand temptation and trial; and the trial must result in his victory over the animals whom he was to rule.[39] Adam had to establish the higher image, God's image, within himself by asserting his superiority over the animals brought before him to be named. He was to name the animals: that is (in biblical usage), to assert his superiority over them, but he was not to lust after them.[40] This was the test Adam failed:

It was, therefore, only because man failed in the first temptation, or in the first moment of it, succumbing to lust for an external helpmate, for self-reproduction such as animals have, and thus losing desire for an internal helpmate . . . that woman was produced from him. For now

39 In a footnote (7,227), Baader explains that "this ability to be tempted on the part of man resided (as J. Böhme says) in the already infected *limus terrae* (slime of the earth) in Adam". He had explained earlier (7,226 fn.) that Böhme's notion, regarding a certain element of corrupted nature which Adam was to govern and restore, was present in him [Adam] as *limus terrae;* his task consisted in overcoming this *limus.* In other words, man faced the challenge of overcoming part of himself in temptation: namely, the "worldly element" (*Welt-Theil*). That is precisely what "the poet" cited by Baader is describing:

> Von der Gewalt, die alle Wesen bindet,
> Befreit der Mensch sich, der sich überwindet.

> (From the power that binds all things fast,
> That man frees himself, who conquers himself.)

40 Baader explains the deep significance of names in a footnote (7,227ff.): "What I name and what bears my name belong to me (*ist mir gehörig*) (is mine [*hörig*] or follows my bidding). In the Holy Scriptures, name and power stand for the same thing exactly, and whoever has no insight into this nature of the name understands nothing about the scriptural doctrine of prayer as invocation of a name . . ." (See also 4,235.) G. MARCEL: *Problematic Man*, pp. 46–49, presents some very interesting and analogous views.

(after he had lusted in that way), it was obviously no longer good that man should abide among the animals. But this condition of it no longer being good for Adam to be alone, mentioned in chapter two, was because of his by no means innate lust, not because God had somehow done wrong by making man alone in the first place. (7,229; see also 10,295; 14,121)

Only this interpretation, says Baader, makes sense out of Adam's sleep, during which Eve was formed. Both the sleep and the formation of Eve from Adam were saving actions of God which prevented Adam from an even more profound plunge into animality. (See 9,210, 145; 12,280.) At this point, Baader takes pains to reject any identification of his view with that of the Gnostics, who would make matter itself evil and marriage an abomination (7,229). Baader sees man's relationship to woman under a double aspect: (1) on the one hand, he sees in woman a constant reminder of the original fall from God; (2) on the other, he recognizes in her a helpmate given him by God to aid in making good the loss he suffered through his sin. Man and woman help each other reestablish the pristine fullness of man. They complement each other's incompleteness. The paradox in their relationship is that "the woman always exercises only a secondary role with reference to the man, both in good and in evil; yet, it depends on her alone whether she will give birth to God or to the devil for him" (7,230).

Baader sees another important role assigned to woman in the third chapter of Genesis (verse 15) where God says to the serpent: "I will put enmity between you and the woman, between your seed and her seed; he shall crush your head, and you shall lie in wait for his heel". Adam acquired an external helpmate, for purposes of procreation, because he turned away from "the internal helpmate" that was part of him prior to his fall. But, in fact, as Genesis 3,15 indicates, the internal helpmate Adam lost is not *totally* lost to him; she is present, in a certain sense, in the external helpmate whom Adam acquired: i.e., in her "seed".[41] That is why the serpent addressed himself first to woman in the second stage of the temptation of man: i.e., at the tree. In the long run, the woman's seed triumphed over the serpent's seed, "because the one who was born of the Virgin Mary is the same one who had to leave Adam because of his sin" (7,230–31). The name Eva was transformed into Ave![42]

41 In the second book of *Fermenta Cognitionis*, Baader speaks of the "woman's seed" in connection with restoring the image of God in man. He calls it the corporeal or female principle in that image, a principle made dormant through sin but capable of being reactivated through Jesus Christ, as anticipated in God's providence from eternity (2,225). One may note that in a citation from the third book of the same work (p. 256 fn.) Baader also speaks of "serpent's seed" and "woman's seed" as types of evil and good lust or desire. See also BAADER: *Sämtliche Werke* 4,254; 14,156; 15,304, 619; E. SUSINI: (Ed.): *Lettres inédites* 1,311.
42 Without identifying its source, Baader, at this point, cites the following verse in a footnote:

If Adam had successfully passed his first trial (at the naming of the animals), he would not only have confirmed his own androgynous perfection but would also have profited the whole of nature. And Adam had another chance – at the tree of paradise. (Man's spiritual dissolution was completed in stages.) Baader believes that Genesis insists on this point: the full realization of man's fall to animal status came only with the fall at the tree of paradise. The first fall was a case of misdirected lust – it remained on the level of thought and imagination (*gleichsam ideell oder magisch*).[43] Only after the second fall did Adam and Eve feel any shame at their nakedness (Genesis 3,7; see also *Sämtliche Werke*, 2,231). If they had not failed in this second temptation, they could have irrevocably prevented the coming to power of man's "ventral life" (*Bauchleben*) and its struggle for supremacy with man's higher powers.[44] As the situation stands now, man's life has been so bestialized that he can hardly free himself from

"Eva et ave produnt inverse [*sic*] Nomine quam sit,
Femina grande malum, Femia [*sic*] grande bonum
Eva parens mortem portendit, Ave que [*sic*] salutem[.]
Perdidit Eva homines, quos reparavit Ave.

(Eva and Ave appear with their names inverted,
A woman brings great evil, a woman brings great good,
Eva giving birth means death, but Ave means life;
Eva brought ruin to those whom Ave restored.)". (7,231)

43 It is a general principle with Baader that no spiritual entity reaches a state of perfection without finding an *embodiment* or corporisation of itself. Thus, he cites the axiom which he liked so well: "Vis ejus integra, si conversus in terram (Its force is integral, if converted into the earth)". Elsewhere, he calls this principle "that fundamental principle of all true religion, poetry, and physics" (13,198). In the matter at hand, the principle applies thusly: sexual differentiation first assumed its full form when it was no longer merely internal but rather "conversus in terram"; it then became "earthly or animal". (See also 7,231 fn.; 8,279.) Baader attributes the axiom to "Hermes", undoubtedly the mythical "Hermes Trismegistus" (thrice-great Hermes), to whom the ancient Egyptian "Hermetic" writings are also attributed (*Sämtliche Werke* 4,427; see also 1,249; 2,3, 63, 87, 99, 257, 331; 4,123, 280; 5,123; 13,198; 15,586). C. G. JUNG: *Mysterium Conjunctionis*, has much to say about Hermes Trismegistus.

44 For Baader, the terms "belly" and "heart" (body) are ideal types of the purely physical (bestialized) body, as opposed to the spiritualized body. The distinction is based on such passages in St. Paul's epistles as I Corinthians 6,13: "Food is only meant for the stomach, and the stomach for food; yes, and God is going to do away with both of them. But the body – this is not meant for fornication; it is for the Lord, and the Lord for the body". (See also Romans 16,18 and Philippians 3,19.) In scriptural usage, generally, "heart" represents the inner man, the source of both good and evil thoughts. Giving oneself over to purely sensual activity makes one's life a *Bauchleben*. (See also *Sämtliche Werke* 10,128ff., 295; E. SUSINI (Ed.): *Lettres inédites* 1,298, 315.) See also E. BENZ: *Adam. Der Mythus vom Urmenschen*, p. 17.

"the animal, the earthly, the belly", in thought and feeling. There are, however, exceptions; in various kinds of ecstasy, man rises above animal demands and into the region of the life of the heart or the breast (*des Brust- oder Herzlebens*) (7,232–33). In a condition like that of "magnetic ecstasy",[45] all earthly life can be suspended, just as a sufficiently pure level or moment of love for a woman can silence all sexual desire.[46]

Lecture eight of the fifth book of *Speculative Dogmatik* (9,207–20) deals largely with the question of androgyny. For all of its repetition – many of the points made earlier are recapitulated – new points of view and emphases are introduced, and they help to round out the general picture. Baader rejects the position of some exegetes: that God formed man "from the slime of the earth" (using the earth as a kind of raw material) in the same way that he formed the animals. The point is relevant because man's original androgynous perfection, in contrast to pristine sexual division among the animals, would not allow man and animals to be formed from the same material. Baader would establish, at least in principle, a specific difference between animals and man on the level of sexual differentiation.

Baader never wearies of rejecting misunderstandings of androgyny that would equate it with impotence or sexlessness; or, at the opposite extreme, with hermaphroditism. As he understands it, androgyny is a specifically Christian notion, disbelief in which gives material aid to those who do not believe in the doctrine of the glorified body – which is part and parcel of belief in resurrection of the body (9,210–11). Another misunderstanding to be avoided is that of regarding a man solely and exclusively as male and a woman solely and exclusively as female. The fact is, says Baader, that both sexual powers ("fiery" or male and "watery" or female[47]) are present in both man and woman: fire, though,

---

45 We have noted earlier (biographical sketch) that Baader was strongly interested in phenomena like magnetism, clairvoyance, somnambulism, ecstasy, and the parapsychological in general. The index volume of the *Sämtliche Werke* contains many references on the subject.

46 The footnote which appears at this point reads: "One recalls in this connection that beautiful oriental myth, according to which the man of paradise was able to digest in his mouth and propagate his kind from the heart with a kiss" (*Sämtliche Werke* 7,233). Baader indicates elsewhere that he attributed deep significance to the kiss – for example, in a letter to Dr. von Stransky (January 22, 1839): "Don't take what I say about the kiss as a joke. For early Christians, the kiss was practically a sacrament" (15,610). "Brute animals do not kiss" (7,236). "St. Bernard calls the Holy Spirit the kiss of the Father and the Son" (7,236). See also BAADER: *Sämtliche Werke* 10,85; 15,612; E. SUSINI (Ed.): *Lettres inédites* 1,300.

47 The symbolism of fire and water for male and female is taken over from Jacob Böhme. See, for example, BAADER: *Sämtliche Werke* 3,274; 7,234; 12,323, 325; E. SUSINI (Ed.): *Lettres inédites* 1,298. See also Chapter 2, note 3 .

is dominant and water recessive in males, whereas the relationship is reversed in females. "Thus, there is no contradiction in thinking of the normal relationship of both powers in one individual; several phenomena in the animal and plant worlds suggest this sort of thing" (9,211).

At the very beginning, God did not simply create man; he also gave him a heavenly helper, the androgynous Sophia, to aid him in giving birth to God's image (inwardly at first) and to destroy the possibility of his becoming male and female (see, for example, 12,380, 388; *Lettres inédites* 1,298). But, even after man's fall and his loss of androgynous integrity, the same Heavenly Sophia continues to aid him in recovering that pristine perfection: "for (according to Paul [Galatians 3,28]) in God, (Christ) there is neither male nor female" (9,212; see also 7,238; 10,247 fn.).[48]

Another distinction Baader occasionally makes (see 9,212; 14,143) is that between "good" androgyny and "evil" androgyny. Humility and nobility characterize the former, pride and baseness the latter. Man's present situation is such that sexual differentiation cancels out not only good but also evil androgyny. Thus, although man's condition could be vastly improved by restoring original androgyny, it could also become much worse; it could become totally diabolical. Negative androgynous features, as well as positive ones, are now divided between the sexes. At least theologians, says Baader, should have known better than to lose hold of the idea of androgyny. Mary gave birth without male intervention, and Adam could have given birth without external female intervention had he not sinned (9,212).

The concept of androgyny is analagous to that of cause and ground: the androgynous condition corresponds to their complete union while their bisexual condition corresponds to their total separation. God the Father generates the Son in an androgynous manner, which helps explain Eckehart's assertion that "all temporality comes into being through, and consists in, separation of Father and Son" (9,213; see also 2,523; 13,277). The "solar, external tincture" is bisexual (in man and woman, fire and water) and is, therefore, a double tincture; incomplete principles and causes, however, are all one in the eternal tincture because Father and Son are one. Divine androgynous fire (Sophia or

---

48   The first part of a long footnote, from the second of three circular letters entitled *Über den Paulinischen Begriff des Versehenseins des Menschen im Namen Jesu vor der Welt Schöpfung* (4,325–422), deals with this role of Sophia: "The spirit who is sent to each of us as individual members (according to Paul) by the Head (in whom the formative Spirit of all members dwells as center) is, in fact, the formative Idea. In accordance with this Idea, every member ought to grow and develop (with the help of his Head and other members). Just as the Savior (in the Head or as the Head) is wedded to heavenly humanity (Sophia) as the center and is androgynous, so should each member also participate in this marriage (Ephesians 5,32) . . ." (4,352).

the Idea) will always remain a mystery in the natural world. It should be neither profaned nor explained away (9,213).

During the entire lecture, Baader speaks of the interrelation between ground and cause: all existing things are polar in nature; and every acting cause can act only within the setting or context of its "middle" or ground.[49] This principle is valid for all seeing, speaking, and doing. Baader llustrates the point by drawing an analogy to the act of seeing:

> But this middle or grounding for seeing is at the same time separation, and in that separation a uniting of the poles of: (a) seeing into the inner (into the hidden depth), and (b) seeing into the outer. It is a case of concentrated and excentrated vision. For it is only in relationship to the middle that the spirit sets out (without permanently departing) both into the depth and into the height, and then comes back with its revelation (*eröffnend*) into the middle. What people call the concept of seeing is simply the concept of this inner and outer seeing, in fact, and their mutual entry and exit (harmonization) through the middle. The principle of identity, A=A, which logicians take to be tautological (and therefore non-significative), in fact, expresses precisely the balancing out of the poles (of innerness and outerness). This A=A signifies in a proper sense the identity (agreement) of the ideal and the real middle, from which identity, the identity of inner and outer, is but a consequence. The high point is the middle – as opposed to the concentrated and excentrated depth of hiddenness . . . (9,214; see also 8,176–78; 15,574–78)

The relationship of all this to the subject at hand is easily seen. Baader speaks of androgyny as the union of two partial causal factors (*Causalitätshälften, Halbcausalitäten*) in a positive ground or middle. The opposite would be the separation of these causal factors in a negative ground or middle. The two factors may exist in harmony (androgyny) or in disharmony, but they never separate totally from one another. Baader understands sexual androgyny as simply the paradigmatic illustration of the polarity of all existing things. In the continuation of the passage just cited, Baader invokes Böhmean symbols to help him describe various manifestations of the androgynous character of reality. He speaks of the sharp and the bitter (Böhme's first two "natural forms"), of depth (innerness) and height (outwardness), of ascent and descent, of nobility-

---

49 See Chapter 2 for a discussion of the importance of "the middle" or "the center" in Baader's thought. H. SEDLMAYR: *Verlust der Mitte*, Salzburg 1948, seems clearly dependent on Baader's notion of "the center", as well as other aspects of Baader's thought. Sedlmayr's central thesis is that the "sickness" of nineteenth- and twentieth-century art is primarily due to a "loss of the center": i.e., a loss of God and his image (man) in modern art. Among other references to, and citations from, Baader's thought, Sedlmayr includes Baader's "deep insight": "How a man stands before God determines the way he is related to himself, to his fellow-man, to nature, and to the spiritual world" (p. 138). Sedlmayr again addressed the subject in a later work: H. SEDLMAYR: "Der Gedanke der Mitte bei Franz von Baader", in: *Wirklichkeit der Mitte. Beiträge zu einer Strukturanthropologie. Festgabe für August Vette zum 80. Geburtstag*, edited by J. TENZLER, Freiburg im Breisgau and Munich, 1968, pp. 309–18.

humility and baseness-pride. He speaks of fire and water, man and woman, food (woman) and hunger (man) – all correlative notions.[50] One can say of each pair what Baader says of "fire and water spirits": "Fire and water spirits are only half-spirits, which constitute the whole spirit in their union" (9,216; see also 13,82). This calls to mind Baader's note: "Man and woman, says J. Böhme, are half-persons" (12,281). Essential to proper understanding of polarity is "the third", the element in which opposites unite.[51] This is, once again, a key element in Baader's whole way of thinking.

But, as we have said, one does not understand this general law of double causality (polarity) meeting in one ground or middle, as long as one does not expand the notion of the duality of that causality to triplicity. For not two, but only three, suffice to produce or enclose a fixed middle (thus, a figure). One should not so understand this triplicity of causality (as grounded either negatively or positively) as though the ground were the third element . . . (9,216; see also 2,360)

In the fourteenth lecture of *Vorlesungen über Societätsphilosophie*, Baader makes this point with explicit reference to the matter of sexual difference. After calling hermaphroditism "the highest deformity or monstrosity", he says:

What we call maleness and femaleness in the temporal-animal condition of human nature are not simply entities educed from separation or dissolution of androgyny (as the primitive image of God); they are merely products of the extinction or vanishing (fading away) of that image of God. In fact, it always happens that duality in formation comes to be and consists solely in the *caput mortuum* of a vanished triad, so that one can conclude from duality and abnormality of form to inner disharmony of the ground or center of that formation . . . (14,142)

A crucial distinction must be made between the two types of grounding which beings may possess: a being grounded in nature; and a being grounded as a child of God (or the devil). These are two very different things. All created beings, including devils, are grounded (in the first sense) in God, since no created thing can subsist without essential reference to God. But grounding in sonship can vary, since it is established, in part, by the creature's own liberty and love. Thus, Christ called some people who were about to stone him "children" of the devil, but not the devil's creatures. The law of the Gospel is that no creature can be born of the Son unless he dies to his purely natural life in the Father. Baader explains:

50   Novalis frequently used the analogy of food and hunger as symbolic of woman and man. See F. GIESE: *Der romantische Charakter*, pp. 331, 336ff.
51   See the appropriate entries – e.g. "Dreizahl", "Dualismus", and "Polarität" – in the index volume of BAADER: *Sämtliche Werke* for numerous references to this idea.

185

The eternal will to nature, which is God the Father, is deeper than nature (it is its *a priori*), and the creature must first surrender his own proper will or will-spirit to this primitive will. If he does that, then that primitive will (the Father) shall lead the creature out of his nature-based anxiety (*Angstnatur*, Böhme's term) into his other will, the will of the Son: i.e., into freedom. He will take him outside the realm of his fire-torture through God's holy fire into light. There, for much that he has given, he receives everything in return – not for his own glory or power, but for God's glory. For it is God in him [as will] who is his will, and it is God in him as deed who is his deed . . . (9,217)

All of this is just another way for Baader to define man's basic vocation: "Every creature is unripe and immature", he says a bit further on, "if he has not yet shared in the sonship" (9,217), and *"Creatura, quae Filium non sapit, Deo Patri Creatori non sapit* (The creature who does not know the Son, does not discern the Father)" (9,218).

Baader connects all this with the concept of androgyny by recalling the views of Böhme and Paracelsus concerning imagination and magic as the key to all production.[52] One can see this principle at work in the life-functions of animals (e.g., nourishment and propagation), in which the *primus motor* is imagination, appetite, or desire. Woman is "food", man is "hunger": they complement and fulfill each other. Even in the divine Trinity, Baader sees the conjunction of eternal harsh fire-potency with gentle light-potency (Sophia) as producing the Son. He then goes on to consider the original androgynous character of the "Unground",[53] which combines elements of will and mirror, another instance when the imagination-principle is applied (9,218-19).

The essay *Über den verderblichen Einfluss, welchen die rationalistisch-materialistischen Vorstellungen auf die höhere Physik, so wie auf die höhere Dichtkunst und die bildende Kunst noch ausüben* (3,287–310) contains another of Baader's more extensive treatments of the problem of androgyny (especially pages 301–10). Fritz Giese remarks that art history affords yet another illustration of the fact that Baader "seemed to encompass, almost to spring beyond, the entire Romantic movement". He singles out Baader's theory of androgyny, as presented and developed in the just-named essay, as the best evidence for this fact.[54] Baader argues that one of the most striking proofs of the inability of religious poets and artists to free themselves from purely materialistic ideas is precisely the way in which they understand the problem of the relationship of the sexes. This shows that "understanding of this deepest mystery of human nature has not been provided them by theologians and philosophers, because

52 For "Image of God", see Chapter 3.
53 For "Unground", See the explanation offered in Chapter 2.
54 F. GIESE: *Der romantische Charakter*, p. 381

the latter, almost without exception, do not possess such understanding" (3,301). Baader reminds us that Scripture calls the rupture of man's relationship with God "adultery", and that through his first sin, man lost the capacity for reproducing himself without the use of animal organs. This sin occasioned the formation from Adam of an external wife, and man became a divided being.

The earliest writers say that it was precisely because of his female characteristics that Adam committed this first sin. These female features can in no sense be construed as Heavenly Sophia (as some writers have thought). Instead, it was the presence of Sophia in man that enabled him to maintain both his male and female characteristics in the harmonized equilibrium (*Temperatur*) of his first state. Only with Sophia's aid could man establish that androgynous perfection in himself. But Adam sinned, and Sophia departed from him. Man *disintegrated* into male and female, into Adam and Eve. (See also 13,357.) The two "tinctures", fire (wrath) and water (mildness), were separated; consequently, man and woman can see the sin of Adam objectified in each other.

Though Baader disclaims any intention of covering the subject thoroughly, he emphasizes two points in particular: (1) Some mystics have interpreted man's relationship to God as that of woman to man in the usual sense, but this is foolish nonsense.[55] (2) The experience of temptation was necessary for Adam if he was to preserve and confirm his original androgeneity. Had he passed the test, he would have settled once and for all the question of whether he was to remain androgynous or become bisexual. Temptation was a summons to radically destroy – within himself – the possibility of separating into male and female.[56] Victory over temptation would have made him definitive king of creation (3,302–03).

55 In the "explanatory supplements" to his essay, *Der morgenländische und abendländische Katholicismus* . . . (10,89–254), Baader takes up the same theme as part of a lengthy footnote: ". . . I must, furthermore, note the fact that several ascetics, especially female ones, have sought this restoration of the image of God through Christ (as heavenly bride and heavenly bridegroom) only in a bad sense: they have, in fact, looked for it through a marriage union of male and female with Christ, not in inner rejection and destruction of male and female desire. In this life, man and woman are supposed to help each other achieve that destruction, but they cannot do so if they are not both bound together in the same Christ about whom Paul says (Galatians 3,28) that he is neither male nor female . . ." (10,247 fn.). The text Baader cites may imply his meaning, but it actually says: "And there are no more distinctions between Jew and Greek, slave and free man, male and female, but all of you are one in Christ Jesus".

56 Baader explains in a footnote why temptation is necessary: "If this capacity [for becoming male and female] were going to be destroyed, it must first be aroused as such. Here is the key to understanding the need for temptation to test a creature. This is not temptation for evil's sake, but for the sake of good: in Adam's case, it came from the evil one; but in the one [temptation] that Lucifer (with all the angels) had to undergo as a test, it did not come from the evil one" (*Sämtliche Werke* 3,303).

Baader insists that we cannot understand "the central idea of religion, namely that of the image of God", if we do not have a clear notion about man's androgynous nature. That painters and sculptors have vaguely sensed this is evident from the fact that they have made the Madonna the central figure of religious art. (See also 15,156.) It is a shame that theologians have been of no help to them in this area, and that they themselves have so often failed to be true to their own intuitions. A figure of Christ, the Madonna, or an angel should evoke not the slightest sexual response in the beholder.[57] In one of his lectures on Böhme, Baader says:

> There is no sexuality in androgyny, whereas in the snake,[58] both sexes are inflamed next to one another. What a remarkable irony of divine androgyny! It is the triumph of Christian art that in the Madonna (earthly) femaleness does not manifest itself. The hermaphrodite, on the contrary, arouses both man and woman. (13,132)

The fact is that pagan art has emphasized the direct opposite of androgyny: i.e., sexual organs in polar opposition to one another, hermaphroditism, and the like.[59] Baader uses some very strong language to express his repugnance for sexuality that does not rise above the level of mere physical impulse:

> There is no cause to wonder [at pagan hermaphroditism or *Venus barbata*], since in the relationship of the sexes – taken by itself and without the exorcism of (religious) love, which is the sole principle of all association and which can elevate unfree bondage (passion) to the level of free union – there is no evidence of anything like striving toward a return to androgyny, to reintegrate human nature in man and woman. Instead, both physical and psychical evidence shows the same orgiastic, loveless, egoistic, and self-seeking striving on the part of man and woman. Each tries to inflame the double hermaphrodite passion in and for himself; each wants to tear from the other what he needs for that stimulation. In loveless coition, the maximum of selfishness in both man and woman seeks satisfaction. Woman serves man and man serves woman as an instrument for the purpose. Thus, satisfaction of sexual desire consists not simply in despising personality, but even in hating it. (3,304–05)[60]

---

57 Compare with Georg Koepgen's position, as quoted in C. G. JUNG: *Mysterium Conjunctionis*, pp. 373ff.

58 The snake or serpent (Genesis 3) is the symbol for Satan, the diametrical opposite of the harmony and integrity of androgyny: i.e., God's image.

59 On this theme, see J. SAUTER: *Baader und Kant*, pp. 519ff., and H. REICHEL: "Baader als Kunstphilosoph", *Zeitschrift für Aesthetik*, 6 (1911), especially pp. 543–44.

60 Compare with 6,15: "The difference between free love and an unfree drive manifests itself especially in sexual desire, which is often present in company with cordial inner hatred. In fact, we see sexual desire not only diminish, but even completely die out when true love enters". Baader has a low opinion of sexual drives and orgasm – they need to be "exorcized" by love. See, for example, BAADER: *Sämtliche Werke* 2,179, 382; 7,237; E. SUSINI (Ed.): *Lettres inédites* 1,298; or, this passage from H. SPRECKELMAYER: *Die philosophische Deutung des Sündenfalls bei Franz von Baader*, p.

Baader complains that even great Christian artists, in depicting Christ, the Madonna, and angels, have often failed to understand that their proper subject was an androgynous figure. That is why their work sometimes appears lifeless and why many have preferred the "flesh-pots of Egypt" (i.e., pagan art) to it. But any attempt to revive ancient pagan art is also affectation, a silly endeavor to roll back the pages of history and recapture an age that is dead. In handling the theme of sexual love, poets have an even more dismal record than plastic artists. Sexual love is the focal point of all poetry, as everyone knows, but what ungodly things the poets have done with it! Secular poetry has mishandled the subject miserably, with its sentimentality, frivolity, utilitarianism, and even its diabolical character (3,306).

Androgyny, Love and Marriage

The significance assigned by Baader to the myth of androgyny is best understood by considering the decisive role it played in his assessment of human love and marriage. He did not simply adopt the myth as a matter of curiosity. Rather, he reconsidered it, expanded it – in a unique way – and appropriated it. In so doing, he used it as the basis for a new and more spiritual understanding of human love. Baader himself says (in his commentary on *Genesis*) that this is the main point of the entire matter:

I return now to the main subject of the essay: i.e., to showing the consequences that we can draw from the second chapter of Genesis for founding a theory of love and marriage (for marriage is always in love, although love is not always in marriage).[61] The higher significance of sexual differentiation in man manifests itself already in a genetic fashion, through the separation of man and woman from one another. It is documented by the fact that this separation took place in the breast or heart area, since man's breast or heart was, as it were, split into two halves. What fell to man's lot from the heart was the harsh element (in this abstraction), and what fell to woman's lot (in the same abstraction) was weak gentleness and softness. It is only in free reunion or concreteness (love), that these factors will stimulate, free, and complement each other,

281: "Therefore, true love begins to exist only beyond the vital-animal sphere. It realizes itself", says Spreckelmayer citing Baader, "between man and woman in sexual love . . . only then . . . when both are no longer inwardly man and woman" (9,221 fn.).
61 Baader's declaration: ". . . denn die Ehe ist immer in der Liebe, wenn schon dies nicht immer in jener . . . " (7,233) contrasts with the view of Schleiermacher and Schlegel; they equate love with marriage, maintaining the permanent, life-long character of both. For them, there is no such thing as "failure" of love or marriage. The only thing that "failure" proves is that love and marriage never existed between two people.

so that one would have to say that fire provides power, strength, and warmth to water, while water provides gentleness (cooling) to fire when they unite productively (as humid heat). (7,233–34)[62]

It is not enough, however, that man and woman try to complement each other by drawing on the strength of what each has to offer in his or her own right. It was sin against God that led to the disastrous separation in the first place; and it is only by means of a reunion with God, through Christ the mediator, that things can be made right again:

> We should not look for the root of love and marriage only in the breast or heart region. Beyond that, I maintain that all deductions of the principle of love and marriage do not go deep enough if they suppose they can establish that bond in anything other than union of man's and woman's heart or will in God: i.e., in Christ as restorer and representative of our lost original nature. That restoration is none other than that of the image of God in man. Thus, those who are bound to each other in love and marriage have bound and obliged themselves to effect this restoration of their original nature together and mutually, each one of them acting as surety for the other, not like the unmarried who are alone and who have to do this each for himself. (7,234–35)

Baader sees the relationship of woman to man described in Genesis as a mixed one. Woman is not only wife to her husband; she is also, in a sense, his "daughter". The New Testament analogue for this argument, says Baader, is St. Paul comparing the relationship of man to woman with that of Christ to the community (Church), or with that of head to body (Ephesians 5,21ff.; see also I Corinthians 11,3–16).[63]

62 Part of the long footnote to this text reads: "These ancient researchers into nature demonstrate, with respect to the dualism of sexual powers, the dualism of innerness and outerness, of spirituality and corporeality, and the invisibility and visibility of every existing thing with the principle: Pater in Filio, Filius in matre (The father is in the son, the son is in the mother) . . . " (7,234). The expression "Pater in Filio, Filius in matre" appears often in Baader's work. It designates, among other things, father as the *in sich*, animating, subjective principle and mother as the *aus sich*, corporative, and objective principle (8,177ff., 190). It goes on to say that "the highest is also the deepest", that the Father of everything is also the Mother of everything, that the one who contains all things and is within them all – above them and yet without them – is also the one who is beneath them all and surrounds them" (3,344). On the same subject, see further, BAADER: *Sämtliche Werke* 1,410; 4,187; 8,112; 9,99, 170; 10,43; 13,246; 14,90, 240. On the question of the "harsh element" (male) and "weak gentleness and softness" (female), H. SPRECKELMAYER: *Die philosophische Deutung des Sündenfalls bei Franz von Baader*, p. 278, remarks that "metaphysically interpreted, man is determined by his intelligence in a more decisive sense than woman is, and the form of his sin is pride. Woman is more thoroughly formed by her 'soul', and her sinful posture is that of baseness". Compare to *Sämtliche Werke* 7,236 fn. 2.
63 Baader provides an analogy for this hybrid-relationship by citing "an old exegete", who says: "Insofar, as we are flesh of his flesh, he (the second Adam) is our father;

In Baader's theory of androgyny, the *embrace* assumes unusual significance. According to "the osteologists", human arms are nothing more than elongated ribs. When a man embraces a woman, "it is as though he were trying to reincorporate her into his thorax (breast or heart) whence she came" (7,236–37).[64] Brute animals do not embrace, any more than they love. We must distinguish the embrace from copulation, which takes place in the "abdominal region", not in "the heart region".[65]

Baader believed that copulation, *per se* and abstractly, is the exact opposite of anything like an act of union, love, or marriage. Of itself, it is the epitome of self-seeking and despiritualization of the sexes – just an animal act. This animal act receives its "exorcism", so to speak, only through the embrace: i.e., through love (7,237). In a letter to the Russian Prince Elim Mestchersky, dated July 23, 1832, Baader asserted: "I maintain, in fact, that just as natural will leads only to concubinage and not to marriage, that same natural will never leads to honest [political] subordination" (*Lettres inédites* 1,411). Baader even sees a close connection between lust to kill and destroy, on the one hand, and lust to copulate on the other.[66] Interestingly, it is a psychological commonplace

insofar, however, as he inserts us into his rib (his pierced side) and raises us up to a state of union of 'spirit-flesh' (*Geistfleisch*) with him, he is our 'blood-groom' (*Blut-Bräutigam*)" (7,236). Compare this last phrase with Exodus 4,25, where Zipporah says to Moses: "Truly, you are a bridegroom of blood to me".

64 The first part of the footnote about embracing reads: "The animal does not know the experience of taking someone to one's heart, or embracing, or the kiss. The mutual embrace (I in you, in your embrace or 'setting', and you in me) is what conditions the union, which is why the union of higher and lower can take place only through compromise (*Ausgleichung*). *Amor descendendo elevat* (Love elevates in descending). Saint Bernard calls the Holy Spirit the kiss of the Father and the Son. Two people who kiss each other really breathe together, and what comes to be through the union of both spirations works, in turn, on both of them . . ." (7,236–37). Novalis attached great significance to the embrace; see, for example, F. GIESE: *Der romantische Charakter*, pp. 328, 335.

65 See note 44 above.

66 Concerning this peculiar juxtaposition of ideas, Baader writes: "There is all the less reason for being surprised about that, since extremes touch on each other everywhere in this temporal life: lust borders on pain, genius on madness, the heroic deed on crime, life on death, and heaven on hell" (7,237 fn.). In *Über die Analogie des Erkenntnis-und des Zeugungstriebes*, Baader likens both lewdness and the desire to kill to an all-consuming rage that aims at overpowering another human being and consuming him to suit one's own purposes. "Therefore, the real meaning (spirit), the tone (*Geist*), and purpose of lust to kill and lewdness are one and the same . . ." (1,44). (See also 6,13; 14,424.) Friedrich Schlegel, cited in translation by H. G. SCHENK: *The Mind of the European Romantics*, London (Constable) 1966, p. 219, says something similar: "Voluptuousness is consummated when it becomes a divination of death, and death when it becomes lust". On the contrast between (isolated) passion and love, see also BAADER: *Sämtliche Werke* 1,236; 6,15; 8,294; 10,344 fn., 345; 14,402; 15,624. On love and chastity, see 11,188.

today to assert that the main intent of a rapist is not so much lustful as it is hostile or even murderous, an assumption which the not infrequent combination of murder and rape seems to corroborate.

St. Paul says in I Corinthians (11,11–12): "However, though woman cannot do without man, neither can man do without woman, in the Lord; woman may come from man, but man is born of woman – both come from God". To Baader, this means that Paul is designating "the Lord as restorer of the basis for our lost androgynous nature" (7,238). As he says elsewhere:

The concept of the redeemer of man can, therefore, be no other than the concept of someone who, working interiorly, will free man from his divided state and the strain of it, and will resolve tension in unity of being. He will free man's heart from bonds of darkness and his head from bondage to coldness;[67] and thus, as Heros and Eros at once, will re-establish the original androgynous essential unity of light and love in man. (10,6)

In the resurrection, man and woman will not be "glued together" again to form a complete human being. (Aristophanes misinterpreted Plato's conception of androgyny in this sense.[68]) Christ will be "bride" to the person who was formerly male, not by marrying either one in the usual sense, but by elevating both to the higher unity of androgyny (7,238).

Few exegetes, remarks Baader, have noted that the serpent in Genesis became an ugly beast only after the Fall of man. The "older authors" (who are not named) did notice this, and they have made the not implausible surmise that the serpent may originally have looked something like the way man looks now.[69] In any case, the important thing is to realize that "not only man and his surrounding nature have suffered such transformation and deformation, but also that distortion of both of them stood (and now stands) in a causal nexus with an original misdeed of man" (7,238–39).

---

67 Baader held that love is not blind and that thought is not (or should not be) divorced from affection; hence, the expression used here: "free man's heart from bonds of darkness and his head from bondage to coldness".

68 See PLATO: "The Symposium", 189A–193D, in *The Dialogues of Plato,* translated by B. Jowett, New York (Random House) 1937, volume 1, pp. 315ff.

69 Baader explains that if Adam had successfully withstood temptation (the second one, the one instigated by the serpent), not only would he and Eve have won paradise permanently, but the serpent itself would have been freed from the power of evil too. Man was to bring either a blessing or a curse on creation. Genesis describes man in the first chapter as a cultivator and benefactor of nature: ". . . [Genesis] shows us, then, that the origin of man's love for nature is in religiosity or in man's love for God, and the true principle of culture is to be found in love of nature. For when the apostle says that whoever does not love his brother (neighbor) does not love God either . . . you would also have to say that whoever does not love nature and lovingly foster it does not love God or his neighbor either . . ." (7,238–39 fn.).

That man's crimes today do not seem to exercise a very deleterious influence on him and on nature does not mean that they never did: for man once stood on a much higher plane than nature, and nature was then much more susceptible to the good and evil effects of his actions (7,239). Baader concludes his remarks on Genesis by defending the need to go beyond the literal text, claiming that he is merely following the lead of St. Paul in his epistle to the Galatians (4,21-27), where Paul explicitly declares that the Old Testament spoke allegorically in telling the story of Abraham, Sara, and Hagar and in describing their relationship to a free Jerusalem above and an enslaved Jerusalem here below.

Though the way in which Baader handled the theme of love between the sexes in his previously-cited essay concerning the baneful influence of materialism on the arts (*Über den verderblichen Einfluss, welchen die rationalistisch-materialistischen Vorstellungen auf die höhere Physik, so wie auf die höhere Dichtkunst und die bildende Kunst noch ausüben*) is similar, he does introduce some fresh nuances. He is, for example, particularly forceful in stating the equation: Christianity equals integrity, and integrity equals androgyny. And while the first part of this chapter concluded with Baader lamenting the way in which secular poets abuse the theme of love, he clearly expects better things of religious poetry:

At least religious poetry should never lose sight of the higher significance of this love of the sexes, for it is no other and no less than the solid bond into which both lovers enter before God, who is love in all its forms. They enter that union in order to help each other restore the inwardly eradicated and destroyed virginal image of God and body. Only from the standpoint of that context can we understand the sacramental element of such union, because only that kind of goal for that union transcends time and reaches the plane of eternally true being. What is purely earthly or purely temporal has no capacity, as such, for being a sacrament, nor does it need such capacity. Man should help woman to free herself from her womanliness (as incompleteness), and woman, in turn, should help man, so that in both of them the full primal image of man will inwardly emerge again. Both of them, instead of being half-men (and to that extent half-wild),[70] will become whole men again: i.e., Christians. For the expressions: to have become a Christian, to be born again, and to have recovered integrity of human nature are synonymous. Whoever shows me a Christian, shows me someone who is at least engaged in his reintegration; and whoever shows me a man engaged in his reintegration, shows me a Christian. It is of greatest importance in our own time to highlight this concept of Christianity as reintegrated humanity. Only that theology which portrays sin as disintegration, and redemption and rebirth as reintegration of man, is going to win out over all its foes, And when Scripture says that the old Adam must die so that the new Adam can live, we should realize that the old Adam is precisely

---

70   Baader defines his use of the term "wild": "Wildness is to be understood here, of course, in a higher sense, as alienation from divine life and from the household of God" (3,306 fn.). Baader believed that anyone who defies the law of his being as implanted in him by God is in fact "wild": that is, outside his proper region.

the man and woman whom we bear in ourselves, but the new Adam is just like the first person, fashioned unto the image of God, neither man nor woman. (3,306–07)

In the continuation of this passage, Baader outlines the salient points of a theory in which the meaning of sexual love is seen as an aid to any poet who might wish to dramatize the theme. Baader thought that the work of such a poet could compete with Goethe's *Faust.* After recalling man's fall from androgyny into bisexuality, Baader speaks of the guiding role Sophia plays in inviting man and woman to find their way back to integral humanity. He speaks of her as "the light that enlightens all men who come into the world" [said of the Word of God in John 1,9]. If she unites with the souls of a man and a woman, then the basis for genuine love between the two is laid. That union is a "higher constellation (about which people know no further cause, because it is itself the first cause: it is love that finds people, and not people who find love)" (3,307).

Every individual tries to restore the original androgynous image of God within himself, but people in love realize that they need each other's help to be successful. It is in this sense that one can speak of a sacrament of love or marriage; it is also why people say that "marriages are made in heaven". Sophia is active in love between the sexes, supplying both to man and woman the element each of them lacks.[71] Sophia's presence in their love explains the idolatry of sexual love and the moment of ecstasy achieved in it. It is the fault of lovers if such ecstasy is but a transitory experience.

In a favorite turn of phrase, Baader notes that love is not just a gift, but a task to be fulfilled (*eine Gabe und Aufgabe*) (3,308). The task that lovers must undertake is the time-transcending one of re-establishing God's image permanently in themselves. They are not only to reproduce themselves externally in their children, but also internally, as sons or children of God. Since the Fall, God's image in man has become a "ghostly", non-substantive, departed sort of spirit. Only through the incarnation of the Word of God in Christ has the image of God become substantive or real again. Thus, Christ was able to tell his followers after his resurrection that it was really he who was present, not just his spirit. That "real presence" referred to by Christ coincides with the concept of integrity. A departed soul (separated from its body) is not integral, any more than a corpse is an integral person.

---

71   "When Adam was broken up (*zerbrochen*), he lost the female part of the corporeal make-up of the virginal image, just as Eve left behind the male part in him. When rebirth takes place, therefore, the same Virgin appears as female to the man and as male to the woman, although the Virgin is intrinsically neither male nor female" (3,308 fn.).

Adam's sin first occurred internally, and only then was it manifested externally (in bisexuality). Conseqeuntly, recovery of God's image must also take place first internally, while man is still (externally) bisexual. St. Paul says that the Lord will do away with bisexuality. Thus, the deeper significance of sexual love is not identical with sexual desire at all, but rather with the mutual help man and woman give each other in reintegrating their humanity in God's image. It is in this sense that Christianity is reintegration (3,309).

In a final note, Baader argues that the disagreeable element ("the cross") in love is inseparable from the agreeable, because the new inner creation of love is not possible without destruction of the old. Even the polarity of sexes, considered in the abstract and not sacrificed to love, constitutes part of the cross that lovers in this world must bear and help one another endure. All of this goes counter to the sentimental and simplistic apotheosis of masculinity and femininity in which poets usually indulge – in fact, they are simply deifying the animal in man. Baader's closing word is the suggestion that, by including "the adversary", the devil (the enemy of all love, marriage, and rebirth), poets have sufficient material – related to his theory of love and sexuality – for a much more authentic essay into this area than they have managed to produce to date (3,310).

Baader's ideas about the relationship of the sexes, love, and marriage contrast sharply with notions prevalent in the eighteenth century.[72] He singles out for particular censure Kant's concept of marriage as a mere "rental contract" arrangement (5,116, 174, 281) and of love as primarily a form of self-gratification rather that self-giving (2,179; 5,264, 282); he finds these ideas extremely impoverished and shallow. Needless to say, Baader would also consider Freud's idea of "love" a horror. Of course, Baader was not alone in his assessment of eighteenth-century and Kantian views of love and marriage. Philosophers such as Fichte, Schelling, Hegel, and Krause – and, for the most part, the entire Romantic movement – also left Kant far behind in this area. (See, for example, 5,281 fn. 2.)

The Romantic movement pioneered a major change in society's view of love, marriage, and the place of woman, and the subject is significantly represented in the thought of Schleiermacher, F. Schlegel, Novalis, Tieck, Brentano, and Arnim.[73] A new and superior conception of woman was a vital element in Ro-

---

72 The most thorough study of this subject is P. KLUCKHOHN: *Die Auffassung der Liebe in der Literatur des 18. Jahrhunderts und der deutschen Romantik* .
73 See also P. KLUCKHOHN: *Das Ideengut der deutschen Romantik*, pp. 60–78; and P. KLUCKHOHN: *Die deutsche Romantik*, pp. 136–53. See also H. G. SCHENK: *The Mind of the European Romantics*, pp. 151ff.

manticism. Whereas eighteenth-century Enlightenment thinkers tended to view man and woman as equals by virtue of their reason and different only in their physical-sexual functions (paying little heed to the place of feeling or of psychological differences between the sexes), Romantics, with their intense regard for feeling and for the uniqueness of the individual, stressed the special contributions that woman brings to man's life and vice-versa. They began to see man and woman in a unique and differentiated but complementary relationship; in their view, it was a relationship filled with religious overtones. No longer was the eighteenth-century dictum, "friendship is a union of souls, marriage one of bodies", acceptable; no longer was marriage simply "four legs in a bed". The intimate connection, even identity, between the physical and the spiritual in love (a consequence of unity of body and spirit) was a basic Romantic conviction that represented something new, even revolutionary, vis-à-vis the eighteenth century. Physical love was seen as an expression of inner feeling, a manifestation of the soul. Love embodied loyalty and stability to such a degree that not a few Romantics simply equated love and marriage; "divorce" signified only that no love and, therefore, no marriage had ever existed in the first place.[74] The anti-institutional view of marriage adopted by some Romantics led, in practice, to many bizarre relationships; in theory, it led to increased pressure for dissolving marriage as an institution.[75] Man and woman began to be considered "partners", a development made possible only by the new conception of woman created by Romanticism. As Fritz Giese puts it: "The essentially new element between the fixed poles of pre-Romanticism and Baader is the woman as a living person".[76]

It is not without good reason that Giese mentions Baader as the *terminus ad quem* of Romantic speculation about love and marriage. For it was Baader, "the philosopher of love", who "led the Romantic conception of love to its apex",[77] and whose aphorisms on love "belong to the most beautiful and profound that have ever been written about love and the task of marriage".[78] Although Baader shared and stressed the positive advances registered by Romantic speculation as a whole, he did not, as it were, simply gather up its nuggets. Nor is it simply length of exposition or beauty of expression that make his thought so noteworthy. To an extent that far surpassed the efforts of any of his contemporaries,

---

74   See P. KLUCKHOHN: *Das Ideengut der deutschen Romantik*, pp. 60ff, on these points.
75   See F. SCHNABEL: *Deutsche Geschichte im 19en. Jahrhundert*, volume 1, pp. 254ff.
76   F. GIESE: *Der romantische Charakter*, p. 392
77   P. KLUCKHOHN: *Die Auffassung der Liebe in der Literatur des 18. Jahrhunderts und der deutschen Romantik*, p. 524.
78   P. KLUCKHOHN: *Die deutsche Romantik*, p. 148.

Baader's theory of love and marriage was grounded in his metaphysics of religion and in his philosophy of human nature – even his philosophy of the world as a whole. His speculation went far beyond Romantic sentimentality or the "pop psychology" of his day; his was truly a "philosophy of love". Many Romantics spoke of love as religious in nature, but none took that position as seriously or developed it as systematically as Baader. In this context, it should be noted that Baader's view of androgyny, with its decisive consequences for his theory of relations between the sexes, contributed much toward making his speculation unique in this area. Several Romantics touched on the theme of androgyny, and Ritter, in particular, developed the notion at some length, but, all in all, androgyny "may in no way be considered an ideal of Romanticism in general. Polar opposition of the sexes should rather find fruitful synthesis in love and marriage".[79]

Baader considered marriage a divinely established institution (7,229). Its object is the mutual help man and woman lend each other in overcoming their incompleteness: i.e., in recovering the lost image of God. Love is the fruit of marriage (10,345) as well as the incentive for marrying. What was once lost can be recovered with the aid of Christ. The "original marriage" can be reestablished:

If we are saddened at the dangers to which things generated and produced by man (taken in their broadest sense) are exposed, we are, nonetheless, confident "that by virtue of the saving, eternal, and incarnate love accessible to every man, that original marriage (this word too is to be taken in the broadest sense) is still possible, and that this possibility renders marriage an indissoluble and holy alliance in every stage and region of this union" . . . (9,146)

"Original marriage" is, of course, not union between separate male and female individuals, but, rather, union of all the constituent elements of human nature in androgyny or integrity. This also involves "marriage" between man and God, whose image in man makes man androgynous.

According to Baader, it is the redemptive and liberating power of Christ (which power is the "seed of the kingdom of God"), working in the lives of married people, that makes marriage a sacrament (6,24). Thus, in the sixth book of *Fermenta Cognitionis*, Baader speaks of man's duty to free himself from the "spirit-animal image" (*Geistthierbild*), which is accomplished by reestablishing the original heavenly image. This is what rebirth means. Man and wife help each other achieve this goal, first inwardly and then corporeally in the resurrection.

79 P. KLUCKHOHN: *Das Ideengut der deutschen Romantik*, p. 68. See F. GIESE: *Der romantische Charakter* for a detailed delineation of the applicability of Kluckhohn's statement.

Furthermore, this is where the concept of marriage as a sacrament, as the Church understands it, belongs. In other words, the purpose of marriage as sacrament is mutual restoration of the inner heavenly and angelic image in man and woman. One can say, in this connection, that the man, if he is as he should be, is really the one who would inwardly (spiritually) cease to be a male animal any longer; similarly, the woman, if she is as she should be, would no longer inwardly be a female animal. This is the only way both of them could restore the idea of humanity in themselves again. (2,382)[80]

Baader's conception of the relation between man and wife is patterned on the organic model, a point of view he adopted directly from the Bible:

It can be said, with regard to two members of one and the same organism, that one member does not have power over the other, because the same unity to which they are subordinate resides in both of them. In this sense, Paul says this of two people (man and woman) joined in love – and Christ says it too – that man and woman truly united become one body: i.e., a body that sublimates their separate bodily character. We might mention in passing that, from all of this, one gets a very different concept than the usual one of both androgyny and celibacy. Likewise, the only correct concept of the sacrament of married love and loving marriage [flows from this]. For that concept rests on the knowledge that, just as lovers are able to love each other only to the extent that God's love abides in each of them, so also they cannot love God in turn, if they do not love each other or are unfaithful to each other. (10,286–87; see also 15,623, 625)

In the fourteenth lecture of *Vorlesungen über Societätsphilosophie* (14,55ff.), Baader is again explicit about the essential role played by love in marriage if true reintegration is to take place.

If one considers attentively the inner action of true love, one is easily convinced that through this love both man and woman perfect themselves, at least interiorly, to the androgynous state. Woman helps man to love, and he helps her to wonder, so that the mystery and sacrament of true love consist in solidarity of the bond between two lovers, each of whom helps the other and himself, too, to restore androgyny as pure and integral humanity that is neither male nor female: i.e., not a half-entity (14,142–43).[81]

It should be noted that sacramentality of love is not conferred on married partners by the Church, but by each other (given the fact that God has so ordained the relationships between the sexes). In a letter to Dr. von Stransky, dated

---

80 See BAADER: *Recension der Schrift: Essai sur l'Indifference en matière de Religion, par M. l'Abbé F. de la Mennais,* 5,126 fn., which expresses substantially the same idea, but uses the categories of nobility and humility (component elements of love) and their caricatures, baseness and pride.
81 Baader continues his consideration of androgyny at this point by shifting from "good" androgyny to "bad" androgyny, which, instead of overcoming selfishness, drives it to the limit of pride, base servility, and false self-sufficiency. True love unites two persons to an angelic image; false love unites them to the devil's image (14,143).

November 22, 1839, Baader speaks of his own forthcoming marriage to Marie Robel and asks von Stransky's prayers on his behalf: "for the prayer of friends is the only thing that they and the priest can and should give as a blessing in this matter. Even the Romans themselves teach that the sacrament of marriage stands without the priest's blessing" (15,634). In asserting this position, Baader's theology is perfectly orthodox: according to Catholic theology, it is not the Church that "marries" people; it merely (officially) witnesses what the married people themselves accomplish.

Just as there can be both good and bad kinds of androgyny,[82] so can there be good and bad kinds of marriage. Number thirty-three ("Über Ehen") of *Socialphilosophische Aphorismen aus verschiedenen Zeitblättern* (5,247ff.) makes this point very clearly. The entire number reads:

If we recognize that a truly organic union of the sexes in mind and spirit, or a pure marriage, cannot come about or last except through mediation of a principle or agent that is superior to both members, we will also see that this higher binding principle is a religious one, whatever sort of understanding we might have of the connection. We will also recognize that it is only by virtue of that mediation that man and woman will be able to complement each other in mind and spirit so as to reach the integral image of man (God's image). For if the efficacy of such a higher formative principle is lacking, then marriage degenerates either to nullity or something very run-of-the-mill, or even deeper into positive evil. For in the first case, the man and woman are or become indifferent to one another in mind and spirit; what they are doing amounts to running an external business together, something like "Hans Stein and Company". In the second case, they do indeed unite in mind and spirit, but in a bad sense, so that man complements his pride with woman's servile snake-cunning, while woman combines this quality of hers with the man's pride; the result is that the two together constitute a demonic image. No one should believe that in this pluralistic world there has ever been a marriage in which each one of these three forms did not really manifest itself in its turn, or, at least, in which each one did not strive and attempt to make itself dominant in the marriage. One would not believe, I maintain, that in this complex world there is anything other than mixed marriages. The fact is that a true marriage itself cannot be given (*gegeben*) to men; it can be offered them only as a lifelong task (*aufgegeben*). (5,339–40)[83]

In a related vein, Baader wrote to Baron Boris von Uxküll, on January 8, 1826, describing the protean character of marriage in words taken from St. Martin and ending with this statement:

. . . finally, the respect given to this bond [of marriage], as well as the attacks that are made on it (especially by those sects that deny the sacrament of marriage), become, in every civil and

---

82 In addition to 14,143, see also 9,207–220, especially 9,212.
83 Not only marriage, but love in general, is something that is not simply "given" (*gegeben*) but also set before one as a task (*aufgegeben*). See BAADER: *Sämtliche Werke* 5,347 where Baader has a paragraph entitled "Gegebene und aufgegebene Liebe".

religious respect, a source of harmony or disorders, of blessings or anathemas (the devil is an enemy of marriage), and they seem to link *heaven, earth,* and *hell* with human marriage [italics are Baader's]. (15,434; see also 14,143)[84]

On the question of dissolubility or indissolubility of marriage, Baader states his position, in a more or less incidental way, in the twelfth lecture of *Vorlesungen über Societätsphilosophie* (14,55ff.). He speaks there of the dissolubility or indissolubility of associations and social communities in general. The stand he takes is that, when the law forbids dissolution of a given association, this prohibition coincides with the prohibition against stealing and killing. The ground for this equation is that an organic community or association is a new creation, a new living entity. To dissolve it is to destroy a living bond between people. "And it is in this sense that the Lord's statement makes sense: What God (the living One) has joined together in one life, man should not separate [see, for example, Matthew 19,6]" (14,131). Here, the intimate connection linking Baader's philosophy of love to his social philosophy becomes manifest once again. He considered his reflection on love "a propaedeutic to social philosophy", because "according to my view of it, the formation of society goes from love into the legislative, and from this latter into executive or power-wielding [forms]: theocracy, aristocracy, monarchy" (15,443; see also *Lettres inédites* 4,202, 220).

In this same lecture, Baader goes on to speak of three kinds of associations people can establish: those that can be dissolved before death; those that are dissolved by death; and those that last for eternity (14,132). He does not indicate explicitly into which category the marriage union falls, but the whole discussion, here and elsewhere, makes it quite clear that he considers marriage an indissoluble sacramental bond. (See, for example: 5,281; 14,47, 132, 408.) However, Hans Reichel's declaration that "Baader's concept of marriage is that of the Catholic Church"[85] seems hard to justify if one takes into account the central role allotted to the myth of androgyny in Baader's thought about Christian marriage. In characterizing sexual relationships, Baader distinguishes between the external *Associéschaft* and the internal *Societät:* the first is a mere liaison or concubinage; the second is a life-relationship, an organic union (14,408). In

---

84 Baader's combined French-German text reads as follows: ". . . enfin le respect porté à ce lien, ainsi que les atteintes, qui lui sont faites (besonders von jenen Secten, welche das Sacrament der Ehe leugnen) deviennent sous tous les rapports civils et religieux, une source d'harmonie ou des désordres, des bénédictions ou d'anathèmes (der Teufel ist ein Feind der Ehe) et semblent lier au mariage de l'homme le *ciel,* la *terre* et les *enfers".*

85 H. REICHEL: "Die Sozietätsphilosophie Franz von Baaders", *Zeitschrift für die gesamte Staatswissenschaft,* 57 (1901), p. 226.

the study-notebooks devoted to St. Martin's *Des Erreurs et de la Vérité* (12,81ff.), Baader cites St. Martin's view that any law code that allows divorce for any grounds other than adultery is acting on a false principle (12,144). Baader offers no comment on that position, apparently agreeing with it. It is interesting to observe that Friedrich Schlegel and Friedrich Schleiermacher, both of whom strongly opposed anything resembling Kant's legalistic view of the marriage "contract", "came, without any theological grounding for it whatsoever, to the conclusion that the possibility of divorce is contrary to the very essence of marriage: to declare a divorce is simply to say that no marriage existed".[86]

In addition to his extensive and systematic treatments of androgyny and relations between the sexes, Baader often touches on these subjects in passing, frequently emphasizing a particular aspect of one or the other in a way not duplicated elsewhere. In a passage from *Fermenta Cognitionis*, for example, one in which Kant's notion of love as an essentially self-serving emotion is being attacked,[87] Baader argues that love is love only to the extent that it is *not bound* by desire or need or nature (although it is not separated from them either). The consecration of sexual passion (the apex of selfishness and lovelessness) through love in the marriage union is a perfect illustration of his point. He comments:

The ideal in animal copulation (so-called love) is to unfold the eternal race in the decline of the individual, but the ideal of human love is to unfold the eternal race by unfolding the uniqueness of the person who is posited in accordance with his eternal uniqueness (as a member of the whole). This unique element thus stands for everything in the eyes of the lover. Here we have a case of the Whole (God) shining through in the transfigured uniqueness of the person. (2,179–80 fn.; see also 14,379)[88]

Fermenta Cognitionis offers yet another aperçu on the theme. In number twenty-nine of the fifth book (2,360ff.), Baader says: "The concept of love is that of a triad – that is, of unifying differentiating and differentiating unifying" (*Der Begriff*

---

86 P. KLUCKHOHN: *Die deutsche Romantik*, pp. 146–47; P. KLUCKHOHN: *Das Ideengut der deutschen Romantik*, p. 72.
87 "Kant, for example, reasons no better about love than a blind man about color when (following Spinoza's definition: *Ideo bonum est, quia appetimus*) he defines love as inclination toward what brings us advantage . . ." (2,179). In E. SUSINI (Ed.): *Lettres inédites* 4,89, Baader makes hate equivalent to egoism or self-seeking.
88 This quotation calls to mind many passages found in R. JOHANN: *The Meaning of Love;* for example, the reference to a community of love as "a whole made up of wholes" (p. 36); or the statement: "It is the presence of this Value [God] in the creature that is the creature. Hence, each creature is a unique value, yet communing in its uniqueness with every other creature in *the* Unique Value" (p. 38).

der Liebe ist jener der Trias, nemlich des einenden Unterscheidens und unterscheidenden Einens). In other words, the harmonization of two unlike entities.[89] The same holds true, in an opposite direction, for hate: it juxtaposes the unlike and separates the like. Baader continues:

Thus, without (original) dissimilarity, there would be no love, just as without original similarity there would be no hate. This is also why only the bad (animal) sexual difference testifies to itself as such in man, because true uniting works in an arresting and hindering way, since, in fact, everything that underlies sexual differentiation is at the same time a condition for harmonizing love itself. This harmonization always manifests itself as productive (creative), whether it be in time (in numerical procreation) or outside of time, producing only new energies (*Kräfte*) and not new creatures. If St. Paul says (Ephesians 5), then: "Husbands should love their wives (as the head loves the body and the Lord the Church) and let the wife fear (reverence) her husband",[90] this text has to be matched with the one that says: "God has loved us first in Christ [see I John 4,10, 19]".[91] In other words, condescension on one side is always necessary if ascent on the other side, a counter-love, is to be possible and their conjunction (love) is to be real.

Where pure heavenly Love looks with creative glance, Counter-love returns to her from the image of that glance (2,360).

In relations between man and woman, man takes the role of one who "descends": i.e., he is the one who is supposed to take the initiative in loving his wife. It is her task to respond to that "descent" with her own "ascent", to reciprocate his action. (See also 14,423.) A man cannot love a woman who will not reciprocate his descending action with her ascending response; a woman can-

---

89 Much of what Baader has to say about how love works is cast in sets of complementary factors. The following passage, from his essay *Über das durch die französische Revolution herbeigeführte Bedürfnis einer neuen und innigeren Verbindung der Religion mit der Politik*, is a typical example: "A relationship of union presupposes unlikeness between those who unite, since there is only aggregation or heaping up in the case of likes. Connection, looked at as an act (reality or action), is nothing more than constant inner accommodation (bringing closer, bringing together) of something that is outwardly unlike (removed, separated). This unlike element (high and low, superiority and dependency, superfluity and lack), when united through love, expresses itself in the relationship and community of the noble and the humble. It is between these two poles that the life of love itself breathes and hovers. An important and illuminating consideration is the fact that, in case love dies, those two poles or elements of love are transformed and appear now as pride and baseness; and between these two poles, hate or the striving to flee (*Fliehstreben*) appears instead of love" (6,15–16; see also 4,175, 185, 194).

90 Baader's reference to Ephesians 5 actually combines elements of two verses: "Husbands should love their wives just as Christ loved the Church" (verse 25), and "let every wife respect her husband" (verse 33).

91 His reference to I John 4,10 should read: "This is the love I mean: not our love for God but God's love for us when he sent his Son to be the sacrifice that takes our sins away"; chapter 4, verse 19 reads: "We are to love, then, because he loved us first".

not reverence a man who turns to her without love. As St. Paul teaches, both man and woman, head and body, Lord and community, are subject to the same unity. (See also 6,87.) It would be wrong to overlook the reality of the triad in this case, as though unity (totality) existed in just one (the man) of the two people who come together. "Woman makes sense only in and with man, and man can propagate himself only in woman" (2,361).

Finally, with reference to "bad" differentiation of sexes, Baader uses one of his favorite illustrations from the field of mathematics to underscore the inherent limitation of anything that exists in isolation from its complementary correlative: ". . . since the root of matter is a fraction (1/2), every raising of the power of that fraction (as reaction against man's spirit), in accordance with the nature of all fractions, can only manifest itself by dividing" (2,361). Thus, every accentuation of one of the sexes, in isolation from the androgynous whole, leads to an ever-diminishing hold on the reality of the integrity of man.

With regard to the integration of sexes in an androgynous whole, Baader remarks – in a footnote at the beginning of lecture nine of book five of *Vorlesungen über speculative Dogmatik* (9,221) – that "this integration does not consist in the fact that both parties mutually complement each other from their own resources (*aus sich*), but that they both find completion in one and the same higher element (androgyny)". To illustrate the point, he analogically cites an agreement reached by two people: it is not as though each person gives the other a "piece" of the idea they agree upon, but rather that they help each other arrive at the point at which "the same idea is present in each of them in its entirety". Every member must help every other member to be fully a member, because "only when the spirit is fully present in all of them, can the spirit be fully present in each of them". That is what constitutes solidarity of membership. The animal world bears witness to the fact that both sexes are present in each animal, though one set of sexual characteristics is present in each only in a dormant way. Among human beings, the situation is such that:

man as soul seeks the womanly image for his male image, and woman as soul seeks the male image for her female image. We can also say that true love between man and woman in sexual union occurs only when both of them are no longer inwardly man and woman. For, if Adam had not first been inwardly differentiated (but not separated) as male and female, he would not have become so outwardly. (9,221 fn.)[92]

92 In a related passage from *Vorlesungen über Societätsphilosophie*, Baader says "In fact, it is not merely religion that talks about a dying out of maleness and femaleness as two upstart, false and evil selves, but rather, if one is attentive to the inner action of true love, one will be easily persuaded that through this love both the man and the woman complement each other, in an inward way at least, to the condition of androgyny. The reason is that the woman helps the man to love, and he helps her to wonder; accord-

An interesting problem-area, connected with the relationship of the sexes, concerns *equality*. Both Johannes Sauter and Hermann Spreckelmeyer discuss this topic in relation to Baader's thought.[93] Sauter observes that "Baader does not speak of any difference in worth of the two sexes in the sphere of Bios and Psyche", and then reviews a number of opinions about the metaphysical superiority of one or the other sex. Especially noteworthy are the remarks of M. Marcuse, who thinks it very possible that all our ideas about women are filtered through purely male thought modes (*Denkaffekte*), and Simmel, who holds that "the principal concepts of modern philosophy, such as reason, person, individuality, truth, etc., which are passed off as universal human categories, basically have a purely male character". Spreckelmeyer judges that "Baader's metaphysics of love is predominantly masculine-oriented, because Adam serves as its point of departure. But in itself, it is thoroughly grounded on the principle of mutuality, which, in turn, is structured into a hierarchy of being". While many argue that the sexes, based on the notion of "equal sharing", complement each other, Spreckelmeyer believes that the " 'opposition' between man and woman, metaphysically considered, appears to be one of superiority-subordination".

The chief argument supporting this point of view is linked to Baader's speculation about the meaning and function of names. In this regard, a footnote found in the essay, *Alle Menschen sind im seelischen, guten oder schlimmen, Sinn unter sich Anthropophagen* (4,221ff.), is instructive:

I observe here that in the Scriptures a name stands as an attribute distinct from a person but still inseparable from him. That is why the woman has no name of her own, since she (considered as married to her husband) has no personality of her own. This is why (according to the teaching of the Hebrews) the seven spirits take the name of the spirit who is related to them (to Sophia or glory) as a husband is to his wife . . . (4,235)[94]

We have seen in the commentary on Genesis that "woman always exercises a secondary function to her husband, both in good and in evil" (7,230). In a

---

ingly, the mystery and sacrament of true love consists in the solid union of the two lovers in the task of aiding each other and themselves in the work of restoring androgyny as pure and integral humanity, which is neither male nor female: i.e., not partial . . ." (14,142–43).

93 J. SAUTER: *Baader und Kant*, p. 463; H. SPRECKELMEYER: *Die philosophische Deutung des Sündenfalls bei Franz von Baader*, p. 276.

94 H. SPRECKELMEYER: *Die philosophische Deutung des Sündenfalls bei Franz von Baader*, p. 276 fn., observes: "From Baader's 'anonymity' a direct path leads to Kierkegaard's 'substantial devotion', which indicates the decisive metaphysical determination of the 'essence' of woman . . ." See note 40 above.

footnote found in book three of *Fermenta Cognitionis*, Baader again takes up the problem of superiority between the sexes:

In the above-mentioned respect, one could say now that woman is superior to man, inasmuch as she is the bearer of lust (of the image) which inflames his desire. But just because she is, in the first place, an unconscious bearer of this image, she is inferior to man, because she first arrives at consciousness of this image through the help of the awakening power of man. This holds true both for good and bad lust, for the woman's seed and for the serpent's seed. For every woman is at once an Eva and an Ave (Maria), and it is for the most part up to the man whether the one or the other of these two forms comes to assert itself in her. (2,256 fn.)

Baader seems to be saying here that woman's identity is inexorably tied to that of man: she is "defined" by her relationship to a man.[95] While Baader cannot – in any sense of the word – be styled a misogynist, his views concerning relationship between the sexes clearly take a male-dominated orientation as their point of departure.

Giese identifies several areas in Baader's theory of androgyny which lack clarity.[96] The role of Sophia in making man androgynous is the major one, but the relation of androgynous man to the figures of Jesus and Mary is also cloudy. In addition, Baader should have defined the precise relationship of the present intersexual state of man to the androgynous state of the future more carefully.

All of these charges have some validity, although, in the matter of androgynous man's relationship to Sophia and to Christ, Baader's position would have been clearer to Giese had he not restricted his attention almost exclusively to texts dealing with androgyny alone. Further consideration of Baader's views on the image of God in man and Sophia's contribution to it, as well as to the vital role that imagination ("magic") and love play in making man actualize God's image and androgynous integrity within himself, would have made Baader's position less uncertain.

In his struggle against Enlightenment philosophy, Baader felt it his duty and calling to revive important streams of mystical thought and insight that had been overwhelmed and overlooked in the floodtide of rationalism. In particular, he judged it an especially urgent task to see that the treasures of Böhme, St. Martin, and Oetinger were brought back into circulation. He owed much to these men, particularly in his struggle to elaborate a theory of androgyny. But, says Giese, "the organization of the problem of androgyny is the incontestable achievement of Baader. And there is no doubt that he goes far beyond St.

---

95   H. SPRECKELMEYER: *Die philosophische Deutung des Sündenfalls bei Franz von Baader*, p. 277.
96   F. GIESE: *Der romantische Charakter*, p. 385.

Martin in doing so . . . The question of relations between the sexes [in Romanticism] was closed with Baader's theory".[97] Consonant with Giese's declaration is Ernst Benz's statement that "Franz von Baader did not simply repeat the myth of androgyny in the form in which he had received it; rather, he developed it further in an independent way . . ."[98]

Benz lists three ways in which Baader's treatment of androgyny represented a significant advance. First, Baader put order and coherence into the disconnected and confused fragments of Böhme's exegesis of scattered biblical passages;[99] he made a meaningful whole of many parts. Second, "Baader developed traditional ideas about androgyny into the basis for a positive understanding of marriage, and saw in the idea of androgyny the possibility for spiritualizing relationships between man and woman in love, marriage, and friendship". The central goal of marriage becomes the recovery of lost unity and the completing of human nature, a "reintegration process" that is effected through love grounded in God. Man and woman see in one another the element lost to each of them through Adam. They desire to restore God's image (Sophia) in themselves, and married love is a means to that end. "Christ is the true androgynous figure in the redeemed world and the restorer of our lost original nature". Third, Baader undertook to modernize the myth of androgyny. He did so by considering the goal of Christianity to be the reintegration of man, a

---

97 F. GIESE: *Der romantische Charakter*, p. 386
98 E. BENZ: *Adam. Der Mythus vom Urmenschen*, p. 210.
99 F. GIESE: *Der romantische Charakter*, p. 380, supplements Benz's position on this point: "It may be that Böhme's presentations seem intricate, confused and obscure; the basic idea is clear and, as usual with Böhme, full of deep intuition. Everything else is only a more or less appropriate application and shifting of meaning. We see this basic idea [of androgyny] attain full resurrection for the first time in Baader's commentary. Baader applies the modern apparatus of science, as it were, to Böhme's intuition. He eliminates all the unclear points and mystifications. One would like to say that he becomes more philosophical. He uses textual criticism and draws word for word (in that, already catholic) from the truth of Moses's text. Beyond that, he does not fail to take account of the accomplishments of natural science; he links up with doctrines on polarity. Besides that, we must show directly how he pays tribute to modern medicine: he explains (indirectly) his concept of androgyny, using physiological expressions in order to define it more sharply; and, in addition, refers to early classical esthetic theory in the process. Besides this, he remains in touch with the present by linking the notion of development contained in the theory of androgyny with ethical points of view. The latter are especially congenial to him, since he does explain things theosophically. His idea is the same as Schleiermacher's: the problem of love has to be resolved religiously, but entirely in a biblical way – with more discipline than Hardenberg used. In that way, Baader becomes the center of gravity (*Sammelpunkt*) for the whole of early Romantic speculation. But he carried this synthesis within himself: he united things less in a self-conscious way than intuitively and 'by nature' ".

reintegration which was to be achieved by restoring the fullness of primal androgeneity. Sin is disintegration; marriage is the means for the divided sexes to help each other achieve integration. Benz closes with the observation that "these thoughts have had an extremely powerful impact on the notions of love, marriage, and friendship held in the circle of German Romanticism and German Idealism, and have also radiated out to the Romantic literature and philosophy of other countries".[100]

The foregoing discussion of androgyny completes the picture: it, together with material introduced in chapters one and two, yields a general but coherent overview of the way in which Baader viewed God, man, nature, and their varying interrelationships. All of the structural elements essential to Baader's *Weltanschauung* are present and accounted for. From start to finish, the commanding position of love in the whole is unmistakable. His mystical view of God as substantial love, as the one who creates and restores man out of love, is clearly and repeatedly stated. And as every product reflects its producer, so man reflects God in an eminent way in all of creation. Consequently, God's image – Eros or Sophia – resides in man as the principle whereby man loves both God and other men. The Fall of man, the rejection of love, resulted in a fissure in man's very being, a fact reflected in the separation of the sexes. Man's only salvation is to rediscover his integrity as God's image. Eros-Sophia invites man to renew androgyny by way of love and marriage. The indwelling of Sophia-Eros alone can reinstate every man in his vocation of reflecting the God who is love:

How a man is related to God determines how he is related to himself, to other men, to his own nature, and to the rest of nature (15,469).

---

100 E. BENZ: *Adam. Der Mythus vom Urmenschen*, pp. 211–12, says that Baader separated himself from Schelling most decisively in the realm of his views about androgyny. Schelling, especially in his later thought, was strongly influenced by Böhme and Oetinger, but he consciously excluded the myth of androgyny. He did, however, take much interest in their speculation on Sophia.

Chapter 5
Propositions Taken from a
Philosophy of Love

Conformation is information. [See also: 2,20 fn.] The creature cannot achieve perfection except by thinking, willing, and acting in God. A man can arrive at true freedom only on the basis of a positively established ground. The freedom and lightness, yes even the grace, of movement is conditioned by a solid foundation. To the extent that a creature has patterned itself in conformity with divine self-grounding, it is united to God and shares in his Love. God is Love. Philosophy of love must, therefore, be the central teaching. Depth of soul (*Gemüthes*) parallels depth of mind. The more superficial a person's feeling is, the shallower his speculation. Man's love for God is like God's immanence or indwelling. A person can indeed withdraw himself from God's indwelling (*Inwohnung*), but not from his presence by power (*Durchwohnung*). If he loses God's love, he then falls subject to his power. He must express God: how he does that makes no difference for God, but it does for him.

Vorlesungen über speculative Dogmatik (8,187, number 40)

The true riddle of philosophy, which the philosophical philistines have left unsolved, is the riddle of birth-giving and creative love.

Über die Vernünftigkeit der drei Fundamentaldoctrinen des Christenthums vom Vater und Sohn, von der Wiedergeburt und von der Mensch- und Leibwerdung Gottes (10,29 fn. 2)

The essence of Franz von Baader's thought on love is contained in two essays: *Sätze aus der erotischen Philosophie* (1828); and *Vierzig Sätze aus einer religiösen Erotik* (1831).[1] As their titles suggest, these essays consist of pithy, aphoristic

1 These two essays are found in BAADER: *Sämtliche Werke* 4,163–78, and 4,179–200, respectively. As previously noted, Paul Kluckhohn contends that "Baader's fragments *aus der erotischen Philosophie* and *aus einer religiösen Erotik* and others belong to the most beautiful and most profound that have ever been written about the essence of love and the task of marriage" (P. KLUCKHOHN: *Die deutsche Romantik*, p. 148). But Baader's thoughts about love and marriage are not limited to these two essays. Indeed, he addresses both subjects frequently and the principal points made elsewhere have been

propositions or paragraphs which sum up, in relatively brief compass, the quint-essential thoughts of the "professor of love" (15,627) on his favorite subject. These aphorisms, however, are but the flower of Baader's thought. Without considering the whole plant – its roots and its stem, the soil and climatic conditions that provide it with nourishment – it would be impossible to understand love as Baader understood it. In logical terms, these propositions are like enthymemes: i.e., conclusions whose premises are implied but not explicitly stated. Both contain a great deal of previously-discussed material; but in each essay, some new elements are introduced for the first time. A chapter will be devoted to the propositions found in each of these two essays.

Baader's point of departure in *Sätze aus der erotischen Philosophie* is his observation that religion and love, though of central importance to life, are often considered unworthy of serious consideration. They are, supposedly, simply "matters of the heart". The fact is, says Baader, that religion and love are intimately related to each other, and are "the highest gifts of life". The happiness of individuals and the well-being of societies depend on the place allocated to religion and love in their schemes of values and priorities. One would suppose that a person could do nothing more important than get a clear idea about them. But people, by and large, are intellectually and spiritually lazy. In addition, the prejudiced notion that "feeling ceases where thinking begins" had been given new life by both Rousseau and Jacobi. Baader often entered the lists to combat this view: for example, in the following passage taken from *Über die Nothwendigkeit einer Revision der Wissenschaft natürlicher, menschlicher und göttlicher Dinge, in Bezug auf die sich in ihr noch mehr oder minder geltend machenden Cartesischen und Spinozistischen Philosopheme*:

It is precisely in these rare moments of inward union between one's affective and apperceptive sides that truly creative and original nature comes to the fore (e.g., in poetic or artistic enthusiasm, as in any other). It is just in those moments, moments that people consider most unnatural to a person, that one feels most at home and natural – those moments, I say, in which one's feeling or affection perfectly coincides with one's apperception and knowledge. The earth-bound person (*der verirdischte Mensch*), on the other hand, feels the discord between the two to a greater or lesser degree all his life: in every case, he feels (or enjoys) only what he does not know or grasp, and he knows only what he does not feel. Or else, he finds himself attracted to something he cannot respect but must despise and is unable to be attracted to what he must respect. Love

systematically collated into the text of this study, especially in this chapter and Chapter 6. Many important studies devoted to Baader's philosophy of love have already been cited, particularly in Chapters 2, 3, and 4, but that list should be expanded to include the following works: H. GRASSL: "Eine Philosophie der Liebe", *Hochland* (1950-51) pp. 374–85; P. KLUCKHOHN: *Das Ideengut der deutschen Romantik,* Tübingen (Max Neimeyer) [4]1961, pp. 60–77; and P. KLUCKHOHN: *Die deutsche Romantik,* Bielefeld and Leipzig (Velhagen and Klasing) 1924, pp. 136–53.

lives in its own element, precisely in that reunion of feeling with knowledge; when the two separate, love dies out and unhappiness sets in for a person. (10,281)[2]

Laziness and prejudice have caused people to be more ignorant about religion and love than almost any other thing in life. (See, for example, 15,408.) People regard these realities as purely emotional affairs, experiences that have nothing to do with thinking; some are even convinced that *not thinking* about religion and love is a necessary condition for experiencing them. In short, blind empiricism is the order of the day. "It is no wonder, then", concludes Baader, "that for so many people both their religion and their love maintain themselves only in a chiaroscuro of their reason" (4,165).

All eighteen of the propositions enumerated in Baader's essay deal with some aspect of love, but they are not ordered in any analytical or logical progression. No attempt has been made to reorganize them, and the discussion which follows will proceed seriatim, following Baader's own order.

Proposition 1 (4,165–67)

Baader describes love's essence as an act of union and harmonization, an act in which the differences between two people are subjected to a higher third element: namely, Eros. (See, for example, 1,232). One of the clearest statements that he makes about this relationship may be found in *Vom Geist und Wesen der Dinge*. He begins that essay by noting that uniting is godly work, whereas dividing is devilish work. There is no unity, he contends, without an act of subjection to a higher third element in which two formerly separated entities unite. Thus, unity calls for humility. (See, for example, 1,59.) Shortly thereafter, he goes on to describe the "inner economy of love":

. . . lovers themselves would be, so to speak, simply visible servants, priests and agents of a higher Eros ("God is Love"), who makes himself known invisibly in their midst whenever they come together in his name. One could rightly say, then, that it is not so much that lovers love one another, but rather that a Higher Being loves himself in and through them. This Higher Being divides and separates Himself, so to speak, in two individual lovers so that he will be able to touch, find, and sense Himself in that way. Thus, the common view of love – which claims that love involves mere exchange of selfhood between lovers, and that both lover and beloved go outside themselves and into one another – would be erroneous. If that were so, these lovers would be doing no more than exchanging the limits of their own narrow existence; but they

---

2   Baader attacks Rousseau and Jacobi for their one-sided overemphasis on feeling. See, for example, BAADER: *Sämtliche Werke* 1,65ff., 90; 2,371, 494; 5,236; 6,139. See also Chapter 2, where Baader insists on the close and indispensable connection between knowledge and love.

could not, in fact, be raised above themselves into a freer and, as it were, heavenly existence. That is possible only if both of them are elevated to, and find each other suspended in, a higher third . . . (1,61–62)[3]

Thus, lovers perfect and complement each other only through Eros, to whom they subject themselves: "for every union comes into existence only through subjection" (4,165). Every union requires some sacrifice of independent individuality by each party to the union. (See, for example, 1,255.) Union is thus superior to whatever one surrenders in order to achieve it.

Baader makes three observations about love that might be styled the "three laws of love": (1) Only unlikes are capable of and need harmonization, just as different sounds – not identical (unison) sounds – produce a musical chord.[4] In *Fermenta Cognitionis*, he points out that:

The concept of love is that of a triad, namely that of differences that unite and of unity that differentiates, a harmonization (accommodation) of two unlikes . . . This holds true in an opposite sense for hate: it combines things that are unlike and separates those that are like . . . (2,360, number 29).

(2) The accord and harmony of love arise in the very act of establishing them, not before or after; "consequently, you cannot understand love apart from loving, nor unity (*unitas*) apart from uniting (*unire*), nor life (*vita*) apart from living

---

3   At the point in the text where it is stated that "a Higher Being loves himself in and through them", Baader has appended the following explanatory footnote: "Only God is able, in loving himself, to be self-sufficient and happy in his love; and insofar as he loves himself through and in his creatures, he makes them happy. Every creature who wants to be like God in this matter, i.e., in self-love, is barring his own happiness, because he blocks the process of God's self-love, which moves and courses through him . . ." (1,61). For more on this subject, see Propositions 28 and 33, Chapter 6; BAADER: *Sämtliche Werke* 1,229–33; and 5,263–65. See also 1,254ff.; 9,411 fn.; and 14,127ff.

4   "In unison, we hear no dissonance, but the latter can occur. In accord [harmony], dissonance is sublated and overcome – there is no more cacophony to fear" (*Vorlesungen über speculative Dogmatik,* Book I, lecture 18, number 41: 8,187). The concept of love as harmonization of disparate entities is also explained in lecture five of *Aus Privatvorlesungen über Jacob Böhmes Lehre mit besonderer Beziehung auf dessen Schrift: Von der Gnadenwahl:* "If many powers are to give up their will in favor of unity, then each individual power must be accorded its own will, a *vita propria.* If two people in love did not have their own proper individuality (*Eigenheit*), they could not surrender themselves to one another, and if differentiation were to perish in unity, it would simply end up as indifference. To the extent that I love the other, I deny myself and posit that other; to the extent that I deny the other, I find myself denied. Hate is, therefore, unproductive" (13,79 fn. 2). See also BAADER: *Sämtliche Werke* 11,181ff.; 12,200.

(*vivere*)". (3) We must distinguish two stages or moments in all love.[5] In the first stage, the lovers are, indeed, "in unison", but only because their love for each other is still in an untested stage. Their unity consists merely in the fact that no real difference has yet asserted itself between them. This is a condition that conceals radical capacity for differentiation and dissolution of the union. That capacity must first be extirpated if love is to attain the second stage of true accord, that of tried and tested love.[6]

The distinction between these two stages of love sets the scene for one of Baader's favorite axioms about love: namely, that we must not consider love simply a pure gift (*ein Gegebenes*), but rather, a task to be performed (*ein Aufgegebenes*). (See also: 3,298 fn.; 5,347; 9,361 fn.) "We accomplish a great deal towards developing a philosophy of love if we come to see that love (of God and of man) is not simply a 'given' or something that allows itself to be given, and is not something to be enjoyed in passivity and idleness" (4,166). We have to "establish the good" (2,91 fn.), not take it for granted. "What we love, we do not leave undone" (14,457). True love (*amor generosus*) is active. (See 4,166; see also 9,367, 408.) To begin with, love is given, but lovers must cooperate to develop it into the tested perfection of love's second stage. In its unexperienced innocence, a love of the "given" sort may be full of charm and intoxication, but it is fundamentally feeble and even carries the hidden seed of death within itself. The spirit of evil heads a large number of forces in this world that are hostile to love (15,601). Thus, the elimination of that lability characteristic of untried love is not a "given" for lovers; on the contrary, it is their basic challenge as lovers to achieve that end in their love.[7] Baader notes, at the conclusion of Proposition 1, that union in love assumes a differing character, to the

---

5   See *Vorlesungen über speculative Dogmatik*, Book I, lecture 16 (8,137–42), for parallel coverage of the two stages of love. On the first page of that lecture, Baader remarks that "three of the most important themes of general dogmatics, namely those of human freedom, the image of God in man, and God's love for man" converge. All of the substantive and relevant points made in that lecture are to be found (in equivalent form) in *Sätze aus der erotischen Philosophie*. On the two stages of love, see further BAADER: *Sämtliche Werke* 13,306; 14,106, 111, 159.

6   Tried and tested love is the ideal and goal of all incipient love, but courtship, as the "springtime of love", also has its charms. See, for example, BAADER: *Sämtliche Werke* 11,206; 15,622, 625.

7   Baader's footnote reads: "In this way, we are rid of those tedious presentations of love as idle pleasure, both in asceticism and in romantic poetry; we also see why the happiness that the yet untested person enjoys is at first only an accidental and unearned happiness, a happiness which contains the element of uncertainty within it (i.e., the possibility of lapsing from it). As the ancients put it: *Dii omnia laboribus (doloribus) vendunt* (The gods sell all things to labor [pain]) (4,166).

extent that those united in love stand on differing levels. He talks about a "genealogical tree" of love (4,167) that explains the intimate relationships between love of God, of man, and of nature. In his short essay, "Zusammenhang des Cultus und der Cultur", *Socialphilosophische Aphorismen aus verschiedenen Zeitblättern*, number 4, he offers the following related thought:

As God's love condescends to man (*amor descendit*), and elevates man if he opens his heart to that love, so also does this love spread horizontally in the form of love of those like us (brotherly love, love of man) and reach downwards to raise non-intelligent nature and creation up to it. Cult, humanity, and culture have, therefore, one and the same source . . . They rise and fall together. Where one of these three loves is lacking, so is the other; where one is re-awakened, the other two soon join it. Not only does a person not love his brother if he does not love God, and vice-versa; rather, it is also true that whoever does not love God, does not love nature either, and whoever does not love nature loves neither God nor man. The just man, says Scripture, has pity on his animals; the farmer says that stock does not thrive under the hand of the scoundrel . . . (5,275, number 4). (See also: 4,198, number 37; 5,258, 311; 6,41; 7,239; 9,361; 14,105.)[8]

Proposition 2 (4,167–68)

Baader next considers the problem of how to overcome the labile character of love's first stage. The first possibility is that lovers will successfully refuse every solicitation that would lead them to separate. In other words, lovers are tempted to allow real differences to come between them, but they overcome that temptation. Their victory confirms and solidifies their love for each other. Indeed, temptation is a necessary prerequisite for such confirmation in love.[9]

---

8   See *Elementarbegriffe über die Zeit als Einleitung zur Philosophie der Societät und der Geschichte*, number 21, where Baader maintains that "earth corresponds in the material order to what man corresponds to in the higher order . . . just as there is only one man in the universe, so also is there just one earth"(14,44ff.). He speaks there also of man's natural love for the earth and especially for his own piece of property. Baader complains often of "mobilization" of values in a predominantly money-oriented economy. See BAADER: *Sämtliche Werke*, the index volume, for dozens of references under such headings as *Erde, Cultus, Cultur*. See also J. SAUTER: *Baader und Kant*, pp. 361, 366ff., 435ff. Almost all of the major studies dealing with Baader's social philosophy address this issue.

9   Baader devotes considerable attention to the significance of temptation. F. HOFFMANN: *Vorhalle zur spekulativen Lehre Franz Baaders* explains the issue as follows: "Temptation is the means whereby a spiritual being makes the transition from a state of indetermination to that of determination. Without temptation, there is no verification, just as there is no victory without battle. Hence, the deep seriousness, yes, even the lethal danger of all life. But if there were no hell to overcome, there would be no heaven to win. So life does not present itself as absence of death, but rather as

The second possibility is that lovers fail the test and, instead of having to contend with the mere *possibility* of separation, are now faced with overcoming the *reality* of difference and separation. Removal of actually existing differences between lovers is called reconciliation.

Baader's understanding of reconciliation, like so much of his thought, is profoundly influenced by the Bible. Thus, for him, immediately given or "natural" love is "natural" in the same sense that St. Paul used the word when he described the first man, as he came from the hand of God, as "natural" man. Man had to lose that condition of immediacy to God before he could become a "spiritual" man (*Geistmensch*). Baader seems to be saying that the mere fact of existence as a human being is not enough to make someone truly a person; he has to *act as a person*: i.e., use his freedom to appropriate and make his own all of those human values for which he has the capacity. God deals with his creature, man, according to the nature he has given him. But man is free. Hence, he needs to appropriate personally what he ought to make his own; only when he has done so has he made it his own. Accordingly, it is not purely natural and given love that is true love, but only love that is mediated through temptation. Some things cannot be inherited.[10] Mediated love is spiritualized love, supernatural love, love that is not cut off from nature, but love that is not confined to it either. This is "second-born" or "re-born" love, a loving relationship quite different in kind from untested love. Baader remarks that, as far as God's love for man is concerned, it is only in the second stage of love that he manifested himself as a true Father to his creatures. (See also 10,344.) Baader then invokes the motif of Augustine's *felix culpa*: reconciled love is preferable to "innocent" (i.e., untested) love. Here, too, God can elicit an even greater good out of antecedent evil.

Proposition 3 (4,168)

In the case mentioned above, when lovers are tempted to separate but do not do so, their transition from the first stage of love to the second stage is free and unhindered. But in the second case, when lovers fail the test and separate from one another, the matter is different. There is a real and positive block in their

overcoming and confining death, just as death is not absence of life but its limitation. Now, temptation has confirmation as its goal . . ." (p. 47). See BAADER: *Sämtliche Werke* 1,151–320; 2,412, especially 249ff.; 8,124ff.; and 14,99–109. See also J. SAUTER: *Baader und Kant*, pp. 455ff.

10 Compare with the following lines, J. GOETHE: *Faust*, Part 1: "Was du ererbt von deinen Vätern hast, / Erwirb es, um es zu besitzen". (What you have inherited from your ancestors, / You yourself must earn, in order to possess it.)

way, one which must be removed if they are to enter love's second stage. The word "sin", Baader observes, comes from the word to "separate" or "divide" or "put asunder".[11] The sin that separates man from God is a real obex, as far as we are concerned; similarly, a lover who "falls away from" his beloved puts a positive block between them, and establishes tension between them which the principle of reconciliation has to overcome and resolve[12].

Proposition 4 (4,168)

Here, Baader invokes a principle that is of controlling importance to his whole body of thought. A short but coherent statement of that principle occurs in a letter which he addressed to Prince Constantine von Löwenstein-Wertheim on February 24, 1831:

At this point, I allow myself the liberty of making the following assertion, because it is, in fact, the quintessence of my philosophy. How a man is related to God will tell you how he is related to himself, to other men, to his own nature, and to the rest of nature. If he exists in a state of tension with God, then a like tension exists within himself, with regard to other people, and with nature. (15,469)

In *Vorlesungen über speculative Dogmatik,* Baader specifies this general principle with respect to love:

The situation is the same for knowing as it is for loving; or rather, the two are identical in this case. *Cognovit eam* (he knew her); for it is only to the extent that a man is conscious of being loved by God, for example, that he acquires the capacity not only to love God in return (*Anteros*) but also to love himself, others, and even nature beneath him. (8,230)[13]

11 The German text reads: "Das Wort Sünde kömmt von Sondern, Trennen (asunder), und man sieht darum die Richtigkeit jener Behauptung ein, dass die uns von Gott trennende Sünde allerdings bezüglich auf uns etwas Reales ist . . ."
12 At this point, Baader adds the following footnote: "In the old German language, tense speech or contradiction (*Spann- oder Widerrede*) were taken as synonymous. And as far as the word reconciliation (*Versöhnung*) is concerned, it means (with reference to family love, i.e., God's love) establishing the above-mentioned filial or childlike relationship of creature to Creator in the second stage of love"(4,168). See also Chapter 6, footnote 52.
13 Baader goes on to argue his cardinal epistemological principle: i.e., that we must be known and loved by God before we can talk of knowing or loving in our own right. He reduces all other positions to self-apotheosis, the absolute summit of pride. In a footnote, he rejects any claim that man can love God without being loved by God: "People have found the assertion very touching and noble 'that man is able to love God even without being loved in return', but there is overweening pride at the base of this state-

Inasmuch as every relationship of creature to creature is conditioned by its relationship to God, it is not surprising to find similarities in the dynamics of these relationships on the horizontal as well as the vertical plane. Man needs to be reconciled with God because he has offended God through sin; he may also need to be reconciled on the purely human level in order to repair injured love. (See also 1,301.) Because of obstacles placed in the way by unreconciled disagreement, there is no free transition possible from the first to the second stage of love. For the Bible-saturated Baader, the message from Matthew 5,23 becomes virtually second nature:

So then, if you are bringing your offering to the altar and there remember that your brother has something against you, leave your offering there before the altar, go and be reconciled with your brother first, and then come back and present your offering.

The first task is to become reconciled.

Proposition 5 (4,168–69)

"The concept of reconciliation involves both a mutual reconciliation of God with humanity and the reconciliation of men among themselves which flows from it . . ." Once again, the principle of the Center applies: sin does not exist directly between people but only through the common Center; they offend *God first* and directly; they offend other people second and indirectly. It follows that rectifying an offense (i.e., reconciliation) must also begin with God: it is only the Love that God is that will supply the love required to rebuild injured love. The same principle applies with respect to nature: right relationship with God mediates right relationship to nature. Instead of considering nature something foreign and strange or unfriendly [Goethe's *Naturscheue*], man should feel at home in nature. The general conclusion is: "Wherever there is true love, or whenever love really makes the transition from its first stage of givenness to its second and higher stage, there lies at the base of it a religious (connecting [*reliirende*]) loosing or redemptive action (agent)".[14]

ment, because precisely that love for God in man is only *Anteros* or counterlove; man can, therefore, not surpass God in magnanimity" (8,231). Love for God is the highest love that man can exercise (11,142ff.; 12,195). With the expression *cognovit eam* (he knew her), Baader is of course referring to biblical usage, according to which when a man "knows" his wife, he has relations with her, and the result of this (carnal) "knowledge" is a child.

14 A footnote to this passage reads: "Because fine art and true cultivation of nature proceed only from love of nature, and because this love proceeds only from reconcilia-

Proposition 6 (4,169)

Daily experience illustrates what reconciliation in love can accomplish. We need only compare the state of love before and after reconciliation or, best of all, in the act of reconciliation itself. There is a widespread prejudice that the best love is one that has experienced no misunderstandings or quarrels and, accordingly, has never needed repentance or forgiveness (which together make up reconciliation). But it is a fact that even the best of loves does not bring two souls together in perfect harmony from the very beginning; at its best, love merely brings together two souls that are *capable* of achieving harmony if they work together to rise above differences between them. Baader illustrates from experience. How often it happens in the love of parents, or friends, or a man and woman that a deep rift between persons who love each other may condition the most profound and inward reunion. The heart's blood which is spilled in misunderstanding is sometimes the very "cement" (*Kitt*) of a deeper and more lasting union. "She loved much, said the Lord about his most dear friend, for much has been forgiven her". (See Luke 7,47.)

Proposition 7 (4,170)

In reviewing the dialectical progress of love in its various stages of attraction – unfaithfulness (unfaithfulness in all its forms is a sin for lovers), pain of contrition, and humility of forgiveness – one must keep clearly in mind that it is freely-accepted pain and freely-exercised humility that are at issue. If they are not freely accepted, if they are simply external formalities, their effect is the very opposite of love. In the same way, the prick of conscience does not make the sinner any better, at least not of itself: the Moral Imperative is no substitute for religion and love.[15] Devils believe in God and tremble on that account, but

tion, there is no doubt that a religious soul or one reconciled with God is the first prerequisite for true art" (4,169 fn.).

15 Baader rarely missed an opportunity to chastise Kant's ethics and religious philosophy. The footnote which he added at this point is a characteristic example: "It is really remarkable how our modern philosophers have been able to settle on the idea of making religion dispensable through morality (the so-called Moral Imperative), and how they have sought to find salvation or the savior not in the dative (*im Dativ*) but solely in the Imperative (of conscience). As if it were not so that this Imperative (as the demand of the believer) simply appears simultaneously with insolvency of the debtor, pointing to that insolvency but not lifting it, just as, in the case of an organism, coercion or necessity appears simultaneously with impotence" (4,170). See Chapter 6, Propositions 9ff., for an explanation of how love "fulfills" the law without imposing the rigidity and burdensomeness which the law entails when it is isolated from love.

this does not mean at all that they are religious or loving; their faith and conviction is simply a fact that they cannot deny.[16]

Proposition 8 (4,170–71)

Baader says that love is closely related to sympathy. He gladly cites Plato's remark that love is the daughter of superfluity and poverty. (See also: 1,235; 3,400, 517 fn.; 7,333; 8,262, 264; 9,115 fn., 189, 322; 10,4; 13,87; 14,345; E. SUSINI [Ed.]: *Lettres inédites* 1,180.) If one agrees, says Baader, it follows that "love is the daughter of forgiveness and repentance (*Tochter des Verzeihens und Reuens*): i.e., of reconciliation, because only the rich soul forgives and only the poor soul needs forgiveness". But about one thing we must be clear: we have no capacity, within the confines of our natural self-seclusion, either to forgive or to be sorry. We can forgive or be truly sorry only "in the power of Love: i.e., in God, who is Love, and who penetrates and encompasses the limitations we have". As Baader points out in *Fermenta Cognitionis*:

> In that way, then, God's love for his creation manifests itself as a daughter of compassion. That is why men can have true and active – not just passive – compassion only from God. Every expression of it is a religious act. For Scripture says: God has first loved us and our love for him is just a reaction (*Rückwirkung*) to his love for us [see I John 4,19] – which love, however, would have no object were it not for our inferiority. (2,352)

Consonant with this point of view, Baader goes on (in Proposition 8) to say that, if ever true contrition and forgiveness (reconciliation) come about, we can be sure that the people involved did not achieve their success on their own (*ex propriis*). We must conclude that a higher mediating force is at work among them, a force to which the estranged parties submit themselves. To one, that mediation affords the riches of forgiveness; to another, the strength of humility: "every true act of reconciliation, therefore, must be understood as a religious act which manifests that higher mediating force".[17]

16   Baader alludes here to James 2,19, where James argues the insufficiency of faith without works: "The demons have the same belief [in God], and they tremble with fear". Elsewhere, Baader states that "there is really no such thing as an atheist (*Gottesleugner*), because there is no being that can shake itself loose from God; it is, therefore, false to make religion, in general, consist in the creature's dependence on God, since even the devils must recognize this dependency" (1,415; see also Chapter 6, Proposition 21, for a continuation of this citation). Though Schleiermacher's name is not mentioned, Baader's rejection of the position that religion consists in dependence on God alone flatly contradicts the central thesis of Schleiermacher's *Reden über die Religion* (1799).

17   In a footnote, Baader here suggests that someone should undertake the task of writing a historical survey of the failures experienced by man while trying to find substitutes

Proposition 9 (4,171–72)

The statement that a mediator stands above those who need mediation, argues Baader, has general validity. God reveals himself in a more profound manner through his reconciling and mediating love than through his justice (the Law), which is the creature's norm of mediation. Baader maintains that in an organically free union, such as that which links governor and governed in society, a higher mediating principle is necessary. Without it, society suffers from infringements "from the top down" in the form of despotism or "from the bottom up" in the form of revolution. It is clear that this principle can only be a spiritual or moral power which stands above both parties; in other words, the mediating principle can only be religion. "We must reject as superficial every theory of state that pretends to be able to explain the origin, stability, and restoration of the state in a naturalistic way, without reference to religion and its mediating, reconciling, harmonizing power . . ." The theory of the state must also take account of the fact that society itself, if it accepts the principle of the religion of love, is also called upon to go beyond its first stage (i.e., its "natural state") to a higher second state.

Baader's views in this area are subsumed under the much larger issue of authority and organization in society. In a small essay entitled "Über den Begriff der Autorität", *Socialphilosophische Aphorismen aus verschiedenen Zeitblättern*, number 11 (5,294–99), he first disposes of several unsatisfactory claims to authority, and then concludes: "In general, we cannot understand authority in a materialistic or purely utilitarian sense . . ." He finds that authority cannot come from man himself, nor from anything less than man; it must come from something superior to him since the very idea of society includes that of superiority and inferiority.

But if subordination conditions association, then the bare dualism of master and servant (higher and lower) will not suffice, unless both of them are in turn subordinated to a third or first party. In other words: since only God is above man, both governor and governed become and remain free and secure, relative to one another, only by virtue of their common subjection to one and the same – not human, but divine – law: i.e., they serve one and the same God . . . (5,296)

He cites possible aberrations into despotism and laxity by governors, and compares them to the servility and revolution of the governed. He then adds:

for the mediating action of religion. Ruling and serving without love has led to selfishness in place of true selfhood and to a frantic search for constitutions, because the true constitutive principle of society has been lost. Constitution makers seem to be followers of Fichte, "since their constituting of the state is a Fichtean self-positing" (4,171).

In any case, both civil and religious society can exist without the effective appearance of authority in them so long as authority already rests in them. In this connection, one can distinguish three stages of society: (a) natural society, in which only love rules . . . (b) civil society, the form society assumes when love is injured or lacking and law asserts itself . . . (c) political society in the narrow sense, which emerges when even the law is broken; it then asserts itself by force . . . (5,296–97)

Baader talks about the combination of physical and moral power, a union which constitutes the "wonder and the mystery of authority". Significant for our present purpose is Baader's remark that "true civil and religious society is the love that I here called natural; both civil and political society serve only as means to secure or restore that end" (5,297). Baader goes on to argue that true authority must liberate both the one who exercises it and the one who submits to it, a point he drives home even more sharply in the essay, *Über die Zeitschrift Avenir und ihre Principien*:

The religion of redemption (Christianity) is, therefore, the religion of man's liberation from God, from himself, from other men, and from nature and creation. [It] . . . restores to man the proper love of self, of man, and of nature. Thus, religion alone establishes society. (6,41)

Throughout his work, Baader consistently pursues this point of view. "Every association and society comes to be and consists solely in love of neighbor" (5,258). The secret of society lies in "consubstantiating love (*konsubstantiirende Liebe*)" (6,81). Baader's essay on the French Revolution (*Über das durch die französische Revolution herbeigeführte Bedürfnis einer neuen und innigeren Verbindung der Religion mit der Politik*) begins with the words: "Love, says Paul, does no harm to one's neighbor; love fulfills the law" (6,13). A passage found further on in this essay reads:

Religion states, therefore, in its chief commandment, "Love God above all, and your neighbor as yourself", that is the principle of all communal life. Love frees man from his fellow man, though it in no wise separates them from one another; instead, it unites them in the most inward and indissoluble way, in a life of mutual helpfulness and advancement. Love manifests itself, therefore, as the truly organic and organizing principle, just as hate shows itself to be disorganizing and non-organic. (6,15)

Love is also the "Christian principle of association" (4,232); it alone makes one free (4,186). (See also 15,443.)[18]

---

18 More work has been done on Baader's social thought than on any other aspect of his philosophy. See particularly: J. SAUTER (Ed.): *Franz von Baaders Schriften zur Gesellschaftsphilosophie*, his major work on the subject; and J. SAUTER: *Baader und Kant*, pp. 383–529. See also H. GRASSL (Ed.): *Franz von Baader. Gesellschaftslehre*, Chapter 1, note 9; Baader's thought on love and organism, Proposition 17 in this chapter; and BAADER: *Sämtliche Werke* 9,31–32.

Proposition 10 (4,172)

Baader offers two arguments to corroborate his views about reestablishing love and union through reconciliation: (a) Reconciliation does not simply restore a man to the first stage of innocence or the first stage of his relationship to God (there is no way to do that); instead, it transfers him immediately to the second stage of love. (b) A general law of life states that every organic reunion constitutes a more profound and solid reality than the union that has been broken or damaged. This is so

because the uniting principle, when actual separation or even merely solicitation to it occurs, has to re-gather its energies within itself in a more profound way for a new emanation; by means of this deeper emanation drawn from itself, it unites what has to be united in the same relationship – [but] more deeply and inwardly.

Baader provides several analogies. A child who has been saved from some physical or moral danger often becomes immeasurably dearer and more precious to those who love that child simply because of the trying experience. Similarly, a person's feeling of health and euphoria, following a serious illness, is often much more intense than the feeling of health experienced before the crisis. "And so Scripture says that there is greater joy in heaven over one sinner who repents than over ninety [*sic*] just men who need no repentance" [see Luke 15,7]. Finally, we can readily observe that a fracture or cut of any kind produces, in an organism, a durable callous or scar that serves as future protection.

Proposition 11 (4,172–73)

Here, Baader applies his ideas about love and reconciliation in an extremely far-reaching way. Indeed, it encompasses the whole range of what theologians call "salvation history", focusing particularly on the incarnation of the Word of God in Christ. In Proposition 10, Baader had stated, as a "general law of life", that life, when forced to respond to a reaction against it, seems to draw more deeply upon its own inner resources: its "emanations" become more profound. The highest significance and manifestation of this law, says Baader, is to be found in God Himself. God has observed that law in his three successive "emanations", those which mark the three epochs of world history. There is no doubt that some kind of world-catastrophe occurred even before the creation of man: indeed, man's primitive vocation was to restore and harmonize a disordered and fallen universe. It was against the background of such a first world-catastrophe that God "went deeper into himself" and produced the emanation which we call man. After the second world-catastrophe, which came about by virtue of man's own fall into sin,

God "collected himself" for a third and most profound emanation of his innermost being (that of Love or Jesus). Not until this last emanation was the way paved for the goal of the now-indissoluble union of creature with Creator, or God with world, and at the same time the highest elevation of the creature; not until then could this come to pass.

In *Über den christlichen Begriff der Unsterblichkeit im Gegensatze der älteren und neueren nichtchristlichen Unsterblichkeitslehren*, Baader remarks that Böhme and other theologians consider "this more profoundly conceived divine act, . . . an act of saving and restoring love, the absolutely greatest miracle, greater even than the act of creation . . ." (4,282). Here again (as in Proposition 6), it is only the heart's blood given in sacrifice which supplies the joining element needed to effect an everlasting bond.

Proposition 12 (4,173)

"But with this blood-offering, the heart's blood (*ame principe* [*sic*]) of every single man has become fluid and freely manifest again; man was freed and redeemed from the rigidity of his own selfhood . . . " (See also 9,404 fn.) It was that rigidity which had previously made it impossible for him to make the transition from the first to the second stage of love. Man's exclusive and closed personality is opened up again by virtue of the action of this "divine blood-warmth" (*göttliche Blutwärme*). It is only because God gave himself freely for man that man is able to give himself freely not only to God, but also, through and in God, to his fellow man. Given man's ability to love God, one can then further admit his capacity for loving other men and nature itself in a fitting manner.

Proposition 13 (14,173-74)

If the third epoch of the world (see Proposition 11) is really the one in which we find ourselves, says Baader, we ought to be able to detect some signs of its presence.[19] We need only compare man's capacity for love, as manifested be-

---

19 In a footnote to this passage, Baader points out the mutual relationship that exists between history and speculation. He begins by noting that, methodologically, reconstructing the past from the present is too often neglected, and he continues by claiming that this neglect is responsible for the erroneous view that history and speculation can get along without one another. Speculation penetrates through the "apparent time"

fore or outside of Christianity and as practiced within it. Baader finds that a comparative analysis of morals, customs, social institutions, and laws – to the extent that they relate to sexual love and marriage – shows enough differences between Christian and non-Christian people to substantiate his assertion. There is even a remarkable difference, he feels, between gentlemanliness, " as it was exercised in pre-Christian times", in the Christian era, and in the "partially post-Christian times" in which he lived. He notes that it is only through Christianity that women have attained civil liberty and honor. Thus, women have every reason to be devoted to Christianity. He refers to woman as "custodian of love" (*Bewahrerin der Liebe*), a kind of consecrated phrase with him (see Proposition 14). A further reason why lovers should be devoted to Christianity is that only people who are reconciled with God (and thus with other people likewise reconciled with God) can really unite with one another: i.e., love each other.

Proposition 14 (4,175)

Baader often seems to regard woman as more naturally suited to love than man. For example, in a letter addressed to Dr. von Stransky on October 3, 1839, he enclosed a copy of a very short essay on love for Frau von Stransky[20]. His accompanying note reads:

For your wife, I enclose a little essay from my philosophy of love, which talks about the greatest mystery of love, and accordingly of life, in an understandable way. This heavenly music sounds more exquisitely in the hearts of women than of men. Men should simply try to supply the text for that music to the ladies. (15,626)

Baader continues to develop the theme of woman's superiority in love by calling her "the custodian of love":

in which we live to the "true present", which is the basis for the past and future. A true prophet sees into the future (and the past) only by virtue of the fact that he has insight into the true present, in which all past and future are contained. Thus, God is "I am, Who am" [Exodus 3,14] and "the One who is, and who was, and who is coming" [Apocalypse 1,4, 1,8; 4,8]. If you tell me that Christ entered into history 1800 years ago, says Baader, your telling me serves the purpose of having me look for him and find him in the world today; had you not told me, I would not have looked and found, but your telling me would have been to no avail if I did not look and find. Paul argued in much the same way when he told those who denied the resurrection that, if Christ has not been raised, they were still in their sins [I Corinthians 15,17]. (See also BAADER: *Sämtliche Werke* 4,173–74 fn.)

20 The essay is entitled "Die Liebe selber ist ein Kind der in Liebe sich Verbindenden" and was published as Proposition 37, *Religionsphilosophische Aphorismen* (10,343–46). For a discussion of this essay, see Chapter 6, Proposition 34. See also: E. SUSINI (Ed.): *Lettres inédites* 4,388.

I call woman the custodian of love because, as everyone knows, as far as men are concerned, it is not love but lust that takes the initiative; love simply comes after lust. On the contrary (in normal circumstances), lust follows love as far as women are concerned. The fact is that a woman, in general, is less capable of abstracting the two things than a man is.

Baader's point here seems to be that a woman generally reacts more spontaneously to a man's *personhood* as a whole than he reacts to her personhood. He has a tendency to see things and even persons as serving a particular function, as a means to an end (in this case, pleasure): hence, the reference to the capacity for abstraction. From these observations, Baader concludes the following: "what a man consciously gives a woman in this respect (lust) is the lesser thing, but what she gives him (love) is the better thing". Baader disposes of two possible objections to this position. In the first place, woman's exalted role in love between the sexes cannot be demeaned by reference to misuses of it (*abusus optimi pessimus* [the abuse of the best is the worst]).[21] Nor, can one argue, that it is precisely woman who arouses lust in man and precisely the man who incites love in woman. Baader reasons that a woman arouses lust in a man unconsciously and blamelessly, whereas she gives her love to man consciously and knowingly.

Proposition 15 (4,175)

Love between a man and woman that remains in the category of bare "naturalness" (i.e., love in the first stage) is insufficient to achieve a true and complete union; it lacks nobility and humility, the essential elements of love. It is "unable to free personality from objectivity". (This last phrase is particularly noteworthy because it anticipates a major argument regarding the dynamics of interpersonalism found in Baader's later thought.[22]) Wherever these two basic elements of love coalesce, there love has already assumed a religious character. If these qualities are lacking, then their perverted opposites, pride (arrogance, the will to despotism) and baseness (servility), manifest themselves; their bitter fruits are division and contrariety of sexual powers, a barbarous (*wilden*) state of marriage and hostility in society. This being the case, one can see how sexual love achieves its positive effects in society: beginning with the family, it acts in a religious way to preserve society and exorcise it. The family is thus "the asylum of both religion and love".

21 The footnote here reads: "Deepest degradation of woman in Eve has been more than abundantly counterbalanced through glorification and nobility won for her in Mary (Ave)" (4,174).
22 See Chapter 6, Proposition 28.

Proposition 16 (4,175–76)

When sexual love enters its higher (second) stage, and in the process assumes a religious character, it affects the sharing of fortune and misfortune (*communio bonorum et malorum*) among lovers and married people: i.e., it lends that sharing a deeper significance.[23] Baader says that the highest good (*summum bonum*) life has to offer man is the potential for realizing in himself, even during his life on earth, the original divine disposition to reestablish his "idea", the image of God within himself. In man's present condition, this process must begin through reconciliation with God. A new dimension is added in the case of people who are bound to one another in love. Because of their union, they have given up their aspirations to independent self-fulfillment in favor of a common lot and destiny. They share both their struggles toward fulfillment and the pain of realizing that imperfections remain. But they also share the joys of their individual and joint successes. In a word, the process of reconciliation is a communal one for them, and "one can say that true love pursues the lover in this respect up to the very gates of hell itself".

The direct antithesis of love's sharing spirit is, of course, selfishness and egoism. Almost any of the propositions found in either of Baader's two major essays on love could be invoked as testimony against egoism. Statements which appear throughout his work point in the same direction: God is love. Since the practice of true love is virtue, love gives of itself; sin, consequently, is egoism. For example, Baader notes in *Gedanken aus dem grossen Zusammenhange des Lebens*: "One can see, then, how sin consists in the fact that a creature wills himself and not God, and how love is denial of self-will and how self-will is denial of love" (2,20). *Über den Begriff der Zeit* contains the following observation: " . . . giving love is fundamentally nothing other than affirming the object of love through denying one's self" (2,83 fn.). In *Der morgenländische und abendländische Katholicismus mehr in seinem innern wesentlichen als in seinem äussern Verhältnisse dargestellt*, Baader cites Meister Eckehart's dictum that anyone who lives in time, and for time, and derives the meaning of his life from it, is purely egoistical and unloving: "all this worldly love is simply self-love and, consequently, no love at all; man lets go of his self-love to the extent that he abandons lust for the temporal world" (10,117; see also: 2,491, number 29). The first four pages of *Recension der Schrift von Professor J. Ch. Aug. Heinroth: Über die Wahrheit* (basi-

---

23 "Every joy not shared becomes pain for one in love, just as every pain shared is dissolved in consolation and almost in enjoyment (*Lust*); this also holds true for man's love of God, and it explains the origin of prayer, because human joy automatically completes itself in prayer of thanksgiving just as human pain is resolved in prayer of petition" (4,176 fn.).

cally, an extended book review: 1,97–132) stress the same incompatibility of egoism and love.[24] It must be pointed out, though, that Baader in no way advocates abolition of self through love. On the contrary, he argues that the only way to achieve genuine self-discovery and self-determination is through love, which, paradoxically, exacts self-denial: ". . . one who freely loves allows himself to be determined (filled) by his lover, without, thereby, losing his self-determination . . ." (8,233–34). It is the gospel message all over again: "Anyone who loses his life for my sake will find it" [Matthew 10,39]; and "Unless a wheat grain falls on the ground and dies, it remains only a single grain. . . Anyone who loves his life, loses it" [John 12,24–25]. Nor does Baader argue for a "Platonic" type of Christianity, one which says, in effect, that all true values are to be found in "another world", so that we may properly love nothing in "this world". His constant concern is, rather, to set forth the conviction that "this world" is not of itself, for itself, or from itself: it is good because God made it good. It does not exist apart from God. It should not be apotheosized: "You should not be God; you should be in God" (12,474). "Whoever seeks himself, does not find himself; whoever seeks God, finds Him and himself" (12,477).

Proposition 17 (4,176)

When two people in love marry, the effect of what they do goes far beyond the ambit of themselves. Their marriage is not simply for their own sakes. In fact, any marriage entered into for other than purely selfish reasons is an institution that aims not only at its own perpetuation but also "propagation of the restoration of the image of God in man". Thus, a good marriage is a blessing for all of humanity; a bad marriage is a curse on the whole race.[25]

---

24 On the same theme, see BAADER: *Sämtliche Werke* 1,99–102, 301, 397; 2,508; 8,222, 231; 9,301. See also Chapter 6, Propositions 13 and 28.

25 Baader, of course, does not regard marriage and love as public affairs in all respects. In a letter to Marie Robel (his wife-to-be), dated September 26, 1839, he speaks of the privacy of love. To speak about love in broadcast tones would be to prostitute it and degrade it; it would be casting pearls before swine. "Love is summer in the heart, but the world outside is wintry; should I open the door to it so as to freeze along with it? The world not only does not believe in love, but even mocks it, despises it, and hates it . . . Love should also be our house-prayer (*Hausandacht*), and it is true to say of it what Christ said of prayer: that one should not pray and shriek in the open market-place . . . one should pray to the Father in secret . . . We two have become one, and no third party, male or female, should be thrust into that unity. If we were to stop being one, we would be loveless, we would be, therefore, Godless, burdened by God and empty of God (*Gottlos oder Gottschwer und Gottleer*). Dear Marie, to me that is the sacrament of love" (15,625; see also 15,628–29 for more of the same).

What Baader says here suggests another fundamental tenet of his views on love: namely, its organic character. Indeed, Josef Siegl comments:

Baader's entire philosophy of life is dominated by the organic idea, which comprises the notion of organic articulation and working out of divine love in the world-organism . . . Baader sees in the cosmos, in the universe, a living organism filled with the divine idea . . .[26]

A few examples from Baader's own work will suffice to illustrate the point. In the sixth lecture of *Vorlesungen über Societätsphilosophie*, he observes:

But pantheists misunderstand this mutual interpenetration and intercommunication of single members and individuals. They confuse the entire thing with mutual destruction of those members through amalgamation of their essences with one another. The reason is that they have not grasped the secret of the function of love as positing oneself by way of mutual emptying of self . . . for love is the proper organizing or structuring principle which holds together the manifold or fullness in unity and imparts unity to the manifold. Through love, the whole is assured of its own constant renewal and rejuvenation in and through its members, while the members are renewed and rejuvenated in the whole and among themselves. It could only be an invention of love to impart or communicate its own existence to another in such a way that the stability and renewal of this other is a condition for love's own renewal and existence . . . (14,85)

The lecture continues with a fuller treatment of love and organism developed from that point of view.

A somewhat different approach is offered in a passage found in the eighteenth lecture of *Vorlesungen über speculative Dogmatik*, Book I:

It is only through communal service and communal rule that life can maintain itself. Submission has to be universal. If only one member submits itself to another, no union results. All the members look "upwards" in service, just as they all face "downwards" in ruling. This presupposes a common substratum, which is body in the broadest sense. In every *communio vitae*, all members affirm the whole; the whole, in turn, "sublates" (*hebt . . . auf*) itself in all the members, affirms them, and is thus affirmed by them in turn. In this mutual dying-for-one-another and giving-life-to-one-another consists the process of life and the miracle of love. Everyone finds himself only to the extent that he does not seek himself, but rather seeks all the others. St. Paul says: "When one part is hurt, all parts are hurt with it [I Corinthians 12,26]." The power of love comes from God; a creature can, *ex propriis*, love only himself. Life is not just "hanging on" – i.e., rigidification – but rather process; one can say here: *omnia fiunt eadem, sed aliter* (All things become the same, but in a different way). Every member, since it is posited again in its "sublation", is continuously renewed and preserved . . . (8,162)[27]

A final example of how Baader weaves together the organic idea and love is found in the following excerpt drawn from the first number of *Religionsphilosophische Aphorismen*:

26   See J. SIEGL: *Franz von Baader. Ein Bild seines Lebens und Wirkens*, p. 23.
27   On the notion of sublation, see Chapter 1.

Scripture designates this organic perfection of the organism by saying that God, as the absolutely – primitively – first living Being, will be all in all with reference to creaturely life; for . . . temporal life is related to eternal life as mechanism is to organism; hence, we will understand God's kingdom as completely organic. From the many proofs . . . that such a higher organism develops itself from the lower, love can give us an example (and here we speak of true sexual love, prescinding from passion). For in love, separateness and difference in mind and body strive for and anticipate organic union; if lovers are kept apart by their differences, it is their own fault. For true love (*Amor*), holds its torch up to heaven; while blind desire (*Cupido*), buries it in the mud of material sensuality and is, therefore, death. – So it can be said in the same way of two members of one and the same organism, that one member does not dominate the other, because they are both subject to the same unity that abides in them. Paul speaks similarly of two persons (man and woman) bound together in love; Christ, too, says in like manner that a man and woman truly united are one body: i.e, they become one body, which "sublates" their separate corporeal condition. From all of this, one gets a very different picture . . . of the sacrament of married love and of loving marriage than is usual. For the notion of this sacrament rests on the knowledge that, just as lovers are able to love one another to the extent that the love of God dwells in them, they are also unable to love if they fail to love one another, or if they are unfaithful to one another. (10,286–87)

Love makes the difference between mere mechanical juxtaposition or interaction and truly organic community, "from which fact one might meanwhile draw the conclusion that love is the universal organizer (*organisateur universel*)" (10,146). Every organic structure, including the state, depends on harmonious cooperation of external force and internal love (6,16). Love is order (12,379). Love is life, and life is organic; thus, love is organic. For Baader, more than for any other Romantic, this is basic truth: he is the only one of the Romantics to carry this point of view so far.[28]

Proposition 18 (4,176–78)

Finally, Baader believes that his view of love enables us to discern a higher meaning in the idealized conceptions that lovers often entertain about each other and about love itself at the beginning of their relationship.[29] He regards

28   On the notion of the organic and its intimate link with love, see BAADER: *Sämtliche Werke* 2,5; 4,238; 5,310; 6,16, 19, 83; 7,389; 8,73, 171; 9,119; 13,180ff.; 14,197, 476; 15,270, 272, 443. See also: J. SIEGL: *Franz von Baader. Ein Bild seines Lebens und Wirkens*, pp. 23ff.; and F. BÜCHLER: *Die geistigen Wurzeln der heiligen Allianz*, pp. 53–55. See also the major studies of general scope: e.g. those written by J. SAUTER, E. SUSINI, and D. BAUMGARDT.

29   *Vorlesungen über religiöse Philosophie im Gegensatz der irreligiösen älterer und neuerer Zeit*, number 28, states as its thesis that "the creature knows himself in truth (in his original state [*Urbild*]) only in God, just as the beloved knows himself only in his love". Baader argues that "one who is loved finds and sees his true worth and content (the better or best and

the infatuation of early love as "that natural phantasmagory of sexual love". Its effect is to make lovers in the first stage of their love seem "more beautiful, more lovable, more perfect, and better" to each other than they really are. Baader feels that lovers ought to consider rapture or ecstasy as an encouraging summons to work together to become inwardly and truly all that the "phantasmagory" suggested they were. There is a natural disposition in them both to seek the content of that phantasmagory by a kind of divination.[30] In other words, there is a natural foundation and possibility in them that makes their imaginings not entirely fantastic and unworkable. What usually happens, however, is that "the first glow of love's rosy dawning is gradually transformed into a gray cloud". Instead of seeing that first glow of love as an indicator of possibilities for themselves, lovers misuse it "in a mutual, idle, vain, and vacuous self-mirroring". What they should have accepted as encouragement and challenge, they dissipate in vanity.

Baader then returns to the controlling themes embodied in his philosophy of love: image of God, loss of original androgynous perfection, and the roles of Sophia and Christ. Jacob Böhme, he says, has shown how man's lust for the earthly led to a distortion of God's image in him and to his separation into two sexes. But God did not abandon man: his heavenly wisdom continues to be a guiding star for men, pointing out the way of return to their lost homeland. Sophia, God's wisdom, is present in the soul of every man and every woman. If Sophia establishes union *in solidum* between those souls, that is betrothal and results in the bond of love and marriage. Sophia brings about the union: she is man to the woman and woman to the man, the same "inner helper and angel" to both. Baader holds that it is Sophia's presence in a pair of lovers that explains the ecstasy of love and its "magic moment".[31] Generally, it is the fault of lovers that evidence of Sophia's presence in them (her *Durchblicken*) is not always manifest. "The higher, time-transcending goal of love is, therefore, pre-

---

finest part of himself) not in himself or from himself, but only in the one who loves him [and similarly] wins self-knowledge, as a gift of love, [only] through that person who loves him. This rapture (ecstasy), involving the best part of himself with the one who loves him and idealizing it through that person, constitutes the transport of love . . . " (1,229). Baader concludes his remarks with the following words: "I observe, finally, that if it happens that a person in love is blind with respect to the failings of his beloved, it also happens that a person who does not love is blind with respect to the apotheosis of what deserves love. But there is the difference here, that blindness is separable from (full and complete) love, but it is not separable from lovelessness" (1,232-33). See also: E. SUSINI (Ed.): *Lettres inédites* 4,291.

30 ". . . als gleichsam im Lichtspiel divinatorisch . . ." (4,177).
31 Baader here uses the metallurgical term *Silberblick*. It refers, literally, to the gleam or glint that silver emits in the refining process; but it is also used, figuratively, to mean "bright moment" or "lucky chance".

cisely this communal (*solidaire*) restoration of the image of God or Sophia . . . in both lovers, whereby both of them are reborn as God's children". The path of reintegration will follow that of original disintegration, but in reverse: just as Adam's sin, and his consequent loss of androgyny occurred first inwardly and only then outwardly (in the corporeal manner described in Genesis), so man must also first inwardly repair the damage done. "In other words, love should aid both man and woman to recover from their incompleteness and inwardly restore the full image of man".

An important aspect of this position is that a certain measure of disagreeableness, or "the cross", is inseparable from love's agreeableness, "because a person must depart with aversion from that into which he once entered with inclination". A good deal of independent self-love has to be overcome if the higher goals of love are to be served, "for the still abstract inner maleness, 'otherness', and femaleness, which in their selfishness are opposed to love, are the cross which lovers in this world must help one another carry and tolerate". (See also 4,268; 15,248–49; *Lettres inédites* 1,404). Baader suggests that the process, by means of which the rebirth of love in two lovers occurs, would make a much more suitable subject for dramatic treatment than the usual offerings of poets and writers on the subject of love.[32] Time and again, Baader links the notions of sorrow and love. "The true Christian ought to submit himself to the sufferings of love, which the redeemer has taken upon himself . . ." (12,203). ". . . A lover reproaches himself if he has stilled the pain of separation from his beloved through distraction. For in this case, the pain of separation brings union" (12,236). "Because God made himself assume the role of organ,[33] he freely exposed himself to suffering. Love made itself suffer, so that it could heal" (12,208; 12,356; 14,365). "Nothing, says St. Martin, illuminates the mind as much as tears of the heart . . ." (10,5 fn.).

These texts are enough to suggest that suffering linked to love can be of various kinds and be caused by different factors. No matter. Love is always worth the pain, because "the path from pain to joy goes through love" (12,344). Love, as such, will suffer willingly: "Love suffers whatever it wills and because it wills" (12,355). Several points made by Baader in the earlier propositions of this essay, particularly about achieving the second stage of love (i.e., tested love) and the depths of true reconciliation, suggest that not every aspect of

---

32 See the essay *Über den verderblichen Einfluss, welchen die rationalistisch-materialistischen Vorstellungen auf die höhere Physik, so wie auf die höhere Dichtkunst und die bildende Kunst noch ausüben* (3,287–310, especially 301–10). The subject is covered in some detail in Chapter 4.
33 For the distinction which Baader makes between principle and organ and instrument, see Chapter 1.

sorrow and suffering in love is bad. In his commentary on St. Martin's *De l'Esprit des Choses* (*Erläuterungen zu Sämtlichen Schriften von Louis Claude de Saint-Martin. De l'esprit des choses*), Baader noted:

No bond is effected in time without pain and suffering. Men call misery misfortune, but, in fact, it is good fortune to the extent that, without it, they could not be led to true and permanent happiness. God must, so to speak, constantly begin over again in conducting men to the goal that his love has bestowed on them. (12,339)[34]

Baader concludes his essay by stating, with conviction, that his treatment of love contributes to proving that love is a subject about which one can and should speculate. One needs all the intellectual enlightenment about love that one can get, because "the wretchedness of purely earthly Eros and the excellence of heavenly Eros consist in the fact that the former is blind and the latter is clairvoyant". As Baader puts it in the ninth lecture of *Vorlesungen über speculative Dogmatik*, Book II:

One has to see that an independently existing being manifests itself only in its image, that it is only the union of mind through love that declares the mystery of mind. If, therefore, someone says that love sees without benefit of image, you must not misinterpret that, as certain "mystics of feeling" (*Gefühlsmystiker*) have, as though love were blind or made itself blind to serve its own greater pleasure; rather, the meaning is that love looks at the original (*Urbild*), not the copy (*Abbild*). It is you I want, not your possessions, says Paul [I Corinthians 12,14] (8,243 fn.) (See also 1,232ff., 298 fn.; 14,376.)

---

34 See Chapter 6, Proposition 26, for a more detailed discussion of this point.

Chapter 6
Forty Propositions Taken from a Religious Philosophy of Love

> I refer you to my composition published by the Franz Press a few weeks ago: *Vierzig Sätze aus einer religiösen Erotik.* I do so with the confidence that you will not, as people so often do, conclude that the work is of little consequence simply because it is short. I also hope that you will not think that, just because it has to do with love, it does not concern the deepest and highest object of all speculation.
>
> *Vorlesungen über Societätsphilosophie*, 1831–32 (14,79–80)[1]

Franz von Baader composed *Vierzig Sätze aus einer religiösen Erotik* in 1831 and dedicated it to Miss Emilie Linder, a friend with whom he corresponded.[2] The few lines of dedication refer to the essay as "a voice that recalls in friendly fashion the holy bond of love among the Three Graces of our better and eternal life: religion, speculation, and poetry – and therefore, fine art also" (4,181).[3] The format is similar to that followed in *Sätze aus der erotischen Philosophie,* but the individual propositions are both more numerous and, in general, considerably shorter. Indeed, they approach the aphoristic or apothegmatic style to a greater extent than do the brief essays of *Sätze aus der erotischen Philosophie.*

1   In a letter addressed to Montalembert on September 16, 1831, Baader writes that it was "not without some trepidation" that he had *Vierzig Sätze aus einer religiösen Erotik* published, "for there are mysteries dealt with herein, which should not be revealed to everyone . . ." (E. SUSINI [Ed.]: *Lettres inédites* 1,406).

2   BAADER: *Sämtliche Werke* 15,427–85 contains nine letters from Baader to Miss Linder, beginning with letter number 140 and ending with number 191. See H. GRASSL (Ed.): *Franz von Baader. Über Liebe, Ehe und Kunst,* pp. 70ff. and 230ff.

3   Baader's dedication refers to Miss Linder's artistic activities in Rome. The litany-like reference to religion, speculation, poetry, and fine art reads like a chant formula whose text varies a bit at times. Compare, for example, the association of religion, life, faith, love, and knowledge in the introduction to *Fermenta Cognitionis,* Book IV, (2,276). See also Baader's citation of WINDISCHMANN: *Über Etwas das der Heilkunst Noth thut:* "Where complete faith, uninterrupted hope, and motherly love are faithfully preserved at all times, there art will also experience blessed prosperity" (14,386).

Baader prefaces the essays of *Vierzig Sätze aus einer religiösen Erotik* with the following two sentences, both of which summarize much of his thought about love:

Most people believe that it is entirely up to them, if they so wish, to refuse to wonder at what they truly should wonder at; to love what they should [truly] love; to believe in what they should [truly] believe in; and to serve their rightful master. But these people usually realize, only too late, that by acting in such a fashion they lose their freedom and fall subject to necessity: they wonder at what merits no wonder; they love the unlovable; they believe in the unbelievable; and they must serve someone who has no rightful claim on their service. (4,183)[4]

The principles enunciated in these two sentences include some of Baader's deepest and most characteristic thought. They center around a truth that is axiomatic for him: namely, that the human condition, as such, does not allow us an option on the question of whether we will encounter mystery, or believe in anything (anyone), or love anyone (anything), or serve anyone (anything). The only option available (and it is not an unlimited option) is what or whom we choose to reverence, love, believe in, or serve. In *Über das Revolutioniren des positiven Rechtsbestandes als Commentar zur Schrift: Einiges über den Missbrauch der gesetzgebenden Gewalt,* Baader writes:

It is an error on the part of philosophers and theologians when they hold that knowledgeable disbelief is the opposite of ignorant faith, because it is only through belief in B that someone wins the ability to disbelieve in A. So you can say to a person: show me what you do not believe in, and I will show you what you do believe in; or, you can say to him: show me the authority against which you are revolting, and I will show you the one to which you are submitting . . . (6,66)

The passage continues with an almost verbatim repetition of the passage cited just above (4,183).

In *Vorlesungen über speculative Dogmatik,* a related idea is expressed:

Simply because a person does not respond to a feeling to which he ought to respond, or, simply because he does not listen to or believe someone to whom he should listen and believe, it does not mean that he stops feeling, or listening, or believing altogether. It merely means that he surrenders himself to another feeling, that he listens to and believes someone else, just as by forgoing the liberating service of love and honor, he surrenders himself to servile service without love or honor. If a person insists on knowing in a situation when he should be believing, he will be reduced to believing in a situation when he should be knowing. This distortion or metastasis of activity and passivity will necessarily manifest itself as deformation in a person and as suffer-

---

4   For a related text (10,281), see the introduction to Chapter 5. See also the passage from *Socialphilosophische aphorismen* (5,349) cited under Proposition 12 below.

ing for him, because it contradicts the law of his constitution. In that way, also, the so-called Godless person thinks indeed that he is really free of God, but what happens is that he merely exchanges free relationship to God and free immanence in him for unfree relationship and unfree immanence. (8,207)

Although Baader makes no reference to Augustine while developing these ideas, his standpoint is reminiscent of the Augustinian dictum: "The person who, knowing the right, fails to do it, loses the power to know what is right; and the person who, having the power to do right, is unwilling to do so, loses the power to do what he wills". A person cannot live in a vacuum. If he thinks, wills, and acts in the world, he also devotes himself to certain ends, believes in certain values, expends his love and commitment in some direction or other.[5] "What we do not desire, love, or hate, what does not affect (touch) us, that is nothing for us. Our whole existence is in feeling" (12,341). Baader, however, is not only intensely conscious of the overwhelmingly *subjective* importance of feeling, he also insists – with great force – on the *objective* consequences of loving the right or the wrong thing or person. There is some truth in existentialist assertions about "creating your own future"; but there is an even more fundamental counterbalancing truth: *you become like what you love.* Freedom is not sufficient by itself; it must be allied with truth. If ultimate truth is not something man himself creates, but is rather something to which man is subject, and if such truth ultimately resides in God, then man is not *absolutely* free and without restraint. He must, in fact, sanctify his freedom: if he is not ultimately *from himself,* he cannot ultimately be *for himself* in an absolute sense. His hold on existence is far too precarious to support unlimited freedom. This is what Baader felt in the marrow of his bones, and this is what he argued in public forums which increasingly tended to apotheosize either man or nature in some form or other.

Proposition 1 (4,183–84)

"St. Martin says that man wanted to be man without God, but God did not want to be God without man".[6] In order to create nature and man, God needed only to unleash his power and glory, to "let himself go". But to redeem fallen man, God almost had to "do violence to himself". The "violence" consists in

---

5   On this theme, see Proposition 20 below; see also Chapter 3, especially the first half; and BAADER: *Sämtliche Werke* 7,17 fn.

6   St. Martin's remark is found in *De l'Esprit Des Choses,* Part 2; see Baader's notation of it (12,254); see also: E. SUSINI (Ed.): *Lettres inédites* 1,340.

the fact that God had to (or chose to) "empty himself of his glory",[7] in a manner of speaking, so that weak and fallen man could receive and bear his aid. "Only love understands and is able to make this sacrifice". In this, as in so many other instances, the distinctive mark and activity of God's love serves as paradigm for all love. Divine *kenosis* finds an analogical counterpart in all love. In a short essay entitled "Über ein Wort der heiligen Theresia", *Socialphilosophische Aphorismen aus verschiedenen Zeitblättern*, number 2 (5,271–73), Baader cites St. Teresa's statement that "the flame of divine love was enkindled and supported in her only by virtue of burning away her natural selfhood". Elsewhere, he elevates this thought to the level of a law for all love:

The egoist who would like to pleasure himself with the light and warmth of love, but wants to know nothing about burning away or sacrificing his selfishness, shows that he is as ignorant as those apes who would like to warm themselves at a fire made by men, but who do not know how to keep the fire going by adding fuel to it. At the bank of love, says the enlightened St. Martin, a person receives everything in return only after he has invested everything. The poet's word applies here in the deepest sense:

> If you do not invest your life,
> You will never gain your life.

Moreover, what is applicable *par excellence* to divine love – namely, that it comes to fruition only if it is sublated (sublimated) – holds good for every other love, since any love is worthy of the name only to the extent that it participates in divine love. For only God is Love as a substantive, just as only he is Reason or Reasonableness; in man (or creation), love or reason are just adjectives . . . (5,273; 12,211)

Kenosis is a constantly recurring element when Baader speaks of love, simply because "union in love demands complete mutual self-emptying of the lovers", a feat which they cannot manage by themselves, for it is "only when each of the lovers gives himself entirely to God in an immediate way that God gives the other completely to each of them" (9,269–70). There is no love without self-giving.[8]

7　The allusion here is to St. Paul (Philippians 2,5–8):

In your minds you must be the same as Christ Jesus: His state was divine, yet he did not cling to his equality with God but emptied himself to assume the condition of a slave, and became as men are; and being as all men are, he was humbler yet, even to accepting death, death on a cross.

The Greek word for "emptying oneself" is *kenosis*, which has found its way into theological and biblical language as a standard term.

8　See also BAADER: *Sämtliche Werke* 14,85, cited under Chapter 5, Proposition 17. Other texts dealing with kenosis and love include: 1,231; 3,412 fn.; 8,259; 10,3 fn., 247–48; 13,79 fn. 2, 241, 328; 14,79, 117, 127, 150, 252. Many of the Propositions which follow in this chapter bear on the theme to a greater or lesser degree. Other related passages include: 6,114 fn.; 13,84, 226.

Baader develops his first point by considering what the notion of "condescension" entails. He observes that a created being does not grasp whatever stands above it, and, therefore, expresses wonder at it. It is, consequently, all the more difficult to grasp how God, the superior being vis-à-vis man, is able to condescend to the level of man or go even lower. "Our philosophy has not yet clearly understood this condescension", although a good clue to a solution lies in the word "substance", which designates a ground or grounding or underpinning for something else. ("Substance" is derived from the Latin *sub* [beneath] and *stare* [to stand].) Baader thus suggests a general principle governing the relationship between producer and product and applies the principle to God:

Every producer establishes a harmonious relationship to his product, or unites himself to that product (without confusing producer with product) by assuming a position as mother, which places him as far beneath that product as his position as father places him above it. As the creature sublates (sublimates) itself in God, so does God sublate himself in the creature. But if this normal, mutual process of sublation is once disturbed, and the creature who wishes to sublate himself with respect to the father is instead immediately suspended or suppressed by the mother, one can see that rectification of this abnormality can come only from the mother, not the father. Consequently, a more profound emanation of motherliness is required. One can see here the function of womanliness in both a good and a bad sense. (4,184)

This opaque and abstruse utterance touches on a subject which Baader addresses in a considerable number of scattered texts: the father-mother principle as it manifests itself in production of all kinds. This principle has direct relevance to love, because love is an intrinsically creative, active, and productive reality.[9] Thus, love consists of both paternal and maternal aspects: "as the paternal aspect, productive love supplies the content (*Fülle*), the inner and hidden element, the life-giving or body-giving factor; as the maternal aspect, it supplies the form (*Hülle*) and provides the shape, it makes manifest and expands . . ." (10,328). This statement appears in a small essay: "Die zeugende, hervorbringende Liebe ist väterlich und mütterlich zugleich", *Religionsphilosophische Aphorismen* number 32 (10,328–32). Here, Baader argues the correlative character of these two principles, showing how the passive character of the one is directly proportioned to the active character of the other and viceversa – each serves as a complementary ground of operation for the other. The differing functions of father and mother are illustrated in the axiom: *Pater in filio, filius in matre.*[10] Father and mother are united in and made parents in their

9   See Chapter 2, particularly the section on creation.
10   Baader's description of the generative process by means of the formula *Pater in filio, filius in matre* is reminiscent of Plato in *Timaeus*, 50c–d: ". . . For the present, we have only to conceive of three natures: first, that which is in process of generation; secondly, that in which the generation takes place; and thirdly, that of which the thing

child. (See also 12,272, 314.) The child, thus, represents a "higher third" with respect to his parents:

Every union of two elements is mutual ecstasy (in a third element) . . . Content (*Fülle*) (expansion, father, thinking, the male) looks for form (*Hülle*) (contraction, mother, willing, speaking, the female), just as form looks for content, because both act only in unison . . . For content is actually content only in the form, whereas form is simply something that holds its content . . . (1,221)

A footnote found in *Über den Begriff des gut – oder positiv – und des nichtgut – oder negativ – gewordenen endlichen Geistes* addresses the matter somewhat differently:

What is called "volatile" and "fixed" here is father and mother, as the two-fold relation of producer to product, both with respect to making it and with respect to preserving or destroying it. Every product can come only from "the middle" of the producer, and this middle must, therefore, be established by means of the producer's "pulling himself together" by way of contracting (descent or extraction) what is volatile (what is free, heaven) and, correspondingly, expanding (ascent or insertion) what is fixed (what is unfree, earth). (7,172 fn.)[11]

Just a few pages earlier, Baader had noted that "the producer posits his product in the middle, between himself as the inner (father) and the outer (mother)" (7,159 fn.). Because of the kaleidoscopic way in which he juggles symbol and image, these few passages illustrate how difficult it can be to ascertain precisely what Baader means. When speaking of father and mother, for example,

generated is a resemblance. And we may liken the receptive principle to a mother and the source or spring to a father, and the intermediate nature to a child . . ." (PLATO: *The Dialogues of Plato*, translated by B. JOWETT, volume 2, p. 31). Hans Grassl notes that "Baader has reworked this axiom principally from Jacob Böhme, Paracelsus, and Saint-Martin". Grassl also notes the following remark, which he found in Baader's copy of SAINT-MARTIN: *De l'Esprit Des Choses* (translated by G. H. SCHUBERT as *Vom Geist und Wesen der Dinge*, Leipzig, 1812): "Father and mother see one another only [through the child] by way of the child; they express wonder at, love, and intermingle with each other only in him, and in this way generate him ever anew". H. GRASSL (Ed.): *Franz von Baader. Über Liebe, Ehe und Kunst*, Notes, p. 246. See also Propositions 9 and 10 below. On the same axiom, see further BAADER: *Sämtliche Werke* 1,410; 5,160 fn.; 8,112, 177ff., 190; 9,99, 170; 10,10 ff., 43; 13,246; 14,90, 240; E, SUSINI (Ed.): *Lettres inédites* 4,338. See also BAADER: *Sämtliche Werke*, the index references (volume 16) to *Vater* and *Mutter*.

11 In the original, this difficult passage reads: "Was hier volatil und fix heisst, ist Pater et Mater, als die zweifache Relation des Producenten zum Product, sowohl in der Zeugung, als in der Erhaltung, als auch in der Hinrichtung. Jedes Product kann nur aus der Mitte des Producenten kommen, und diese Mitte muss also durch Sichzusammennehmen des letzteren hergestellt sein, durch Sammlung (Descensus oder Heraussetzen) des Volatilen (Freien, Himmels) und durch entgegnende Expansion (Ascensus, Hineinsetzen) des Fixen (unfreien, Erde)".

he may use such paired terms as heaven-earth, content-form, inner-outer, higher-lower, active-passive, mind-body, subject-object, expansion-contraction, thinking-willing, free-unfree, volatile-fixed, fire-water – to name but a handful of the more common combinations which he employs. The similarity between the polar opposites, father and mother, and the male-female polarity that is part of all reality is also immediately apparent.[12] The central point Baader seems to be making, with his many references to the mother-father principle in Proposition 1 of *Vierzig Sätze aus einer religiösen Erotik*, is the requirement for strict correspondence and correlation between these two aspects: neither may be over-emphasized or slighted – "the highest must also be the most profound. Only the universal Father *(Allvater)* can simultaneously be the universal Mother *(Allmutter)* . . ." *(Über den solidären Verband der Religionswissenschaft mit der Naturwissenschaft*, 3,344).[13]

Proposition 2 (4,184)

A merchant makes entries in his debit-ledger for goods which he receives; conversely, he makes entries in his credit-ledger for items which he sells. Baader finds an analogy in this business practice for "transactions" that take place in love:

In a similar way, love manages its trade-book. For inasmuch as my beloved gives herself to me, I become indebted to her, and to the extent that I give myself to my beloved (having faith in her), she becomes indebted to me. But even God cannot give himself to me if I do not permit it, if I do not rely on him or believe in him. On the other hand, he is also unable to withdraw himself from me if I give myself to him with faith in him, and he thereby becomes, so to speak, a debtor to me. (4,184)

Assessing debits and credits, however, involves more than a simple question of give-and-take At issue, rather, is the more specific matter of exact proportion: what one man gives, another takes, and vice-versa. A note from Baader's study-book on St. Martin shows that this principle applies to love as well:

The greater the sacrifice, the greater the reward. This does not happen in a mechanical way, but by inner necessity. The expression has something almost disturbing about it, but what the author [St. Martin] says about it is true: "Happy is the one among us who makes the greatest sacrifice! At the exchange-bank of love, as at any other, the person who deposits the most capi-

---

12   See Chapter 4, part one.
13   In addition to the 58 references listed under *Vater and Mutter* in BAADER: *Sämtliche Werke*, the index volume (16), see also: 9,310; 10,27 fn. 1, 336 fn.; 12,97, 278, 320, 384, 468, 534; 13,247, 257; 14,247, 417; 15,169, 639 fn.

tal draws the most interest". But, of course, someone motivated [solely] by interest in making [this] deposit would not deposit anything. (12,211)

On the question of whether God can "escape" the person who believes in him and loves him, Baader's own principles allow no room for anything like a debate. Given that all true love emanates from God, and is mediated by God, it can hardly happen that God would attempt to "flee" something which he himself is inspiring. In the light of Baader's view of God as Erotic Center, St. Paul's words seem singularly appropriate: "It is God, for his own loving purpose, who puts both the will and action into you" (Philippians 2,13). As Baader wrote in a letter to Marie Robel, who became his second wife: ". . . commission of sin is already punishment from God, and the beginning of that punishment is, as the common folk say, abandonment by God, after man has inwardly abandoned his God and turned his heart from him" (15,629). This is a view that echoes the patristic dictum: *Deus non deserit, nisi prius deseratur* (God abandons no one unless he is first abandoned).

Proposition 3 (4,184–85)

The reciprocity associated with the dynamics of love is thoroughgoing: to the extent that love is perfect, mutuality of love is still more complete. Everything proceeds in love by a kind of "doubling". Love is an "overcharging".

To the extent that I possess my beloved, I have mastery over her and am her lord; to the extent that she possesses me, she has mastery over me and is my mistress. If I can bring some joy to someone I love, doing it relieves me of a responsibility and of suffering; and if I can take away some pain from that person, doing so brings me joy. In both cases, then, I owe as much gratitude to my beloved as my beloved owes me. One can say, in that respect, that love overcharges in everything. (4,184–85)

Thoughts like this did not come to Baader only late in life. As a young man of twenty-four, he confided to his diary for April 19, 1789:

To possess a human heart, to find joy in a person! A man in love has become richer by a whole person; he feasts on two lives at once! Someone who loves only himself sucks miserably on his own paw, like a bear in a wretched winter's cave. A meager diet indeed!

" ––– How rapturous
And sweet it is, to feel oneself exalted
In a beautiful soul, to know
That our joy brings flush to another's cheeks,

That our fear trembles in another's breast,
That our pains moisten another's eyes"!
(11,185, 207)[14]

Proposition 4 (4,185)

Advancing the same theme, Baader argues that love cannot be a one-way street. Loving initiative from one side requires loving response from the other to keep it alive. Both sides must give and take.

One could say, then, that a lover is already thankful to his beloved for the fact that she allows herself to be loved by him. But, looking at the matter a little more carefully, it seems clear that I can love only someone who loves me in return and who allows me to love in return. In this sense, God complains so often in the Scriptures that so few people are willing to let themselves be loved by him, and even then so feebly. And that is why, even though he is Love itself, he is able to love so few men effectively, and even these to such a limited extent due to their own fault, no matter how much he wants to love them. (4,185; 5,264; 15,602)

The following passage, from *Vorlesungen über religiöse Philosophie im Gegensatz der irreligiösen älterer und neuerer Zeit*, trenchantly makes the point that one can love only someone who loves in return:

If the law of equivalence between action and reaction holds anywhere at all, it holds for love. Someone who trangresses that law, and thinks he can take someone's heart while holding on to his own, is punished by love's withdrawal from him, which renders him to that extent love-less or less capable of love. In fact, the heart he has devoured does as little to enrich his own heart as the soul of a murdered man gives life to his murderer. A person never really comes into possession of something he ought not to take. Besides that, love also punishes the robber and deceiver by taking from him the ornament of his own lovability. *Scias autem nihil amabilius esse, quam ipsum amorem* (Know that nothing is more lovable than love itself). The same law manifests itself in the loss of one's heart, when one sets it on the heartless and the temporal. (1,297–98)[15]

Proposition 5 (4,185)

"From this it follows that nothing is really worthy of love itself, because in the realm of the spirit and the soul, worthiness, receptiveness, and merit are one"

14 On the reciprocity of love, see further BAADER: *Sämtliche Werke* 2,227, 229, 412, 458–59; 8,37; 12,452, 460.
15 On "setting one's heart on the heartless", see Proposition 31 below.

(4,185). "Love is the source of all perfection" (12,212). Baader makes his point, simply but powerfully, in a brief poetic statement found in "Die Liebe selber ist ein Kind der in Liebe sich Verbindenden", *Religionsphilosophische Aphorismen*, number 37:

Only for so long as they loved did they live!
For only love (like life, which love is) has no Why or Wherefore, nothing that would precede it; hence, love alone is an absolute end in itself (end or perfection of all things, as well as their beginning), to which everything else serves as means. It is true to say:

> Love, it is said, has no law.
> Why not?
> Because love itself
> Is the supreme law!
> (10,344–45; see also 14,482; and *Lettres inédites* 4,243.)[16]

Baader is consistent with his own principles: everything goes back to "God is Love". In a very real sense, for Baader, all love begins and ends with God. Hence, God's love for his creatures is also, in an important sense, love of himself: i.e., love of the goodness in these creatures, which is his own gift and his own presence in them (but see also 14,418). Conversely, all genuine love of creatures for God and for each other is, in fact, simply a form of their cooperation with *his* presence, the presence of Love, in them. Baader holds that a person may reject God's love, but he cannot create a *positive* substitute for God in his life. For the rejection of God is sin, but sin is essentially distortion and disfiguring, not independent creation. It might be styled "nihilating": i.e., performing an action that produces no self-subsistent result but exists only in reference to some positive good that it denies or distorts.[17] It is with this in mind

---

16 The last four lines appear in French in Baader's essay:

> L'amour, dit-on, n'a pas de loi.
> Pourquoi?
> Parceque l'amour lui-même
> Est la loi supreme!

See Proposition 34 below for a commentary on the essay in which these lines appear.

17 Even when Baader argues that evil is "not simply history (*histoire*), but real and effective power (*puissance*)" (2,464, number 10), its reality and effectiveness is that of an obex, a barricade or hindrance, not a positive substitute for good. Baader usually speaks of sin and evil in negative terms: e.g., "The origin of sin is failure to commit oneself to the good: i.e., neglecting to integrate and fix oneself in God. This non-affirmation, as failure to deny oneself with respect to God, affirms the creature against God and denies [God]" (14,419). Sin is setting one's will in a direction that precludes God entirely: i.e., an *attempt* to do so, since it cannot be carried out in fact (2,45 fn.). Baader compares sin to thirst: "Thirst is not a thing, yet it can torment you. How could it be that sin would not eternally gnaw at

that Baader says: "If the good man proves that God exists, then the evil man proves that only God exists" (13,138). Thus, "nothing is worthy of love except love itself": a thing is lovable in direct proportion to God's presence in it.[18] Worthiness, receptivity, and merit coincide, because they are all functions or qualities of the one Love who is all in all.

Proposition 6 (4,185–86)

Here, Baader takes up one of his favorite descriptions of love: namely, that it is a combination of *Erhabenheit* and *Demut*, nobility and humility. Connecting these two qualities expresses the all-encompassing character of love, at once infinite in its sublimity yet attentive to the smallest detail of truth. These things can be ascribed to God (Christ) too, limitless in majesty, yet "taking the form of a slave".[19] Baader's statement reads:

Nothing can be more erroneous and simple-minded than to confuse freely condescending humility of love with unfree baseness, or its nobility with arrogance. The fact is that in their androgynous unity, humility and nobility constitute love. As soon as love – as such and as a power (*pouvoir*) – vanishes, sexual difference emerges as force (*violence*), and weakness comes forth as arrogance or tyranny and servility; these things are wedded to one another as in a barbarous marriage (*als in einer wilden Ehe*)". (4,185–86)

How the polarities of nobility and baseness, on the one hand, and humility and arrogance, on the other, are related, is described in *Über die Analogie des Erkenntniss- und der Zeugungstriebes*:

you, sinner"? (12,435). See also BAADER: *Sämtliche Werke* 2,19, 35; 10,103; 12,491; 14,229, 270, 332ff., 340, 402, 452; E. SUSINI (Ed.): *Lettres inédites* 1,180 fn.

18 R. JOHANN: *The Meaning of Love*, p. 38, says substantially the same thing: ". . . What I love in myself or another is a subsistent likeness of God. Thus, the ultimate oneness of value is assured. God the Creator, present in all, is loved in all and above all . . ." In light of their insistence on *creatio ex nihilo*, it is clear that neither Johann nor Baader can properly be accused of pantheism. Neither says that all things taken together are God, or that all things are a "part" of what God is, for only God is subsistent being. Only God exists in the most proper and fullest sense: God alone can and must exist; everything else may or may not exist, hence is contingent being dependent on God. The terms "existence" and "being" apply to God and to creatures only in an analogical sense; only God can say "I" in its full and complete meaning. Of course, Baader's theosophical position in general, his preoccupation with the thought of mystics like Eckehart and Böhme in particular, and his contemporaneity with German Idealism and Romanticism (with their varieties of pantheism) and with Krause's panentheism might tend to make a reader suspicious about Baader and pantheism. See also BAADER: *Sämtliche Werke* 5,230.

19 On *kenosis*, see Proposition 1 above.

Love has two elements: nobility and humility. Only when love perishes do these elements transform themselves in and through their separation. Then they appear as pride and baseness, two qualities one cannot regard as educed from love, but rather as products of love's dissolution; their presence always attests to such a past and ongoing process of dissolution. (1,48 fn.)[20]

Proposition 7 (4,186)

"Only love makes a person truly broad-minded (liberal), because only the lover does not separate right (ruling) from duty (serving), nor possessing from being possessed or letting oneself be possessed" (4,186). Only love finds the golden mean between despotism and servility because it subordinates all relationships between people to their common higher relationship to God. In the political sphere, Baader thus rejects theories of absolutism, which would make people dependent on the grace of the king. But, he also rejects theories advanced by the Jacobins or Rousseau, which would make the king just an officer of the people, one dependent on their sovereignty. Both rulers and ruled are subject to God (6,41; see also 5,343; 10,352). Just as love is sublime and yet humble, so it not only rules, but also serves. Baader's reference to possessing and being possessed is elucidated by a proposition examined in *Vorlesungen über religiöse Philosophie im Gegensatz der irreligiösen älterer und neuerer Zeit,* lecture 47:

Legitimate possession frees both the higher (possessing) agent and the lower (possessed, belonging, obedient) element . . . This proposition . . . becomes clear through the single observation that the higher, possessing agent is freed through his possession with regard to his own manifestation, because the agent receives from his possession the powers he needs to express himself; likewise, the agent possessed is, thereby, freed, because it is only through being possessed by the higher agent that he is grounded and made independent . . . (1,282)

In other words, "possessing" an inferior being enables a superior being to express one of his powers through that inferior; conversely, "being possessed" by a higher being grounds the inferior's freedom to act within a certain range of activity. Thus, a teacher can freely teach the student whom he "possesses" – [though] he could not teach if he had no students; the student can learn freely, because he has a teacher who "possesses" him. (See 1,161; 1,177 fn.) *Sätze aus der Bildungs- und Begründungslehre des Lebens,* number 37, throws additional light on the principle that "only true possession frees one":

---

20 The linking of *Erhabenheit* with *Demut* is a consecrated formula for love in Baader's thought; see BAADER: *Sämtliche Werke* 2,316, 340; 4,151; 5,125, 272; 6,16, 19–21, 321ff.; 8,129, 177, 290; 9,215, 274; 10,3, 118; 12,459; 13,62, 106, 390; 14,143, 159, 468; 15,296, 449, 598, 602; E. SUSINI (Ed.): *Lettres inédites* 1,452 and 4,338. See also Chapter 2 above.

But man can appear as a god (*als Gott*) in this lower nature only when and to the extent that God has appeared in him as in a nature inferior to God: only to the extent that God possesses him (dwells in him organically) can he possess (also organically) this lower nature. (2,118; see also 5,283ff.)

This amounts to restating an axiom already cited in Chapter 5: man's relationship to God determines his relationship to himself, to others, and to all of nature. Thus, if a person is to love anything rightly, he must love God rightly: he must be "possessed" by God's love if he is to have the freedom to "possess" anything else through his own love.

Proposition 8 (4,186)

Baader says that it is not possible for anyone to escape every sort of relationship to God:

Both a person who loves God and one who hates him bear witness to him unceasingly. For, just as the good man praises and thanks God in good fortune and entreats him in ill fortune, so the evil man curses God in pain and bad fortune and defies him in good fortune. (4,186)

Similar declarations may be found scattered throughout Baader's work. For example: "The good man and the evil one will different things, but both do what God wills" (12,211). ". . . God makes every person good or evil, as the person chooses; for doing is determined by willing" (13,295). Baader's standpoint is that God exists, whether we like it or not, and he will have his way with man and with all creation, either by way of reciprocated love or else by his power (see also 15,311).

Proposition 9 (4,186–87)

One of the most interesting aspects of Baader's understanding of love is his treatment of love and law. Once again, his controlling ideas are largely derived from the Bible: in this case, especially from the epistles of St. Paul.

Although the entire Christian religion rests on the knowledge and conviction that "God is Love", many theologians and moralists still speak about our duty toward God and men as though duty and love were not fundamentally the same thing.[21] Now if, in fact, it says in Scripture that all

---

21 A long footnote in *Über Religions- und religiöse Philosophie im Gegensatze sowohl der Religionsunphilosophie als der irreligiösen Philosophie* reads, in part:

commands are subsumed under one command of love of God and neighbor, then clearly Scripture commands love itself as a duty. But it would obviously be impossible to command this love or duty if it were merely an appetite or a passion. This command to love merely expresses, therefore, that every person has the power to open himself up to, or close himself off from, the emotion of this love that freely offers itself to him and solicits him. Moreover, the identity of obligation and love is already clear from the fact that they both express union. For the word duty or obligation comes from "being-interwoven-with" or "being-bound-to", and the difference between the two is only that duty (the law), as power that merely penetrates, pushes (*presse*) toward union, whereas love, as something that fills and indwells, attracts (*attire*).[22] That is why love frees us from the pressure of the law, just as entry of air into an airless body frees that body from [external] air pressure.[23] The connection that is still one-sided and, therefore, unfree in the case of duty, becomes mutual and, therefore, free in the case of love. In this sense, Scripture says that love *fulfills* the law [Romans 13,10] and, in the same sense, the Word, or personified (in a human way) desire of God for reunion with man, is called the nourishing or filling Word. (4,186–87)

In an extended book review entitled, *Recension der Schrift von Professor J. Ch. Aug. Heinroth: Über die Wahrheit,* Baader takes issue with Heinroth's contention that the first instance in which truth freely offers itself to man is through law. Baader argues, rather, that law is an expression of divine will "that asserts itself only when man's will has already departed from love of God (unity of will with God); it is only then that God's will asserts itself as limitation or confinement of man's will". Indeed, says Baader, "there is no law for the just man (the loving man), as St. Paul says: the lover is, therefore, free of the law (*gesetzfrei*), just like God himself, although he is not lawless (*gesetzlos*) or opposed to law (*gesetzwidrig*)" (1,129–30). The reason is not hard to locate in Baader's own principles. As he notes, just a few lines further on, the Christian religious view

What John says about God's love and brotherly love applies here also: i.e., that he who is not for his Lord . . . is already against him . . . In which connection it should not be forgotten that love descends, or that love of the higher by the lower being is only reactive love (*Anteros*) with respect to the love that has condescended to it, although this return-love is a free act on the part of the inferior person returning it; man has the power, after all, either to open his heart or to close it to the solicitation of this love. Thus, Kant's error was one that radically eliminates all religiosity when he maintained that love cannot be commanded (I. KANT: *Gesammelte Schriften,* volume 4, p. 17) and, thereby, made a lie of the command regarding love of God and neighbor; this fact has not prevented many simpletons from accrediting Kant's moral principles to their own so-called Christian moral systems . . . (1,327)

22 Baader often uses *durchwohnen* and *inwohnen* to distinguish between presence by power and presence by love. And it is that distinction that is here being emphasized: ". . . die Pflicht (das Gesetz) als nur durchwohnende Macht zur Verbindung treibt (*presse*), wogegen die Liebe als erfüllende und inwohnende anzieht (*attire*) . . ."
23 For more on this analogy, see 2,511 fn. On love as something that "fills", see also BAADER: *Sämtliche Werke* 2,20; 12,212, 275.

is one in which "the same truth is at once Giver and Recipient, Lawgiver and Fulfiller of law" (1,130).

One of the things that disturbed Baader most about subject-centered philosophies, such as those of Kant and Fichte, was the standing they gave to law and the position they took on the question of law's provenance. *Vorlesungen über speculative Dogmatik,* Book V, number 18, contains a fine exposition of his views on the subject. He notes that the *Subjectivitätsphilosophie* understands the ethical law of will as absolutely autonomous; "in other words, not as law entrusted to man's keeping, but as law that he himself makes and gives to himself, although the idea of obliging oneself in this sense is not any less ridiculous than the idea of embracing oneself". Baader argues that making one's own law leads to recognizing oneself as lawgiver too: i.e., as God, since "the idea of an impersonal law is as bad as the idea of an unlawful personality (*einer ungesetzlichen Persönlichkeit*)". Subjective philosophy, says Baader, has failed to see that everything that affects my will or strives to determine it must itself be another willing that is distinct from my willing.

This willing manifests itself either in a law of will as a power that only penetrates (*durchwohnt*) my will [by force], or in one that also dwells within (*inwohnt*) my will [by love]. In the latter case, it does not manifest itself as law, although it is, nonetheless, a willing that is distinct from my own. The same thing holds true here as in the case of air: air exerts pressure only on airless bodies, but it supports and frees air-filled bodies in which it "indwells". Paul also says that a person is no longer "under the law" when the lawgiver has entered into him and dwells in him as a spiritualizing principle . . . (See 9,263–64; see also 5,507ff.)

Baader's explanation is of a piece: "Properly speaking, only God can fulfill his law in me . . . only in fulfillment of the law is there happiness" (12,430; see also 9,122). "If love gives itself to the law, the result is that the law subjects itself and gives itself up to love" (13,310). To the extent that love fulfills the law, coercion vanishes.

. . . in other words, constraint placed on the will as compulsory obligation linked to law makes itself perceptible as an imperative or demand (as authority) in the same degree in which inclination of will (love-obligation, with its dative [*mit ihrem Dativ*]) vanishes.

Love, it is said, knows no law.
Why not?
Because love itself
Is the supreme law (14,481–82).[24]

24 On law and love, see further BAADER: *Sämtliche Werke* 1,142 fn. 2, 241–45; 2,92, 213, 294, 461; 3,296; 4,407; 5,297; 6,64 fn. 2, 307; 7,319, 415; 8,19; 9,31–32, 417; 11,180; 12,432; 13,303, 390; 14,114, 408. See also, such general sudies as: F. HOFFMANN: *Vorhalle zur spekulativen Lehre Franz von Baaders,* pp. 23–25; J. SAUTER: *Baader und*

Coercion or compulsion is thus just a "court of second instance" in man's relationship with God: if man returns God's love with his own, law in its stark guise of heavy obligation does not exist. That is why Baader maintained in *Sätze aus der erotischen Philosophie*, number 9, that the revelation of God as love was more profound than his revelation as justice or law.

Before proceeding to Proposition 10, Baader digresses briefly to reconsider the dictum: *Pater in filio, filius in matre*. He says that this phrase expresses the double relationship of every product to its producer: a producer, as father, is more subtle (*subtiler*) in nature than its product and cannot be grasped by the product, whereas a producer, as mother, can be grasped – in this capacity, the producer nourishes and fills its product. Thus, the producer stands superior to its product in its role as father (heaven) and beneath it in its role as mother (earth).[25]

Proposition 10 (4,187–88)

Baader returns to the theme of love and law:

The burden of duty or of law indicates emptiness, therefore, a lack of indwelling, because something is heavy when it does not have its supportive center within itself and experiences that center only as penetrating (*durchwohnend*) it. Lack of love and heaviness of heart are, therefore, synonymous, just as darkness, as a burden to the eyes, is lack of light. (4,187)

It is the same point Baader makes so often when he distinguishes *Durchwohnung*, presence by power, from *Inwohnung*, presence by indwelling in love. We feel the law as weight and burden when it functions like a mechanical force; love transforms that mechanical pressure into organic freedom and spontaneity. In the external forum, a person may do the same thing: i.e., "keep" the law either way; but in the internal forum, only love has the spirit of the law abiding in it. On the surface, Baader seems simply to be stating a truism, or even a tautology: a person does what he wants to do gladly or spontaneously; he feels constrained, however, when doing what he does not want to do. But Baader says much more than that. He says that something is out of order if we feel law (God's law, in any case) as oppressive, for "the law governing man is *constitutive* [my emphasis] and is, therefore, burdensome for man to the extent that he

Kant, pp. 239, 256; H. MERTENS: *Untersuchungen zu Franz Baaders historischpolitischen Arbeitsgebiet*, Freiburg 1926, p. 33; H. GRASSL (Ed.): *Franz von Baader. Gesellschaftslehre*, pp. 40ff. The theme is touched upon often throughout the literature.
25 See note 10 above.

does not fulfill it" (12,214). Law describes man's intrinsic being: who he is and where he belongs. Baader makes this clear by taking the word *Gesetz* (law) as a derivative of the verb *setzen*: to place, to put, to fix, to plant, to erect. Thus, "law" (*Gesetz*) expresses the notion of "a-being-placed" (*ein Gesetztsein*). The task for a freely-created being is to confirm himself voluntarily in this position. For the creature is well off where he has been placed. By establishing himself in that position, a created person recognizes that he is made and defined by God" (13,137). By fulfilling his law through love, he exercises the highest measure of freedom, because every being "is free in its own region and only there; only there does it have no law" (8,266). For "law is not something that is originally negative; it becomes negative only through false reaction to it" (12,164). Baader likes to cite Goethe's couplet:

> The master manifests himself first in limitation,
> And only the law gives liberty. (2,330; 5,192; 8,41; 13,189)

The concept of "region" is a notion which Baader employs copiously when attempting to define one level of reality in relation to other levels of reality. If someone or something is in its proper "region", vis-à-vis realities surrounding it, then he (it) can act freely and feel no adverse pressure or hostile environment. One who feels constrained by a rightful law is "in the wrong region" or is "out of place"; responding to that law with love, on the other hand, "fulfills" the law and dissipates its burdensomeness.[26] Freedom and love sit comfortably together only if truth – the truth of one's being – sits with them. It is, of course, not difficult to find numerous traces of this concept in Baader's (mostly) subsequent thought; one need only recall such terms (largely Existentialist) as *Entfremdung* or alienation (of many kinds), *Geworfenheit* or "thrownness", "no exit", dislocation, the *déracinées* or "uprooted", *Sitz im Leben* or "place in life", "the man without a country", or even the biblically-based Christian term "pilgrim" (Hebrews 11,13; 13,14; I Peter 2,11), the City of God and the City of Man, etc. But for Baader, ultimate alienation is alienation from God the source. It is the sort of alienation St. Augustine implies when he says in the first paragraph of his *Confessions*: "You have made us for yourself, O Lord, and our hearts will have no rest until they find their rest in you". Any other alienation is superficial by comparison. Indeed, if this alienation persists into eternity, it is what the theologians call hell.

---

26 Baader uses the term "region" to complement other terms that define the constitution or range of activity of a being: e.g. ground and cause, center and periphery, original and image. For a particularly thorough study of Baader's *Begründungslehre*, see F. KÜMMEL: *Über den Begriff der Zeit*, pp. 87–121, especially pp. 87–100.

In the second part of Proposition 10, Baader goes back again to the father-mother principle:

The old Germans called "being in a foreign country" the same as "being in misery". A person in misery, however, is one who has lost his mother and finds himself [with] a strange mother, a step-mother (*in einer fremden oder Stiefmutter sich befindet*), in a region or medium, that is, with which he is incompatible. That is because a child is elevated or lowered by his natural mother in the same proportion in which that child elevates or lowers himself with respect to his father. This helps to explain the statement that there is no being who does not have the duty of reproducing his own father [*Ésprit des Choses* 1,267]:[27] i.e., with the help of its mother. For the mother gives herself in the same proportion to her child, as the child gives himself to his father and wants him. Or, to use the word *Aufheben* in a Hegelian sense, one could say that in the same proportion as the son sublates himself (*sich . . . aufhebt*) in his father, the mother sublates herself in her son, normally speaking, whereas in abnormal circumstances, she withdraws herself from him as a step-mother. (4,187–88)[28]

Proposition 11 (4,188)

In Proposition 11, Baader argues that purely selfish love is not possible; attempts at it simply provide evidence of the inner emptiness that results from failure to love what is worthy of love.

Nothing is more foolish than to believe in an effective or accomplished self-love (*Philautie*), because a person is no more able to love himself than he is able to embrace himself. A person who wishes to love and express wonder about himself is, in fact, really trying to refute, by means of the testimony of others, his doubts concerning his own worthiness to be loved or admired. His efforts are always unsuccessful, the result being that he always ends up inwardly empty. Self-love and self-wonder, therefore, are invariably evidence of this emptiness (which is the subject's own fault): as perpetual frustration, they serve as punishment for having failed to give one's wonder and love where it was really due. (4,188)

An elucidation of precisely this point is found in Baader's essay *Über die sich so nennende rationelle Theologie in Deutschland:*

It is precisely this assertion that sounds so strange to many people – namely, that the ultimate motive for a will can itself be only another will, that one can technically will only a willing. That is proved by someone who is in love with himself, an egoist who wills only his own. For here is an individual who – in order to be able to love himself, i.e., will his own willing, enter into himself, fill and nourish himself constantly – continually wears himself out in a useless and ridiculous way in trying to "double" himself, because he cannot embrace himself in any other way. (2,507–08)

---

27   Baader cites St. Martin's principle in French: "qu'il n'y a pas un être qui ne soit chargé d'engendrer son Père". The same axiom is relevant to much of what was said about the function of imagination in Chapter 3.
28   See note 10 above.

It is a constant mark of true love and hate that "true love is love of all (not only oneself), just as true hatred is hatred of all, not only others, but also oneself" (14,424).[29] "Free self-emptying through love" (14,79) can scarcely come to pass through self-love, its opposite. The ultimate reason why we cannot effectively or directly manage selfish love, it appears, is simply because one would have to be God himself to do so. Baader takes his own statement, that the last motive for willing can only be another will, in dead earnest: to love only oneself means to live for oneself only, a condition which presupposes that one comes from oneself, and is, therefore, totally self-sufficient, which amounts to proclaiming onself God. Thus, one can define sin as pride, or as lovelessness, or as a lie. For what one loves and how one loves is bound up intimately with the explanation of one's life as a whole:

Whatever (whoever) gives me life, for that do I also live, with and through him do I live. I live with and for the one who gives me life: I do his will; he lives in me. For living and dying are dual: I live and die always for another; and even the egoist who lives only for himself, must first lyingly deny this other in himself. (12,180)

Baader's statement that emptiness and incapacity in love are punishment for the misuse of love is similar to much of what he says about prayer. He writes, for example, in *Alle Menschen sind im seelischen, guten oder schlimmen, Sinn unter sich Anthropophagen*, that "Prayer is at once a gift of God and a task for man: to be unwilling to pray is sin; to be averse to prayer, and finally to be unable to pray, is punishment for it . . ." (4,234). Baader often connects the notions of love and prayer. Indeed, "prayer is the offspring of love and the salt of wisdom" (12,210). Baader is not simply the "professor of love" (15,627); he also teaches "a philosophy of prayer" (14,487; see also 15,536). The affinity of these ideas is due, of course, to the fact that prayer belongs to the category of love: it is the human response in love to the divine initiative of love.[30]

29 This statement, by Baader, is found in a marginal note to: C. DAUB: *Judas Ischariot, oder das Böse im Verhältniss zum Guten*, 2 volumes, Heidelberg 1816 and 1818, volume 2, p. 328. It appears in French and without quotation marks: "L'amour vrai est l'amour de tous (pas seulement de soi-même) comme la vraie haine est la haine de tous, pas seulement des autres, mais aussi de soi-même" (14,424).

30 Prayer, for Baader, is simply a response to a person's recognition of the fact that he is a creature who owes his life and what he does with it to the creator. "What the plumb-line is to an earthly builder, that is prayer (*Sursum corda* – Thy will be done) for man building interiorly and eternally" (15,310; see also 2,35). In a lengthy footnote which appears in the essay *Über Kants Deduction der praktischen Vernunft und die absolute Blindheit der letztern*, Baader scores Kant for totally misunderstanding the nature of prayer. His main point is the charge that failure to pray is equivalent to self-deification. He rejects Kant's equating of prayer with mere expression of one's own wishes (as in *Religion innerhalb der Grenzen der blossen Vernunft*), partly because such a view overlooks the fact

Proposition 12 (4,188-89)

Baader speaks again of mutuality in love, the emphasis falling this time on reciprocal respect and the freedom that marks the exercise of love.

Every man, the noblest as well as the least, needs to express wonder and respect and also needs to be respected, to love, and to be loved. We can only fear and shy away from someone who does not respect us or who despises us, even if we acknowledge him as a superior. We cannot love someone who is disinclined toward us. For only free inclination is love; only someone who is master of himself can give himself or be himself received by someone else. One just "takes" a man who has no self or has lost his self, and one does not thank him for it. (4,188–89)

The last sentence is interestingly echoed by Addie Bundren in Faulkner's *As I Lay Dying*: "So I just *took* Anse [my emphasis]". In Addie's only interior monologue, she makes it abundantly clear that her husband Anse was "dead" and had no self, except in the sense of inert woodenness. And of course – as Baader would suggest – she did not thank Anse for "taking him".

A paragraph entitled "Über ungemischte und gemischte Liebe und Ehe", from *Socialphilosophische Aphorismen*, addresses itself specifically to the themes of wonder, respect, and freedom in love and marriage:

Man, who is simultaneously soul and mind, lives as mind only through the emotion of admiration, just as soul or heart [lives only] through the emotion of reverence (adoration). Since man outdoes woman in his capacity to admire, and she outdoes him in her capacity to revere, they need each other to complement each other. Now, if it happens in the relationship between sexes that each of the parties is inclined only toward something that he admires and esteems, and respects only that which attracts him, that bond of love or marriage is an unmixed one; on the contrary, that bond manifests itself as a barbarous (*wilde*) marriage as soon as it happens that the two parties who are joined together, or rather bound together, are inclined only toward what they cannot admire and respect and what cannot elevate them and free them, and they have to admire and respect what they cannot incline toward at all. To break up a barbarous marriage like that is mutual liberation, just as to break up a true bond of love is mutual loss of freedom. (5,349)[31]

Baader refers to the importance of wonder and reverence and their close connection with love in numerous contexts;[32] one of the more striking is found in

that prayer is primarily an act of adoration and thanksgiving and, partly because even a prayer of petition does not begin or end with the petitioner; instead, it is itself a gift of God – God is himself "the giver of the petition" in true prayer. The real sin is rejecting God's gift of prayer: i.e., failure to pray, which is its own punsishment, inasmuch as it rejects God himself. (See, for example: 1,18–20 fn.) Texts which link prayer and love include: BAADER: *Sämtliche Werke* 2,347; 4,106, 409; 5,343; 12,343, 486; E. SUSINI (Ed.): *Lettres inédites* 4,248.

31 See note 4, above, and *Sämtliche Werke* 4,183 (cited in the introduction to this chapter).
32 On the connection between wonder, reverence, and love, see Chapter 2.

an essay entitled *Über den Affect der Bewunderung und der Ehrfurcht*. Baader there insists that "man's mind is truly and everywhere oriented only toward wonder, and it does not rest until it has penetrated to what is alone worthy of wonder . . ."[33] Baader continues with a statement which he considers to be of great importance: "just as the heart finds its rest in being enveloped in reverence with love, so the mind finds its rest in wonder,[34] and the better part of the human soul lives and preserves its life through these two emotions". In fact, if these emotions are lacking in too pronounced a degree, a man is sick:

If milieu and a man's style of behavior bring him to the point that his mind (*sein Kopf*) has nothing more to respect and revere, and he cannot respect what he loves and does not love what he must fear (*achten*),[35] then his psychic life is in decay and is sick, just as all life decays when it lacks its proper nourishment . . . (1,30–31)[36]

In the second part of Proposition 12, Baader discusses the freedom necessary to give oneself in love or to receive someone in love. Indeed, love is the highest act of sovereignty a person can exercise, because through it he disposes not simply of things that he owns or administers but of his very self.

33   Baader adds a footnote at this point: "Rest for a living being is not inactivity but rather: 'il n'y a de repos ou de sabbat pour un être, qu'autant qu'il ne peut librement développer toutes ses facultés (There is no rest or sabbath for a being, as long as he is unable to develop all of his faculties freely)' ". See ST. MARTIN: *Ministère de l'Homme-Esprit*, p. 137 (1,30 fn. 3).

34   Baader's text, to this point, is italicized. At the beginning of a footnote which he added to this statement, Baader remarks: "This proposition seems to be completely new, and it goes contrary to the hitherto prevailing opinion which holds that wonder is supposed to cease precisely at the onset of knowledge. But this is really saying only what Kant, for example, says: that our reason is really oriented always toward ideals and principles of reason only . . ." (1,31).

35   The footnote to this clause reads: "With that, of course, love ceases to be love and becomes mere inclination (passion); likewise, respect ceases to be respect and becomes simply (unfree) fear and aversion. This is an observation about which Kant was not clear in his investigations of the feeling of respect" (1,31 fn. 2).

36   Baader speaks of the incompatibility of fear and love in the following places: BAADER: *Sämtliche Werke* 2,94 (with respect to Kant's Categorical Imperative), 194, 345; 4,125 fn.; 6,38; 14,456. F. HOFFMAN (Ed.): *Franz von Baader. Sämtliche Werke*, notes, at the end of the essay, *Über den Affect der Bewunderung und der Ehrfurcht* (1,25–32), that Baader was really aiming it against Jacobi's "deism of feeling", just as he had aimed his first essay, *Über Kants Deduction der praktischen Vernunft und die absolute Blindheit der letztern*, (1,1–23), against Kant's "deism of understanding". Baader did not, however, lose his balance and fall into the opposite extreme of pantheism; he remains firmly grounded in genuine theism, says Hoffmann (1,32 fn.).

Proposition 13 (4,189)

Reciprocity is again the theme, this time on the paradigm level of "give and take" in love:

The giver is not the gift, nor is the gift the giver, yet the giver gives himself in his gift to the extent that he loves [the recipient], and the recipient receives the giver in the gift to the extent that he loves him. If I do not give you myself (my heart) in my gift, then I do not love you, and if you do not receive me in my gift, then you do not love me. (4,189; see also 1,162, 164)

Here again, the interchange does not take place directly on a horizontal or an across-the-board plane: "Where friendship and love join hands, both giver and receiver are blessed, since the same God who gives to one creature through another gives back to the latter through the former" (15,634). Since love is essentially mysterious, it is essentially indefinable. But giving and receiving have always been considered meaningful descriptions of what transpires in the dynamics of love. Baader makes abundant use of them, for example, in lecture seven of *Aus Privatvorlesungen über Jacob Böhmes Lehre mit besonderer Beziehung auf dessen Schrift: Von der Gnadenwahl*:

To the extent that I love the other, I deny myself and posit that other; to the extent that the other loves me, he denies himself and posits me. And so love is a constant mutual process of giving and receiving. To the extent that I deny another, I find myself denied. Hate is, therefore, unproductive. This is the truth of [the saying]: one for all and all for one. (13,83)

In supplementary remarks to *Der morgenländische und abendländische Katholicismus* . . . Baader speaks about "the law of love itself: love fulfills itself only by fulfilling the beloved, just as one who illuminates fills himself with light; or just as I possess only the word that I give, I receive only the breath that I emit. Give, and it shall be given to you, or":

Love stands before us with full heart,
Asking that we take from her;
For to stem the tide of giving,
Is all that brings her pain. (10,245–46 fn.)[37]

---

37 The German verse reads:

Liebe steht mit vollem Herzen
Bittend dass man ihr soll nehmen;
Denn den Fluss des Gebens hemmen,
Das allein nur macht ihr Schmerzen.

Living, loving, and knowing are not dead artefacts but living processes; give-and-take are as vital to them as circulation is to blood.

Moreover, as an intelligent creature, man does not produce anything solely from and for himself, but rather only receives life, love, and knowledge in order to pass it on in turn. He maintains continuity of his own existence (his reproduction) only when he freely and unrestrictedly gives and receives. Thus, any constriction of that circulation must necessarily show itself as constriction of his own existence. And so we see that a person who wants to have knowledge all by himself (from himself and for himself) falls subject to the same idiocy[38] to which he would succumb if he wished to love all by himself and to lock up within himself any love he received: i.e., in this case, as in the other, to reduce the three persons of a society to his own person (as a monodram). (*Über die Freiheit der Intelligenz*, 1,137 fn.).

In *Vorlesungen über religiöse Philosophie im Gegensatz der irreligiösen älterer und neuerer Zeit*, number 51, Baader throws a different light on the give-and-take of love when he discusses give-and-take in prayer:

For in the act of prayer, man exercises an act of humility and self-abasement before God: i.e., an act of receiving God as giver; man exhales so that he may inhale. I say he receives God "as giver", because a person may otherwise respond to a gift (i.e., what the giver *has*, but not what he *is*) simply by likewise giving something he has. But in this case, he has to give and open himself entirely to the giver. For freely receiving (as in love), is fully correlative to freely giving. In other words, a credit corresponds to every debit; receiving is one with *il credere*, with faith. What a person gives (himself to God, in this case) gives him credit with God, just as he also owes God what he has received from God, namely himself. (1,298)

In the footnote appended to this text, Baader cites St. Paul's "It is you I want, not your possessions" (II Corinthians 12,14), and comments: "Every honest lover who loves from the heart says the same thing to his beloved, and she to him". Just as good is diffusive of itself (*bonum est diffusivum sui* – Aquinas), so love gives (14,346). The world finds it hard to understand that love is truly disinterested, that it really gives without ulterior motive, that it simply gives (15,625).

Baader's point about giving oneself through one's gift strikes home in the experience of everyone. Unfortunately, it is relatively easy to make the subtle but crucial transition from giving a gift as *representing* and symbolizing oneself, to giving that gift as *substituting* for oneself. Conversely, one can receive a gift primarily as an objective quantum of value or advantage rather than as a vis-

---

38 Baader uses the word *Idiotismus*. From the context, it seems clear that he is playing on the etymology of the word: the Greek *idios* means "one's own, personal, private". From that primary meaning, the reference was extended to include: "the peculiar or distinct; hence, the strange". Baader is calling "private knowledge" or "private love" a kind of idiocy.

ible sign of the giver's self-giving. Love determines, in every case, what is given and what is received.[39]

Proposition 14 (4,189)

Happiness depends on the worthiness of the object in which one seeks satisfaction or fulfillment. In other words, it is not simply enough that we incline toward something to ensure that possessing it will make us happy; the object of our love must be worthy of it:

The only person who is really unhappy or luckless is one who can muster no inclination towards what he must respect and even fear, and whose inclination chains him to something that he has to despise. (4,189; see also 12,460)[40]

Illustrations of Baader's point are, of course, easy to identify. On the one hand, they are found in the various philosophies of absurdity and hopelessness so rife in the modern era; on the other, in the phenomena of alcoholism, drug addiction, gluttony, avarice, etc., that, in varying degrees, characterize the lives of countless human beings.

Proposition 15 (4,189-90)

Baader rounds out what he said about the role of love in giving and receiving by considering how love manifests itself in every good deed and in art.

It is rightly pointed out that we can attract a heart and bind it to us only by doing good. But effective will to do good is itself already a good deed and is, in fact, on principle, the central good deed; [it is,] therefore, the greatest [thing] that a person or free being can do for another. Without it, no other good deeds exist; consequently, none is recognized as such, nor do any produce gratitude. (4,189)

The main point corresponds with Kant's central moral conviction that "nothing in the world – indeed, nothing even beyond the world – can possibly be conceived that could be called good without qualification except a good will".[41] Baader's argument that God is quintessentially love, combined with his idea of

39 On the link between giving and loving, see further BAADER: *Sämtliche Werke* 1,160–64; 2,257; 8,343; 11,182, 255; 12,387, 466, 486; 13,180.
40 See Chapter 5, note 3, where 1,61 fn. is cited on this point.
41 J. COLLINS: *A History of Modern European Philosophy*, p. 517.

God's immediacy as Center to every act of love, provides the strongest possible metaphysical foundation for such a conviction. In Kant's argument, however, it is not at all clear where or how a finite human being comes to have a good will. Baader, on the other hand, speaks of a certain "benevolence of nature" that enables an artist to produce his work:

Thus, the good work that nature or the poet (artist) presents to our esthetic sense also stems from benevolence, and is similarly recognized as such. So too beauty, as lovableness, stems from love, and ugliness from hate, and *Charis* or *Grazie* are one with charity (grace or inclination). (4,189–90)[42]

In "Über Gemüth, Liebe und Kunst", *Religionsphilosophische Aphorismen*, number 44, Baader speaks of the link between great ideas, love, and art:

If our mind is once really taken with a great idea, it will soon overflow with ardent love for people. See to it that great thoughts do not die out among you ... All visible forms are merely copies of inner ones and must not be separated from them – *omnia sacramentum* (All things are a sacrament). All art, all creativity is love, a total giving (going into) of desire for the object, not the visible object, which appears only as a result, but the invisible object (idea, desire) present to the inner sense.

> The triune God, – Father, Son, and Spirit –
> Shows himself in beauty as his idea. (10,350–51)

It is common enough to say of a good artist that he is "gifted". Embodied in Baader's conception of such a "gift", however, is the intimate connection he sees between it and love, benevolence, perfect freedom, and grace: in short, with God. So, for example, he remarks in *Fermenta Cognitionis* that true faith and genius are not bound to any formulas; they work, rather, hand-in-hand with God, the supremely free Being: i.e., with Love. He concludes: "So also the artist produces nothing worthwhile if he does not pursue his work *con amore* (2,294–95). The artist's ability is "a gift (talent, genius): i.e., a grace or gratuitous endowment" (9,274). But it is a gift we must not separate from love and wonder:

> If you take wonder from us, and with it love,
> Pray, tell us, then, where art and poetry would be! (9,274)[43]

---

42 The second sentence of this passage involves a play on words in German: "Wie denn die Schönheit als Lieblichkeit von Liebe, die Hässlichkeit von Hass stammt, und die Charis oder Grazie mit der Charitas (Gnade oder Zuneigung) dieselbe ist". Lovableness (*Lieblichkeit*) and love (*Liebe*) are appropriately matched in English; but hatefulness does not quite strike the precise tone of *Hässlichkeit* (ugliness, nastiness) and, consequently, cannot be as readily matched with hate (*Hass*). See 3,356 on the same point.

43 On the link between art and love see also BAADER: *Sämtliche Werke* 4,213; 9,163, 274; J. SAUTER: *Baader und Kant*, pp. 499–529; D. BAUMGARDT: *Franz von Baader und*

Proposition 15 concludes with a statement that addresses itself to the notion of beauty:

For the rest, as far as the beauty of material forms is concerned, the affinity of "beautiful" (*schön*) with "forbearance" (*Schonen*) is all the more fitting, since it is indeed only the indulgent mercy of God which conceals from our eye – under a beautiful veneer (as with a beautiful appearance) – the awkwardness, yes, even the hideousness, which matter conceals within itself. Appearance (*Maja*) in itself is, however, neither truth nor lie; it becomes a lie only through the intention of one who presents it as such; likewise, it becomes deception only through the fault of one who takes it for something that it is not. (4,190)

Baader seems to be saying here that beautiful appearance is all right as far as it goes, but we should not ascribe more importance to it than it deserves, nor should we be deceived by it. True love, in any case, is something much greater than response to external beauty, just as beauty in art goes beyond the merely superficially beautiful.[44] In a paragraph entitled "Über den Nexus zwischen Schön und Erhaben", *Religionsphilosophische Aphorismen*, number 34, Baader argues, *ex professo*, that beauty is a quality which, far from being synonymous with mere pleasing appearance, includes the basic characteristics which he ascribes to love itself.

Generally, people do not esthetically explain the concepts of the sublime and the beautiful in terms of their mutual relationship. The sublime, abstractly conceived as power – and, consequently, forbidding and depressing – would excite only fear and terror if it did not, at the same time, function in a condescending and elevating way. But this leaning (*Neigung*) is grace (for the word grace in German comes from inclination [*Zuneigung*]), and without grace inclination is not beautiful, for everything beautiful condescends (*Charis, Charitas*), while everything ugly hates and repels. Just as power without affection (*Zuneigung*) is only fearful (and, therefore, not beautiful), so, likewise, inclination without power or without sublimity is not beautiful. If we call beauty the uniform of love, that beauty must always include the expression of sublimity and humility (*Erhabenheit und Demut*), because love contains both of them. (10,333–34)[45]

die philosophische Romantik, pp. 336ff.; E. SUSINI: *Franz von Baader et le romantisme mystique. La philosophie de Franz von Baader*, volume 3, pp. 577ff.; J. SAUTER: "Franz von Baaders Aesthetik", *Archiv für Geschichte der Philosophie*, new series, 38 (1927), pp. 34–63 (especially pp. 46ff); H. REICHEL: "Baader als Kunstphilosoph", *Zeitschrift für Aesthetik*, 6 (1911), pp. 525–45 (especially, pp. 527, 532, 541–44); H. SEDLMAYR: "Franz von Baaders Gedanken zur Kunst", *Philosophisches Jahrbuch der Görres-Gesellschaft*, 68 (1960), pp. 361ff.

44   See BAADER: *Sämtliche Werke* 10,350–51.

45   The question of the sublime and the beautiful commanded considerable attention in eighteenth-century thought. See, for example: E. BURKE: *Philosophical Inquiry into the Origin of our Ideas of the Sublime and the Beautiful* (1756); and I. KANT: *Beobachtungen über das Gefühl des Schönen und Erhabenen* (1764). Fritz Strich notes that Schiller's notion of tragedy is bound up with this distinction: "The sublime man is, therefore, the tragic form of the classical man or the classical form of the tragic man, into which he can transform himself, if fate no longer allows him beauty" (F. STRICH: *Deutsche Klassik*

Beauty and love belong so closely connected that one can say neither is truly "of this world":

> But if love appears as a foreign guest who is not at home in this world, the same thing is true of the beautiful, for it is only the beautiful that is lovable, as the word "lovely" (*Wunderschön*)[46] expresses – which word indicates indemonstrability or incomprehensibility of the beautiful: i.e., its divinity. The distinction between sublime and beautiful, which is coming to be adopted by the esthetes, has, therefore, no other meaning than that the beautiful is sublime in free descent and the sublime is the beautiful in ascent. This solidarity of the beautiful and sublime (of affection and esteem) is substantiated by the fact that love vanishes when its gift, the beautiful, is no longer recognized as a free gift . . . (*Der morgenländische und abendländische Katholicismus . . .* 10,117–18; see also 9,164 fn. 1; 10,345 fn.)

Baader subscribes to Plato's observation that two people in love seek each other and bind themselves to one another to help each other produce the beautiful (1,44; 9,122; 12,266).[47] It lends itself admirably to that purpose, for, in Baader's terms, it is simply another way of saying that two people in love complement one another's deficiencies in their common aim of saying "yes" to the Love at work in them, thus establishing the image of that Love within themselves. "In all languages, the beautiful and the lovable are predicated after love, and the ugly (*das Hässliche*) after hate (*Hass*): as all beauty comes from love, so all ugliness comes from hate. The beautiful is what does good, just as evil makes what is ugly . . ." (*Über den solidären Verband der Religionswissenschaft mit der Naturwissenschaft*, 3,356).[48]

Proposition 16 (4,190)

We should freely perform and freely accept good deeds. We should acccept them without humiliation, just as we should perform them without pride. Baader would apparently approve of the common expression, "much obliged".

und Romantik, Bern and Munich [Francke] [5]1962, p. 310.) See also: I. KANT: "Analytic of the Beautiful", *The Critique of Judgment*, translated and introduced by Walter Cerf, Library of Liberal Arts, 1963; pages livff. include a chronological listing of major works on esthetics from Muratori to Hegel. S. H. MONK: *The Sublime*, Ann Arbor, Michigan (Ann Arbor Paperback) 1960, is an important study devoted to this theme; it includes abundant bibliographical references (pp. 237–46). In a footnote found in BAADER: *Vom Segen und Fluch der Creatur*, the incompleteness of both power without love and love without power is asserted in a similar fashion (7,99).

46 Baader plays on the word *schön* (beautiful) and *wunderschön* (lovely, very beautiful): something beautiful has a dimension of mystery or miracle (*Wunder*) about it; hence, it is indemonstrable.

47 See PLATO: "Symposium", 206B–07A, *The Dialogues of Plato*, volume 1, translated by B. JOWETT, New York 1937, pp. 330–31.

48 See BAADER: *Sämtliche Werke* 3,355–56 for a general discussion of the beautiful, the pleasing, the ugly, and allied notions.

If, then, the benefactor establishes a cordial bond with the recipient of his bounty, this bond should be a free – i.e., a mutual – one. The recipient should be just as willing and happy to let himself become obliged, as the giver is to oblige him. A person who can give without pride can also receive without humiliation (pressure), and a person who accepts something with humiliation could give something only with pride. (4,190; see also: 1,163)

Proposition 17 (4,190)

I Peter 4,8 states that "love covers over many a sin". Baader believes that the need for love is so vital that it can even excuse a certain measure of gullibility and deception.

The need to feel respected and loved is so genuine and strong that it not only excuses the weakness of one who is too easily prone to believe anything in this regard and lets himself be deceived, but sometimes will excuse even the man or woman who practices the deception, if he or she is not malicious about it. (4,190)

Proposition 18 (4,190-91)

Baader makes a plea for diligent and mutual attentiveness in love, a constant willingness and effort to please.

If we rightly reject coquettishness as exaggerated and deceitful fawning, we should, neverthe-less, not forget that friendship and love cannot last if friend or lover stops trying to oblige and thus no longer seeks to please. For it is precisely [such] pains-taking, even scrupulosity, in this matter, which is the sign of love. Love always gives much, with just a little, for the very reason that love always considers the great deal that she gives as too little, but the little she receives as too much. (4,190–91)

Baader seems to have maintained this point of view in his personal life too: in the little note he wrote to his fiancée Marie Robel on September 25, 1839, he apologetically regrets that he cannot deliver "this handbag" (see *Lettres inédites* 4,27) personally and "with a kiss strengthen your assurance that no matter how small a thing you receive from me, at least it does not come from a small heart" (15,624; see also 15,628). In *Über den solidären Verband der Religionswissenschaft mit der Naturwissenschaft*, Baader discusses the various meanings of "beautiful" and "pleasing". He distinguishes principally between merely external qualities that are pleasing and internal qualities that are pleasing. It is preferable, he argues, to win the love of a woman who has good qualities of mind and charac-ter, even though she may not be so physically attractive, than to win over a woman who is physically beautiful but lacks good moral qualities. "An intelligent, well-bred, and capable woman is able to make herself pleasing, indifferent, or unpleasing whenever and to whomever she wishes. A coquette is one who wants to dally with everyone and to please no one" (3,355–56).

Baader considers the effort to please so much a part of love that he says in the passage which follows immediately that "the will to please another, to be agreeable to him – i.e., to do for him what pleases him – is and is called love". He describes this as an active attitude, which not only meets someone half-way but even "seeks out his pleasure, not simply to support it, but to renew it constantly and to increase it". It is with this attitude in mind that the giver's gift, no matter how splendid, will seem an inadequate symbol of himself if he truly loves; the recipient, if he truly loves, pays little heed to the external gift as such – he is likely to find it excessive – but receives the giver through it.

Proposition 19 (4,191)

We cannot reduce love and religion to mere functions of reason without destroying both of them.

In our rationalistic age, one in which even cattle breeding and manure-production have been rationalized, people will naturally rationalize both love and religion in the same way: i.e., purify them from the scrupulosity [of love] as superstition; but, in fact, they throw out the baby with the bath by so doing. (4,191)

The word "scrupulosity" refers to Proposition 18 (4,190–91), where Baader speaks of the scrupulosity with which love takes great pains to please. Love tends of its very nature to do "too much": i.e., to exceed the law of reason alone, a law characterized by justice and strict proportions and ratios. Love is richness, superfluity (the "daughter of superfluity and poverty"), kenosis, gift of self, losing one's life in order to find it, and a host of other things that are not "reasonable". If we insist on subsuming everything under the law of reason, then we extinguish love – "throw out the baby with the bath". Baader fulminates every bit as much against the rationalism of Spinoza and Descartes as he does against the one-sided emphasis on feeling of Rousseau, Jacobi, and the Pietists. He repudiates the manner in which Kant shortchanges life and experience: for, "instead of thinking, [Kant] researches the laws of thinking; instead of loving, the laws of loving; instead of living, the laws of living; instead of digesting, the laws of digestion" (12,350). Rationalism knows nothing of nobility and humility, only of their caricatures: "To rationalism, true humility looks like a pleasant sort of weakness; rationalism knows no nobility except under the form of pride" (13,62). It is also the spirit of rationalism that has led to loss of love for the earth, for one's roots in a given locale and culture (15,444–45). Baader by no means opposes reason, but he strongly opposes the apotheosis of reason, which, in his view, would result in the death of life and love. The ultimate mystery of life and reality are much larger than reason.

Proposition 20 (4,191)

Service and self-sacrifice are so completely identified with true love that they cannot be separated from each other.

Loving is serving the beloved so thoroughly that, conversely, service easily produces love. Loving is gladly suffering and enduring privation for the loved one. And, if someone had nothing more, or knew of nothing more to do or to do without, or to suffer for that loved one, he would cease loving. (4,191)

As far as Baader is concerned, love and self-sacrifice for the beloved would seem to be subsumed under Leibniz's law of the identity of indiscernibles. Christ says: "A man can have no greater love than to lay down his life for his friends" (John 15,13). If a person cannot give *more* than his life in love, Baader would say, he cannot give anything *less* than some part of his life if he is to love at all.

Baader appeals for service, not servility. The qualities of love are easily distorted when they are not mediated through the Center:

Accordingly, one person not only should not love another person directly and apart from God, but cannot really do so; the same thing holds true for faith and obedience of men among themselves. It is precisely because of this that harmonization – impossible apart from Christendom – exists between freedom and subordination, ruling and serving, knowledge and faith, both in spiritual and in secular governance. For only the free and liberating spirit of Christianity delivers man from the arrogance of liberalism and the slave-mentality of servility. (*Bruchstück eines Commentars zu Jacob Böhmes Abhandlung über die Gnadenwahl,* 13,329; see also 6,21 fn.; 9,296 fn. 2)

In *Socialphilosophische Aphorismen,* number 8, Baader argues that "every legitimate and free subjection leads to true freedom and is the ground for it, just as every false and illegitimate freedom leads to deserved unfree subjection" (5,286ff.). He maintains that unwillingness to serve God freely, uprightly, and happily leads ineluctably to a kind of "service" that is exacted by force. Once again the distinction between *Inwohnung* and *Durchwohnung* is the issue. After referring to man's service of God, Baader adds:

[One must consider] that loving is serving; accordingly, as Adam Müller notes, the secret (of the unity of service and freedom) consists simply in the fact that one serves with love (*con amore*) while the ruler, for his part, makes this serving with love or well-meaning service as easy as possible for the one who serves. We have seen that, if the "belongingness" and love by means of which a servant becomes a member of the family vanish, his true freedom vanishes also. (5,288)

Based on this text, one might think that Baader's views about love and service simply echo contemporary conservative thought by recognizing the provenance of all authority from God and by giving willing service to all in authority. But there is no doubt that Baader makes all love of every kind a form of service. In *Vorlesungen über religiöse Philosophie im Gegensatz der irreligiösen älterer und neuerer Zeit*, number 3, he makes this point clear by citing a couplet, then in common usage in "our philosophy" (i.e., the philosophy of the time), and commenting on it:

> If you wish to live, you must serve,
> If you wish to be free, you must die!

One can grant this statement without hesitation, inasmuch as life in a certain region – as life from that region and, therefore, also for it – necessarily expresses serving that region. To break off that service necessarily results in dying for that region or leaving it. This holds true both for worship of God and for service of the world; yes, even for the service of love;* consequently, the question comes down to the matter of which master one refuses to serve (with love), the legitimate or the illegitimate.[49]

*[footnote] Everyone who loves, serves; only in serving does he love. Thus, one could also write the proposition above in this form:

> If you wish to love, you must serve,
> If you wish to be free, you must give up love! (1,161)

Service and giving-of-self are closely related concepts when considered in the context of love. The passage just cited continues by dealing primarily with the implications of giving and receiving, but the transition is easily made to the theme of serving:

One consequence of what we have said above is that free acceptance is a mutual thing. That is why the poet rightly says: "If you want to take, then give". Only in giving can I take . . . just as one who loves serves in freedom. To the extent that service is not simply compulsory service, it has to be *con amore*. Whoever serves an external master (another man) for God's sake (to please God), is the only one who serves freely. Only when love of God (religiosity) perishes in a person or in people do relationships of service manifest themselves in their oppressive and brittle hardness, just as limbs become rigid when the warmth of life that inwardly harmonizes all things vanishes. God, says Scripture, does the will of (serves) those who love or serve him. Ruling and serving are reciprocal. (1,163)

Baader varies the content and the expression, but the main point remains constant: "All living, as loving, is serving; only in the service of that love does life show that it opposes the foes of that love" (1,245).[50]

49   See the introductory pages to this chapter.
50   On service and love, see also BAADER: *Sämtliche Werke* 1,32ff.; 4,151 fn. 1; 5,292ff.; 8,162, 172; 9,107; E. SUSINI (Ed.): *Lettres inédites* 4,320.

Proposition 21 (4,191–192)

We have seen that service, in some form or other, is an essential part of man's life. Only *loving* service, however, is worthy of man.

It is not service as such that makes one unfree and humiliates, but only the kind of service that destroys respect and love. Loving service (*Liebesdienst*) is, therefore, liberating and ennobling or elevating. Nothing can be more foolish than to wish to "liberate" people by abolishing service and, accordingly, love. That would serve only to make them an unheeding rabble. (4,191; see also 8,207; 14,339, 450, 457)

Baader's point here is the same as that made in the foreword to *Vierzig Sätze aus einer religiösen Erotik*: everyone must serve; but, one must choose an object worthy of service and by so doing love and be elevated. We become like that which we love. Without worthy service performed in love, no one can find fulfillment: love and service "fill" us.

"Whoever wishes to exalt himself (i.e., 'fill' himself in an immediate way) will be humbled (emptied), and whoever humbles himself (i.e., empties himself of himself, gives up his false self-sufficiency) will be exalted (truly filled)", says Christ. (*Über den biblischen Begriff von Geist und Wasser, in Bezug auf jenen des Ternars*, 10,3 fn.)

Freedom for man is not defined by the absence of ties or service, but in establishing and pursuing worthy service:

The religion of redemption (Christianity) is, therefore, the religion of man's liberation from God, from himself, from other men and spirits (*Intelligenzen*), and from nature. That is because this religion, freeing man from the tension that held him captive and from his strife with God, makes God unburdensome again; it restores his inclination and love for [God]. At the same time, it liberates man from his own burdensomeness to himself, as well as from the burdensomeness of other men, of creation, and the world; it restores to him a proper regard and love for himself and the world, because it gives him the power to sustain himself and the world. *Da mihi punctum et coelum terramque sustinebo* (Give me a point [fulcrum], and I can hold up heaven and earth). (1,415–16)

In Baader's thought, freedom and liberation have nothing to do with "causal gaps" or "vacuum" theories. For him, God is a totally free Being because he is totally self-sufficient and grounded in himself. God is the absolutely and infinitely free Being because he is pure act and encompasses, within himself, all possible causality; he is the only being who is absolute and unlimited self-determination. Freedom, for man, consists in accepting one's definition, one's proper ground and "region", the law of one's being; it is self-determination too, not in an absolute sense (such as God's), but within the context that defines the limits of his freedom.[51] Freedom and truth must not be separated. "The truth will make you free" (John 8,32).

Proposition 22 (4,192)

Baader continues to develop the theme of service.

If you complain that you have to serve, just remember that no one in the world does not serve, and, indeed, often enough not just his superior but his inferior. But no one is too great or too small for loving service, or for service with love, for even God serves someone who willingly and honestly serves him, says the Scripture. Good will or love is the best element even in the meanest service; in fact, that man is a fool who, through lovelessness or bad will, makes it impossible for one serving him to do so with good will: i.e., to serve him well. (4,192)

St. Paul advises that whatever we do, in word or in work, should be done for the honor and glory of God (Colossians 3,17). Baader's version of that thought would, no doubt, advise: whatever you do, in word or in work, do it all with love and for Love.

Proposition 23 (4,192)

Love prompted by admiration is an important prerequisite for good service in government too.

Therefore, you secular and spiritual authorities, if you wish men to serve you willingly and well, see to it that they can love you. In order to enable them to love you, see to it that they can

---

51 *Vorlesungen über religiöse Philosophie im Gegensatz der irreligiösen älterer und neuerer Zeit,* number 13, explains: "Not only is that person unfree who is not grounded in himself (and whose grounding principle, at least in a full sense, does not dwell in him), nor is it merely one who is externally prevented from manifesting himself; the person who does not fully command the instruments necessary for him to manifest himself must also be called unfree. Lack of freedom for a living being is lack of integrity: want of, or mutual opposition of, its helping principles or organs which mediate the total traffic between the individual being and unity in integrity. Lack of freedom is, thus, incompleteness. Therefore, God alone is absolutely free, since only he is self-sufficient. Seeking and desiring are unfree, because unwhole. But we must not consider the free desire of love, which gives us fullness and satisfaction, the same as unfree need" (1,177 fn.). As Baader writes elsewhere: "Freedom of a being . . . is its capacity to fulfill the law of its constitution and to establish itself in it . . ." (6,302). Baader wrote a great deal about problems associated with freedom, and references to many of the major sources are indexed in BAADER: *Sämtliche Werke,* volume 16. Besides the general studies on Baader, see also: H. TUEBBEN: *Die Freiheitsproblematik Baaders und Deutingers und der deutsche Idealismus.*

admire you. For only admiration (*Bewunderung*) brings about free subjection, and anyone who wishes to be considered an authority should show himself worthy of admiration: i.e., he should be at once noble and condescending or loving. Grace (*Gnade*) comes from "descending" or "lowering" (*Gnieden oder Niedern*). The sun "goes to grace" (*geht zu Gnaden*), said the ancients: i.e., it goes down. (4,192)[52]

As Baader sees it, wonder or admiration are constant companions of love. Without *Bewunderung*, there is no mystery, no reverence, no prayer, no basis for love: it is the foundation for all religion.[53] In *Vorlesungen über religiöse Philosophie im Gegensatz der irreligiösen älterer und neuerer Zeit*, number 30, Baader states his thesis as follows: "Our reverential love of the good, together with our subjection to it, stems only from the admiring respect we have for it and our recognition of it as the true" (1,234). "To destroy the emotion of *Bewunderung*, or to stifle it, amounts to a radical destruction of religion" (1,235). It also destroys all true love and entails apotheosis of the human.

Proposition 24 (4,192)

"Only love is truly courteous or polite, whereas lovelessness is always coarse, no matter how polite and well-behaved it might want to be" (4,192). More succinctly: "Love is polite, hate is coarse" (12,291). The point here is that loveless "correctness" or rule-keeping is mere formality, i.e., hypocrisy: it conveys no respect or regard for a person. Politeness that flows from love, on the other hand, is just one aspect of the taking-pains-to-please that marks true love (Proposition 18). It conveys reverence and respect, a certain wonder in the face of mystery.

Proposition 25 (4,192–93)

In *Sätze aus der erotischen Philosophie*, Proposition 7 and following, Baader had already addressed the point to which he now returns:

52   Other passages in which the idea of grace is linked with that of love include: BAADER: *Sämtliche Werke* 9,116; 10,38; 13,88, 371; 14,149; E. SUSINI (Ed.): *Lettres inédites* 4,214. It should be noted that Baader's use of etymological derivations is, in general, highly questionable. His main source for such matters was *Die Teutsche Sprache aus ihren Wurzen* by Johann Evangelist Kaindl, a Benedictine archivist from the abbey at Prifling. The work appeared in four volumes between 1815 and 1824 at Regensburg-Sulzbach. (See 13,219–20.) H. GRASSL (Ed.): *Franz von Baader. Über Liebe, Ehe und Kunst*, pp. 241–42 compiles a substantial amount of evidence documenting the unreliability of this work.
53   See Chapter 2 for the link between love and *Bewunderung*.

Just as every human heart needs respect and love, it also needs forgiveness. But only love forgives, and she forgives gladly, because the humility and sorrow that turn to her enable her to develop the richness and fullness of her own tenderness. True contrition does not have to do with having injured or offended someone who can punish us for it, but rather someone who forgives us or is ready to forgive us. (4,192–93)

In other words, contrition and forgiveness are correlative notions, each describing the state of love that characterizes one of the formerly estranged parties in the act of reconciliation. For the contrite person, sorrow should not be based on fear; rather, one should feel sorrow for having offended against love. For the forgiving person, forgiveness should not be a shout of triumph over a morally vanquished and inferior adversary, not even satisfaction that justice has been vindicated; rather, it should be the surpassing joy of the father whose prodigal son has returned – to paraphrase a bit, "this love, which was lost, has come back again" (Luke 15,32)!

Proposition 26 (4,193)

Love is essentially a kind of union in being: it naturally produces a community of experience between lovers, not simply in joy but especially in sorrow.

Without suffering with someone, there is no rejoicing with him . . . A person can not only say that he gets to know his friend and beloved in time of need, but even that friendship and love first take root in tribulation and necessity. In prosperity and good fortune, people get only as far as camaraderie (with women and with men). Even if the plant of love shoots up without tears, it is, nonetheless, not without roots in this dew.

> Who never ate his bread in tears,
> Who never sat on his bed weeping
> Through pain-laden nightly vigils,
> Does not know you, you heavenly powers. (4,193)[54]

In this context, it appears that the familiar words of the traditional marriage ritual – "for better or for worse, for richer or for poorer, in sickness and in

54　The poem cited by Baader is taken from J. W. GOETHE: *Wilhelm Meister.* The lines are spoken by the harp-player. See J. W. GOETHE: *Goethes Werke in Vier Bänden,* Hamburg (Hoffman and Campe) 1956, volume 4, p. 84. The German text reads:

> Wer nie sein Brot mit Tränen ass,
> Wer nie die kummervollen Nächte
> Auf seinem Bette weined sass,
> Der kennt euch nicht, ihr himmlischen Mächte!

Baader's citation of this poem is not precise: in the second line, he substitutes *schmerzdurchwachten* for *kummervollen.*

health" – accord the place of honor to what a married couple must *suffer* together, for it is suffering that does the most for their love. Shortly after the wife of Crown Prince Constantin Lowenstein-Wertheim died in 1835, Baader sent the prince a circular entitled *Über den christlichen Begriff der Unsterblichkeit im Gegensätze der älteren und neueren nichtchristlichen Unsterblichkeitslehren.* He began by offering his sympathy and followed with some remarks about sorrow and grief in life. "Time can assuage such wounds, but not heal them, and it would, in fact, be bad if time could do that . . ." It would make a man heartless and insensitive if his heart could so petrify. For the poet says:

> Do not dry up, do not dry up,
> You tears of unfortunate love!
> Ah, to even an eye but half-dry,
> How barren and dead the world appears!
> Do not dry up, do not dry up,
> You tears of undying love![55]

Here, the poet is expressing the great truth which has been confirmed in all times and places and continues to be confirmed: "that in this world (as a rule) immortal love is unfortunate love", and that love manifests itself only as a fleeting moment (eternal moment) in time or temporality (which flees truth and cannot stand up to it), like a flower that quickly opens and closes itself only at midnight – this is also the "tragic" significance of the cross . . . (4,267–68)

The suffering and sorrow connected with love are directly related to the fact that love unites two persons: the suffering and pain of each become the suffering and pain of both through their love. "When, therefore, Christ speaks on several occasions of his being inwardly moved by compassion, the cause is that which dwells in man's profoundest being, i.e., God, who not only *has* love for creation but *is* this love, so that his thinking, willing, and doing of love is

---

55 The poem cited is one of Goethe's *Lieder.* See J. W. GOETHE: *Goethes Werke in Vier Bänden,* volume 4, p. 48. The German text reads:

> Trocknet nicht, trocknet nicht,
> Tränen der ewigen Liebe!
> Ach, nur dem halb getrockneten Auge
> Wie öde, wie tot die Welt ihm erscheint!
> Trocknet nicht, trocknet nicht,
> Tränen unglücklicher Liebe!

Once again, Baader's citation is inaccurate: he substitues *unglücklicher* for *der ewigen* in the second line; *Wie öde und todt* for *Wie öde, wie tot* in the fourth line; and finally, *unsterblicher* for *unglücklicher* in the last line. See also: E. SUSINI (Ed.): *Lettres inédites* 4,260.

essential and spontaneous for him alone" [my emphasis] (4,408). "In the free compassion of love, there is not just the same [amount of] sensitivity as [one finds] in unfree compassion, but more intense sensitivity" (4,407 fn. 3). Baader cites St. Martin's statement that "God can bring time to its goal only through suffering, because time is a teardrop of God (*eine Thräne Gottes*)". He goes on to speak of teardrops of eternity too; they are tears of joy, whereas those of time are tears of sorrow. Joys of eternity will supplant those of time for all who achieve and establish their spiritual re-birth. "For only tears of pain, true tears of time, will remain to us and become life for us, whereas no trace of the joys of this life will remain" (12,339).[56]

Proposition 27 (4,193)

The dynamics of contrition and forgiveness involve "confession" of sin, the effects of which Baader examines in the following remarks:

Love forgives the contrite person: i.e., the one who honestly confesses to her. Every plant dies if someone exposes its root or brings it to light. The penitent does this with the sin or lovelessness that has taken root in his soul and that, even as indifference, is already incipient hatred. One could say, then, that the contrite penitent is betraying the evil in himself to the good, just as he had betrayed the good in himself to evil in committing his sin; for there is no sin that does not attack the root of good and to that extent expose it. (4,193)

It is interesting to note the way in which Baader defines sin: it is simply love-lessness or hatred. There is no real middle ground. As Baader wrote on the first page of the Alliance-document:

... someone who knew man profoundly remarked "that every one who does not love his brother is already (at heart) a murderer".[57] Consequently, there is no room for indifference here: "He who is not with me, is against me" (Matthew 12,30), and where the spirit of love does not dwell, there lives the murdering spirit ... (6,13; see also: 5,258)

The only cure for past sin is love, love of the one who has been offended and forgives as well as the loving sorrow of the sinner who rejects his sin. Ulti-mately, in Baader's scheme of things, the only cure for sin is Love: i.e., God, freely accepted and loved in return by man.

---

56 See Chapter 5, Proposition 18. Baader frequently links love and sacrifice. See, for example, BAADER: *Sämtliche Werke* 7,345, 357; 8,169, 255; 9,165, 397, 401; 10,349 number 43; 12,203, 211. See also: this chapter, Proposition 2.

57 Here, Baader adapts I John 3,15. The text should read: "to hate your brother is to be a murderer".

Proposition 28 (4,194–95)

Baader was much preoccupied with the significance of *eating* and its implications for life and human community. He touches on that interest in the first paragraph of Proposition 28.

It is not visible, palpable food that really feeds and nourishes us, or, as the French expression significantly says: "gives substance" to us; it is, rather, an invisible, secret power that is concealed or incognito in it. When we eat food and let it work in us, it is through that secret power that those forces establish effective community with us as in a kind of *communio vitae*, which is the object for which those powers produced the food.[58] If the sun in the sky nourishes, blesses, and communicates itself to plants with its light and warmth – since what the sun does not bless or consecrate does not prosper – it is as though the sun were saying to them: "Take and eat, it is I".[59] But the sun does not divide itself into countless hosts, and remains ever the same in the sky. (4,194; see also: 14,487)

In "Über die Eucharistie", *Religionsphilosophische Aphorismen*, number 2, (10,290ff.), Baader makes the same point at greater length, using the same (solar) analogy:

Take and eat, says the sun to all earth-dwellers, it is I; only when you eat me in this way, only when this new food is in you do I remain with you and in you, subjecting you freely to me, while I continue to remain above you. Every true union of love, as Ruysbroeck says, is mutual eating and letting oneself be eaten: i.e., mutual burning and cooling, acting and resting, consuming and feeding; false or bad love is love wherein no filling, cooling, or nourishment take place, and the *horror* and *dolor vacui* emerge in abstract fashion. For food conditions and mediates active rapport with the one from whom it came, and it is, therefore, not food that directly strengthens me or makes me ill; rather, it is those higher or deeper powers to which I am elevated or become subject, an affective community with them when I eat or let this basis of rapport develop and work in me . . . (10,291–92)

This is the language of image and symbol, not always clear and unambiguous. But the general thrust seems apparent enough, especially when compared with Baader's other statements on the subject. "One has to suffer with someone if one is to rejoice with him. This connection is to be understood only as a mutual sacrifice, just as every process of nourishment is a sacrifice of food" (12,416). In love, the "food" is metaphorical: God "feeds" us by giving us his love as

---

58 The German reads: ". . . sondern eine unsichtbare, heimliche Kraft, welche in ihr verhüllt oder incognito ist, und durch welche, so wie wir die Speise in uns nehmen und auswirken, jene Mächte in effective Gemeinschaft mit uns treten, als in eine *Communio vitae*, welche Mächte zu diesem Zwecke diese Speise erzeugten".

59 Baader's allusion is to the Christian Eucharist. See Matthew 26,26ff. On Baader's copious use of symbol, see J. SAUTER: "Der Symbolismus bei Baader", *Blätter für deutsche Philosophie*, 1 (1928), pp. 348–66.

nourishment; in a sense, we also "feed" God by responding to his love, because "God does what we will if we do what we should and what he wills. When we love, we enter into God in a determining fashion (*Liebend gehen wir bestimmend in Gott ein*)" (12,416–17). "To allow someone to express wonder at us is to nourish him. Reverence is thanksgiving. To be admired (*Bewundertsein*) is loving and condescending to the admirer, 'in order to elevate him' " (12,417). The idea here seems to be that "to allow someone to express wonder at us" is equivalent to declaring or revealing the deeper levels of our personality to another in an outgoing way; it is offering our self to a loving response from the other – it "nourishes" the other's need for loving and sharing of another person. This line of thought becomes clearer if we study the essay, *Alle Menschen sind im seelischen, guten oder schlimmen, Sinn unter sich Anthropophagen* (4,221ff.). In that work, Baader speaks of the "mutual transmutation" that takes place in the process of nourishment. "The one who eats gives himself in return to the one nourishing him, since he allows food to take its effect in him and, thereby, brings fruit to the one who nourishes" (4,230). In other words, a person who lets himself be nourished is actively cooperating with the will of the one who wishes to nourish him; in a sense he "aids" the latter to realize his creative and life-giving potential.[60] Baader continues:

God himself says that his word should not come back to him empty, but rather should bear fruit. This is the sense in which Novalis says that lovers transfigure one another by eating from one another (*von einander essend*); in the same sense, Christ says that he reveals, transfigures, and glorifies the Father, while the Father does the same to him; the Spirit does likewise to both of them and they to the Spirit . . . (4,230)

More of the same may be found in the essay *Über die Wechselseitigkeit der Alimentation und der in ihr stattfindenden Beiwohnung* (14,59ff.; see especially p. 479). Just six months after Baader's death, Ludwig Feuerbach's *Das Wesen des Christentums* appeared. Feuerbach's materialistic axiom: man is what he eats (*Man ist, was man isst*) was worlds removed from Baader's *Weltanschauung*. But Baader would, nonetheless, have subscribed to the notion that one becomes like or is identical to what one eats; he would simply have distinguished varying sorts of things man can "eat" and emphasized the importance of spiritual

---

60 This case is analogous to the teacher-student relationship described in Proposition 7 above: each acts as "liberator" to the other, but in differing senses. On this principle, see 1,161, where the discussion of the teacher-student relationship concludes with the following axiom: ". . . the liberator must in turn liberate his own liberator (. . . der Erlöser seinen Erlöser wieder erlösen muss)". Substantially the same point is made in the scholastic axiom: *Causae sunt causae invicem, sed in diverso ordine* ("causes act as causes to one another, but in a different order").

nourishment, especially love. Baader would say that we become like the sum of the various sources of nourishment that we "ingest", not just in a physical sense but also on other levels. Through love in particular we make something our very own, even as we give ourselves to it: the reciprocity is ineluctable.[61]

In the second paragraph of Proposition 28, Baader discusses interpersonal relationships in a manner highly suggestive of Martin Buber's later I and Thou distinction.[62] Baader says:

As a person, I cannot, of course, immediately possess or enjoy another person as such, for that would be to degrade him to the level of an impersonal chattel or thing. Thus, *materia* is from *mater*, and in this sense, every self-giving to a lover is a self-offering to the lover. Without insight into this constant mutual interpenetration and withdrawal of personal self into impersonal nature (of course in a different sense than that used by the *Naturphilosophen*), without insight into this self-realizing and self-emptying process, one does not understand a thing about either [person or nature]. – From this, one can also understand the originally androgynous nature of mind: i.e., that every mind, as such, contains its nature (*Terre*) within itself, not outside itself. Thus, true love becomes actual only if both lovers mobilize their capacity for alternate self-realization and self-emptying. (The presence of that capacity in both of them is presupposed.) Ignorance of the original androgynous nature of man is, moreover, so great that people have even confused Eve's issuance from Adam as a second human being with the division of sexual powers in each of them that came about on this occasion; but, at the same time, they thought of androgyny as something absolutely impotent for reproductive purposes. In the normal sexual relationship (through love), the man helps the woman to wonder and she helps him to love; or, the man helps the woman in himself toward maleness, while the woman helps the male within herself toward femaleness. On the contrary, in abnormal (loveless) sexual union, the woman helps the man develop serpentine [baseness], while he helps her develop satanic pride.[63] (4,194–95)

What really establishes two persons in an I-Thou relationship is love, not passion. Inspired by a passage which he had read on page 127 of *De trinitate ac mysteriis Christi–Alcuini Levitae libri tres, D. Carolo Imperatori dicati* (Strasbourg, 1530), Baader makes two remarkable observations regarding the I-Thou relationship. Both anticipate some of his later thought about love and interpersonalism.

---

61 Compare Baader's diary entry: "Both love and friendship free people from bonds under which they sigh: friendship, from serving vanity which provides no nourishment for the heart and in its perennial dissatisfaction causes the heart to atrophy and be lamed; love, from slavish coercion that shrivels up the heart and kills it" (11,260). See also: E. SUSINI (Ed.): *Lettres inédites* 4,350; Proposition 29, this chapter; and Chapter 3.

62 M. BUBER: *I and Thou*, New York (Scribner) ²1958.

63 On "serpentine baseness" and "satanic pride", see Chapter 4, especially the commentary on the second chapter of Genesis.

One could express this better by saying that I and Thou (we) issue out of (in) love, than by saying that we make this love through our union; at any rate, they are new people who thus issue forth (as members). (14,447)

Fulfillment of desire is the perfecting of that desire, not, as people (in time) think, its cessation or extinction; thus, union in love is what first posits persons, while animal union confuses them. (14,447; see also: 14,402)[64]

Thus, love creates the I-Thou relationship. The experience of love is so profound that it produces a situation of "ecstasy" (Greek *ek*= outside of; *stasis* = standing) or "being-outside-oneself". (See, for example, 14,313.) Existence in love is equivalent to existence in the beloved, hence the kenosis necessary for love to occur.[65] It is axiomatic for Baader that the lover finds himself in the beloved and vice-versa. If that is so, his conclusion that there is no I-Thou apart from love is valid.

It holds true for every reciprocal union (bond, or in the old German language, marriage) that each of the two or more contracting parties is or becomes a whole (something personal) only in that union; one must also say that two people who love each other do not love themselves in each other, but rather that each of them first finds himself in the other . . .*
 *[footnote] What is given up or perishes in the union is precisely the incompleteness and lack of truth in the existence of those who unite with one another . . . (*Vorlesungen über speculative Dogmatik*, Book 5, number 17, 9,261)[66]

64 Baader's words read: "Man kann besser sagen, dass ich und du (wir) aus (in) der Liebe hervorgehen, als dass wir diese Liebe durch unsere Union machen; wenigstens sind es neue Menschen, die so hervorgehen (wie Glieder)" (14,447). "Die Erfüllung des Verlangens ist dessen Vollendung, nicht, wie man (in der Zeit) meint, dessen Aufhören oder Erlöschen, wie die Union in Liebe die Personen erst setzt, die animalische sie confundirt" (14,447). One may profitably compare Baader's suggestions with Hegel's discussion of the Master-Slave relationship in the preface to G. F. HEGEL: *Phänomenologie des Geistes* (1807). Hegel argues that the self comes into existence only by way of recognition of that self through another. In this area, as in so many others, Baader vindicates his claim to being simply a "seed-peddler" (*Samenhändler*) and not one who sells fully grown plants (2,238). Indeed, all of his work – and not just the single large work which goes by that name – might be styled *Fermenta Cognitionis*.
65 On *kenosis*, see Proposition 1 above.
66 Baader immediately applies his point – i.e., that persons in love do not love themselves in one another but rather find themselves there: "It is because people have not understood this mutual complementarity through and in union that they have not understood the dogma either: *Pater Deus, Filius Deus, Spiritus Deus, non tres Dii*" (9,261). Baader's citation is from the Symbolum "Quicunque" (Athanasian Creed), but he does not quote its wording exactly. It should read: ". . . ita Deus Pater, Deus Filius, Deus (et) Spiritus Sanctus: et tamen non tres dii . . ." See C. RAHNER (Ed.): *Enchiridion Symbolorum*, Freiburg [31]1947 p. 17, number 39.

Elsewhere, the formulations vary a bit, but the end result is the same: e.g., "When I love, I do not see myself in the other; instead, I lose myself in him and find myself again only because the other loses himself in me" (12,364). In other words: when in love, one finds oneself in the other. What, then, is true self-love? "Love is true when the lover's separation is self-division (*Selbsttrennung*). This is true self-love. It is the mystery of love as true love of self – Eckehart" (12,468). In *Vorlesungen über Societätsphilosophie*, number 11, Baader talks about the continual renewal of the creature by the creator's presence in it and love for it: God in the creature and the creature in God – in those capacities, they constantly "renew" each other. He finds an analogy for this arrangement in the dynamics of love:

. . . a lover constantly finds himself in, is rejuvenated by, or is re-born only in his beloved, because he never looks for himself in himself but always in the one he loves. So the dictum – "Set your hearts on [your heavenly Father's] kingdom first . . . and all these other things will be given you as well" [Matthew 6,33] – is explained through love, since the "departed" existence of one who loves is always, in reality, simply added to him or given to him. It is precisely this continual finding of oneself that constitutes the reward for losing oneself in the beloved – that is the ongoing miracle of one's continual resurrection out of and in the beloved. (14,117)

One of the radical differences between the effects of love and those of knowledge is that love affects the *essence* of both lover and beloved, whereas knowledge does not (14,318; see also 8,243 fn.; 11,205; 14,204). Indeed, love involves an *ekstasis* precisely because it goes beyond those qualities that are touched upon or abstracted in love; it affects the whole person. *Effectus amoris est mutua inhaesio, ut amans sit in amato, amatum in amante* (the effect of love is mutual inherence, so that the lover is in the beloved and the beloved in the lover), cites Baader from Thomas Aquinas, and then adds: "Just as the thing known is in the knower (but not essentially, as in willing and in love)" (14,312; see also 14,208).[67] Baader sometimes refers to the reciprocity of interpenetration experienced by two lovers as "taking birth" (*Eingeburt*) in one another:

The concept of mutual "taking birth" as precondition for mutual conformation is, moreover, already contained in the idea of love, although this mutual birth-taking takes place differently between creature and creator than it does between two creatures. (*Vorlesungen über Societätsphilosophie*, 14,106, 113, 124)

---

67   Baader studied Aquinas's works rather extensively, but not until he was fully matured intellectually. (See 15,64.) BAADER: *Sämtliche Werke* 14,197–348, is filled with excerpts from Aquinas's works, including a considerable section from the *Prima Secundae* of the *Summa Theologiae*. See especially pp. 309–24 on *Amor*.

Baader speaks of the "identity of the eye with what it sees, and of lover with beloved" (12,424), which is why "the lover manifests the beloved" (12,466). For "love is and accomplishes an exchange of personality, an interchange of substances. Differences between these substances, if I might say it this way, is the condition for love. Love accomplishes mutual assimilation . . ." (11,182). "Every union is a mutual affair. One who loves me abides in me, and I in him . . . " (14,449).[68] "The lover is in the beloved (mutual entry)" (14,207, 208). *Vorlesungen über religiöse Philosophie im Gegensatz der irreligiösen älterer und neuerer Zeit,* number 28, proclaims the following as both title and thesis: "The creature knows itself (in its original) only in God, just as the one who is loved knows himself only in the one who loves him" (1,229). The extended discussion which follows is devoted largely to the ways in which lovers interpenetrate.[69]

. . . therefore, love and limitation to one's own subjectivity are diametrically opposed . . . In fact, it is the most clever invention of love that she freely empties herself of her existence and, indeed, of the best part of it, in order to be able to thank another, not herself, for its recovery or its proof and possession, and in that way is able to bind that other indissolubly to herself. As J. Böhme says: this is the greatest miracle – that God has made two out of one, which, nevertheless, has remained one . . . When I love, I posit my "middle" in the loved one. *Anima est, ubi amat, et sentit, ubi amat* (The soul exists where it loves and senses where it loves.) . . . The fact that two beings are really two comes from the fact that they are both relatively "wholes"; that they are one, comes from the fact that each is half of the other. For them to unite, so that each may be half of the other, each must "halve" himself: i.e., enter into the other with part of his being, leaving the other part behind . . . (1, 229–31)

Baader diagrams this process, but then proceeds to reject it with the observation that "properly speaking, such a union can take place only in a third element" (1,232).[70]

The statement *Anima est ubi amat* is particularly significant. It expresses and explains how will, imagination, and love work. It states, in four words, precisely what all of the foregoing evidence about lovers finding themselves in each other attempts to document. Baader develops his argument in the following two passages:

Of great importance, therefore, is the principle: *Anima est, ubi amat* – particularly, in the expanded form I give to it: *Anima est, ubi amat, et quamdiu amat* (The soul exists where it loves and for as long as it loves). "Only for as long as they loved, did they exist", says the poet: i.e.,

---

68   Baader develops this thought at greater length and illustrates the dynamics of personal interchange with a diagram.
69   See note 71 below.
70   See Chapter 5, Proposition 1.

location and duration for a voluntary being are only in feeling (*im Affect*), but feeling is based in the image (*imago*). If what you love exists everywhere and always, or if it is taken up into the "everywhere" and "always", then you yourself exist everywhere and always; for love works by imagination and is magic; love has the radical power of making itself like what it loves . . . (*Vorlesungen über die Lehre Jacob Böhmes mit besonderer Beziehung auf dessen Schrift: Mysterium Magnum*, number 15, 13,221–22; see also 8,127; 10,16 fn. 2).

For those in love, as for the magnetic clairvoyant, the statement holds true: *Anima est ubi amat.* For your treasure – that is, your mental image (*Geistbild*) – is where your heart is: i.e., its Here and Now is solely in its feeling. Lovers exist only, love only, feel only, where their will-image (*Willens-bild*) is and where it is in rapport [with something]. Everything that lies in between is of no importance to them; in fact, we observe that intensity of feeling corresponds exactly to the magnitude of the distance in time and space that is destroyed in the process . . . (*Vorlesungen über speculative Dogmatik*, Book I, number 18, 8,155–56)[71]

This peculiarity of love is one of the factors that distinguishes it from pleasure: pleasure requires actual physical presence of whatever causes it, but love does not (14,311).

Proposition 29 (4,195)

We speak at times of a "heart-to-heart talk". Baader speaks here of heart-to-heart nourishment:

Properly speaking, a heart does not nourish or give substance to anything other than another heart. Feed it any other food or delicacy and the heart remains empty. Just as a person loves and eats only from another person, so can one person be poison and death for another. How foolish, then, are those people to be called who are so careful and scrupulous in choice of food for their stomachs, yet so inattentive and indifferent in choice of food for the heart. (4,195)

Baader continues by developing a thought introduced at the beginning of Proposition 28: Man does not live by bread alone (Matthew 4,4) any more than man is body alone. A specific level of nourishment, he argues, corresponds to each level of existence:

A person lives for that from which he lives; that is, what lives in us. We do its (his) will because it is only in so doing that we are able to achieve the union we need with the source that nour-

---

71 *Anima est ubi amat (et quamdiu amat)* translates as "The soul exists where it loves (and as long as it loves)". Baader uses this principle extensively; see, for example, BAADER: *Sämtliche Werke* 2,501; 3,281; 4,242; 7,372; 8,102; 9,199, 265; 12,291, 341, 480–81; 13,382; 14,100, 311, 449; 15,628; E. SUSINI (Ed.): *Lettres inédites* 1,472. See also: Chapter 3. Baader adopts Jacob Böhme's and Paracelsus's idea that "love . . . has the radical power of making a lover similar to the thing he loves". (See, for example, 8,127; 10,16 fn. 2.)

ishes us and to maintain the connection. That is why Christ says: "Only he who does my word will know that it is from God and brings him to God". He also said to his disciples at Jacob's well "that it was his heavenly food, to do his Father's will".[72] (*Alle Menschen sind im seelischen, guten oder schlimmen, Sinn unter sich Anthropophagen* 4,233)

Just as the whole universe before man's creation was too small a place for God to enter and find his rest, "so also is the whole starry heaven too small a place for man to pour out his heart; only another human heart gives him the room to do that" (15,608). A heart atrophies and decays without the love-nourishment of another heart.

Proposition 30 (4,195)

The notion of the Center never leaves Baader; without it, nothing else makes any sense to him. So also, and indeed especially (since the Center is quintessentially Love), is the case of love:

If there were no Central Heart (*Cœur-Centre*), and if people as a community could not take substance [sustenance] from and restore themselves from and in this Heart, then they would not be able to take substance [sustenance] from one another either, and a person would have to "spit out" another, as actually happens sometimes. (4,195)

The heart stands for the innermost core; it is the "perfected middle" (*vollendete Mitte*) (1,205) of any personal being; it is "the first and the last" (*Lettres inédites* 1,170) for a person's life. "The heart" also stands for love, of course; and in Baader's scheme of things, it is perfectly right that God should be the "Heart" of reality in both senses: as the ultimate core of all being; and as love, the "central law".[73]

Proposition 31 (4,195–96)

If a person does not watch his "heart-diet" carefully, he runs the risk of some fearful consequences:

72 Here again Baader cites loosely. His first scriptural reference seems to be John 7,17 and should read: "If anyone is prepared to do his will, he will know whether my teaching is from God or whether my doctrine is my own". The second, "cited" by Baader in the third person, should read: "My food is to do the will of the one who sent me and to complete his work . . ." (John 4,34).
73 See J. SAUTER: "Der Symbolismus bei Baader", *Blätter für deutsche Philosophie*, 1 (1928), p. 354.

Do not set your heart on things or persons that are heartless, much less on the evil-hearted. All poisonous and bloodthirsty insects and worms are bloodless or cold-blooded; so also are all cold-hearted people who are the heart's bloodsuckers and poisoners or murderers. (4,195)

Ever since the negative spirit has become doctrinaire and holds men's minds captive, there has arisen a crowd of heart-chilling, withering and poisonous, soul-vitrifying or soul-decaying, philosophic, religious, and moral systems that are, for the most part, worse than their authors, since the latter are more obsessed than possessed. (4,195–96; see also *Lettres inédites* 4,79, 307)

Vorlesungen über religiöse Philosophie im Gegensatz der irreligiösen älterer und neuerer Zeit, number 51, contains an analagous passage which sheds additional light on Baader's meaning:

If someone speaks to something incapable of speech (*welches selber das Wort nicht hat*), he "loses" his word on it; in similar fashion, he loses his heart or his love if he sets his heart on objects that have no heart, or what is worse, that are heart-killing (bloodsuckers of the heart). St. Martin says, therefore, that man, by his becoming earthly (*durch sein Irdischwerden*), "divorced love out of his life". Indeed, do the vacuousness, lamentation, and pain of our lives have any other cause than this continual loss, this bleeding to death of our love on behalf of things that are themselves either loveless or incapable of love, or that even kill love with their cold scorpion's poison? Are we not, then, everywhere surrounded by that kind of *miroirs nuls* and *miroirs faux* of our hearts? Now, if a person has let the better part of himself descend to the lower and the worse, if he has "divorced" himself, then this evil element has indeed infected him, but he has, in turn, infected that evil element with a good element that is foreign to it . . . (1,295–96)

At times, Baader betrays this kind of sentiment in just a word or two: for example, in speaking of "the heart-consuming aspect of all worldly pleasure. Man loves in it a heart that is no heart" (12,386; see also 9,44 fn.; 14,353). A footnote which appears in *Über den Begriff der Zeit* says, in part:

. . . if someone gives himself completely over to this external world, it happens that this world not only fails to nourish him interiorly or leaves him empty, but rather, since it unceasingly pulls him totally toward the external, empties him out more and more like a true bloodsucker; or, if one will allow the use of a new word, like a true "heart-sucker" (*Herzsauger*). That is why I said in my little essay *Über das heilige Abendmahl* . . . that in this world we find ourselves under the power of a being that does not cease eating our body and drinking our blood (our soul). Finally, whoever completely identifies or confuses himself with this external world will eventually end up believing that he is of the same idle (empty or inwardly null) nature as it is. Unfortunately, this belief is only all too common among our modern philosophers, who call themselves *Naturphilosophen*; this belief is the *proton pseudos* (first or fundamental illusion) of their philosophy. (2,89–90)

Proposition 32 (4,196)

Necessities of various kinds may bring men together, but their staying together requires something more lasting than transitory emergencies. So, also, with regard to love: it takes persevering effort and constant renewal to make it what it should be. It is possible for something like frivolity or accident to bring people together; even a crime could do it. But it does not follow that their staying together is an accident or a crime, because it lies within a person's power to make a better situation out of a bad one. So, for example, necessity or some baser requirement may bring people together, but the bond developed between them outlasts the necessity. So, also, every natural love is something put to us as a task, the task being to make something better out of it through our cooperation (4,196).

Nothing human is permanent; everything needs to be re-created or re-made if it is not to die. This holds true not only for the body, with its need for food and rest, but also for the soul: basic life-orientation or deep love can also "wear out".

Many people show that they are no less ignorant in this regard than orangutans, who chase indians away from the fire they had made and warm themselves by it, but who are too ignorant to keep the fire going by adding fuel to it. How often, then, do we see natural love of the sexes, love of children, love of parents, love of brothers and sisters, love of tribe or country, etc., go out or be extinguished in short order for the same reason. (4,196; see also 5,273)

Proposition 33 (4,196–97)

A large and important part of Baader's philosophizing is devoted to the subject of time and eternity. Indeed, one could organize his whole philosophical thought around these two ideas.[74] Hans Reichel summarizes Baader's thought succinctly:

The integer of time is eternity. Time, says Baader, is the differential of eternity. (3,377; 14,67) We can understand time speculatively only from the standpoint of eternity: as its integer (14,89). To posit time as an *a priori*, as Kant does, and to make it, thereby, indestructible and non-deducible, is superficial. (14,56, 65ff.)[75]

Baader's statements about time and eternity include some of the most fascinating things he ever wrote. Proposition 33 addresses the subject only briefly:

---

74   BAADER: *Sämtliche Werke*, volume 16, the index volume, requires several pages to indicate the chief references to *Zeit.* See F. KÜMMEL: *Über den Begriff der Zeit;* H. REICHEL: "Die Sozietätsphilosophie Franz von Baaders", *Zeitschrift für die gesamte Staatswissenschaft*, 57 (1901); C. LINFERT (Ed.): *Franz von Baader. Über den Begriff der Zeit. Über den Zwiespalt des religiösen Glaubens und Wissens*, Basel (Benno Schwabe) 1954.
75   REICHEL: "Die Sozietätsphilosophie Franz von Baaders", p. 198.

You complain about the transitoriness and vanity of all these loves, although you were able to, and had the duty to, transform the transitory into the permanent by making it free of time, instead of, conversely, "giving fodder" (*füttern*) to time, so to speak. (4,196; see also 2,519 fn. 1; 10,346)

The whole thrust of Baader's approach to time is to make it useful in the context of eternity: "Time has been given to us so that we will become free of time" (12,419). Every moment counts: "That time is past (lost) from which we have not taken its worthwhile content; that is time which we have not consumed, but rather 'given fodder to' " (12,332). "A fraction never yields a whole, and can never replace the whole. That is why living in time and whiling away time are never without a Beyond and an Ought" (7,84 fn. 2). Baader's thought is full of statements of this kind. The following passage, found in *Socialphilosophische Aphorismen aus verschiedenen Zeitblättern*, clearly outlines his views about the relationship between time and love:

A person becomes (or thinks he becomes) more or less like the activity he pursues and like whatever he loves, or that from which and for which he lives. It is, therefore, no wonder if we see that a person who constantly dedicates his eternal love and his eternal powers to temporal confusion stamps the character of temporality . . . on all that he does or makes. Since he does only what is temporal, it is no wonder that he believes himself to be only temporal. With the time he had at his disposal . . . as with a small coin, he should have procured the gold of eternity for himself. But by the day and the hour he trades in eternity for time and, instead of putting time to death, lets himself be put to death by it. (5,264–65; see also 1,64–65; 2,18–19; 5,273; 10,345–46)

To every person is allotted a certain measure of time in this world. Everyone is supposed to use the time that he has been given to bring himself closer to the source of his being: i.e., to God. Misused or unused time puts one in a relatively worse position, which is aggravated in proportion to the amount of time badly used. The following passage, which appears in *Über den Evolutionismus und Revolutionismus oder die posit. und negat. Evolution des Lebens überhaupt und des socialen Lebens insbesondere*, develops this argument:

Every individual person (or every people [*Volk*]) who neglects to appropriate for himself the supports (*Hilfen*) that are at his disposal, afresh every day and every hour, or who neglects to set aside and overcome the barriers that continually block his way – (and who thus, in a passive sense, abides with the old) – leaves past time behind him as a double debt of time and, so to speak, as undigested time. Instead of the past, as an already resolved problem, leading him onward into the future, instead of finding himself increasingly freer of time, stronger through time (*zeitkräftiger*) and *therefore really younger*, the burden of time and the chains of time increase constantly for him as time goes on. Finally, this burden and crisis make him seize the desperate expedient of declaring that time and history are bankrupt; he thinks that if he simply decrees the beginning of a new calendar, as those madmen did at the first outbreak of their revolution, then his whole time-debt would be wiped out. We see here, once again, how and why every revolutionary movement (which breaks away from and rejects the continuity or tradition of history in a selfish way) is simply the consequence of neglected and omitted evolution . . . (6,101)[76]

Thus, time seems to be a neutral category: we can use it to lead us in the right direction, or we can invest it wrongly, and then it proves lethal. The test for Baader, as for all persons whose thinking is mystically oriented, is eternity. The crucial question is the one St. Bernard of Clairvaux constantly put to himself: *Quid hoc ad aeternitatem?* (How does this [thing, action] relate to eternity?) Time is a testing-ground for eternity. "Time is both gift and punishment. The entire nature of time (*Zeitnatur*) is a work of the merciful love of God" (12,417). All of this relates immediately to love, for love is itself eternal, not merely as popular love-songs would have it but as Baader's principles require. If the eternal God is love, and we are made in his image, it is easy enough to see what Baader thinks about how we should spend our time. In a letter to Marie Robel (September 23, 1839), Baader wrote: "You are right, dear Marie; the heart of man, as the only immortal thing in him, ages and winters only if the sunshine of eternal love does not fall upon it and does not awake eternal spring and eternal youth in it" (15,623).

It is true that Baader is affected here by the love he felt for the young woman he was shortly to marry; on the other hand, what he says is perfectly consonant with, indeed required by, what he had always held about love. In a letter to his friend Dr. von Stransky (October 12, 1839), Baader writes of his love for Marie. Among other things, he says that "love as God's gift to nature and creation is a miracle; we understand even less how we could have lived earlier without this love, or how it would be possible to outlive it in the future. For when the eternal enters into time, time forgets about past and future" (15,627). Baader's letter to Marie Robel of October 28, 1839 links their love for each other quite explicitly to love for God:

. . . our love does not shift with the wind. We love each other eternally, since we love each other in the eternal God, or rather we love God in us, and we would be defecting from God if we were to defect from each other. (15,628)

Just as the principle *Anima est ubi amat* overcomes limitations of space and distance, Baader's concept of love also removes limitations of time: love is eternal (10,344); its goal transcends time (Proposition 18, 4,177).[77]

76 Baader develops this theme throughout the entire essay (6,73–108). Mention of the "new calendar" refers, of course, to the new Revolutionary (Republican) Calendar decreed by the French National Convention in 1793; it was made retroactive to September 22, 1792.

77 See H. REICHEL: "Die Sozietätsphilosophie Franz von Baaders", p. 200.

Proposition 34 (4,197)

As Baader had already pointed out a number of times in *Vierzig Sätze aus einer religiösen Erotik*, nature needs nurture, even in love (especially in love). Newly conceived love is a fragile child.

Every new love (not excluding religious love) that comes into our lives, without any action or merit on our part, is like a newborn child, tender but also fragile and in need of assiduous care. For the newborn child is at first only the immediate fruit and image of the substance of the parents, but it must develop into the active personal image of their spirit and heart. (4,197)

In a sense, two people are "parents" of the child that is their love; in another sense, that child is parent to them: ". . . Love is the child that remains within parents and gives birth to them anew" (12,266). In the letter he wrote to Dr. von Stransky on October 12, 1839, Baader expresses his pleasure "that you have found my idea of love as a child born of and in lovers, and giving them re-birth in its turn, a fitting notion . . ." (15,626–27). The most complete statement of this analogy formulated by Baader appears in "Die Liebe selber ist ein Kind der in Liebe sich Verbindenden", *Religionsphilosophische Aphorismen*, number 37, (10,343–46). The essay begins with the following thought:

Just as we speak of children of love – and, in fact, all children should be such – we should realize, above all, that love itself, in its origins, is just a child. It is, however, a child whose loving parents conceive it within themselves and give birth to it within themselves, unlike the child to which they give birth "from" themselves through reproduction. Parents ought to take great pains with this child within them; they ought to protect it and, to their joy, happiness, and glory (*Herrlichkeit*), they ought to raise that child in them to be large and strong . . . (10,343)

Baader goes on to ask: What is the origin of such a child? This prodigy (*Wunderkind*) is as much a third party with respect to its parents as any natural child is, despite the fact that the child that is love dwells inside them permanently. Philosophers and theologians have left the question unanswered. Baader answers by noting that God, "who is himself birth-giving and creative Love", is not satisfied with merely creating man; he also wishes to be re-born in man, to become God a second time, so to speak: i.e., he wills to be not simply Creator but Father to his creation. Baader proceeds to list some more contrasts between a natural child and the child that is love. Parents might rejoice in both kinds of children, but we should not forget that, in procreating a physical child, parents are working in a way that is largely blind and purely instrumental, like animals. Another difference is that children eventually leave home and parents and, in a sense, "commit them to the past", but "the very opposite must be said of the child that is love itself. Here is a child who not only never leaves her parents, so long as they do not abandon her, but in whom their life really begins (rather than ends): i.e., eternal divine life, because God himself eternally lives only because he eternally loves" (10,344).

Baader then posits that love is an end in itself, coextensive with life, an absolute *a priori*, alpha and omega, law above all laws.[78] So far as natural children are concerned, we must observe that marriages without children occur frequently enough, as do marriages in which children bring no joy to their parents; but "the marriage of true and honest souls is invariably fruitful, however, because it always enjoys its marvelously gracious fruit of love, its marriage-blessing" (10,345). We should remember that Christ speaks of an end to marriage in the physical sense in heaven; he says that men will be like the angels in heaven: i.e., there will be a union of spirits, of souls (see Matthew 22,30; Mark 12,25). This kind of spiritual marriage and fruitfulness is already foreshadowed on earth by people who love one another, so long as sensuality does not blind them. We should perceive the truth of Faust's statement, as far as the purely physical aspects of pleasure are concerned:

> When full of desire, I yearn for pleasure,
> And in pleasure I long for desire. (10,345)[79]

Sensual pleasure, in its own right, leads to death. Lust does not last: it is too closely linked to time and matter to survive long. To concentrate on it in isolation is to neglect the inner child of love and cause her to depart.

Baader concludes by remarking on the foolishness of one who claims to find no evidence for the presence of such eternal love within himself. Such a claim is easily ascribable to the fact that such a one has devoted his whole life and time to "foddering time", rather than offering up what one does in time for eternal ends.

Proposition 35 (4,197)

In Proposition 1 of *Sätze aus der erotischen Philosophie*, Baader drew a distinction between tried and untested stages of love. Now, he returns to the same theme:

Only that is permanent and immortal which has thoroughly destroyed transitoriness and mortality within itself. So also in love: only he is faithful and stable in it who has destroyed infidelity

---

78   For the continuation of this text, see Proposition 5 above.
79   The German text reads:

> In der Begierde lechz' ich nach Genuss,
> Und im Genuss verschmacht' ich vor Begierde.

and lability within himself, at least as a natural disposition and possibility (*posse mori*, as Augustine says), even when it has never come to actual infidelity or fall. Those who maintain the necessity of an actual fall are telling us, in effect, that a girl cannot get married in any way other than by a previous fall, or that a man can achieve knowledge of truth only by retracting to a lie. (4,197)

Proposition 36 (4,197)

The point is continued:

Just as God created man sinless – that is, innocent – and created nature unspoiled, but did not create them incapable of sin and corruption, and just as God willed that man should destroy the capacity for sin and corruption in himself through his own effort, cooperation, and merit (by way of trial or temptation), the same is true for every other love, because all love must pass from its first, immediate, and natural condition of innocence through temptation to its tested condition of stability. (4,197)

Proposition 37 (4,198)

Man's fall from God's favor was not a necessary thing, but the temptation to fall was necessary; the same applies to love in general.

Further, man's infidelity and fall from and against God were not necessary; man could have withstood and overcome temptation without succumbing to it. But temptation was necessary because, if man had not passed through it, he could not have attained a tested or tried and permanent condition of being connected to God. All of this is valid in its own way for every love – i.e., for human love and for love of nature – as a principle of culture and fine art. (4,198; see also 4,167)

In the next paragraph, Baader discusses the various dimensions of God's love: vertical, horizontal, and vertical once again. The descent-ascent relationship is part of either one of two vertical relationships: from God to man, and from man to nature.

Just as God's love lowers itself to man, raising him up toward it, so it broadens itself out as human love on the horizontal level, and reaches downwards as love of nature, raising the latter up to it. But if genuine love (or inclination toward it) is to establish the true subordinate relationship of nature to man, the intelligent creature will have to overcome a double temptation here too: either to misuse nature in a despotic way, giving no thought to God, or in a servile way (which also gives no thought to God), by making himself subordinate to it. In the first instance, the intelligent creature forgets that God is absolute Lord of nature; in the second, he forgets that God is his only immediate master. Lucifer fell in the first temptation, man in the second one. (4,198; see also 5,258–59; 6,41; 14,105)

As always, man is a crossroads. He is lord of creation, but only in a mediate sense. He did not create or constitute nature, nor does he preserve it in being; his lordship is borrowed or derivative. On the other hand, man is made in God's image. His worth and destiny are such that he may not prostitute his love in either an exclusive or a dominant way to nature, in which he is indeed immersed but which he surpasses.

Proposition 38 (4,198–99)

Beginning with Proposition 4, *Sätze aus der erotischen Philosophie* had much to say about reconciliation in love. Baader now takes up that theme again.

If a lapse or infidelity in love has actually taken place, it does not mean that all is, therefore, lost, as long as the possibility of reconciliation has not already been destroyed, either in the fall or after it. Reconciliation does not simply rejoin what has been separated or turned away from another; instead, so long as a person freely accepts the pain of reconciliation (which is at once a death-pang and a birth-pang), it makes what has been spoiled even better, and it binds up what has been separated even more firmly, just as reconciled friends and lovers find themselves more strongly, more inwardly, and more indissolubly bound to one another than they were before their fall. (4,198–99)

The next paragraph introduces some new factors into the notion of reconciliation. First, there is the etymological link Baader finds among the words son, sun, and reconciliation. Next, there is the distinction he draws between reconcilable and irreconcilable infidelities. The pivotal point of the latter distinction is, not surprisingly, the kind of opposition to the Center that motivated the crime which resulted in separation. Direct and total opposition to the Center constitutes an irreconcilable crime, whereas indirect opposition can be rectified in time.[80] In drawing this distinction, Baader might also have had Christ's words in mind: "And so I tell you, every one of men's sins and blasphemies will be forgiven, but blasphemy against the Spirit will not be forgiven . . ." (Matthew 12,31). Because time allows a chance for redemption and reintegration, one can say that "accordingly, temporal nature manifests itself as the first

80   In a brief passage in *Gedanken aus dem grossen Zusammenhange des Lebens*, Baader discusses the interconnectedness and interpenetration of "the central, divine, life-process with the partial one of an individual creature". He argues that, just as it is not a matter of indifference where one aims an electrical spark or the focus of a burning mirror, "neither is it a matter of indifference for a person . . . in what direction he turns the focus of his power, his desire and his love . . ." (2,18–19). Thus, one has to be "aimed" properly vis-à-vis the divine Center.

religion. It is merciful Love which temporizes with her erring children . . ." (2,79). Thus, time is "a gift as well as a punishment" (12,417). On the one hand, time indicates a less-than-perfect relationship of man to God, since permanent right order, vis-à-vis God, has not yet been established; on the other, man can use the time available to him to rectify his relationship to God for good. Time will ultimately decide whether one ends up in direct opposition to the Center or by uniting freely and lovingly with it. Baader observes:

The words son (*Filius*), sun (*Sol*), and reconciling or expiating have the same root.[81] Christ died on the cross, says Meister Eckehart, "that he might make peace and reconciliation (*Friede und Sun*) between God and us". According to the note made in the text, one must, moreover, distinguish between an irreconcilable fall or infidelity and treachery, and one that can (in time) be reconciled. We must regard irreconcilable crime as the kind that takes place in a central direction, and thus as total or direct opposition; but contrary, non-total opposition, which takes place in an oblique direction, switches immediately into the circling, boomerang-like movement of time; from this, the identity of the concepts of time and of restoration is clear. For, if a person uses time well, he can rectify or straighten out his still-indirect orientation toward the Center. Just as oblique opposition entirely exhausts itself [if one uses time well], so also, as in the case of improper use of time, oblique orientation toward the good exhausts itself entirely, and opposition against the Center becomes total and direct. (4,199)

Proposition 39 (4,199–200)

Man's fall from God stirred God's love to unprecedented activity: God sent Love itself, his Son, to achieve reconciliation.

The fall of proud Lucifer did not affect God so profoundly, but the fall of weak man, misled by sensuality, did affect God deeply. But because this fall went straight to God's heart, the saving and helping love of God went forth from this heart and began the work of reconciliation with the incarnation (for this began at the moment of the Fall): i.e., God began to effect an indissoluble union between himself and man and, through man, with the world. This work is the ongoing history of the world in its broad outlines, just as it is the history of the life of every individual man on the small scale. Love is and was with God, as John says, when he created the world and man; but when man fell, Love left God and came into the world as the redeeming Word. (4,199–200; see also 12,281)

This unique and final sending of God's Love into the world is what Baader referred to (in *Sätze aus der erotischen Philosophie*, Proposition 11) as the "third and most profound emanation of his innermost being". *Speculative Dogmatik*, Book I, Lecture 18, also mentions this "third and profoundest emanation of his

---

81 Again, Baader plays on the similarity of several German words: "Die Worte Sohn (Filius), Sonne (Sol), so wie Söhnung, Sühne haben dieselbe Wurzel".

Love (Jesus)", and says that it was "only through this third emanation that the double goal of creation (i.e., highest elevation of the creature and its indissoluble union with God) was made attainable, and with that the kingdom of God was founded" (8,152). A rather unusual formulation of what took place is stated in a note Baader made in his commentary on St. Martin's *Le Nouvel Homme* (*Sämtliche Schriften von Louis Claude de Saint-Martin: Erläuterungen zu De l'esprit des choses*): "The father can be father only to his son. Since man lost his sonship (did not confirm his participation in it), God had to give himself as Son to man, so that God could find and sense himself again in him as Father" (12,254).

In the second paragraph, Baader returns to a point alluded to in the first: namely, that the incarnation began at the moment of the Fall.

One could say that at the moment of the Fall of man, God's heart made provision for him (*sich an ihm versah*), although in a sense opposite to the usual one: namely, because the unformed was again hereby reformed (*das Unförmliche hiemit wieder reformirt ward*). The ray of divine love, or Jesus (according to the interpretation of Hebrews), entered directly into Sophia (the proper matrix of all archetypes) at the moment of the Fall; in the archetype of man, Jesus became a spirit-man (*Geistmensch*). With that, the natural incarnation in time began. On this rests the triple name of the Savior: Jesus, Christ, and Mary's Son. (4,200)[82]

It was in connection with God's loving response to man's plight after the Fall of man that God promised Adam and Eve a Redeemer (Genesis 3,15). Baader views the incarnation as a process that goes on until the end of the world (7,304 fn.), since man can respond to God's love with his own until that time and thus extend the range of those effectively touched by the incarnation.

Proposition 40 (4,200)

What happens on a grand scale between God and mankind is mirrored on a small scale in the lives of individuals.

Similar mysteries take place in every human breast, which allows the work of reconciliation to go on within it, because the central process repeats or mirrors itself in every partial one. For what lover would not have inwardly felt that he "goes deeper" into his own heart in forgiveness and reconciliation, that he "takes hold of himself" more profoundly in that heart and in the thought of restored relationship with one who has broken with him, to replace their broken and distorted relationship. With this newly conceived and derived desire and hope (*Verlangen und Imagination*), which are themselves creative, would this lover not enter into and renew the repentant person and establish a closer tie with him? What lover, I say, would not have observed

---

82 See BAADER: *Sämtliche Werke* 9,409 for a discussion of St. Martin's understanding of how "the emanation of divine love, Jesus", bears, in addition, the name Christ and Mary's son.

that it is only the heart's blood flowing in sacrifice in this process, which supplies the "cement" for that more inward and more lasting bond of love and friendship ("consanguinity" in a deeper sense)? About this one can say what Moses's wife [Zipporah] said: you have become a blood-bridegroom (*Blutbräutigam*) to me. (4,200)

To every person who has honestly and cordially gone through the process of reconciliation, therefore, one could exclaim: You are not far from the kingdom of God! (4,200)

Not far from the kingdom of God is anyone, in fact, who sincerely and honestly loves, for God is Love!

Conclusion

Summary of the Argument

The principal objectives of this study were stated at the outset: (1) to show that love is the key to all of Baader's thought – to document the fact that Baader's thought about God, man, and the world is fundamentally a "philosophy of love"; and (2) to gather, by means of direct quotation or paraphrase, all that Baader (in his published works and correspondence) had to say on the subject of love, and to do so systematically and comprehensively.

That love is of central importance to Baader's thought is, of course, not a new discovery. All who have concerned themselves seriously with Baader have recognized that fact, and all of the major studies devoted to Baader and his work include sections of greater or lesser length on the subject of love. Until now, however, no one has attempted to meet both of these goals.

In Baader's scheme of reality, the cardinal truth about *God* is that God is love. Although all descriptions of God are essentially inadequate, Baader felt that his was the least inadequate. Love is itself mysterious; yet, all who experience it feel that they are somehow brought into closer contact with ultimate reality. Love is essentially a creative and productive force, an overflowing of abundance and fullness; consequently, creation could have been motivated only by love. In its richness, love also forgives, restores, and rebuilds; hence, redemption springs from the same love as that manifested by the Creator. Love is much more than feeling; it is never separated from knowledge, and it vitally affects the quality of knowing. Love is one with life itself. It is as sublime as it is humble, as bounteous in giving as it is in forgiving. Love is full of wonder and transcendent mystery; yet, it is as close to the innermost essence of all things as their nuclei. Love is the absolute summit of freedom, the polar opposite of compulsive passion; only through love, can a person give or dispose of himself totally.

Love is and does all of these things and immeasurably more. The mystic begins with God, "the center", and works "from the inside out". For the mystical Baader, these notions about God as love were neither "Romantic" speculation nor "rhapsodic" revelation – neither were they lacework, trimming, frosting, or *fervorino*. Baader's standpoint was decisively determined by his absolute belief that the Ground of all being is a personal God, and that love is what God is.

In Baader's view, the cardinal truth about *man* is that he is "created to the image of God": Sophia or Eros (the likeness of the trinitarian God) is meant to reside in man. Since "love is divine in all its forms", human exercise of love is possible only if God (Sophia-Eros) dwells in man. Every product reflects its producer; man's dignity, therefore, consists in his ability to love in a manner analogous to that of his maker. Consequently, he can do marvelous things. Through the magic of imagination and love, he can transcend time and space, for "the soul exists where, and for as long as, it loves". Through love, man can effect organic union with others in society, for "love is the organizational principle par excellence". Man's very personality is formed through the experience of love: the loving encounter makes the man. Love touches the very essence of one who loves, as well as that of the one who is loved. Love is communion of life between people: what a person loves is his nourishment – either in a good or a bad sense. Love is destiny, for we become like that which we love. It is only as God's image that a person truly loves, for love is not a "one-to-one" relationship between people: it takes place only in the "higher third", Sophia-Eros. It is not so much that people find love, as it is that love finds them. Since a man becomes like that which he loves, religion, for him, is the practice of truly loving God and his neighbor, just as God does. Man came from a God who is love, and he is oriented back toward that same love. He can make his way to it only by living a life of love.

But love (which is intrinsically free) cannot be forced. A man can refuse to accept God's love, an action which constitutes sin, or he can choose to reciprocate it. Since there is no love except through God, to reject God is to create one's own hell. To repudiate God's love is to repudiate his "image". As a result, God's naked *power* replaces God's love as the characteristic ethos of his relationship to man (*Durchwohnung* instead of *Inwohnung*). God's "child" becomes God's "slave", but with a standing invitation to rejoin the family. Baader held that the human race bears the mark of primal sin, not only because of the moral-spiritual tensions with which it wrestles but even in its very body. Man is divided and incomplete – the separation of the sexes is a clear sign of that condition. As God's image, he ought to be androgynous or integral; he ought to bear the fullness of humanity in himself. Sexual differentiation is the sign of man's dissolution, but all is not lost. Sophia-Eros invites man, by means of human love and marriage, to recapture the lost part of his humanity and to reestablish the integrity that should be his as God's image. Consequently, the sacrament of love and marriage is also the sacrament of reintegration or wholeness. Love is once again the center of focus: by receiving Sophia-Eros, man receives substantial love. He comes to share in God's very being as "son and image of God". This is man's calling and fulfillment.

For Baader, the cardinal truth about *nature* is that its welfare is determined by man, "the king of creation". If things are as they should be with man, they are as they should be with nature as well. Things can be "right" for man only to the extent that he maintains a proper relationship to God. The nature of that relationship, as God intended, is one of love. How a man is related to God (i.e., love, Sophia-Eros) determines how he is related to himself, to other men, and to nature. If things are as they should be in the hierarchy of loves, then all is well on every level. Hence, his concept of love is the key to all of Baader's thought. It tells us who God is, who man is, and what nature is. It tells us what organizes society, what defines a person, and what determines man's destiny – i.e., where human salvation or destruction lies. And it tells us when and how things will be right with the physical universe as well.

All of the views which Baader held about the nature of God as love – the effects of that love on man as God's image, and the repercussions that man's love or lack of it have had on himself and on all of nature – provided the foundation and context for his *aphorisms* on love, for the aphorisms are grounded in these presuppositions and organically spring from them. Thus, Baader's key position on love – that it is a harmonization of unlikenesses in a "higher third" – has no appropriate context without his prior assumption that Eros-Sophia, the image of God, conditions the possibility of all love: "lovers are, so to speak, only the visible ministers, priests, and agents of a higher love (God is love)". Similarly, Baader's understanding of the testing and trial which takes place in love, the forgiveness and reconciliation which occur in love, and the equation of love with sacrifice, are all predicated on the paradigm of man's relations with God, a paradigm in which God (love) demonstrates the essential behavior pattern that love follows.

In love, a person should be as thankful for being able to give as for being able to receive; in fact, the two acts so interpenetrate that they are inseparable – as in the divine Trinity. Only because God is love is it true that love is an end in itself. No one can love "in order that . . ." By definition, nothing is more sublime or noble than God. For that very reason, nothing can match the humility of God in choosing to become incarnate. But nobility and humility, in combination, are characteristic of love at any level. Baader calls love true liberalism, because it balances the will to rule with the will to serve. But here again, the ruler of all became the servant of all in order to show the true nature of love's rule. The aphorisms continue to be consistent with their presuppositions.

Love fulfills the law "from the inside", so to speak. Like genius, it observes the rule without being constricted by it. Love is the spirit of the law, and where the spirit of the law is present, all constraint vanishes. Love is one with reverence and respect: inseparable from one another, they both bear witness to the divine spark that is their ground. Love gives nothing except itself, and it receives nothing except another self. "Gifts" are only symbols of that underlying giving and receiving. No more perfect example can be found than the giving and receiving that constitute the Persons of the Trinity, just as every gift of God to man is a gift of himself in differing forms. Love does not measure and mete out with rational precision: God's love for man does not function in this fashion, nor can any other type of love so function. The service that love gives is an ennobling one, not a debasing one, because the object of all love is to find God in oneself and God in others.

In the aphorisms, Baader connects love with sorrow and both with "the cross"; he demonstrates, by his choice of words, that even in this particular tragedy of love it is God who represents the model. Love needs appropriate nourishment, for it can be either strengthened or weakened. "Nothing can nourish a heart except another heart", and so, "all men are man-eaters". But for Baader, this was already true in the Trinity, where the divine Persons eternally "nourish" each other while it (the Trinity) "nourishes" every creature with its love. By loving creatures, God loves himself in them; to the extent that a person truly loves, he also loves the divine presence (Sophia-Eros) in the object of his love. Thus, the process of loving is a process of increasing approximation to divinity: perfect love would be apotheosis. The "re-birth" that is called salvation is, in fact, the birth of love in a person; for, if that occurs, God is present and salvation is achieved. Ultimate fulfillment comes about only through union with the ultimate source of being. Love is God's gift of himself, but it is also a challenge to the recipient and becomes the task of his life (*Gabe und Aufgabe*). True acceptance and appropriation of that gift "substantiates" it into oneself permanently – one becomes like that which one loves.

Reactions to Baader's views vary – from the almost unrestrained enthusiasm of Franz Hoffmann, who would see in Baader "the philosopher of the future", to Arthur Schopenhauer's curt dismissal of him; he found "Baader, next to Hegel, the most nauseating scribbler". Most scholars wish neither to make Baader's thought the model for a future philosophy nor dismiss it as simply the product of an over-heated fantasy life. Baader's philosophy of love, at least, is noteworthy for possessing a quality missing from much that is said about love: it provides a metaphysical framework for a philosophy of interpersonal relations, an approach that has become popular only since Baader's death. For all of the justly-deserved criticism heaped on him because of the unsystematic and fragmented nature of his work, Baader is, nevertheless, astonishingly integrative and consistent: his theology/philosophy/mysticism of love is harmoniously interwoven with a profound psychology of love, an anthropology of love, a sociology of love, and a genuine theory of marital love. Critics have frequently noted the striking holism which characterizes Baader's thought on love. Novalis, for example, called Baader a "true psychologist". But, unlike many a later psychologist, Baader does not psychologize in a vacuum. He does so only in the context of his general philosophy. In any case, much of what people have found interesting and worthwhile in Baader – his power and fire, his intensity and enthusiasm, the purity and internal consistency of his thought, and its overall credibility – is organically linked to his attitude toward love and the place he allotted it in his thought and life.

The concept of *virtue* was linked by Socrates to wisdom or knowledge of the good. Plato identified the cardinal virtues as wisdom (prudence), justice, temperance, and courage (fortitude). Aristotle spoke of virtue as a habit of excellence in conduct based on a golden mean between excess and defect. He also distinguished moral or practical virtues from the intellectual virtues of wisdom and insight. Christian thinkers, such as Augustine, focused on charity or love as the source of all virtue; they distinguished the natural virtues, originally identified by their pagan predecessors, from the supernatural virtues of faith, hope, and charity, which are infused by God into human beings. Without denying any of these earlier views, Baader identifies the meaning of human life with the theological virtues of faith, hope, and love. Indeed, the subject matter of these virtues is of interest not only in the theological or religious sphere, but in the natural sphere as well. In the final analysis, the essence of human life can be defined by the answers given to the following three questions: What can (should) one believe in? What can (should) one hope for? What can (should) one love? Baader's views are important, not only because they provide a Christian (mystical) answer to these questions, but also because they recognize that every person, of whatever persuasion, *must* answer them if he is to live at all. And to Baader, everyone's story, as convoluted and multi-layered as it may be, begins and ends with love, not merely as a psychological phenomenon but as the source and sense of all being.

The Influence of Baader on Later Thought

Though Baader enjoyed a distinguished reputation among the intelligentsia of the nineteenth century, his stature as a thinker has suffered substantially since his death. The chief reason for this decline was probably his failure to construct a systematic and elegant body of thought. Johannes Sauter, who reviewed the treatment accorded Baader in some twenty histories of philosophy dating from Baader's own lifetime through 1920, predictably found no unanimity of opinion among the scholars who evaluated his significance as a thinker;[1] many, in fact, erred by regarding Baader as either a disciple of Schelling or as a neo-scholastic. Of the twenty, Sauter found Johann E. Erdmann's *Die Entwicklung der deutschen Spekulation seit Kant*, Martin Deutinger's *Das Prinzip der neueren Philosophie*, and Max Ettlinger's *Geschichte der Philosophie von der Romantik bis zur Gegenwart* the most balanced and thoughtful.

While Baader has never been considered a truly significant figure in the history of ideas, a small group of friends and admirers did attempt to establish what might loosely be termed a "Baader school": Franz Hoffmann, together with the other editors of Baader's *Sämtliche Werke* and Martin Deutinger were the prime movers. Their main achievement was getting the collected works published. Hans Grassl recalls that Ringseis, in a rectoral address delivered in 1855, referred to Baader as "the greatest German philosopher", and received assurance from the retired King Ludwig of his "complete agreement" with that assessment.[2] Baumgardt and others have referred to the favorable impact which Baader made on Kierkegaard who, in *The Concept of Dread*, speaks of the "customary power and validity" of Baader's ideas.[3] In the late 1860s, Hoffmann attempted to resurrect Baader's arguments against the Papacy as part of a campaign against the Ultramontanes before, during, and after the first Vatican Council. Other appeals to Baader's thought during the nineteenth century and afterwards have proven to be of little significance. For the most part, however, he remains a virtually forgotten figure.[4]

A remarkable exception to this general picture, however, is the reception accorded Baader's thought by Vladimir Soloviev, "Russia's first great philosopher".[5] Indeed, the coincidence of their *Weltanschauungen* is quite amazing. Both men view God, man, and nature as the three realms of being. Baader's unusual epistemological principle – that men think only by virtue of a primitive thinking on God's part in which men share – was also adopted by Soloviev. For both, purity of soul is a requisite of true knowledge. Soloviev learned from Baader how Descartes's and Kant's epistemology could be circumvented, or at least how it could be religiously grounded. Kant's *a priori* was replaced by the

1   J. SAUTER: *Baader und Kant*, pp. 519ff.
2   H. GRASSL (Ed.): *Franz von Baader. Über Liebe, Ehe und Kunst*, p. 59.
3   D. BAUMGARDT: *Franz von Baader und die philosophische Romantik*, pp. 7, 398; H. GRASSL: *Aufbruch zur Romantik. Bayerns Beitrag zur deutschen Geistesgeschichte 1765–1785*, p. 13.
4   For a survey and digest of references to Baader, from the time of his death until the 1920s, see D. BAUMGARDT: *Franz von Baader und die philosophische Romantik*, especially the introduction, pp. 1–13, and p. 398.
5   J. SAUTER: *Baader und Kant*, pp. 55ff. My summary of parallels between Baader and Soloviev follows the sketch provided by Sauter.

divine primitive thought, and his "thing-in-itself" by the Trinitarian God. For Soloviev, as for Baader, a metaphysics of being and a world of religious faith took the place of transcendental idealism, and it was Baader who introduced Soloviev to the world of medieval mysticism and philosophy. They both sought a bridge from God to man and from idea to reality. "Nature" was no more the opposite of "spirit" for Soloviev than it was for Baader: it was, rather, its proper complement. The role allotted to conscience was crucial for both men: it provided the moral "proof" of God's existence. Neither viewed ethics as utilitarianism, eudaemonism, or hedonism; it was, rather, something grounded in religion. And no amount of skepticism could shake their faith in the existence of God or of good and evil. Both attempted to reconcile gnosis with orthodox religion, and both tended to fuse revelation with mysticism, philosophy with religion, and the human with the divine. Soloviev distinguishes among the three kinds of presence that God may exercise with respect to creatures, stages that correspond to Baader's *Inwohnung, Beiwohnung, and Durchwohnung.* They were both ardent ecumenists. Christ is the middle-point of history for Soloviev and Baader alike. Indeed, Soloviev himself says that his philosophy is practically identical with Baader's world of ideas.

Beyond such general similarities, however, Soloviev's and Baader's philosophies of love – in particular – resemble each other closely. (Baader's *Vierzig Sätze aus einer religiösen Erotik* was translated into Russian, and it seems almost certain that Soloviev must have been familiar with it.[6]) For both, the root of religion was respect (reverence) and love. Indeed, their metaphysics of love is strikingly similar: Sophia and her actions occupy the center-position; and a series of elaborate philosophical arguments founded on the myth of androgyny support their core beliefs.[7] The integration of humanity as the object of sexual love with marriage appears in Soloviev, as it does in Baader, and Baader's ideas about the lover's loving God in the person of the beloved are clearly analogous to the similar views propounded by Soloviev, as were Baader's notions about love as idealization of the beloved, the ascent-descent motif, strict insistence on distinguishing passion from love, the whole complex of ideas about man as the image of God (love), and faith as the foundation of love, etc.[8] It would be interesting to trace, in detail, the intellectual ties which link Baader, Soloviev, and Berdyaev.

6   J. SAUTER: *Baader und Kant,* p. 590.
7   See E. BENZ: *Adam. Der Mythus vom Urmenschen,* p. 267.
8   With respect to Soloviev's ideas on love, see, for example: S. L. FRANK (Ed.): *A Solovyev Anthology,* pp. 150–79. See also: E. B. KLUM: *Natur, Kunst und Liebe in der Philosophie Vladimir Solov'evs,* in: *Slavistische Beiträge,* volume 14, Munich (Otto Sagner) 1965, pp. 161–216.

Close parallels have also been found between Baader's thought and that of Teilhard de Chardin.[9] In all probability, Chardin never read a line of Baader, but the similarity of their major ideas is striking. Both reintroduced modes of thought – particularly those of a mystical flavor – that were common in early Christianity and the Orthodox Church, ways of thinking that had been largely lost or substantially deemphasized by the western Church. Both stressed the cosmic significance of Christianity, eschewing the moralistic-pietistic straitjacket that has confined it in modern times. Their shared view of the incarnation held it to be independent of original sin or a "Fall of man"; for both, the incarnation was part of a cosmological process which involved not only all of mankind, but all of nature as well. In a spirit akin to that of St. Paul, who envisioned a time when all creation shall be "completed" and fulfilled, Chardin speaks of the "omega point" and Baader of cosmic fulfillment. The thought of both men is Christocentric and evolutionary. Both believe in the unity of the spiritual and corporeal, particularly as it is made manifest in Christ. As the "Heros and Eros" of evolution, Christ leads man, the "final creation", to the fullness of divine sonship and the reintegration of nature, man, and God.

Critique of Baader's Work as a Whole

Overall, Baader's work is a curious mixture of the most disparate topics and varied tendencies. While it is riddled with weaknesses, in some respects it also contains a great deal that is consistent and unified.

Enough has already been said about the problems which must be overcome by anyone wishing to understand Baader's work: particularly, its unsystematic character, its prolixity, and its repetitive style. Such basic ideas as the *Cogitor* axiom of his epistemology, the establishment of personality through love, the ties that bind nature (body) and spirit, and any number of other leading notions would, without question, be more easily assimilated if they were developed in a more logical and systematic way. Unfortunately, one of Baader's

---

9   G.-K. KALTENBRUNNER (Ed.): *Franz von Baader. Sätze aus der erotischen Philosophie und andere Schriften*, pp. 25ff. identified these parallels. See also: E. BENZ: "Zum theologischen Verständnis der Evolutionslehre", in: *Perspektiven Teilhard de Chardin. Acht Beiträge zu seiner Weltanschauung und Evolutionslehre*, ed. by H. de TERRA, Munich (C. H. Beck) 1966. In this article, Benz traces the concept of evolution, which Baader (following Herder and Kant) introduced into the philosophy of history and religion in German Idealism, and discusses similarities between Baader's and Chardin's thoughts on the subject. For a comparison between the views of Soloviev and Chardin, see K. V. TRUHLAR: *Teilhard und Solowjew. Dichtung und religiöse Erfahrung*, Freiburg/Munich (Karl Alber) 1966.

chief strengths, his ability to use telling imagery and analogy, frequently becomes one of his major weaknesses: instead of using his talent to illustrate or dramatize an argument, he permits himself to be beguiled into substituting a string of analogies for a proper argument. On occasion, the analogy is even more telling than the argument.

An apparent weakness in Baader's thought – the one-sidedness of his *Cogitor* principle, with its overemphasis on the objective foundation for knowing and its almost total neglect of the subjective – may, in one sense, be construed as a strength: he underplays the human element by minimizing man's free will and its personal contribution to the knowing process. In fact, "the greatest merit of Baader's philosophy . . . consists in its pointing out the objective and positively highest principle of knowledge, which modern philosophy had completely lost sight of".[10] Baader's habit of blurring (or completely ignoring) the lines which separate philosophy from theology, and mysticism or personal experience from either, led not only to faulty methodology, but to a virtual absence of method altogether. Johannes Sauter differentiates between the merits of a systematic body of philosophical thought – its coherence and illumination of problem areas – and its "truth-content". He lauds Kant's "system" for being genuinely noteworthy, without in any way questioning the validity of its content. He credits Baader for recognizing the significance of Kant's achievement (ushering in the age of German Idealism) and weaving into this new philosophical world the "truth-content" of traditional thought.[11] In effect, Baader had many good and important things to say, but failed to give his voice the coherence and compactness of orderly presentation. His refusal to move the metaphysical center of gravity away from God and into man, or man's mind, or into pantheism – at a time when it seemed all the rage to do so – is particularly noteworthy and of great historical importance.

Baader's methodological deficiencies provide sufficient reason to question those who would elevate him to the rank of a great philosopher.[12] Although Deutinger – despite all of his criticism – calls Baader "the most inventive of all German philosophers",[13] such a claim must not be taken too seriously. Though the extent to which Baader foraged in areas of esoteric and half-forgotten mystical-occult lore made him unique among the Romantics and the leading philosophers of his day, it must never be forgotten that much of what made him so

10 M. DEUTINGER: *Das Prinzip der neuern Philosophie*, p. 363.
11 J. SAUTER: *Baader und Kant*, p. 605.
12 E. PRZYWARA: *Ringen der Gegenwart*, 2 volumes, Augsburg, 1922–27 speaks of "the old fairy-tale about Baader as the greatest Catholic philosopher of the modern age", and blames Hoffmann particularly for this kind of exaggeration – especially in F. HOFFMANN: *Acht Philosophische Abhandlungen über Franz von Baader*, Leipzig 1857.
13 M. DEUTINGER: *Das Prinzip der neuern Philosophie*, p. 339.

"distinctive" was derivative, not original. He never tried to hide his debt to the past, nor did he have to: he was, in his own right, a strikingly original thinker. Hegel praised him for reviving and rethinking the ancient traditions for the world of his day; but once again, Baader failed to become what his far-reaching research theoretically equipped him to be: a scholar who carefully, methodically, and systematically works through a mass of largely ignored but highly influential materials and presents them critically to the scholarship of his age. In reviving these older traditions, Baader did, in fact, have a significant impact on the early nineteenth-century German Romantics and Idealists, but he never did become a great scholar/thinker. On the other hand, he was not nearly as undisciplined and obscure as either Jacob Böhme or Hamann.

But one is not yet finished with Franz von Baader. He was much more than a mere polemicist or a gatherer of forgotten wisdom, and he cannot fairly be reduced to the status of an "also ran". Intellectually and spiritually (religiously), he was certainly one of the most remarkable figures in Germany at the zenith of her cultural development – during the age of Goethe and Beethoven, Hegel and Schelling, the Schlegels and the Grimms, and a host of other titans. The intellectual elite among the Romantics and the Idealists took Baader very seriously and were personally much influenced by him. While his bold and far-sighted plans often misfired, conceptions such as the Holy Alliance, the establishment of an ecumenical academy in Russia, and the general ecumenical aims which he espoused were not unworthy of a major thinker. Who can deny the skill with which he analyzed the problems of the proletariat or the national economic structure – especially, the acumen he displayed in identifying spiritual nihilism as the root malaise of his day? From his early critiques of Kant to his later attacks on Fichte, Schelling, and Hegel, he demonstrated a formidable intellect. In his lifelong struggle against the Enlightenment, Pietism, materialism, and spiritualism, he revealed a passionate commitment. And the acuteness of his insights, with respect to cultural diagnoses and premonitions of the future, remains unmatched by any thinker of his age.

Baader's intense and personal religious struggle is as noteworthy as anything which he accomplished during his long and active life. His whole life's work in the sphere of religious-philosophical thought was aimed at reconciling faith and reason, religion and politics, the objective dependence of man on God and the subjective claims of human consciousness – those claims so extolled by Kant and the German Idealists. Baader was not simply arguing academic propositions; his was a life-and-death struggle for the highest values he knew. He refused to reduce life to the passionless, two-dimensional geometry which infused so much of Enlightenment thought. Nor would he accept a Kantian epistemology that left man bereft of "real" knowledge, or a Kantian ethics that made autonomous reason the legislator of morality. Fichte's deification of the ego repelled him as much as Schelling's nature-pantheism and Hegel's logos-pantheism. Baader battled most fiercely in the arena of religious values. He fought for the fullness of life, not merely for one or another aspect of it. He was convinced that no denial of religion, and no surrogate for religion, could provide the degree of fullness which he sought. Within the framework of religion, however, he found a place for pain and suffering, as well as joy and happiness. He also found room for the passionate zest of a Dionysus, as well as the dispassionate claims of Apollonian reason and lofty speculation.

It is a strange fate that has consigned Baader to near oblivion, though he was considered at least the equal of such famous contemporaries as Novalis, Schleiermacher, and Kierkegaard – precisely in the area of their greatest strength: the religious-philosophical sphere. David Baumgardt's conclusion, cited earlier in this study, rings true:

Judged by the pithiness, depth, and enthusiasm of his being, Baader definitely belongs to the most powerful religious minds of the Germanic people. In fact, he surpasses the entire Romantic movement in this respect. Even Novalis's religiosity seems more artificial and Schleiermacher's more a matter of educational acquisition when compared to the deep and mighty natural power of Baader's religious struggle.

There seems to be no reason why Baader should not be considered on a par with Novalis, Schleiermacher, and Kierkegaard as a religious thinker, not only because of his enthusiasm and verbal persuasiveness but also because of his ability as a speculative philosopher.

For more than half a century, Baader and Kierkegaard suffered a parallel fate: the world of ideas had apparently lost sight of them both. It was not so much historical curiosity as widespread spiritual drought, however, that caused both to be revisited in our century; it was, rather, an urgent awareness that a spiritual nihilism, more universal and more intense than any that had existed in Baader's time, was inundating the world and had to be addressed. Men went in search of thinkers capable of putting the old wine of religious and human values into new skins for the thirsty of our age. Kierkegaard has been rediscovered. Baader has not, though his star may be on the rise. That Baader has remained relatively unknown since his death proves no more about his value than it proved about Kierkegaard's. While no summons is being issued for a "back to Baader movement", it seems clear that to know Baader better is not only to know German Romanticism and German Idealism better, but also to know oneself and every man a little better.

Appendix 1
Works Written By Baader
Which Are Cited by Title in the Text

During his long and productive life, Baader wrote and published a vast number of articles, essays, reviews, manifestos, and assorted miscellanea. Many carry lengthy and convoluted titles, some so similar that they are easily confused with each other. In addition, subtitles which appear in several different works are identical to titles used in others. As a result, a number of Baader's essays are inconsistently (and on occasion inaccurately) cited in the secondary literature, making it difficult, at times, to determine precisely which reference applies. For example: in 1815, Baader wrote an essay (in French) entitled *Sur l'Eucharistie* (7,1–14); that same year, he translated the essay into German as *Über das heilige Abendmahl* (7,15–28). However, a section (number 2) of *Religionsphilosophische Aphorismen* (n.d.) bears the subtitle "Über die Eucharistie" (10,290–92).

To minimize potential confusion, all Baader works referred to (by title) in either the text or notes have been cited exactly as they appear in the collected edition of Baader's written works: BAADER: *Sämtliche Werke*. And it is in that form that they appear in the alphabetically-ordered list of titles which constitutes Appendix 1. (Short titles, unless absolutely unambiguous, have been avoided in both text and notes.) In addition to citing each work precisely as it appears in the *Sämtliche Werke*, Appendix 1 also includes cross-references (SEE and ALSO CITED AS) and annotations (NOTE) where appropriate.

The 121 titles which appear in Appendix 1 are associated with 99 different works or parts of works. Twelve (12) of the 121 titles are in fact subtitles – i.e. titles of sections which belong to larger works. Eighteen (18) are ALSO CITED under another title or titles; of these 18, 3 are ALSO CITED under two different titles. Twenty two (22) are short titles, ambiguous titles, or corrupt titles, and the reader is directed to SEE the correct (full) title.

Alle Menschen sind im seelischen, guten oder schlimmen, Sinn unter sich: Anthropophagen, 1834 (4,221–42)

Alles, was dem Eindringen der Religion in die Region des Wissens sich widersetzt oder selbes nicht fördert, ist vom Bösen, 1825 (7,47–52)
ALSO CITED AS: (1) *Über Religion und Wissen*; and (2) *Religion und Wissen*.

Beiträge zur Elementar-Physiologie, 1797 (3,203–46)

Bemerkungen über das zweite Capitel der Genesis, besonders in Bezug auf das durch den Fall des Menschen eingetretene Geschlechts-Verhältniss, 1829 (7,223–40)

Bemerkungen über den in der Beilage zur Augsburger Allgemeine Zeitung vom 17. December 1839 enthaltenen Aufsatz: die römisch-katholische und die griechisch-russische Kirche, 1847 (5,391–98)

ALSO CITED AS: *Über die römische und russische Kirche.*

Bemerkungen über die Schrift: Paroles d'un Croyant (Par de la Mennais), Paris, 1834, 1834 (6,109–24)

ALSO CITED AS: *Über de la Mennais; Paroles d'un Croyant.*

NOTE: First edition: Paris, 1833.

Bemerkungen über einige antireligiöse Philosopheme unserer Zeit, 1824 (2,443–96)

ALSO CITED AS: *Über einige antireligiöse Philosopheme unserer Zeit.*

Bruchstück eines Commentars zu Jacob Böhmes Abhandlung über die Gnadenwahl, n.d. (13,317–30)

Elementarbegriffe über die Zeit als Einleitung zur Philosophie der Societät und der Geschichte, 1831 (14,29–54)

Erläuternder Zusatz zur Recension der Schrift: Über die Begründung der Ethik durch die Physik, 1814 (5,35–42)

NOTE: This essay is a supplement to: *Über die Begründung der Ethik durch die Physik*, Gelesen in einer öffentlichen zur Feier des Namenstages Seiner Majestät des Königs 1813 gehaltenen Versammlung der K. [bayerischen] Akademie der Wissenschaft, 1813 (5,1–34).

Erläuterungen zu Sämtlichen Schriften von Louis Claude de Saint-Martin. De l'esprit des choses, (12,261–366)

Fermenta Cognitionis, 6 Books, 1822–25: Book 1, 1822 (2,137–96); Book 2, 1822 (2,197–234); Book 3, 1823 (2,235–72); Book 4, 1823 (2,273–318); Book 5, 1824 (2,319–64); Book 6, 1825 (2,365–442)

Fragment aus der Geschichte einer magnetischen Hellseherin, 1818 (4,41–60)

Gedanken aus dem grossen Zusammenhange des Lebens, 1813 (2,9–26)

"Hegel über meine Lehre", *Religionsphilosophische Aphorismen*, number 15, n.d. (10,306–09)

Ideen über Festigkeit und Flüssigkeit zur Prüfung der physikalischen Grundsätze des Herrn Lavoisier, 1792 (3,181–202)

"Die Liebe selber ist ein Kind der in Liebe sich Verbindenden", *Religionsphilosophische Aphorismen*, number 37, n.d. (10,343–46)

Der morgenländische und abendländische Katholicismus mehr in seinem innern wesentlichen als in seinem äussern Verhältnisse dargestellt. Nebst mehreren Beweisen, dass Schrift und Natur sich nur wechselseitig auslegen, 1840/1841? (10,89-254)

. ALSO CITED AS: *Über den morgenländischen und den abendländischen Katholicismus.*

NOTE: Table of Contents, volume 10, reads: "inneren" and "äusseren" for "innern" and "äussern".

Aus Privatvorlesungen über Jacob Böhmes Lehre mit besonderer Beziehung auf dessen Schrift: Von der Gnadenwahl, 1829 (13,57–158)

ALSO CITED AS: *Vorlesungen über J. Böhmes Lehre mit besonderer Beziehung auf dessen Schrift: Von der Gnadenwahl.*

Randglossen zu Schriften: Die Seherin von Prevorst, von Justinus Kerner, 1829 (14,358–66)

Randglossen zu Schriften: Les Soirées de Saint-Petersbourg, par J. de Maistre, (Abendstunden), 1821 (14,387–401)

Randglossen zu Schriften: Die Schutzgeister, oder merkwürdige Blicke zweier Seherinnen in die Geisterwelt, von Heinrich Werner, 1839 (14,367–81)

Randglossen zu Schriften: Die Symbolik des Traumes, von J. H. Schubert, 1821 (14,351–58)

Recension der Schrift: Essai sur l'Indifférence en matière de Réligion, par M. l'Abbé F. de la Mennais,
    Paris:1818-23, 1826 (5,121-246)
Recension der Schrift von Professor J. Ch. Aug. Heinroth: Über die Wahrheit, Leipzig: 1824 (1,97-
    132)
    ALSO CITED AS: *Über die Wahrheit.*
Recension von M. Bonald: Recherches philosophique sur les prémiers objets des coinnoissances mo-
    rales, Paris 1818, 1825 (5,43-120)
Religion und Wissen
    SEE: *Alles, was dem Eindringen der Religion in die Region des Wissens sich widersetzt oder selbes*
        nicht fördert, ist vom Bösen, 1825 (7,47-52).
Religionsphilosophische Aphorismen, n.d. (10,283-352)
Religiöse Societätsphilosophie
    SEE: *Vorlesungen über Societätsphilosophie,* 1831-32 (14, 55-160).
Religiöse Societätsphilosophie in siebenzehn Vorlesungen
    SEE: *Vorlesungen über Societätsphilosophie,* 1831-32 (14, 55-160).
Rückblick auf de la Mennais in Bezug auf die Widersetzlichkeit des katholischen Clerus in Preussen
    gegen die Regierung, 1838 (5,383-90)
Sätze aus der Bildungs- und Begründungslehre des Lebens, 1820 (2,95-124)
Sätze aus der erotischen Philosophie, 1828 (4,163-78)
    ALSO CITED AS: *Über erotischen Philosophie.*
"Schlüssel zum Verständnisse des Mysteriums der Liebe", *Religionsphilosophische Aphorismen,*
    number 14, n.d. (10,304-06)
Socialphilosophische Aphorismen aus verschiedenen Zeitblättern, 1828-40 (5,247-368)
Speculative Dogmatik
    SEE: *Vorlesungen über speculative Dogmatik,* 1828-38 (8,1-368 and 9,1-288).
Sur la notion du tems [sic], 1818 (2,47-68)
    NOTE: For German text, see: *Über den Begriff der Zeit,* 1818 (2,69-94).
Sur l'Eucharistie, 1815 (7,1-14)
    NOTE: For German text, see: *Über das heilige Abendmahl,* 1815 (7,15-28).
Über Alimentation und Beiwohnung
    SEE: *Über die Wechselseitigkeit der Alimentation und der in ihr stattfindenden Beiwohnung.*
        Geschreiben im Spätherbst 1838 als Programm zu Vorlesungen über Anthropologie
        und Psychologie, 1838 (14,459-88).
Über das dermalige Missverhältniss der Vermögenslosen oder Proletairs zu den Vermögen besitzenden
    Classen der Societät in Betreff ihres Auskommens sowohl in materieller als intellectueller Hinsicht
    aus dem Standpuncte des Rechts betrachtet, 1835 (6,125-44)
Über das durch die französische Revolution herbeigeführte Bedürfnis einer neuen und innigeren
    Verbindung der Religion mit der Politik, 1815 (6,11-28)
    ALSO CITED AS: *Über die Verbindung von/der Religion und/mit der Politik.*
Über das durch unsere Zeit herbeigeführte Bedürfnis einer innigerer Vereinigung/Verbindung der
    Wissenschaft und der Religion, 1824 (1,81-96)
    NOTE: Text reads: "Vereinigung"; Table of Contents, volume 1, and some sources read:
        "Verbindung." Text reads: "und der Religion"; some sources read: "mit der Religion".
Über das heilige Abendmahl, 1815 (7,15-28)
    NOTE: For French text, see: *Sur l'Eucharistie,* 1815 (7,1-14).
Über das Kirchenvorsteheramt auf Veranlassung der kirchlichen Wirren in der preussischen
    Rheinprovinz, 1838 (5,399-404)
    NOTE: Text gives date as 1834.

Über das pythagoräische Quadrat in der Natur oder die vier Weltgegenden, 1798 (3,247–68)
NOTE: Completed in 1797; published in 1798.
Über das Revolutioniren des positiven Rechtsbestandes als Commentar zur Schrift: Einiges über den Missbrauch der gesetzgebenden Gewalt, Frankfurt a. M. 1832. Hermann'sche Buchandlung, 1831 (6,55–72)
Über das Verhalten des Wissens zum Glauben. Auf Veranlassung eines Programms des Herrn Abbé Bautain: Enseignement de la Philosophie en France, Strasbourg, 1833, Aus einem Sendschreiben an Herrn Christ. Schlüter, Privatdocenten an der philosophischen Facultät zu Münster, 1833 (1,339–56)
NOTE: Text reads: "Wissens zum Glauben"; Table of Contents, volume 1, and some sources read: "Glaubens zum Wissen".
Über de la Mennais. Paroles d'un Croyant
SEE: *Bemerkungen über die Schrift: Paroles d'un Croyant (Par de la Mennais), Paris, 1834,* 1834 (6,109–24).
NOTE: First edition: Paris, 1833.
Über den Affect der Bewunderung und der Ehrfurcht, 1804 (1,25–32)
NOTE: Date in text reads 1804; some sources cite date as 1806.
"Über den Begriff der Autorität", *Socialphilosophische Aphorismen aus verschiedenen Zeitblättern,* 1828-40, number 11 (5,294–99)
Über den Begriff der Ekstasis als Metastasis, 1830 (4,147–62)
ALSO CITED AS: *Über Ekstasis als Metastasis.*
Über den Begriff der Zeit, 1818 (2,69–94)
NOTE: For French text, see: *Sur la notion du tems [sic],* 1818 (2,47–68).
Über den Begriff der Zeit und die vermittelnde Function der Form oder des Maasses, 1833 (2,517–34)
Über den Begriff des gut – oder positiv – und des nichtgut – oder negativ – gewordenen endlichen Geistes, 1829 (7,155–208)
Über den biblischen Begriff von Geist und Wasser, in Bezug auf jenen des Ternars, 1830 (10,1–16)
NOTE: Date in text reads 1830; some sources cite date as 1829.
Über den Blitz als Vater des Lichtes, 1815 (2,27–46)
Über den christlichen Begriff der Unsterblichkeit im Gegensatze der älteren und neueren nichtchristlichen Unsterblichkeitslehren, 1835 (4,257–84)
Über den Evolutionismus und Revolutionismus oder die posit. und negat. Evolution des Lebens überhaupt und des socialen Lebens insbesondere, 1834 (6,73–108)
Über den inneren Sinn im Gegensatze zu den äussern Sinnen, 1822 (4,93–106)
Über den morgenländischen und den abendländischen Katholicismus
SEE: *Der morgenländische und abendländische Katholicismus mehr in seinem innern wesentlichen als in seinem äussern Verhältnisse dargestellt. Nebst mehreren Beweisen, dass Schrift und Natur sich nur wechselseitig auslegen,* 1840/1841 (10,89–254).
"Über den Nexus zwischen Schön und Erhaben", *Religionsphilosophische Aphorismen,* number 34, n.d. (10,333–34)
Über den Paulinischen Begriff des Versehenseins des Menschen im Namen Jesu vor der Welt Schöpfung, three letters to Molitor and Hoffmann, 1837 (4,325–422)
NOTE: The first letter (4,327–40) is addressed to Professor Molitor in Frankfurt; the second (4,341–62), likewise, to Professor Molitor in Frankfurt; and the third (4,363–422) to Dr. Fr. Hoffman in Würzburg.
Über den solidären Verband der Religionswissenschaft mit der Naturwissenschaft, 1834 (3,331–56)
Über den verderblichen Einfluss, welchen die rationalistisch-materialistischen Vorstellungen auf die höhere Physik, so wie auf die höhere Dichtkunst und die bildende Kunst noch ausüben, 1834 (3,287–310)

NOTE: The title, as given in the Table of Contents, volume 3, and cited by other sources, reads: *Über den verderblichen Einfluss der herrschenden rationalistisch-materialistischen Vorstellungen auf die höhere Physic und Kunst.*

Über den Wärmestoff

SEE: *Vom Wärmestoff, seiner Vertheilung, Bindung und Entbindung, vorzüglich beim Brennen der Körper,* 1786 (3,1–180).

Über den Zwiespalt des religiösen Glaubens und Wissens als die geistige Wurzel des Verfalls der religiösen und politischen Societät in unserer wie in jeder Zeit, 1833 (1,357–82)

Über des Spaniers Don Martinez Pasqualis Lehre, 1823 (4,115–32)

ALSO CITED AS: *Über Don Martinez Pasqualis Lehre.*

Über die Abbreviatur der indirecten, nicht intuitiven, reflectirenden Vernunfterkenntniss durch das directe, intuitive und evidente Erkennen, 1822 (4,107–14)

Über die Analogie des Erkenntniss- und des Zeugungs-Triebes, 1808 (1,39–48)

NOTE: The Table of Contents, volume 1, reads: "Erkenntniss – und Zeugungstriebes".

Über die Begründung der Ethik durch die Physik, Gelesen in einer öffentlichen zur Feier des Namenstages Seiner Majestät des Königs 1813 gehaltenen Versammlung der K. [bayerischen] Akademie der Wissenschaft, 1813 (5,1–34)

NOTE: A supplement appeared in 1814. It was entitled: *Erläuternder Zusatz zur Recension der Schrift: Über die Begründung der Ethik durch die Physik,* 1814 (5,35–42).

Über die Behauptung: dass kein übler Gebrauch der Vernunft sein könne, 1807 (1,33–38)

Über Ekstasis als Metastasis

SEE: *Über den Begriff der Ekstasis als Metastasis,* 1830 (4,147–62).

Über die Ekstase oder das Verzücktsein der magnetischen Schlafredner, (drei Stücke), 1817 and 1818 (4,1–40)

"Über die Eucharistie", *Religionsphilosophische Aphorismen,* number 2, n.d. (10,290–92)

Über die Freiheit der Intelligenz. Eine akademische Rede bei Eröffnung der Ludwig-Maximilians-Universität in München, 1826 (1,133–50)

Über die Incompetenz unserer dermaligen Philosophie zur Erklärung der Erscheinungen aus dem Nachtgebiete der Natur. Aus einem Sendschreiben an Justinus Kerner, 1837 (4,303–24)

Über die Nothwendigkeit einer Revision der Wissenschaft natürlicher, menschlicher und göttlicher Dinge, in Bezug auf die sich in ihr noch mehr oder minder geltend machenden Cartesischen und Spinozistischen Philosopheme, 1841 (10,255–82)

Über die römische und russische Kirche

SEE: *Bemerkungen über den in der Beilage zur Augsburger Allgemeine Zeitung vom 17. December 1839 enthaltenen Aufsatz: die römisch-katholische und die griechisch-russische Kirche,* 1847 (5,391–98).

Über die sich so nennende rationelle Theologie in Deutschland, 1833 (2,497–516)

NOTE: The Table of Contents, volume 2, reads: "rationale".

Über die Thunlichkeit oder Nichtthunlichkeit einer Emancipation des Katholicismus von der Römischen Dictatur in Bezug auf Religionswissenschaft. Aus einem Schreiben an Seine Durchlaucht Fürst Elim von Mestchersky Kaiserlich Russischen Kämmerer, 1839 (10,53–88)

NOTE: The Table of Contents, volume 10, reads: "römischen" [sic] and "Sendschreiben".

Über die Trennbarkeit oder Untrennbarkeit des Pabstthums oder des Primats vom Katholicismus, 1838 (5,369–82)

Über die Verbindung von/der Religion und/mit der Politik

SEE: *Über das durch die französische Revolution herbeigeführte Bedürfnis einer neuen und innigeren Verbindung der Religion mit der Politik,* 1815 (6,11–28).

Über die Vernünftigkeit der drei Fundamentaldoctrinen des Christenthums vom Vater und Sohn, von der Wiedergeburt und von der Mensch- und Leibwerdung Gottes. Aus einem Sendschreiben an Freiherrn Stransky auf Greifenels, 1838 (10,17–52)

NOTE: Written in Munich, 1838; published in Nürnberg, 1839.

Über die Wahrheit
SEE: *Recension der Schrift von Professor J. Ch. Aug. Heinroth: Über die Wahrheit, Leipzig,* 1824 (1,97–132).
Über die Wechselseitigkeit der Alimentation und der in ihr stattfindenden Beiwohnung. Geschreiben im Spätherbst 1838 als Programm zu Vorlesungen über Anthropologie und Psychologie, 1838 (14,459–88)
ALSO CITED AS: *Über Alimentation und Beiwohnung.*
Über die Zeitschrift Avenir und ihre Principien. Aus einem Sendschreiben an den Herrn Grafen Carl Montalembert in Paris, 1831 (6,29–44)
Über Divinations- und Glaubenskraft. Aus einem Schreiben an den Fürsten Alex. Golizin, 1822 (4,61–92)
Über Don Martinez Pasqualis Lehre
SEE: *Über des Spaniers Don Martinez Pasqualis Lehre,* 1823 (4,115–32).
"Über ein Wort der heiligen Theresia", *Socialphilosophische Aphorismen aus verschiedenen Zeitblättern,* number 2 (5,271–73)
Über eine Behauptung Swedenborgs, den Rapport des irdisch-lebenden Menschen mit Geistern und Abgeschiedenen betreffend, 1832 (4,201–08)
ALSO CITED AS: *Über Swedenborg.*
Über eine bleibende und universelle Geistererscheinung hienieden. Aus einem Sendschreiben an die Frau Gräfen von Wielhorski, geborne Fürsten Birron von Curland, 1833 (4,209–20)
NOTE: Written in Munich, 1832; published in Münster, 1833.
Über einige antireligiöse Philosopheme unserer Zeit
SEE: *Bemerkungen über einige antireligiöse Philosopheme unserer Zeit,* 1824 (2,443–96).
Über Ekstasis als Metastasis
SEE: *Über den Begriff der Ekstasis als Metastasis,* 1830 (4,147–62).
Über erotische Philosophie
SEE: *Sätze aus der erotischen Philosophie,* 1828 (4,163–78).
"Über Gemüth, Liebe und Kunst", *Religionsphilosophische Aphorismen,* number 44, n.d. (10,350–51)
Über Kants Deduction der praktischen Vernunft und die absolute Blindheit der letzten, 1809 (1,1–23)
NOTE: Written in England, 1796; first published in Berlin, 1809.
Über Religion und Wissen
SEE: *Alles, was dem Eindringen der Religion in die Region des Wissens sich widersetzt oder selbes nicht fördert, ist vom Bösen,* 1825 (7,47–52).
Über Religions- und religiöse Philosophie im Gegensatze sowohl der Religionsunphilosophie als der irreligiösen Philosophie, 1831 (1,321–38)
NOTE: In the Table of Contents, volume 1, the word "sowohl" does not appear in the title and "als der irreligiösen" appears as "und der irreligiöse".
Über religiöse Philosophie im Gegensatz zur irreligiösen
SEE: *Vorlesungen über religiöse Philosophie im Gegensatz der irreligiösen älterer und neuerer Zeit,* 1827 (1,151–320).
Über Swedenborg
SEE: *Über eine Behauptung Swedenborg's, den Rapport des irdisch-lebenden Menschen mit Geistern und Abgeschiedenen betreffend,* 1832 (4,201–08).
"Über ungemischte und gemischte Liebe und Ehe", *Socialphilosophische Aphorismen aus verschiedenen Zeitblättern,* number 41 (5,349)
NOTE: The Table of Contents, volume 5, incorrectly identifies this section as No. 42.

Über zeitliches und ewiges Leben und die Beziehung zwischen diesem und jenem, 1836 (4,285-94)
NOTE: Written in 1836; published in 1850.
Versuch einer Theorie der Sprengarbeit, 1792 (6,153-66)
NOTE: A second edition was published in 1798.
Vierzig Sätze aus einer religiösen Erotik, 1831 (4,179-200)
Vom Geist und Wesen der Dinge
SEE: *Vorrede zu der Schrift: Vom Geist und Wesen der Dinge [De l'esprit des choses] oder Philosophische Blicke auf die Natur der Dinge und den Zweck ihres Doseins, wobei der Mensch überall als die Lösung des Räthsels betrachtet wird. Aus dem Französischen des Herrn von St. Martin übersetzt von D. G. H. Schubert*, 1812 (1,57-70).
Vom Segen und Fluch der Creatur. Drei Sendschreiben an Herrn Professor Görres, 1826 (7,71-154)
Vom Wärmestoff, seiner Vertheilung, Bindung und Entbindung, vorzüglich beim Brennen der Körper, 1786 (3,1-180)
ALSO CITED AS: *Über den Wärmestoff.*
Vorlesungen über die Lehre Jacob Böhmes mit besonderer Beziehung auf dessen Schrift: Mysterium Magnum, 1833 (13,159-236)
Vorlesungen über eine künftige Theorie des Opfers oder des Cultus. Zugleich als Einleitung und Einladung zu einer neuen mit Erläuterungen versehene. Ausgabe der bedeutendsten Schriften von Jacob Böhme und St. Martin, 1836 (7,271-416)
Vorlesungen über J. Böhmes Lehre mit besonderer Beziehung auf dessen Schrift: Von der Gnadenwahl
SEE: *Aus Privatvorlesungen über Jacob Böhmes Lehre mit besonderer Beziehung auf dessen Schrift: Von der Gnadenwahl*, 1829 (13,57-158).
Vorlesungen über religiöse Philosophie im Gegensatz der irreligiösen älterer und neuerer Zeit, 1827 (1,151-320)
ALSO CITED AS: *Über religiöse Philosophie im Gegensatz zur irreligiösen.*
Vorlesungen über Societätsphilosophie, 1831-32 (14,55-160)
ALSO CITED AS: (1) *Religiöse Societätsphilosophie*, or (2) *Religiöse Societätsphilosophie in siebenzehn Vorlesungen.*
Vorlesungen über speculative Dogmatik, 5 Books, 1828-38: Book 1, 1828 (8,1-192); Book 2, 1830 (8,193-304); Book 3, 1833 (8,305-68); Book 4, 1836 (9,1-152); Book 5, 1838 (9,153-288)
ALSO CITED AS: *Speculative Dogmatik.*
Vorrede zu [D. G. H.] Schuberts Übersetzung von St. Martin de l'Esprit des choses
SEE: *Vorrede zu der Schrift: Vom Geist und Wesen der Dinge [De l'esprit des choses] oder Philosophische Blicke auf die Natur der Dinge und den Zweck ihres Doseins, wobei der Mensch überall als die Lösung des Räthsels betrachtet wird. Aus dem Französischen des Herrn von St. Martin übersetzt von D. G. H. Schubert*, 1811-12 (1,57-70).
Vorrede zu der Schrift: Vom Geist und Wesen der Dinge [De l'esprit des choses] oder Philosophische Blicke auf die Natur der Dinge und den Zweck ihres Doseins, wobei der Mensch überall als die Lösung des Räthsels betrachtet wird. Aus dem Französischen des Herrn von St. Martin übersetzt von D. G. H. Schubert, 1811-12 (1,57-70)
ALSO CITED AS: (1) *Vom Geist und Wesen der Dinge*; and (2) *Vorrede zu [D. G. H.] Schuberts Übersetzung von St. Martin de l'Esprit des choses.*
Vorwort zu der kleinen Schrift: Speculative Entwickelung der ewigen Selbsterzeugung Gottes, von Prof. Dr. Fr. Hoffman, 1835 (1,417-18)
"Die zeugende, hervorbringende Liebe ist väterlich und mütterlich zugleich", *Religionsphilosophische Aphorismen*, number 32, n.d. (10,328-32)

"Zur Lehre vom Bilde", *Vorlesungen über speculative Dogmatik*, number 10 (8,93–105)

Zurückweisung der von dem Univers wider mich erhobenen Anklage eines Abfalls von der katholischen Kirche, 1839 (5,405–08)

"Zusammenhang des Cultus und der Cultur", *Socialphilosophische Aphorismen aus verschiedenen Zeitblättern*, number 4 (5,275–76)

Appendix 2
Non-Critical Works Written by Predecessors, Contemporaries, or Successors of Baader Which Are Cited by Title in the Text

Many non-critical works (e.g. literature, philosophy, theology) written by predecessors, contemporaries, or successors of Baader (e.g. Plato, Aquinas, Kant, Goethe, Camus, Buber) are cited in the text or notes. Most are not included in the Bibliography. To provide the reader with an overview of this significant body of material, all such works referred to have been included in the alphabetically-ordered list of titles which constitutes Appendix 2.

AQUINAS, T. (Saint): *Summa Theologiae*
AUGUSTINE (Saint): *Confessions*

BÖHME, J.: *Mysterium Magnum*
BÖHME, J.: *Six Theosophic Points*, edited and with an introduction by N. BERDYAEV
BÖHMER, K.: *Natur, Kunst und Liebe in der Philosophie Vladimir Solov'evs*
BRENTANO, C.: *Godwi*
BUBER, M.: *I and Thou*
BURKE, E.: *Philosophical Inquiry into the Origin of our Ideas of the Sublime and the Beautiful*

CAMUS, A.: *The Rebel*
CAMUS, A.: *Helen's Exile*

DAUB, C.: *Judas Ischariot, oder das Böse im Verhältniss zum Guten*

FAULKNER, W.: *As I Lay Dying*
FEUERBACH, L.: *Das Wesen des Christentums*

GOETHE, J. W. v:. *Faust*
GOETHE, J. W. v.: "Trocknet nicht, trocknet nicht" (lyric)
GOETHE, J. W. v.: *Wilhelm Meister*

HEGEL, G. W. F.: *Enzyklopädie der philosophischen Wissenschaften im Grundrisse*
HEGEL, G. W. F.: *Phänomenologie des Geistes*
HEGEL, G. W. F.: *Vom göttlichen Dreieck*
HEGEL, G. W. F.: *Wissenschaft der Logik*
HEINROTH, J. C. A. *Über die Wahrheit* (reviewed by Baader)
HUMBOLDT, W. F. v.: *Über die männliche und weibliche Form*

JACOBI, F.: *Gefühlsdeismus*
JUNG, C. G.: *Mysterium Conjunctionis*
JUNG, C. G.: *Psychologie der Übertragung*

KAINDL, J. E.: *Die Teutsche Sprache aus ihren Wurzeln,* 4 volumes
KANT, I.: *Beobachtungen über das Gefühl des Schönen und Erhabenen*
KANT, I.: *Kritik der reinen Vernunft* (*The Critique of Pure Reason*)
KANT, I.: *Kritik der Urteilskraft* (*The Critique of [Pure] Judgment*)
KANT, I.: *Religion innerhalb der Grenzen der blossen Vernunft* (*Religion Within the Limits of Reason Alone*)
KANT, I.: *Verstandesdeismus*
KIERKEGAARD, S.: *The Concept of Dread*
KLEUKER, J. F.: *Magikon oder das geheime System einer Gesellschaft unbekannter Philosophen*

LAMENNAIS: *Essai sur l'indifférence en matière de religion*
LEIBNIZ, G. W. Baron v.: *Über die Sicherheit des Reiches*
LEONE EBREO: *Dialoghi d'Amore*
LIST, F.: *National-System der politischen Ökonomie* (1841)

MONK, S. H.: *The Sublime*

NOVALIS (pseud. of Friedrich von Hardenberg): *Christenheit oder Europa*

PLATO: *Symposium*
PLATO: *Timaeus*

RITTER, J. W.: *Fragmente aus dem Nachlass eines jungen Physikers*

SAINT-MARTIN, L. C. de: *De l'Esprit des Choses ou Coup-d'Oeil Philosophique sur la Nature des Êtres et sur l'Objet de leur Existence*
SAINT-MARTIN, L. C. de: *Des Erreurs et de la Verité*
SAINT-MARTIN, L. C. de: *Ministère de l'Homme-Esprit*
SAINT-MARTIN, L. C. de: *Le Nouvel Homme*
SAINT-MARTIN, L. C. de: *Tableau Naturel des Rapports qui existent entre Dieu, l'Homme et l'Univers*
SCHELLING, F. W.: *Über die Weltseele*
SCHELLING, F. W.: *Untersuchungen über das Wesen der menschlichen Freiheit*
SCHLEGEL, A. W.: *Über die schöne Kunst und Literatur*
SCHLEGEL, F.: *Über die Diotima*
SCHLEIERMACHER, F. D. E.: *Reden über die Religion*
SOLOVYEV, V.: *A Solovyev Anthology,* ed. by S. L. FRANK and translated from the Russian by N. DUDDINGTON
NOTE: See BÖHMER, K.: *Natur, Kunst, und Liebe in der Philosophie Vladimir Solov'evs.*

TROELTSCH, E.: *Augustin, die christliche Antike und das Mittelalter*
TURGENIEV, I. S.: *Fathers and Sons*

WINDSCHMANN: *Über Etwas, das der Heilkunst Noth thut*

Bibliography

Collected Writings and Letters

BAADER, F. X. v.: *Sämtliche Werke*, 16 volumes, ed. by F. HOFFMANN (volumes 1-10 and 15), J. HAMBERGER (volume 13), A. LUTTERBECK (volume 16 and part of volume 14), E. A. v. SCHADEN (volume 11), F. v. der OSTEN-SACKEN (volume 12) and C. SCHLÜTER (part of volume 14), Leipzig 1851-60. Reprinted, Aalen (Scientia) 1963. (For a review and critique of this edition, see references to "Hoffmann" in the index of E. SUSINI [Ed.]: *Lettres inédites de Franz von Baader*, volume 3. See also F. X. v. BAADER: *Franz von Baader. Gesellschaftslehre*, ed. by H. GRASSL, pp. 277, 302.)

BAADER, F. X. v.: *Lettres inédites de Franz von Baader*, ed. by E. SUSINI, 4 volumes: volume 1, Paris (J. Vrin) 1942; volumes 2 and 3, Vienna (Herder) 1951; volume 4, Paris (Presses universitaires de France) 1967.

Selected Writings

BAADER, F. X. v.: *Philosophische Schriften und Aufsätze*, 3 volumes, Münster 1831-33.

BAADER, F. X. v.: *Franz von Baaders kleine Schriften*, ed. by F. HOFFMANN, Leipzig 1850.

BAADER, F. X. v.: *Grundzüge der Sozietätsphilosophie Franz von Baaders*, ed. by F. HOFFMANN, Würzburg 1865. (Published in a new edition by A. SCHMID (Ed.): *Summa Schriften*, volume 2, Hellerau 1917.)

BAADER, F. X. v.: *Die Weltalter. Lichtstrahlen aus Baaders Werken*, ed. by F. HOFFMANN, Erlangen 1868.

BAADER, F. X. v.: *Franz von Baaders Leben und theosophische Werke*, ed. by J. CLASSEN, 2 volumes, Stuttgart (Steinkopf) 1886-87.

BAADER, F. X. v.: *Les Enseignments secrets de Martinez de Pasqually*, Paris (Bibliothèque Rosicrucienne) 1900. (Translation of F. X. v. BAADER: *Über des Spaniers Don Martinez Pasqualis Lehre*; *Sämtliche Werke*, volume 4, pp. 115ff.)

BAADER, F. X. v.: *Schriften Franz von Baaders*, in: *Der Dom* series, selected and ed. by M. PULVER, Leipzig (Insel) 1921.

BAADER, F. X. v.: *Franz von Baader und sein Kreis. Ein Briefwechsel*, ed. by F. WERLE, Leipzig (Wolkenwanderer) 1924.

BAADER, F. X. v.: *Franz von Baaders Schriften zur Gesellschaftsphilosophie*, in: *Die Herdflamme*, volume 14, introduced, commented upon, and ed. by J. SAUTER, Jena (Gustav Fischer) 1925.

BAADER, F. X. v.: *Ausgewählte Schriften und Abhandlungen*, ed. by the Franz von Baader Society, Stuttgart (Steinkopf) 1929.

BAADER, F. X. v.: *Seele und Welt. Franz Baaders Jugendtagebücher*, newly revised text by M. JARISLOWSKY, introduced and ed. by D. BAUMGARDT, Berlin (Wegweiser) 1929.

BAADER, F. X. v.: *Lebenslehre und Weltanschauung der jüngeren Romantik*, in: *Deutsche Literatur. Reihe Romantik*, volume 11, texts arranged by W. BIETAK, Leipzig (Reclam) 1936, pp. 146–60, 189–94, 222–32.

BAADER, F. X. v.: *Franz von Baaders Aufsätze*, introduced and ed. by by H. P. JAEGER, Zürich (Hoffmann Library 118) 1945.

BAADER, F. X. v.: *Franz von Baader. Über Liebe, Ehe und Kunst*, selected and introduced by H. GRASSL, Munich (Kösel) 1953.

BAADER, F. X. v.: *Über den Begriff der Zeit. Über den Zwiespalt des religiösen Glaubens und Wissens*, introduced by C. LINFERT, Basel (Benno Schwabe) 1954.

BAADER, F. X. v.: *Franz von Baader. Gesellschaftslehre*, selected and introduced by H. GRASSL, Munich (Kösel) 1957.

BAADER, F. X. v.: *So spricht Franz von Baader*, ed. by F. WERLE and U. v. MANGOLT, arranged by E. KLIEMKE, Munich (Otto Wilhelm Barth) 1954.

BAADER, F. X. v.: *Sätze aus der erotischen Philosophie und andere Schriften*, ed. by G.-K. KALTENBRUNNER, Frankfurt (Insel) 1966.

BAADER, F. X. v.: *Vom Sinn der Gesellschaft. Schriften zur Sozialphilosophie*, ed. by H. A. FISCHER-BARNICOL, Cologne (Hegener) 1966.

BAADER, F. X. v.: *Gedanken über den Staat und Gesellschaft, Revolution und Reform* (1831); *Über das dermalige Missverhältniss der Vermögenslosen oder Proletairs zu den Vermögen-besitzenden Klassen der Societät in Betreff ihres Auskommens sowohl in materieller als intellectueller Hinsicht, aus dem Standpuncte des Rechts betrachtet* (1835), ed. by K. SPRENG, Darmstadt (Wissenschaftliche Buchgesellschaft) 1968.

BAADER, F. X. v.: *Über die Begründung der Ethik durch die Physik, und andere Schriften*, ed. by and with an epilogue by K. POPPE, Stuttgart (Freies Geistesleben) 1968.

BAADER, F. X. v.: "Sobre la noción de tiempo", translated by M. KERKHOFF, *Dialogos* 24 (1989), pp. 139–59. (Translation of F. X. v. Baader:*Über den Begriff der Zeit und die vermittelnde Function der Form oder des Maasses; Sämtliche Werke*, volume 2, pp. 517ff.)

Bibliography

JOST, J.: "Bibliographie der Schriften Franz von Baaders, mit kurzem Lebensabriss", in: *Rheinischer Buch-Anzeiger*, volume 4, Bonn (Friedrich Cohen) 1926.

Books, Articles, and Miscellaneous Contributions to Encyclopedias, Dictionaries, Yearbooks, Festschriften, Historical and Philosophical Surveys, Memorial Tributes, etc.

ABRAMS, M. H.: *Natural Supernaturalism. Tradition and Revolution in Romantic Literature*, New York (W. W. Norton) 1971.

ANONYMOUS: "Franz von Baader und das innere Licht", *Die weisse Fahne. Wegweiser zur erfolgreichen Lebensführung*, 30 (1957), pp. 135–41.

ARNIM, A.: "Ökologie als Heilsgeschichte. Die Gnosis des Herrn von Baader", *Fragmente, Schriftenreihe für Psychoanalyse*, 29/30 (1989), pp. 211–21.

ATTERBOM, P. D. A.: *Aufzeichnungen des schwedischen Dichters Pehr D. A. Atterbom über berühmte deutsche Männer und Frauen nebst Reiseerinnerungen aus Deutschland und Italien aus den Jahren 1817–1819*, German translation by F. MAURER, Berlin 1867.

BACH, H.: "Zur Aktualität des Naturverständnisses der Romantik", *Zeitschrift der Ganzheitsforschung*, new series, 34 (1990), pp. 67–73.

BALL, H.: *Zur Kritik der deutschen Intelligenz*, Bern 1919, pp. 125–71.

BALTHASAR, H. U. v.: *Prometheus. Studien zur Geschichte des deutschen Idealismus*, Heidelberg (Kerle) 1947, pp. 624–35.

BAUMAN, H.: *Das doppelte Geschlecht*, Berlin 1955.

BAUMGARDT, D.: *Franz von Baader und die philosophische Romantik*, Halle/Saale (Max Niemeyer) 1927.

BAUMGARDT, D.: "Ein unbekanntes Dokument zur Kirchenpolitik der deutschen Romantik", *Historische Zeitschrift*, 136 (1927), pp. 514–17.

BAUMGARDT, D.: "Franz Baader", *Das Bayerland*, 39 (1928), p. 84. (This entry is nothing more than an advertisement for materials on Baader, but it is listed in the *Bibiliographie der deutschen Zeitschriftenliteratur.*)

BAUMGARDT, D. (Ed.): *Seele und Welt. Franz Baaders Jugendtagebücher*, newly revised text by M. JARISLOWSKY, Berlin (Wegweiser) 1929.

BAUR, L.: "Baader", in: *Staatslexikon*, volume 1, ed. by H. SACHER, Freiburg (Herder) ⁵1926.

BAUR, L.: " Baader, Franz Xaver v.", in: *Lexikin für Theologie und Kirche*, volume 1, ed. by M. BUCHBERGER, Freiburg (Herder) 1930.

BAXA, J.: *Einführung in die romantische Staatswissenschaft*, Jena (G. Fischer) 1923, pp. 158–64.

BAXA, J.: *Gesellschaft und Staat im Spiegel deutscher Romantik*, in: *Die Herdflamme*, volume 8, Vienna 1924.

BAXA, J.: "Franz von Baader. Zum Gedächtnis seines 200. Geburtstages", *Zeitschrift für Ganzheitsforschung*, new series, 9 (1965), pp. 129–42.

BEHLER, U.: "Franz von Baader und die Wiener Jahrbücher der Literatur. Neue Briefe Baaders an Franz Bernhard von Bucholtz, nebst drei unbekannten Aufsätzen", *Literaturwissenschaftliches Jahrbuch*, ed. by the Görres Society, new series, 13 (1972) pp. 71–123.

BENZ, E.: "Franz von Baaders Gedanken über den 'Proletair' ", *Zeitschrift für Religions- und Geistesgeschichte*, 2 (1948), pp. 97–123.

BENZ, E.: "Franz von Baader und der abendländische Nihilismus", *Archiv für Philosophie*, 3 (1949), pp. 29–52.

BENZ, E.: *Die abendländische Sendung der östlich-orthodoxen Kirche*, Mainz (Akademie der Wissenschaften und der Literatur) 1950, pp. 559–852.

BENZ, E.: *Die Ostkirche im Lichte der protestantischen Geschichtsschreibung von der Reformation bis zur Gegenwart*, Freiburg/Munich (Karl Alber) 1952, pp. 151–60, 405–06,

BENZ, E.: *Schelling. Werden und Wirken seines Denkens*, Zürich (Rhein) 1955.

BENZ, E.: *Adam. Der Mythus vom Urmenschen*, Munich (Otto Wilhelm Barth) 1955, especially pp. 209–36.

BENZ, E.: *Der Prophet Jacob Böhme*, Mainz (Akademie der Wissenschaften und der Literatur) 1959.

BENZ, E.: *Schöpfungsglaube und Endzeiterwartung. Antwort auf Teilhard de Chardins Theologie der Evolution*, Munich (Nymphenburger) 1965, especially pp. 78ff.

BENZ, E.: "Zum theologischen Verständnis der Evolutionslehre", in: *Perspektiven Teilhard de Chardin. Acht Beiträge zu seiner Weltanschauung und Evolutionslehre*, ed. by H. de TERRA, Munich (C. H. Beck) 1966.

BENZ, E.: *Die russische Kirche und das abendländische Christentum*, Munich (Nymphenburger) 1966, especially pp. 118ff.

BENZ, E.: *Franz von Baader und Kotzebue. Das Russlandsbild der Restaurationszeit*, Mainz/Wiesbaden (Akademie der Wissenschaften und der Literatur) 1957.

BENZ, R.: *Lebenswelt der Romantik*, Munich (Nymphenburger) 1948.

BERDYAEV, N.: *Von der Bestimmung des Menschen*, German translation by I. SCHOR, Bern-Leipzig 1935.

BERDYAEV, N.: "Unground and Freedom", introduction to J. BÖHME: *Six Theosophic Points*, Ann Arbor, Michigan (University of Michigan Press) 1958.

BERNHARDI, T. v.: *Geschichte Russlands und der europäischen Politik in den Jahren 1814 bis 1831*, volume 1, Leipzig 1863, pp. 482ff.

BETANZOS, R.: "Franz von Baaders Philosophie der Liebe", in: P, KOSLOWSKI (Ed.): *Die Philosophie, Theologie und Gnosis Franz von Baaders. Spekulatives Denken zwischen Aufklärung, Restauration und Romantik*, Vienna (Passagen) 1993, pp. 51–66.

BEUMER, J.: "Franz von Baader und sein Plan für die Vereinigung der römischen und russischen Kirche", in: *Volk Gottes. Zum Kirchenverständnis der katholischen, evangelischen, und anglikanischen Theologie*, Festgabe for Josef Höfer, ed. by R. BÄUMER and H. DOLCH, Freiburg im Breisgau 1967, pp. 430–54.

BÖHME, J.: *Six Theosophic Points*, introduced by N. BERDYAEV, Ann Arbor, Michigan (University of Michigan Press) 1958.

BONDY, P.: *Das Problem der Gesellschaft bei Franz von Baader*, Erlangen (doctoral dissertation) 1922.

BOWEN, R.: *German Theories of the Corporative State*, New York 1947, pp. 46–53.

BRINTON, H.: *The Mystic Will*, introduced by R. JONES, London (G. Allen and Unwin) 1931.

BÜCHLER, F.: *Die geistigen Wurzeln der heiligen Allianz*, Freiburg im Breisgau (doctoral dissertation) 1929, especially pp. 61–71.

CARRIÈRE, M.: *Schwert- und handschlag für Franz Baader. Zur Erwiederung seiner Revision der Philosopheme der Hegelschen Schule bezüglich auf das Christentum*, Weilburg (Lanz) 1841.

CLASSEN, J. (Ed.): *Franz von Baaders Leben und theosophische Werke*, 2 volumes, Stuttgart (Steinkopf) 1886–87.

COLLINS, J.: *A History of Modern European Philosophy*, Milwaukee (Bruce) 1954.

D'ARCY, M. C.: *The Mind and Heart of Love*, New York (Meridian) 1955.

DEGHAYE, P.: "Jacob Böhmes Theosophie. Die Theosophie in der ewigen Natur", in: P. KOSLOWSKI (Ed.): *Gnosis und Mystik in der Geschichte der Philosophie*, Zürick and Munich (Artemis) 1988, pp. 151–67.

DEMPF, A.: "Schelling, Baader und Görres. Die München Philosophen der Romantik", *Geistige Welt*, 2 (1947), pp. 10–17.

DEUTINGER, M.: *Das Prinzip der neuern Philosophie*, Regensburg (Drews, Arthur) 1857.

DREWS, A.: *Die deutsche Spekulation seit Kant*, Leipzig (Gustav Fock) 1895.

DÜLMEN, R. van: "Baaderiana. Neue Veröffentlichungen über Franz von Baader", *Zeitschrift für bayerische Landesgeschichte*, 3 (1968), pp. 822–31.

DÜLMEN, R. van: "Gegenrevolution und Sozietät bei Franz von Baader", *Jahrbuch des Instituts für deutsche Geschichte*, 3 (Tel Aviv, 1974), pp. 101–18.

DYROFF, A. and HOHNEN, W.: *Der Philosoph Christoph Bernhard Schlüter und seine Vorläufer*, in: *Geschichtliche Forschungen zur Philosophie der Neuzeit*, Paderborn (Ferdinand Schöningk) 1935.

EBERHARD, O.: "Franz Xaver von Baader", in: *Zeugnisse deutscher Frömmigkeit von der Frühzeit bis heute*, Leipzig 1940, p. 38.

ELIADE, M.: *Mephistopheles and the Androgyne*, New York (Sheed and Ward) 1965.

ENGERT, T.: "Franz von Baaders Gedanken über einen romfreien Katholizismus", in: *Das neue Jahrhundert* (a weekly), 20–22, Augsburg (Theodor Lampart) 1910.

EPSTEIN, K.: *The Genesis of German Conservatism*, Princeton, New Jersey (Princeton University Press) 1966.

ERDMANN, J. E.: *Die Entwicklung der deutschen Spekulation seit Kant*, volume 3, ed. by H. GLOCKNER, Stuttgart 1931, pp. 287–314.

ETTLINGER, M.: *Geschichte der Philosophie von der Romantik bis zur Gegenwart*, Kempten/ Munich (Kösel and Pustet) 1924, pp. 109ff.

FEARS, J. R.: *Selected Writings of Lord Acton*, Indianapolis (Liberty Classics) 1985.

FELS, H.: *Martin Deutinger. Auswahl seiner Schriften*, Munich (Kösel and Pustet) 1938, especially pp. 193–222.

FICHTE, I. H.: *System der Ethik*, in: *Die philosophischen Lehren von Recht, Staat und Sitte in Deutschland, Frankreich und England, von der Mitte des 18. Jh. bis zur Gegenwart*, volume 1, Leipzig (Dyk'sche) 1850, pp. 447ff.

FICHTE, J. G.: *Johann Gottlieb Fichtes Sämtliche Werke*, 8 volumes, ed. by I. H. FICHTE, Berlin (Veit) 1845–46.

FISCHER, K. P.: *Zur hundertjährigen Geburtsfeier Franz von Baaders. Versuch einer Charakteristik seiner Theosophie*, Erlangen (Eduard Besold) 1865.

FISCHER-BARNICOL, H. A. (Ed.): *Franz von Baader: Vom Sinn der Gesellschaft. Schriften zur Sozialphilosophie*, Cologne (Hegener) 1966.

FORTLAGE, K.: *Genetische Geschichte der Philosophie seit Kant*, Leipzig (Brockhaus) 1852, pp. 246–55.

FRANK, S. L. (Ed.): *A Solovyev Anthology*, translated from the Russian by N. DUDDINGTON, New York (Charles Scribner's Sons) 1950.

FRANZ, G.: "Franz von Baader", in: *Biographisches Wörterbuch zur deutschen Geschichte*, Munich (Oldenbourg) 1952ff., p. 42.

FROMM, E.: *The Art of Loving*, New York (Harper: Colophon Books) 1956.

FUNK, P.: "Münchener Romantik", *Hochland*, 19 (1921–22), pp. 544ff.

FUNK, P.: *Von der Aufklärung zur Romantik*, Munich 1925.

GAUGLER, E.: "Franz von Baaders Kampf gegen die Alleinherrschaft des Papstes in der katholischen Kirche", *Internationale kirchliche Zeitschrift*, 7 (1917), pp. 240–69.

GERHARD: "Franz von Baader und das altkatholische Christentum", *Altkatholisches Volksblatt*, 56 (1926), p. 75.

GETZENY, H.: "Franz von Baaders Staats- und Gesellschaftsauffassung", in: *Gedanke (des katholishcen München)*, 1932, pp. 175–83.

GIESE, F.: *Der romantische Charakter*, in: *Die Entwicklung des Androgynenproblems in der Frühromantik*, volume 1, Langensalza (Wendt and Klauwell) 1919.

GOEPP, G.: *Essai sur François de Baader*, Strasbourg 1862.

GÖRTZ, H.-J.: *Franz von Baaders "anthropologischer Standpunkt"*, Freiburg im Breisgau and Munich (Alber) 1977.

GOETHE, J. W. v.: *Goethes Werke in vier Bänden*, Hamburg (Hoffman and Campe) 1956.

GOGOLEWSKI, T.: "Versuch einer Synthese der Theologie Franz von Baaders" (in Polish), *Studia Theologica Varsaviensia*, 17 (1979), pp. 273–80.

GONDILLAC, M. de: "Baader et ses correspondents", *Études germaniques*, (1953), pp. 166–71.

GRASSL, H.: "Eine Philosophie der Liebe", *Hochland*, (1950–51), pp. 374–85.

GRASSL, H.: "Franz von Baader", in: *Neue Deutsche Biographie*, 1952.

GRASSL, H.: "Franz von Baader", in: *Allgemeine deutsche Biographie*, volume 1, Berlin 1953ff., pp. 474ff.

GRASSL, H. (Ed.): *Franz von Baader. Über Liebe, Ehe und Kunst*, Munich (Kösel) 1953.

GRASSL, H. (Ed.): *Franz von Baader. Gesellschaftslehre*, Munich (Kösel) 1957.

GRASSL, H.: "Franz von Baader", in: *Staatslexikon: Recht, Wirtschaft, Gesellschaft*, ed. by Görres Gesellschaft, Freiburg (Herder) [6]1957.

GRASSL, H.: "Münchener Romantik, ein Beitrag zu ihrer deutschen und europäischen Bedeutung", in: *Der Mönch im Wappen*, Munich (Schnell and Steiner) 1960.

GRASSL, H.: "Das neue Bild der Münchner Romantik", *Literaturwissenschaftliches Jahrbuch*, new series, 2 (1961), pp. 55–60.

GRASSL, H.: "Franz von Baader als Nachfahre der Alchemisten und Rosenkreuzer", *Antaios: Zeitschrift für eine freie Welt*, 3 (1962), pp. 330–41.

GRASSL, H.: "Hegel an Baader. Ein unveröffentlicher Brief", *Hegel Studien*, 2 (1963), pp. 105–10.

GRASSL, H.: *Aufbruch zur Romantik. Bayerns Beitrag zur deutschen Geistesgeschichte 1765–1785*, Munich (C. H. Beck) 1968.

GRASSL, H.: "Franz von Baader (1765–1841)", in: *Katholische Theologen Deutschlands*, volume 1, ed. by H. FRIES, Munich (Kösel) 1975.

GRAY, R. D.: "Male and Female", in: *Goethe the Alchemist*, Cambridge 1952.

GRÜNDLER, O.: "Franz von Baader", *Hochland*, 21 (1923–24), pp. 147–62.

GÜNTHER, A.: *Vorschule zur spekulativen Theologie*, Vienna 1846, pp. 164–81.

HAFFNER, P.: "Franz von Baader", in: *Kirchen-Lexikon oder Encyklopädie der katholischen Theologie und ihrer Hilfswissenschaften*, volume 12, ed. by H. J. WETZER and B. WELTE, Freiburg 1856, pp. 393–408.

HAFFNER, P.: "Baader, Franz v.", in: *Wetzer und Weltes Kirchenlexikon*, volume 1, Freiburg [2]1882, pp. 1781–91.

HAMBERGER, J.: "The Theosophy of Franz Baader", *The American Presbyterian Review* (later, *Princeton Review*), 18 (1846), pp. 171ff.

HAMBERGER, J. (Ed.): *Franz von Baader. Sämtliche Werke*, volume 13, Leipzig 1851–60. Reprinted, Aalen (Scientia) 1963.

HAMBERGER, J.: *Die Cardinalpuncte der Franz Baaderschen Philosophie*, Stuttgart 1855.

HAMBERGER, J.: *Fundamentalbegriffe von Franz Baaders Ethik, Politik und Religionsphilosophie*, Stuttgart 1858.

HAMBERGER, J.: *Christentum und moderne Cultur*, 3 volumes, Erlangen 1863, 1867, 1875.

HAMBERGER, J.: *Erinnerungen aus meinem Leben, nebst einigen kleinen Abhandlungen*, Stuttgart 1883, especially pp. 83–87.

HARRAS, H.: *Franz von Baader*, Giessen (doctoral dissertation) 1931.

HARRAS, H.: "Franz von Baader (1765–1841), ein Vorläufer und Geistesverwandter Friedrich Lists", *Ständisches Leben*, 4 (1931), pp. 466–82.

HARTL, F.: *Franz von Baader und die Entwicklung seines Kirchenbegriffs*, Munich (Max Hueber) 1970.

HARTL, F.: *Franz von Baader. Leben und Werk*, Graz, Vienna, and Cologne (Styria) 1971.

HARTL, F.: "Die Idee der einen Kirche bei Franz von Baader", *Theologie und Philosophie* (a Quarterly), 48 (1973), pp. 551–57.

HARTMANN, N.: *Die Philsphie des deutschen Idealismus*, Berlin (Walter de Gruyter) [2]1960.

HEER, F.: *Europäische Geistesgeschichte*, Stuttgart (Kohlhammer) [2]1953.

HEER, F.: *Europa Mutter der Revolutionen*, Stuttgart (Kohlhammer) 1964, pp. 578–94.

HEGEL, G. F.: *Hegels Sämtliche Werke*, ed. by G. LASSON and J. HOFFMEISTER, 21 volumes, Leipzig (Meiner) 1905ff.

HEIN, L.: "Franz von Baader und seine Liebe zur russischen orthodoxen Kirche", *Kyrios. Vierteljahrschrift für Kirchen- und Geistesgeschichte*, new series, 12 (1972), pp. 31–59.

HELBERGER-FROBENIUS, S.: *Macht und Gewalt in der Philosophie Franz von Baaders*, Bonn

(H. Bouvier) 1969. (For a response, see: W. PÜSCHEL: "Zur Einordnung Franz von Baaders. Sein Verhältnis zur Jenaer Romantik (Novalis). Replik auf Helberger-Frobenius [*Macht und Gewalt in der Philosophie Franz von Baaders*]".)

HEMMERLE, K.: "Franz von Baader", in: *Lexikon für Theologie und Kirche*, volume 1, ed. by J. HÖFFER and K. RAHNER, Freiburg (Herder) 1962.

HEMMERLE, K.: *Franz von Baaders philosophischer Gedanke der Schöpfung*, Freiburg/Munich (Karl Alber) 1963.

HÖFER, J.: "Zum Aufbruch der Neuscholastik im 19. Jahrhundert. Christoph Bernhard Schlüter, Franz von Baader und Hermann Ernst Plassmann", *Historisches Jahrbuch der Görres-gesellschaft*, 72 (1953), pp. 410–32.

HOFFMANN, F.: *Die spekulative Entwicklung der ewigen Selbsterzeugung Gottes (aus Baaders Schriften zusammengetragen)*, Amberg 1835.

HOFFMANN, F.: *Vorhalle zur spekulativen Lehre Franz Baaders*, Aschaffenburg (Theodor Pergay) 1836.

HOFFMANN, F. (Ed.): *Franz von Baaders kleine Schriften*, Leipzig 1850.

HOFFMANN, F.: *Über das Verhältniss Franz Baaders zu Schelling und Hegel*, Leipzig 1850.

HOFFMANN, F.: *Grundzüge einer Geschichte des Begriffs der Logik in Deutschland von Kant bis Baader*, Leipzig (H. Bethmann) 1851.

HOFFMANN, F. (Ed.): *Franz von Baader. Sämtliche Werke*, volumes 1–10 and 15, Leipzig 1851–60. Reprinted, Aalen (Scientia) 1963.

HOFFMANN, F.: *Franz von Baader als Begründer der Philosphie der Zukunft*, (collected views from the *Sämtliche Werke*), Leipzig 1856.

HOFFMANN, F.: *Acht philosophische Abhandlungen über Franz von Baader*, Leipzig 1857.

HOFFMANN, F.: *Über die Haltlosigkeit unsrer bisherigen wissenschaftlichen Systeme und die im Bedürfniss unsrer Zeit liegende Notwendigkeit, sich allgemeiner der Lehre Franz von Baaders zuwenden*, Elberfeld and Düsseldorf 1858.

HOFFMANN, F. (Ed.): *Grundzüge der Sozietätsphilosophie Franz von Baaders*, Würzburg 1865. (Published in a new edition by A. SCHMID [Ed.]: *Summa Schriften*, volume 2, Hellerau 1917.)

HOFFMANN, F. (Ed.): *Die Weltalter. Lichtstrahlen aus Baaders Werken*, Erlangen 1868.

HOFFMANN, F.: "Ansprache an die Verehrer und Freunde der Baaderschen Philosophie in den Staaten Europas und Vereinigten Staaten Amerikas", *Philosophische Schriften [Franz von Baaders]*, Preface to volume 1, Erlangen (Deichert) 1868.

HOFFMANN, F.: "Franz von Baader", in: *Allgemeine deutsche Biographie*, volume 1, Berlin (Duncker and Humblot) 1875, pp. 713–25. Reprinted in 1967.

HUCH, R.: *Die Romantik. Blütezeit, Ausbreitung und Verfall*, Tübingen (Rainer Wunderlich) ²1951. (1st edition, 2 volumes, Leipzig 1918.)

HÜBSCHER, A.: "Franz von Baader in neurer Sicht", *Unser Bayern*, 2 (1953), pp. 79–80.

IMLE, F.: "Baaders theologische Erkenntnisslehre", *Philosophisches Jahrbuch*, 46 (1933), pp. 464–78.

IMLE, F.: "Baaders theologische Erkenntnisslehre", *Philosophisches Jahrbuch*, 47 (1934), pp. 65–84.

JAEGER, H. P. (Ed.): *Franz von Baaders Aufsätze*, Zürich (Hoffmann Library 118) 1945.

JOHANN, R.: *The Meaning of Love. An Essay Towards a Metaphysics of Intersubjectivity*, Glen Rock, New Jersey (Paulist Press) 1954, 1966.

JONES, R. *Spiritual Reformers in the 16th and 17th Centuries*, (pp. 151–234 on Jacob Böhme), London (Macmillan) 1914. (Boston [Beacon Paperback] 1959.)

JOURDAIN, E.: "Exposition du système philosophique de M. de Baader", *Revue Européenne par les rédacteurs du Correspondant*, 1831, pp. 71–85. (See the same journal, no. 3, for an unsigned letter – probably written by Eloi Jourdain – with the caption: "Remarques sur la philosophie de Baader et sur les objections auxquelles elle peut donner lieu". See SUSINI, E. [Ed.]: *Lettres inédites de Franz von Baader*, volume 3, p. 331, fn. 4.)

JOWETT, B. (Ed.): *The Dialogues of Plato*, 2 volumes, New York (Random House) 1937.

JUNG, A.: *Charaktere, Charakteristiken und vermischte Schriften*, Königsberg 1848.

JUNG, A.: *Über Franz von Baaders Dogmatik als Reform der Sozietätswissenschaft und der gesellschaftlichen Zustände*, Erlangen 1868.

JUNG, C. G.: *Mysterium Conjunctionis*, in: *The Collected Works of C. G. Jung* , volume 14 (Bollingen Series XX), ed. by Sir H. READ, M. FORDHAM, and G. ADLER, New York (H. Wolff: Pantheon Books) 1963.

KALTENBRUNNER, G.-K.: "Sozialrevolutionär, Politiker und Laientheologe. Zum 200. Geburtstag Franz von Baaders", *Zeitwende*, new series, 9 (1965), pp. 151–60.

KALTENBRUNNER, G.-K.: "Franz von Baader als Theologe der Gegenrevolution", *Moderne Welt. Zeitschrift für vergleichende geistesgeschichtliche und sozialwissenschaftliche Forschung*, 6 (1965), pp. 210–17.

KALTENBRUNNER, G.-K.: "Zwischen Romantik und Sozialismus. Der christliche Philosoph Franz von Baader", *Werkhefte. Zeitschrift für Probleme der Gesellschaft und des Katholizismus*, 19 (1965), pp. 212–22.

KALTENBRUNNER, G.-K. (Ed.): *Franz von Baader. Sätze aus der erotischen Philosophie und andere Schriften*, Frankfurt (Insel) 1966.

KANT, I.: *Gesammelte Schriften*, 23 volumes, ed. by VON HARTENSTEIN (critical edition sponsored by the Prussian Academy of Sciences), Berlin (W. de Gruyter) 1902–55.

KAPPES, H.: "Über Franz von Baader", *Theologische Quartalschrift*, ed. by Professors of the Catholic Theological Faculty at the University of Tübingen, 156 (1976), pp. 305–11.

KAUFMANN, M.: "Christian Socialists. III. Baader and Ketteler", *Good Words*, 23 (1882).

KLUCKHOHN, P.: *Die deutsche Romantik*, Bielefeld and Leipzig (Velhagen and Klasing) 1924.

KLUCKHOHN, P.: *Persönlichkeit und Gemeinschaft*, Halle/Saale (Max Niemeyer) 1925.

KLUCKHOHN, P.: *Charakteristiken. Die Romantiker in Selbstzeugnissen und Äusserungen ihrer Zeitgenossen*, Stuttgart (Reclam) 1950.

KLUCKHOHN, P.: *Das Ideengut der deutschen Romantik*, Tübingen (Max Niemeyer) ⁴1961.

KLUCKHOHN, P.: *Die Auffassung der Liebe in der Literatur des 18. Jahrhunderts und der deutschen Romantik*, Tübingen (Max Niemeyer) ³1966, especially pp. 542–53.

KLUM, E. B.: *Natur, Kunst und Liebe in der Philosophie Vladimir Solov'evs*, in: *Slavistische Beiträge*, volume 14, Munich (Otto Sagner) 1965.

KNITTERMEYER, H.: "Schelling und die romantische Schule", in: *Geschichte der Philosophie in Einzeldarstellungen. Die Philosophie der neuesten Zeit*, volume 1, Munich (Reinhardt) 1929, pp. 152–60, 364–91.

KOSCH, W.: "Sailer und die Romantik in Bayern", in: *Geschichte der deutschen Literatur im Spiegel der nationalen Entwicklung von 1813 bis 1848*, volume 1, Munich (Parcus) 1925, pp. 193–236.

KOSLOWSKI, P. (Ed.): *Gnosis und Mystik in der Geschichte der Philosophie*, Zürich and Munich (Artemis) 1988.

KOSLOWSKI, P.: "Franz von Baader. Spekulative Dogmatik als christliche Gnosis", in: P. KOSLOWSKI (Ed.): *Gnosis und Mystik in der Geschichte der Philosophie*, Zürich and Munich (Artemis) 1988, especially pp. 243–59.

KOSLOWSKI, P. (Ed.): *Die Philosophie, Theologie und Gnosis Franz von Baader. Spekulatives Denken zwischen Aufklärung, Restauration und Romantik*, Vienna (Passagen) 1993.

KÜMMEL, F.: *Über den Begriff der Zeit,* Tübingen (Max Niemeyer) 1962, pp. 87–121.

LAMBERT, W.: *Franz von Baaders Philosophie des Gebets. Ein Grundriss seines Denkens* (Innsbrucker Theologische Studien 2), Innsbruck (Tyrolia) 1978.

LAMBERT, W.: "Ideologie und Ideologiekritik bei Franz von Baader", *Zeitschrift für katholische Theologie,* 101 (1979), pp. 127–46.

LÈBRE, A.: "Baader et l'Université de Munich", 1841, in: *Oeuvres,* volume 1, ed. by M. DEBRIT, Lausanne and Paris (G. Bridel) 1856, pp. 387–91.

LÈBRE, A.: "François Baader, étude philosophique", 1844, in: *Oeuvres,* volume 1, ed. by M. DEBRIT, Lausanne and Paris (G. Bridel) 1856, pp. 393–404.

LEHMANN, G.: *Geschichte der nachkantischen Philosophie,* Berlin (Junker and Dünnhaupt) 1931, pp. 87–94.

LEWIS, C. S.: *The Four Loves,* New York (Harcourt, Brace and World) 1960.

LIEB, F.: *Baader und Kant,* Basel (doctoral dissertation) 1923.

LIEB, F.: *Baaders Jugendgeschichte,* Munich (M. C. Kaiser) 1926.

LIEB, F.: "Franz von Baader", in: *Die Religion in Geschichte und Gegenwart,* volume 1, Tübingen [3]1957, columns 803–05.

LINFERT, C. (Ed.): *Franz von Baader: Über den Begriff der Zeit. Über den Zwiespalt des religiösen Glaubens und Wissens,* Basel (Benno Schwabe) 1954.

LINFERT, K.: "Franz von Baader," in: *Die grossen Deutschen,* volume 3, Berlin (Ullstein) 1956.

LINPINSEL, E.: "Auch die Wissenschaft hat ihre Ahnen. Franz Xaver von Baader und die Gegenwart", *Katholische Frauenbildung,* 66 (1965), pp. 356–62.

LÖSCH, S.: *Döllinger und Frankreich. Eine geistige Allianz 1823–1871,* in: *Schriftenreihe zur bayerischen Landesgeschichte,* volume 51, Munich (C. H. Beck) 1955.

LÖWE, H.: "Zwei Hauptvertreter des bayerischen Stammes, Lorenz von Westenrieder und Franz von Baader", in: *Friedrich Thiersch, ein Humanistenleben im Rahmen der Geistesgeschichte seiner Zeit,* chapter 3, Munich 1831.

LÖWENTHAL, L.: *Die Sozietätsphilosophie Franz von Baaders,* Frankfort (doctoral dissertation) 1923.

LÖWENTHAL, L.: "Franz von Baader. Ein religiöser Soziologe", *Internationales Jahrbuch für Religionssoziologie. Religiöser Pluralismus und Gesellschaftsstruktur,* 2 (1966), pp. 231–52.

LÖWENTHAL, L.: "Franz von Baader. Ein religiöser Soziologe", *Internationales Jahrbuch für Religionssoziologie. Religiöser Pluralismus und Gesellschaftsstruktur,* 3 (1967), pp. 201–18.

LOVEJOY, A. O.: "On the Discrimination of Romanticisms", in: *Essays in the History of Ideas,* chapter 12, New York (G. P. Putnam and Sons) 1948.

LOVEJOY, A. O.: "Romanticism and the Principle of Plenitude", in: *The Great Chain of Being,* chapter 10, New York (Harper Torchbook) 1960.

LÜTGERT, D. W.: *Die Religion des deutschen Idealismus und ihr Ende,* in: *Idealismus und Erweckungsbewegung,* volume 2, Gütersloh (Bertelsmann) [3]1929. (See also pp. 108ff. of 1st edition: 1923.)

LUTTERBECK, A. (Ed.): *Franz von Baader. Sämtliche Werke,* volume 16 and part of volume 14, Leipzig 1851–60. Reprinted, Aalen (Scientia) 1963.

LUTTERBECK, A.: *Über den philosophischen Standpunkt Franz von Baaders,* Mainz 1856.

LUTTERBECK, A.: *Lebensepochen Baaders und Charakterisierung seines Systems der Philosophie,* Würzburg 1860. (Included as an introductory essay to volume 16 of Baader's *Sämtliche Werke.*)

MANGENO, E.: "Franz von Baader", in: *Dictionnaire de Théologie Catholique,* volume 2, Paris 1905ff.

MARCEL, G.: *Problematic Man,* New York (Herder and Herder) 1967.

MEIER, P.: "Vision eines Konservativen. Franz von Baader als gesellschaftspolitischer Theoretiker", *Civitas. Monatsschrift des schweizerischen Studentenvereins,* 30 (1974–75), pp. 849–56.

MERTENS, H.: *Untersuchungen zu Franz Baaders historischpolitischen Arbeitsgebiet,* Freiburg (doctoral dissertation) 1926.

MEYER, H.: *Geschichte der abendländischen Weltanschauung,* in:*Von der Rennaissance bis zum Deutschen Idealismus,* volume 4, Würzburg and Paderborn 1950.

MURILLO, J. S. de: "Franz von Baaders Interpretation der kantischen Naturphilosophie", *Philosophia Naturalis. Archiv für Naturphilosophie und die philosophischen Grenzgebiete der Exakten Wissenschaften und Wissenschaftsgebiete,* 23 (1986), pp. 293–319.

NETTESHEIM, J.: "Christoph Bernhard Schlüter über Franz von Baader", *Philosophisches Jahrbuch der Görres-gesellschaft,* 65 (1957), pp. 135–41.

NOACK, L. (Ed.): "Franz Baader", in: *Philosophie-Geschichtliches Lexikon,* Leipzig (Erich Koschny) 1879, pp. 65–87.

NOHL, J.: "Franz von Baader, der Philosoph der Romantik", *Euphorion,* 19 (1912), pp. 612–33.

OSTEN-SACKEN, F. v. der (Ed.): *Franz von Baader. Sämtliche Werke,* volume 12, Leipzig 1851–60. Reprinted, Aalen (Scientia) 1963.

OTTO, R.: *Mysticism, East and West,* New York (Collier) 1956.

PASCALE, C. de: "Franz von Baader und 'der Geschlossene Handelsstaat' ", in: *Erneuerung der Transcendentalphilosophie im Anschluss an Kant und Fichte. Reinhard Lauth zum 60. Geburtstag,* ed. by K. HAMMACHER and A. MUES, Stuttgart-Bad Cannstadt 1979, pp. 259–73.

PIETSCH, R.: "Die metaphysische Grundlegung der Gesellschaftslehre Franz von Baaders", *Zeitschrift für Ganzheitsforschung,* 23 (1979), pp. 67–85.

PLARD, H.: "Lettres retrouvées de Baader", *Études germaniques,* 23 (1968), p. 389.

PLATO: *The Dialogues of Plato,* ed. by B. JOWETT, 2 volumes, New York (Random House) 1937.

POPPE, K.: "Franz von Baaders Lehre zur Übernatur-Natur-Unternatur und zur Unnatur", *Die Drei. Monatschrift für Anthroposophie, Dreigliederung und Goetheanismus,* 31 (1961), pp. 146–62.

POPPE, K. (Ed.): *Franz von Baader. Über die Begründung der ethik durch die Physik, und andere Schriften,* Stuttgart (Freies Geistesleben) 1968.

PRZYWARA, E.: *Ringen der Gegenwart,* 2 volumes, Augsburg 1922–27.

PRZYWARA, E.: "Platonismus. Platon – Baader – Franz Brentano", *Stimmen der Zeit,* 114 (1928), pp. 260–83.

PÜSCHEL, W.: "Zur Einordnung Franz von Baaders. Sein Verhältnis zur Jenaer Romantik (Novalis). Replik auf Helberger-Frobenius (*Macht und Gewalt in der Philosophie Franz von Baaders*)", *Zeitschrift für bayerische Landesgeschichte,* 36 (1973), pp. 333–74.

PULVER, M. (Ed.): *Schriften Franz von Baaders,* in: *Der Dom* series, Leipzig (Insel) 1921.

RASKE, A.: "Der Schöpfungsbegriff Teilhards de Chardin im Horizont der Philosophie Jakob Böhmes und Franz von Baaders", *Zeitschrift für philosophische Forschung,* 38 (1984), pp. 450–68.

RAVERA, M.: "Baader lettore di Joseph de Maistre", *Filosofia,* 37 (1986), pp. 239–50.

REBER, M.: *Franz von Baader und die Möglichkeit unbedingter pädagogischer Zielsetzung,* Erlangen (doctoral dissertation) 1925.

REICHEL, H.: "Die Sozietätsphilosophie Franz von Baaders", *Zeitschrift für die gesamte Staatswissenschaft*, 57 (1901), pp. 193-264.

REICHEL, H.: "Baader als Kunstphilosoph", *Zeitschrift für Aesthetik*, 6 (1911), pp. 525-45.

RENTBEAMTER: "Franz von Baader", *Anzeiger der königlichen Akademie der Wissenschaften*, (Philosophy-History Group, Selections), 50 (1919), p. 31.

RIEBER, A.: "Sexualität und Liebe in ihrem Zusammenhang mit Schöpfung, Sündenfall und Erlösung bei Franz von Baader", *Salzburger Jahrbuch für Philosophie*, 14 (1970), pp. 67-83.

RINGSEIS, E. (Ed.): *Erinnerungen des Dr. J. N. Ringseis*, 4 volumes, Regensburg 1886.

RIO, F.-A.: *Epilogue à l'art chrétien*, Paris 1870.

ROCHOLL, A.: *Beiträge zu einer Geschichte deutscher Theosophie*, Berlin 1856.

ROSENKRANZ, K.: "Franz von Baader, ein Mystiker, aber kein Jesuit", *Neue Studien*, 4 (1878), pp. 106ff. (A review of Baader's *Spekulative Dogmatik*.)

ROTHE, R.: *Theologische Ethik*, 5 volumes, Wittenberg (Kölling) 1867-72.

SAINTE-FOI, C.: *Souvenirs de jeunesse (1828-1835)*, Paris (C. Latreille).

SAUER, H.: *Ferment der Vermittlung. zum Theologiebegriff bei Franz von Baader*, in: *Studien zur Theologie und Geistesgeschichte des neunzehnten Jahrhunderts*, volume 27, Göttingen (Vandenhoeck und Ruprecht) 1977.

SAUTER, J. (Ed.): *Franz von Baaders Schriften zur Gesellschaftsphilosophie*, in: *Die Herdflamme*, volume 14, Jena (Gustav Fischer) 1925.

SAUTER, J.: "Die Grundlegung der deutschen Volkswirtschaftslehre durch Franz von Baader", *Jahrbuch für Nationalökonomie und Statistik*, 123 (1925).

SAUTER, J.: "Franz von Baader", *Der Fels*, 20 (1925), pp. 61-64.

SAUTER, J.: *Die Sozialphilosophie Franz von Baaders*, Munich (doctoral dissertation) 1926.

SAUTER, J.: "Franz von Baaders romantische Sozialphilosophie", *Zeitschrift für die gesamte Staatswissenschaft*, (1926), pp. 449-81.

SAUTER, J.: "Franz von Baaders Aesthetik", *Archiv für Geschichte der Philosophie*, new series, 38 (1927), pp. 34-63.

SAUTER, J.: "Der Symbolismus bei Baader", *Blätter für deutsche Philosophie*, 1 (1928), pp. 348-66.

SAUTER, J.: *Baader und Kant*, in: *Deutsche Beiträge zur Wirtschaftsund Gesellschaftslehre*, volume 6, Jena (Gustav Fischer) 1928.

SAUTER, J.: "Franz von Baader", *Süddeutsche Monatshefte*, 32 (1935), pp. 547-53.

SCHADEN, A. v. (Ed.): *Franz von Baader. Sämtliche Werke*, volume 11, Leipzig 1851-60. Reprinted, Aalen (Scientia) 1963.

SCHÄDER, H.: *Die dritte Koalition und die heilige Allianz*, in: *Osteuropäishce Forschungen*, new series, 16 (1934).

SCHEFFCZYK, L. (Ed.): *Theologie in Aufbruch und Widerstreit. Die deutsche katholische Theologie im 19. Jahrhundert*, Bremen (Carl Schünermann) 1965.

SCHEFFCZYK, L. (Ed.): *Der Mensch als Bild Gottes*, Darmstadt (Wissenschaftliche Buchgesellschaft) 1969.

SCHELLING, F. W.: *Sämtliche Werke*, 6 volumes, Munich (Jubilaeum) 1927ff.

SCHENK, H. G.: *The Mind of the European Romantics*, London (Constable) 1966, especially pp. 103-09.

SCHIEL, H.: *Johann Michael Sailer*, 2 volumes: volume 1, *Leben und Persönlichkeit in Selbstzeugnissen, Gesprächen und Erinnerungen der Zeitgenossen*; volume 2, *Briefe*, Regensburg (Friedrich Pustet) 1948; 1952.

SCHLÜTER, C. (Ed.): *Franz von Baader. Sämtliche Werke*, part of volume 14, Leipzig 1851-60. Reprinted, Aalen (Scientia) 1963.

SCHMID, A.: "Schelling, Baader, Görres", *Jahresbericht der Görres-gesellschaft*, (1879-80), pp. 25-38.

SCHMID, A.: "Franz von Baader", *Summa, eine Vierteljahrschrift*, (1917), pp. 159-63.

SCHNABEL, F.: *Deutsche Geschichte im 19en. Jahrhundert*, 4 volumes, Freiburg (Herder) [3]1955.

SCHULZE, W. A.: "Franz von Baader und der päpstliche Primat", *Theologische Zeitschrift*, 16 (1960), pp. 59-61.

SEDLMAYR, H.: *Verlust der Mitte*, Salzburg 1948.

SEDLMAYR, H.: "Franz von Baaders Gedanken zur Kunst", *Philosophisches Jahrbuch der Görres-Gesellschaft*, 68 (1960).

SEDLMAYR, H.: "Erneuerung als konservatives Prinzip bei Franz von Baader", *Studium Generale. Zeitschrift für die Einheit der Wissenschaften im Zusammenhang ihrer Begriffsbildungen und Forschungsmethoden*, 15 (1962), pp. 264-71.

SEDLMAYR, H.: "Über Wahrheit und Erkenntnis nach Franz von Baader", in: *Wahrheit und Verkündigung. Michael Schmaus zum 70. Geburtstag*, volume 1, ed. by L. SCHEFFCZYK et al., Munich 1967.

SEDLMAYR, H.: "Der Gedanke der Mitte bei Franz von Baader", in: *Wirklichkeit der Mitte. Beiträge zu einer Strukturanthropologie. Festgabe für August Vetter zum 80. Geburtstag*, ed. by J. TENZLER, Freiburg im Breisgau and Munich 1968, pp. 309-18.

SEEBASS, F.: "Franz von Baader 1765-1841. Technischer Theoretiker, mystischer Philosoph, ökumenischer Christ", *Deutsche Rundschau*, 80 (1954), pp. 679-83.

SENGLER, J.: *Über das Wesen und die Bedeutung der spekulativen Philosophie und Theologie in der gegenwärtigen Zeit*, Heidelberg 1837, pp. 415-52.

SIEGL, J.: "Franz von Baader, ein bayerischer Philosoph", *Zwiebelturm*, 4 (1949), pp. 169-73.

SIEGL, J.: *Franz von Baader, Ein Bild seines Lebens und Wirkens*, Munich (Bayerisches Schulbuch) 1957.

SOLOVYEV, V.: *A Solovyev Anthology*, translated from the Russian by N. DUDDINGTON, and ed. by S. L. FRANK, New York (Charles Scribner's Sons) 1950.

SPAEL, W.: *Das katholische Deutschland im 20. Jahrhundert. Seine Pionier- und Krisenzeiten 1890-1945*, Würzberg 1964.

SPAEMAN, R.: "Franz von Baader und die Romantiker", *Die Mitarbeit. Monatshefte der Aktion evangelischer Arbeitsnehmer*, 3 (1954-55), pp. 6-9.

SPRECKELMEYER, H.: *Die philosophische Deutung des Sündenfalls bei Franz von Baader*, in: *Abhandlungen zur Philosophie und Psychologie der Religion*, volume 43/44, Würzburg 1938.

SPRENG, K.: *Studien zur Entstehung sozialpolitischer Ideen in Deutschland auf Grund der Schriften Franz von Baaders und Franz Joseph von Buss*, Giessen (doctoral dissertation) 1932.

SPRENG, K. (Ed.): *Franz von Baader. Gedanken über den Staat und Gesellschaft, Revolution und Reform* (1831). *Über das dermalige Missverhältniss der vermögenslosen oder Proletairs zu den Vermögen-besitzenden Klassen der Societät in Betreff ihres Auskommens sowohl in materieller als intellectueller Hinsicht aus dem Standpuncte des Rechts betrachtet* (1835), Darmstadt (Wissenschaftliche Buchgesellschaft) 1968.

STEGMAN, F. J.: "Franz von Baader", in: *Zeitgeschichte in Lebensbildern aus dem deutschen Katholizismus des 20. Jahrhunderts*, volume 3, ed. by R. MORSEY, J. ARETZ, and A. RAUSCHER, Mainz 1979, pp. 11-25.

STEINBÜCHEL, T.: "Franz von Baaders Descartes-Kritik im Rahmen ihrer Zeit und in ihrer grundsätzlichen Bedeutung", *Wissenschaft und Weisheit*, 10 (1943), pp. 41-60, 103-26.

STEINBÜCHEL, T.: "Franz von Baaders Descartes-Kritik im Rahmen ihrer Zeit und in ihrer grundsätzlichen Bedeutung", *Wissenschaft und Weisheit*, 11 (1944), pp. 24-42.

STEINBÜCHEL, T.: "Romantisches Denken im Katholizismus mit besonderer Berüchsichtigung der romantischen Philosophie Franz von Baaders", in: *Romantik, ein Zyklus Tübinger Vorlesungen*, Tübingen 1948, pp. 87-109.

STÖCKL, A.: "Die Baadersche Philosophie", *Der Katholik*, new series, 1 (1859), pp. 277-95; 513-32; 787-802; 1042-60.

STÖLZLE, R.: "Zwei Briefe des Philosophen Franz von Baader", *Historischpolitische Blätter für das katholische Deutschland*, (1903), pp. 553–56.

STÖLZLE, R.: "Zwei Briefe E.v. Lasaulx' zur Charakteristik des Philosophen Dr. Baader", *Philosophisches Jahrbuch der Görres-gesellschaft*, 17 (1904).

STOUDT, J. J.: *Sunrise to Eternity. A Study in Jacob Böhme's Life and Thought*, preface by P. TILLICH, Philadelphia (University of Pennsylvania Press) 1957.

STRICH, F.: *Deutsche Klassik und Romantik*, Bern and Munich (Francke) ⁵1962.

SUSINI, E.: *Franz von Baader et le romantisme mystique. La philosophie de Franz von Baader*, 2 volumes, Paris (J. Vrin) 1942.

SUSINI, E. (Ed.): *Lettres inédites de Franz von Baader*, 4 volumes: volume 1, Paris (J. Vrin) 1942; volumes 2 and 3, Vienna (Herder) 1951; volume 4, Paris (Presses universitaires de France) 1967.

SUSINI, E.: "Nouvelles lettres inédites de Franz von Baader", *Études germaniques*, 24 (1969), pp. 62–82.

SYBEL-PETERSO, A. v.: "Franz von Baader und das Böse", *Goetheanum (Anthroposophie)*, 12 (1933), pp. 12–15.

THILO, C. A.: "Beleuchtung des Angriffs auf Franz Baader", in: *Die theologisirende Rechts- und Staatslehre*, Würzburg 1861.

TONSOR, S. J.: "Franz Xaver von Baader", in: *The New Catholic Encyclopedia*, New York (McGraw-Hill) 1967.

TRUHLAR, K. V.: *Teilhard und Solowjew. Dichtung und religiöse Erfahrung*. Freiburg/Munich (Karl Alber) 1966.

TUEBBEN, H.: *Die Freiheitsproblematik Baaders und Deutingers und der deutsche Idealismus*, in: *Abhandlungen zur Philosophie und Psychologie der Religion*, volume 20/21, Würzburg 1929.

UNDERHILL, E.: *Mysticism*, New York (Meridian) 1955

UNDERHILL, E.: *The Essentials of Mysticism*, New York (E. P. Dutton) 1960.

VALERIUS, G.: *Deutscher Katholizismus und Lamennais. Die Auseinandersetzung in der katholischen Publizistik 1817–1854*, Mainz (Matthias Grünewald) 1983.

VATERNAHM, T.: "Schopenhauer und Baader", *Schopenhauer Jahrbuch*, 34 (1951–52), pp. 69–73.

VIATTE, A.: *Les Sources Occultes du Romantisme; Illuminisme-Theosophie 1770–1820*, 2 volumes: volume 1, *Le Préromantisme*; volume 2, *La Génération de l'Empire*, Paris (Honoré Champion) 1965. (First published in 1928.)

WEEKS, A.: *Boehme. An Intellectual Biography of the Seventeenth-Century Philosopher and Mystic*, Albany, New York (State University of New York Press) 1991.

WERLE, F. (Ed.): *Franz von Baader und sein Kreis. Ein Briefwechsel*, Leipzig (Wolkenwanderer) 1924.

WERLE, F. (Ed.): *So spricht Franz von Baader*, arranged by E. KLIEMKE, Munich (Otto Wilhelm Barth) 1954.

WERNAER, R. M.: *Romanticism and the Romantic School in Germany*, New York and London 1910.

WERNER, K.: *Geschichte der katholischen Theologie*, Munich (Cotta) 1866, pp. 443–51, 456–63.

WETZER, H. J. and WELTE, B. W. (Eds.): *Kirchenlexikon oder Enzyklopädie der katholischen Theologie und ihrer Hülfswissenschaften*, Freiburg (Herder) ²1882, columns 1781–91.

WHITE, A. and SWAINSON, W. P.: *Three Famous Mystics. St. Martin, Jacob Böhme and Swedenborg*, Philadelphia (David McKay) 1940.

WIMMERSHOF, H.: *Die Lehre vom Sündenfall in der Philosophie Schellings, Baaders und Friedrich Schlegels*, Freiburg (doctoral dissertation) 1934.

WINTER, Eduard: "Neues über Baader", *Hochland*, 26 (1929), pp. 433–36.

WINTER, Eduard.: *Russland und das Papstthum*, volume 2, Berlin (Akademie) 1961.

WINTER, Ernst Karl: "Anton Günther. Ein Beitrag zur Romantikforschung", *Zeitschrift für die gesamte Staatswissenschaft*, 88, pp. 281ff., especially pp. 321–33.

XELLA, L. P.: "La Dogmatica Speculativa di Franz von Baader", *Filsofia*, 28 (1988), pp. 73–88.

XELLA, L. P.: "La Dogmatica Speculativa di Franz von Baader: III. Conoscenza e Immaginatione", *Filosofia*, 27, pp. 379–94.

XELLA, L. P.: "La Dogmatica Speculativa di Franz von Baader: IV. Teosofia e Filosofia della Natura", *Filosofia*

ZELTNER, H.: "Aussenseiter in der Geschichte des Gedankens, Hinweis auf Franz von Baader", *Die Erlanger Universität. Beilage des Erlanger Tagesblattes*, 10 (1957), pp. 3–4.

ZIEGENFUSS, W. (Ed.): *Philosophen-Lexikon*, volume 1, Berlin (Walter de Gruyter) 1949.

ZIEGLER, L.: *Die Menschwerdung*, 2 volumes, Olten 1948.

ZIEGLER, L.: *Die neue Wissenschaft*, Munich 1951.

ZIMMERMAN, R. C.: "Franz von Baader und Goethes vier Ehrfurchten", *Germanisch-Romanische Monatsschrift*, 14 (1964), pp. 267–79.

Index

Bavarian Hall of Fame 78
Beethoven, Ludwig van 12, 14, 298
Benz, Ernst 50, 67 n. 15, 69 n. 21, 76 n. 40,
176, 206, 206 n. 99, 207, 207 n. 100, 295,
296 n. 9
Berdyaev, Nicholas 25, 58, 110 n. 4, 172
Berleburger Bible 169
Bernard of Clairvaux (see also St. Bernard) 281
Blake, William 123
Böhme, Jacob 12, 42, 42 n. 31, 52, 52 n. 64,
53, 54, 54 n. 68, 54 n. 70, 54 n. 73, 55, 58,
64, 65, 67, 72 n. 27, 81 n. 52, 85 n. 61, 88, 88
n. 66, 88 n. 67, 91, 92, 92 n. 74, 92 n. 75, 92
n. 77, 93, 94, 95 n. 83, 100 n. 97, 109 n. 3,
110, 110 n. 4, 113, 118, 119, 122, 137, 138 n.
4, 139,140 n. 7, 143, 146, 150, 150 n. 22, 151,
152, 153, 153 n. 24, 153 n. 25, 154, 154 n.
28, 155,157 n. 30, 159, 160, 161, 162, 164,
169, 170, 176, 176 n. 33, 177, 178 n. 36, 179 n.
39, 182 n. 46, 182 n. 47, 184, 185, 186, 188,
205, 206, 206 n. 99, 207 n. 100, 223, 230,
237 n. 10, 243 n,18, 275, 276 n. 71, 298
Boisserée, Sulpiz 36
Bonaparte, Napoleon 66, 67
Brentano, Clemens 37, 170, 195
Buber, Martin 272
Burke, Edmund 33, 103

Cabbala / Cabbalism / cabbalistic / cabbalists 14, 55, 55 n. 75, 64, 79, 169, 176,
176 n. 33, 178 n. 38
Camus, Albert 24, 73 n. 28, 145
Cartesian (see also Descartes) 47, 83
Categorical Imperative / categorical impera-
tive 100, 151, 165, 253 n. 36
Categorical Ought 117
catoptric image 137, 138, 139
celibacy (see also sacerdotal celibacy) 61,
170, 198
Chardin, Teilhard de 296, 206 n. 9
Christophobia, 73
circulus vitae 95, 149
Civil Service Order of Noblity 64
clairvoyance / clairvoyant 138, 156, 182 n.
45, 232
Claudius, Matthias 52 n. 63, 64
Clement of Alexandria 110
"Cologne Troubles" 77, 77 n. 45
Colossians (book of the Bible) 265

Conseil des Mines of Paris 64
consubstanatial / consubstantiality / consubstantiation / *consubstantialis Patri* (see also
Homousie) 140 n. 7, 143, 143 n. 12, 144, 221
Corinthians (book of the Bible) 181 n. 44,
190, 192, 223 n. 19, 228, 232, 255
cosmic 145, 296
cosmology 31, 32, 53, 175, 296
cosmos 172, 228
cosmosophy 94, 94 n. 82
Cousin, Victor 75
creatio ex nihilo 95, 243 n. 18
creation, theory of creation / creationism
95, 118–26, 135, 139, 143–46, 151–152,
158, 158 n. 30, 176, 187, 192 n. 69, 214,
219, 222, 223, 236, 237 n. 9, 245, 282, 285,
289, 291, 296
cupido / cupid 156, 229

deism / deists / deistic 136, 165, 253 n. 36
Descartes, René 14, 34, 47, 83, 97 n. 89, 112,
156, 261, 294
despotism / despotic 220, 225, 244, 284
Deutinger, Martin 47, 68 n. 18, 77 n. 46, 83
n. 56, 294, 297
devil / devilish / demon(s) / demonic 90,
128, 131, 142, 142 n. 10, 163, 180, 185, 195,
198 n. 81, 199, 200, 211, 218, 219 n. 16
diabolical 183, 189
dieu-machine 94
Ding-an-sich (see also "thing-in-itself") 85
"divine contract" 102 n. 101
Döllinger, Johann Joseph Ignaz von 74, 75
Droste-Vischering, Archbishop von 77 n 45
dualism / duality (see also polarity) 46, 85,
87–89, 92, 190 n. 62, 220
Dynamis logiké 153

Eckartshaussen, Karl von 52 n. 63
Eckehart, Meister 45, 55, 56, 67, 72, 115,
143, 150, 183, 226, 243 n. 18, 274, 286
Eckhardt, Meister (see Eckehart)
ecstasy / ecstatic (see also *ekstasis* and magnetic ecstasy) 48, 86, 162, 182, 182 n. 45,
194, 229 n. 29, 230, 238, 273
ecumenism / ecumenists / ecumenical 29,
30, 34, 295, 298
ekstasis (see also ecstasy and magnetic
ecsatsy) 273, 274

Kleuker, Johann Friedrich 51, 51 n. 62, 52 n. 63, 52 n. 64, 63
Klopstock, Friedrich Gottlieb 52 n. 63
Kluckhohn, Paul 25, 33, 35, 58, 58 n. 83, 111 n. 8, 171, 209 n. 1
Kotzebue, August von 69, 69 n. 21, 70

laissez-faire 103
Lamennais, Félicité Robert de 75, 86
Lasaulx, Ernst von (son in law) 64
Lavater, Johann Kaspar 52 n. 63
Leade, Jane 169
Leibniz, Gottfried Wilhelm, Baron von 67, 77, 97 n. 89, 262
Lenau, Nicolas (Nikolaus) pseud. of Nikolaus Niembsch Edler von Strehlenau 36
Leone Ebreo 169, 170 n. 10
Lieb, Fritz 57
limus terrae 179 n. 39
Linder, Emilie 233, 233 n. 2, 233 n. 3
List, Friedrich 29
Locke, John 63
logical positivism (see positivism)
Logos 158, 159, 164
Logos ekthetos 157, 158, 158 n. 31, 158 n. 32
Logos enthetos 157, 158, 158 n. 31, 158 n. 32
logos-pantheism (see also pantheism and nature-pantheism) 299
Löwenstein-Wertheim, Prince Constantine von 75, 216, 268
Lucifer 124, 141, 143, 187 n. 56, 284, 286
Ludwig Maximilian University 74
Luke (book of the Bible) 218, 222, 267
Luther 140 n. 7
Lutterbeck, Anton 52 n. 64

magia 138
Magie 154
magnes 138
magnetic clairvoyant (see also clairvoyance and clairvoyant) 276
magnetic ecstasy (see also ecstasy and ecstatic) 182
magnetism (see also animal magnetism and Galvanism) 33, 56, 182 n. 45
Maistre, Joseph de 70, 75
Maja 154, 258
Marcel, Gabriel 179 n. 40
Marcuse, M. 204

Marheinecke 72, 72 n. 27, 123
Mark (book of the Bible) 283
Marx, Karl 24, 29, 76, 76 n. 40
Masons / Masonry (see also Freemasons) 49, 49 n. 52, 70
materialism / materialistic 46, 97 n. 89, 98, 186, 193, 220, 271, 298
materialistic atomism (see also atomism) 97 n. 89
Matthew (book of the Bible) 111 n. 9, 150, 200, 217, 227, 269, 270 n. 59, 274, 276, 283, 285
mechanistic world view / mechanism / mechanistic atomism 33, 34–35, 35 n. 11, 95, 97 n. 89, 165, 175, 229, 248
Medieval idealism (see also German idealism, idealism, and transcendental idealism) 117
medieval mysticism (see also mysticism) 49, 52, 295
mercurius 167 n. 3
Mestchersky, Elim (Prince) 56, 68 n. 19, 191
metaphysics / metaphysical(ly) 34, 40, 41, 53, 57, 63 n. 6, 82, 83, 92, 110, 121 n. 32, 149, 164, 172, 190 n. 62, 197, 204, 204 n. 94, 257, 292, 295, 297
microcosm / *microcosmos* 87, 97, 135, 136, 144, 145, 152
microtheos 87, 97, 135, 144, 145, 152
Möhler, Johann Adam 58
Montalembert, Charles Forbes (comte de) 56, 75, 233 n. 1
Moral Imperative 99, 218, 218 n. 15
moral law / morality 42, 99, 100
Mosaic 101, 190 n. 63
Moses (Biblical) 139, 152, 206 n. 99, 288
Müller, Adam 72, 262
mundus machinalis 94
mundus vitalis 94
Munich Academy of Sciences 64
mystical body / Mystical Body of Christ 140
Mysticism or mysticism / mystic(s) or mystical(ly) or mystical thought 12, 14, 31, 32, 38, 39, 40, 42, 43, 44, 48, 49, 50–56, 65, 67, 68, 75, 76, 79, 79 n. 50, 94, 96, 100 n. 97, 105, 107, 109, 110, 115, 117, 118, 126, 171, 172, 175, 176, 177, 187, 205, 207, 232, 243 n. 18, 281, 289, 293, 295, 296, 297

Napoleon (see also Bonaparte) 66, 67, 69

329

National Socialists 68 n. 17
naturalism / naturalistic (see also *Naturphilosophen* and philosophy of nature) 54, 98, 220, 291, 293
nature-machine 94
nature-pantheism (see also pantheism and logos-pantheism) 299
Naturphilosophen (see also naturalism and philosophy of nature) 272, 278
Nazism 68 n. 17
neo-Platonists 168
neo-Pythagoreans 168
neo-scholastic 294
Newton, Isaac 97
Newtonian astronomy 97
Nicholas of Cusa 167
Nietzsche, Friedrich 16, 24, 29
nihilism (see also Spiritual nihilism) 29, 73, 73 n. 28, 242, 298, 299
noetical / noetically 117
Nohl, Johannes 35, 38, 58 n. 83
Nomos 164
Novalis, pseud. of Friederich von Hardenberg 12, 25, 32, 34, 35, 36, 38, 54, 57, 62, 67 n. 15, 77, 95, 95 n. 85, 170, 171, 171 n. 13, 185 n. 50, 191 n. 64, 195, 271, 293, 299

Obscurantaism / obscurantist 40, 49, 68, 73
occulation (see also *kenosis* and sublation) 88
occult / occultism 31, 32, 38, 49, 50–56, 297
Oetinger, Friedrich Christoph 52 n. 64, 55, 55 n. 75, 169, 205, 107 n. 100
Old Testament 101, 138, 193
ontology / ontological / ontologically 83, 104, 117, 121 n. 32, 149, 153, 172
optative 40, 100 n. 96
organicism / organic idea / organic interconnectedness / organic unity / organic principle / organic model 30, 32, 34, 35, 49, 66, 78, 80, 95, 101, 102–05, 108, 132, 165, 171 n. 13, 198, 199, 200, 221, 222, 228, 229, 229 n. 28, 248, 290, 291, 293, 295
Orthodox Church (see also Russian Orthodox Church) 70, 77, 296
osteologists 191

pagan 104, 188, 189
Pahlen (Count) 70
pantheism / panthestic / pantheists see also

nature-pantheism) 12, 24, 43, 44, 54, 65, 89, 90, 91, 91 n. 71, 94 n. 82, 117, 118, 121, 122, 149, 165, 228, 243 n. 18, 253 n. 36, 297
papacy / papal / anti-papal 68, 76, 77, 77 n. 46, 104, 294
Paracelsus, Philippus Aureolus 54, 55, 55 n. 75, 88, 95 n. 83, 100 n. 97, 137, 138, 138 n. 4, 143, 186, 237 n. 10, 276 n. 71
paradise 100, 168, 181
parapsychology / parapsychological 33, 56, 66, 95, 182 n. 45
Pasqualis, Martinez 52, 52 n. 65
Paul, Jean, pseud. of Johann Paul Friedrich Richter 37
Paulucci 68 n. 19, 70
Peter (book of the Bible) 249, 260
Philippians (book of the Bible) 181 n. 44, 236 n. 7, 240
Philo of Alexandria 168
philosophical anthropology (see also anthropology)
philosophy of nature or nature-philosophy (see also *Naturphilsophen* and naturalism) 38, 44, 51, 53, 54, 55, 62, 82, 94–97, 97 n. 89, 98, 145, 170, 171 n. 13
Physiosophy 94, 94 n 82, 145
Pietism / Pietists / Pietistic(ally) 14, 47, 49, 50, 52 n. 63, 57, 68, 70, 169, 261, 296, 298
Plato / Platonic / Platonism (see also neo-Platonists) 24, 46, 83, 93, 110, 111, 112, 114, 121 n. 32, 123, 125, 154, 168, 169, 176, 192, 219, 227, 237 n. 10, 259, 293
polarity (see also dualism) 88, 88 n. 65, 171 n. 13, 206 n. 99, 239, 243, 289
Pordage, John 169
positive philosophy / positive science 40, 79 n. 50, 82
positivism / positivists or logical positivists 108
proletariat 24, 29, 30, 76, 298
Promethean hero 34, 35
Propädeutik 40, 200
Pulver, Max 59, 81 n. 51

quaternary / quaternity 88, 88 n. 67

realism (see also ideal realism) 57, 84, 97
Redeemer / redeemer 47, 53, 143, 156, 231, 287
redemption / redeeming / redemptive 118–26, 135, 145, 197, 206, 221, 235

171 n. 13, 178 n. 36, 183, 183 n. 48, 186, 187, 194, 204, 205, 206, 207, 207 n. 100, 230, 231, 287, 290, 291, 292, 295
Spinoza, Baruch 12, 14, 42, 42 n. 31, 46, 91 n. 71, 113, 116, 116 n. 22, 117, 118, 201 n. 87, 261
Spirit (see also Holy Spirit) 285
Spiritual nihilism (see also nihilism) 24, 29, 30, 298
spiritualism / spiritualization / spiritualized / spiritualizing 53, 98, 298, 299
Spiritualist Conventicles 169
Spreckelmeyer, Hermann 188 n. 60, 204, 204 n. 94
Stattler, Benedict 49
Steffens, Henrik 37, 43 n. 37, 62 n. 5
Stourdza, Alexander 68 n. 19, 75
Stransky, Dr. von 54 n. 68, 158 n. 31, 182 n. 46, 198, 199, 224, 281, 282
Strich, Fritz 258 n. 45
Sturm und Drang 170
subjectivism / subjective philosophy / *Subjectivitätsphilosophie* 40, 83, 247
sublate / sublation (see also *kenosis* and occulation) 85 n. 61, 86 n. 63, 88, 172, 172 n. 21, 212 n. 4, 228, 228 n. 27, 229, 236, 237, 250
supernaturalism / supernaturalist / supernatural religion 49, 98
Susini, Eugène 37 n. 22, 59, 59 n. 63, 61 n. 1, 67 n. 15, 68 n. 19, 69 n. 22, 172 n. 19
Suso, Heinrich 56, 67
Swedenborg, Emmanuel 38, 52, 170

Tauler, Johannes 56, 67, 127, 144
teleology or teleological 31, 149
Teresa of Avila (Saint) 50, 236
Tertullian 158
theism / theistic 24, 40, 42, 65, 253 n. 36
theocentric 103, 104
theocracy 200
theogony 149
theophobia 73
theory of knowledge (see also epistemology) 33, 74, 82, 83–91
theory of revelation 86, 87
theosophy / theosophist / theosophical(ly) 14,

43, 51, 52, 54, 79 n. 50, 94, 94 n. 82, 110 n. 4, 117, 118, 169, 172, 206 n. 99, 243 n. 18
"thing-in-itself" (see also *Ding-an-sich*) 39, 40, 295
Tieck, Ludwig 32, 36, 54, 65, 75, 195
tincture 100 n. 97, 141, 141 n. 8, 175, 178 n. 38, 183, 187
transcendental idealism / transcendental philosophy (see also German idealism, idealism, Medieval idealism) 24, 40, 295
triad / triadic / triadic structure / triadic thought 43, 43 n. 38, 86 n. 63, 87, 88, 88 n. 66, 91, 154 n. 28, 185, 201, 203, 212
Turgeniev, Ivan Sergeyevich 73 n. 28

Ultramontanes 294
University of Munich 44
utilitarian / utilitarianism / utilitarian ethics 39, 39 n. 26, 102, 103, 189, 220, 295
Üxküll, Baron Boris von 70, 71, 199

Valhalla (Bavarian Valhalla) 78
Varnhagen von Ense, Karl August 36, 72, 75
Varnhagen von Ense, Rachel 72
Vatican Council 294
Venus barbata 173, 188
Volksgeist 33
voluntarism / voluntarist 92, 109, 110, 110 n. 4

Wackenroder 32
Weltanschauung (see also worldview) 30, 34, 94, 105, 108, 207, 271, 294
Weltseele (see also World Soul) 94, 95
Wieland, Christoph Martin 170
Winckelmann, Johann Joachim 170
Windischmann 73, 233 n. 3
Winter, Eduard 57, 77 n. 46, 81 n. 51
Wolffian rationalism 38
"World Soul" or "World Spirit" (see also *Weltseele*) 94, 122
worldview (see also *Weltanschauung*) 14, 29, 33, 35 n. 11, 40, 46, 63, 118

Ziegler, Leopold 58
Zipporah (Biblical) 190 n. 63, 288

332

Philosophical Theology
Studies in Speculative Philosophy and Religion

Edited by Peter Koslowski

in Conjunction with:
Alois M. Haas, Moshe Idel, Odo Marquard,
Johann Baptist Metz, Thomas V. Morris, Raoul J. Mortley,
Marco M. Olivetti, Julio Terán Dutari,
Xavier Tilliette, Shizutero Ueda, Falk Wagner

The series "Philosophical Theology, Studies in Speculative Philosophy and Religion," is devoted to investigating issues associated with speculative philosophy, metaphysics, the philosophy of religion, and speculative religion. The term "speculative religion" applies to questions which address religion and theology from a philosophical and speculative point of view, questions which interpret the content of religion and theology by employing rational, speculative thinking. Consequently, works published in the series deal with issues related to the systematic study of the philosophy of religion and natural theology, as well as matters associated with mystical theology, theosophy, and gnosticism – insofar as they lend themselves to the methodology of philosophical inquiry and rational discourse.

The objective of the series is to encourage and revitalize inquiry between philosophy and religion and the tradition of speculative theology. By so doing, it seeks to promote dialogue between speculative religion and the religious philosophies of such non-Christian religions as Judaism, Islam, Buddhism, and Hinduism. Its publications – monographs, conference proceedings, and collections of essays – are designed to serve as an international forum of scholarly inquiry. All are devoted to the synthesis of philosophical-theological thought and emphasize originality and clarity. Works in English and German are considered for publication.

Volumes Appearing in the Series Philosophische Theologie